Cultural Integration of Immigrants in Europe

Studies of Policy Reform

Series Editors

François Bourguignon and Daniel Cohen

This series brings new and innovative policy research to the forefront of academic and policy debates.

It addresses the widest range of policies, from macro-economics to welfare, public finance, trade, migration, or environment. It hosts collaborative work under the auspices of CEPR, CEPREMAP, and the Paris School of Economics.

Titles published in the series

The Economics of Clusters

Gilles Duranton, Philippe Martin, Thierry Mayer, and Florian Mayneris

Cultural Integration of Immigrants in Europe

Edited by Yann Algan, Alberto Bisin, Alan Manning, and Thierry Verdier

Cultural Integration of Immigrants in Europe

Edited by
Yann Algan, Alberto Bisin, Alan Manning,
and Thierry Verdier

OXFORD
UNIVERSITY PRESS

OXFORD
UNIVERSITY PRESS

Great Clarendon Street, Oxford, OX2 6DP,
United Kingdom

Oxford University Press is a department of the University of Oxford.
It furthers the University's objective of excellence in research, scholarship,
and education by publishing worldwide. Oxford is a registered trade mark of
Oxford University Press in the UK and in certain other countries

First Edition published in 2012

Impression: 1

British Library Cataloguing in Publication Data

Data available

Library of Congress Cataloging in Publication Data

Data available

ISBN 978–0–19–966009–4

Printed in Great Britain by
MPG Books Group, Bodmin and King's Lynn

Contents

List of Figures

List of Tables

List of Tables

List of Contributors

Mariya Aleksynska, Institute for Research on the International Economy, Paris

Yann Algan, Sciences Po, Paris

Alberto Bisin, New York University

Amelie Constant, DIWDC, Washington, DC; George Washington University, Washington, DC; Institute for the Study of Labor, IZA, Bonn

Andreas Georgiadis, London School of Economics

Pierre Kohler, Graduate Institute of International and Development Studies, Geneva

Camille Landais, University of California, Berkeley

Alan Manning, London School of Economics

Lena Nekby, Stockholm University

Olga Nottmeyer, Institute for the Study of Labor, IZA, Bonn

Francesc Ortega, Queens College, CUNY

Eleonora Patacchini, University of Rome

Sara de la Rica, University of the Basque Country

Claudia Senik, Paris School of Economics

Thierry Verdier, Paris School of Economics

Jacob Vigdor, Duke University

Klaus Zimmermann, Institute for the Study of Labor and Bonn University

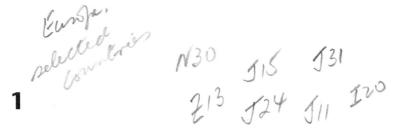

1

Introduction: Perspectives on Cultural Integration of Immigrants

Yann Algan[1], Alberto Bisin, and Thierry Verdier

1.1 Introduction

The concepts of cultural diversity and cultural identity are at the forefront of the political debate in many western societies. In Europe, the discussion is stimulated by the political pressures associated with immigration flows, which are increasing in many European countries, as shown in Figure 1.1. Dealing with the ethnic and cultural heterogeneity associated to such trends is one of the most important challenges that European societies will face. The debate on the perceived costs and benefits of cultural diversity is already intense. This is well illustrated, for instance, in France, where discussions about the wearing of the Islamic veil and the burqa stimulated, in turn, a public debate on national identity. Similarly, the recent vote in Switzerland against the construction of Muslim mosques clearly shows how heated and emotional arguments on ethnic and religious identity have recently become.

Sociologists have been studying the cultural integration patterns of immigrants at least since the late nineteenth century, especially in the context of immigration into the United States. Economists have instead been traditionally mainly interested in assessing the direct impact of immigration flows on market outcomes (especially on the labour market) or on fiscal transfers and public goods provision. The basic question of assimilation for economists has, then, been framed in terms of economic

[1] The research leading to there results for Yann Algan has received funding from the European Research Council under the European Community's Sweath Framework Programme (FP7/2007–2013)/ERC grant agreement number 240923.

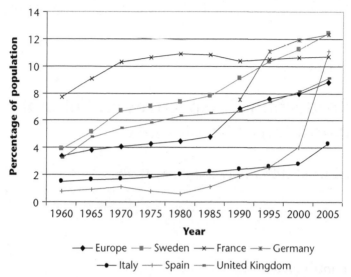

Figure 1.1 Immigration flows in European countries.
Source: United Nations Population Division

assimilation, namely in terms of the dynamics of immigrants' earnings and socio-economic positions relatively to natives. Recently, however, economists have been recognizing that, beyond interactions directly mediated through markets, prices and incomes, other non-market social and cultural interactions could also be important determinants of the socio-economic integration of immigrants. Specific patterns of cultural attitudes of immigrant groups can significantly affect their labour market performances, for instance. The common social phenomenon of 'oppositional' identities, by which certain minority individuals actively reject the dominant majority behavioural norms, can produce significant economic and social conflicts as well as adverse labour-market outcomes.

More generally, social scientists have dedicated a lot of attention to the fact that immigrants' integration patterns can significantly alter the design and the political economy of public policies in the host society. An example of this issue concerns the sustainability of welfare state institutions in the context of multicultural societies. Cultural diversity may indeed affect the sense of community and social solidarity which constitute founding pillars of democratic welfare state systems. This could lead to the erosion of the social consensus for redistribution and diminish the political support for universal social programmes. Public policies aimed at correcting for horizontal inequalities across cultural groups, might end up substituting for vertical redistribution across social classes.

For these reasons, several observers favour explicit public policies promoting, or even requesting, the cultural assimilation of immigrants to the cultural attitudes of natives. Other observers, however, argue that welfare state institutions should be designed to accommodate cultural diversity. These policies would facilitate contacts across communities, promote tolerance, trust, and respect towards other groups and, in the end, would help develop new national identities.

In either case, the study of cultural and socio-economic integration patterns of immigrants seems of paramount importance, as such patterns determine how the expression of cultural differences is translated into individual behaviour and public policy. The imperatives that current immigration trends impose on European democracies bring to light a number of issues that need to be addressed. What are the patterns and dynamics of cultural integration? How do they differ across immigrants of different ethnic groups and religious faiths? How do they differ across host societies? What are the implications and consequences for market outcomes and public policy? Which kind of institutional contexts are more or less likely to accommodate the cultural integration of immigrants? All these questions are crucial for policy makers and await answers.

In this context, the purpose of this book is to provide a modest but nevertheless essential contribution as a stepping stone to the debate. Taking an economic perspective, the collection of essays in this book presents the first descriptive and comparative picture of the process of cultural integration of immigrants in Europe, as it is taking place. We provide in the country chapters a detailed description of the cultural and economic integration process in seven main European countries and in the United States. The European countries include France, Germany, Italy, Spain, Sweden, Switzerland, and United Kingdom. We then provide in the conclusion of the book a cross-country comparison of the integration process using a unified database, the European Social Survey. The conclusion concentrates on the interplay between the cultural and economic integration process across European countries, and discusses how those various dimensions of integration correlate with specific national policies aimed at immigrants' integration.

In this first chapter, building on the recent economics of cultural transmission, we introduce the main conceptual issues which are of relevance to the study of the cultural integration patterns of immigrants and of their interaction with market and non-market outcomes. More specifically, this chapter is organized as follows. In Section 1.2 we discuss briefly the different theories of cultural integration developed in the social sciences. In Section 1.3 we introduce in more detail the economic approach to the study of cultural integration. In Section 1.4 we provide a short overview of the main conceptual issues associated with measuring cultural integration processes. In Section 1.5 we discuss cultural integration in terms of its socio-economic impact on host countries. Finally, in Section 1.6 we conclude with a brief overview of the subsequent chapters included in this book.

1.2 Cultural integration theories in the social sciences

Three main perspectives on cultural integration confront themselves in the social sciences: *assimilation theory, multiculturalism,* and *structuralism.* This section briefly discusses the main elements of each of these conceptual views as well as those of a recent synthetic perspective, called *segmented assimilation.*

1.2.1 Assimilation theory

In the literature on the cultural integration of immigrants, the perspective of assimilation theory has dominated much of the sociological thinking for most of the twentieth century. This approach builds upon three central features. First, diverse ethnic groups come to share a common culture through a natural process along which they have the same access to socio-economic opportunities as natives of the host country. Second, this process consists of the gradual disappearance of original cultural and behavioural patterns in favour of new ones. Third, once set in motion, the process moves inevitably and irreversibly towards complete assimilation. Hence, diverse immigrant groups are expected to 'melt' into the mainstream culture through an inter-generational process of cultural, social, and economic integration.

This view is exemplified, for example, by Gordon (1964), who provides a typology of assimilation patterns to capture this process. In Gordon's view, immigrants begin their adaptation to their new country through cultural assimilation, or acculturation. Though cultural assimilation is a necessary first step, ethnic groups may remain distinguished from one another because of spatial isolation and lack of contact. Their full assimilation depends ultimately on the degree to which these groups gain the acceptance of the dominant population. Socio-economic assimilation inevitably leads to other stages of assimilation through which ethnic groups eventually lose their distinctive characteristics.

Assimilation theory seemed to be rather corroborated by the experience of the various waves of European immigrants that arrived in the

USA between the 1920s and the 1950s. As indicated by assimilation theory, these groups of immigrants followed progressive trends of social mobility across generations and increasing rates of intermarriage, as determined by educational achievements, job market integration, English proficiency, and levels of exposure to American culture (see for instance Alba, 1985; Chiswick, 1978; Lieberson and Waters, 1988). In the 1960s, the classical assimilation perspective was challenged in the USA by the cultural integration patterns of more recent non-European immigrant groups. Instead of converging into the mainstream culture, these groups appeared to preserve their ethnic and religious identities, making cultural differences more persistent than assimilation theory would conventionally predict. Differential outcomes with respect to natives seemed to prevail even after long-term residence in the USA (Kao and Tienda, 1995; Rumbaut and Ima, 1988; Suarez-Orozco and Suarez-Orozco, 1995; and Landale and Oropesa, 1995). Disadvantages were reproduced, rather than diminished (Gans, 1992). Patterns of mobility across generations were observed to have divergent rather than convergent paths (Becker, 1963; Goffman, 1963; and Perlmann, 1988). This evidence turned out to lead to the development of alternative approaches to the study of cultural integration.

1.2.2 Multiculturalism

One such alternative approach is multiculturalism, which rejects the simple integration process proposed by assimilation theory. Scholars from this perspective view multicultural societies as composed of a heterogeneous collection of ethnic and racial minority groups, as well as of a dominant majority group. This view has been forcefully illustrated by Glazer and Moynihan (1970) and by Handlin (1973) in the context of the American society. They argue that immigrants actively shape their own identities rather than posing as passive subjects in front of the forces of assimilation. These authors also emphasize that some aspects of the cultural characteristics of immigrants may be preserved in a state of uneasy co-existence with the attitudes of the host country. The multicultural perspective offers, then, an alternative way of considering the host society, presenting members of ethnic minority groups as active integral segments of the whole society rather than just foreigners or outsiders.

1.2.3 Structuralism

Rather than focusing on the processes of assimilation or integration per se, the structuralist approach emphasizes how differences in socio-economic opportunities relate to differences in social integration of ethnic minority groups. Unequal access to wealth, jobs, housing, education, power, and privilege are seen as structural constraints that affect the ability of immigrants and ethnic minorities to socially integrate. This leads to persistent ethnic disparities in levels of income, educational attainment, and occupational achievement of immigrants (Blau and Duncan, 1967; Portes and Borocz, 1989). Consequently, the benefits of integration depend largely on what stratum of society absorbs the new immigrants. Contrary to the perspectives of assimilation theory and of multiculturalism, structuralism emphasizes the inherent conflicts that exist in the social hierarchy between dominant and minority groups and therefore questions even the possibility of cultural and socio-economic integration of immigrants.

To summarize, assimilation theory, multiculturalism, and structuralism provide different views of the same phenomenon. The focus of assimilation theorists is on immigrants' succeeding generations gradually moving away from their original culture. Multiculturalists acknowledge that the cultural characteristics of immigrants are constantly reshaped along the integration process and therefore may never completely disappear. Structuralists emphasize the effects of the social and economic structure of the host country on the ability of immigrants to integrate into its cultural attitudes and to share its economic benefits. While each of the previous perspectives insists on one specific dimension of the integration pattern of immigrants, segmented assimilation theory provides a synthesis of these distinctive approaches.

1.2.4 *Segmented assimilation synthesis*

The main objective of this line of research is to provide a more complete picture of the different patterns of integration among immigrants in terms of convergent or divergent paths of cultural adaptation. More precisely, this theory envisions the process of cultural integration along three possible patterns: (1) an upward mobility pattern associated with assimilation and economic integration into the normative structures of the majority group; (2) a downward mobility pattern, in the opposite direction, associated to assimilation and parallel integration into the underclass; (3) economic integration but lagged assimilation and/or deliberate preservation of the immigrant community's values and identity (see Portes and Zhou, 1994). This theoretical perspective attempts to explain the factors that determine which segment of the host society a particular immigrant group may assimilate into. Its focus is on how various socio-economic and demographic factors (education, native language proficiency, place of birth, age upon arrival, and length of residence in the host country) interact with contextual variables (such as racial status, family socio-economic backgrounds, and place of residence) to produce specific cultural integration patterns of a given cultural minority group.

1.3 Economic approach to cultural integration

While other social scientists tend to focus on the effects of the social environment on cultural patterns across groups, the starting point of the economic approach to cultural integration is the analysis of individual behaviour, extended to account for endogenous preferences and identity formation. Economists, therefore, emphasize the importance of individual incentives and of the opportunity costs associated with different integration patterns.

1.3.1 *Cultural adoption*

A first simple model capturing the incentives for cultural integration is provided by an analysis of adoption of a common language by Lazear (1999). In this framework, individuals from two different cultural groups (a minority and a majority) are matched to interact economically and socially. Cultural integration facilitates trade across individuals.[2] The incentives for an individual belonging to the minority cultural group to assimilate and adopt the culture of the majority are then directly related to the expected gains from trade that such a strategy provides.

More specifically, consider a simple environment in which each individual is randomly matched with one and only one other individual each period. Let the two cultural groups be denoted A and B, and let p_A and p_B denote the proportions of individuals who belong to culture A and B, respectively. Finally, let A represent the majority group: $p_A = 1 - p_B > 1/2$.[3] A minority individual may encounter another individual of his own group and get an expected gain from trade V_B. Alternatively, he may interact with an individual from the majority group A, in which case he receives an expected gain V_A if he shares

---

[2] Defined broadly to include non-market interactions as well.

[3] In Lazear (1999), the fractions p_A and p_B reflect the proportions of people that speak, respectively, language A and language B. Therefore, bilingual individuals belong to both cultures and $p_A + p_B > 1$.

common cultural elements with that group (i.e. if he made a specific effort at assimilating the majority culture), and a lower gain fV_A (with $f < 1$) if he does not.

When individuals of group B acquire group A's cultural values, they become 'assimilated' into group A. They may still retain some or all of their old culture, but they now have the ability to trade with the majority group. For instance, in the specific case of language adoption, assimilation can be thought of as becoming fluent in the majority language, while possibly retaining the ability to speak the native tongue. It is reasonable to assume that cultural assimilation is costly and resources must be spent to acquire new cultural traits (e.g. to learn a new language). Moreover, these costs may be individual specific. Denote, therefore, by t_i the individual-specific cost parameter that measures (inversely) the efficiency with which individual i acquires the new culture. Formally, t_i is distributed with density and distribution function $g(t_i)$ and $G(t_i)$, respectively. Individuals make their cultural assimilation choices with no coordinated group strategy. When an individual belonging to group B does not assimilate to the culture of the majority, his expected gain is $p_B V_B + p_A f V_A$. On the other hand, when he does assimilate, his expected gain is $p_B V_B + p_A V_A - t_i$. It follows that an individual belonging to group B will culturally assimilate when $t_i < p_A(1-f)V_A$; that is, if the individual cost t_i of acquiring the cultural trait of group A is smaller than the expected benefit $p_A(1-f)V_A$ of such assimilation strategy. Aggregating over all individuals of group B that find it profitable to acquire the cultural trait of group A, the fraction of assimilated individuals in the minority is $s_{BA} = G(p_A(1-f) V_A) = G[(1- p_B)(1-f)V_A]$.

Interestingly, this simple model produces three important implications. First, cultural assimilation is a decreasing function of the fraction p_B of minority group members in society. Hence the smaller and the more dispersed the minority group, the more likely we should expect cultural assimilation for that group. Second, s_{BA} is also an increasing function of the expected economic gain V_A to be obtained by interacting with individuals belonging to the majority. Hence, the larger the economic benefits to be culturally integrated, the larger the incentives to assimilate. Third, cultural integration is increasing with $(1-f)$, namely the degree of inefficiency associated with interacting with individuals of the majority without sharing their cultural traits. Hence, the more important is the sharing of a common culture to enjoy social interactions, the larger, again, are the incentives to assimilate for the minority group. Two additional implications of Lazear's model are also worth emphasizing. From a normative perspective, there is a crucial externality in the assimilation process. Indeed, the larger the fraction of minority individuals which assimilate, the higher are the expected gains from trade for the majority. Clearly, when deciding whether to assimilate, individuals belonging to the cultural minority do not internalize these gains. At least from the point of view of the majority group, this provides a rationale for integration policies which subsidize the assimilation of minorities. Furthermore, this framework can be easily expanded to allow for multiple minority groups. In this case, cultural assimilation will be favoured in the presence of a relatively even distribution of minority groups. The existence of relatively large minorities, in fact, reduces the incentives of each minority group to adopt the culture of the majority. Again, straightforward policy implications can be obtained, favouring even distributions of immigrants by cultural identity.

1.3.2 Identity formation

While the model of Lazear (1999) puts its emphasis on the potential gains from trade associated with the interaction between members of different communities, Akerlof and Kranton (2000) concentrate more directly on cultural identity as an important source of the gains or losses associated with social interactions between different groups. Building on insights from social psychology and sociology, Akerlof and Kranton introduce the concept of social identity in economic models and discuss how it may interact with individuals' incentives. More specifically, identity is defined as a person's self-image, based on given social categories and on prescriptions associated with these categories. Each person has a perception of his own categories and that of all other people. Prescriptions, in turn, indicate which behaviour is deemed appropriate for people in different social categories and/or in different situations. Prescriptions may also often describe ideals for each category in terms of physical and material attributes.

In this conceptual context, Akerlof and Kranton emphasize two dimensions of identity formation which are relevant to understand cultural integration. First, categorizations and prescriptions are learned and acquired by individuals through processes of internalization and identification with respect to others who share these categories, that is, who belong to the same cultural group. This implies in particular that one's self image depends on how one satisfies the prescriptions of the category. Moreover, as identification is a crucial part of the internalization process, a person's self-image can be threatened by others' violation of the set of prescriptions he identifies with. Indeed, prescriptions associated with one group or category are often defined in contrast to those of others. This dimension provides a source of potentially important social externalities when individuals interact with each other. Second, Akerlof and Kranton's cultural identity is not given. Individuals choose assignments to social categories (form their identity) by means of actions corresponding to these categorizations. Hence, incentives can affect the process of identity formation. As in Lazear (1999), the costs of cultural assimilation may relate to different factors such as the size of the groups, the economic gains from trade and interactions, the role of frictions in social interactions and matching.

An important application of this conceptual framework is to the study of oppositional cultures, when minorities adopt cultural categorizations and prescriptions defined in opposition to the categorizations and prescriptions of the dominant majority. Oppositional cultures often correspond to behaviour which requires significant economic costs for members of the minority group adopting the culture. At the heart of the emergence of oppositional cultures, according to Akerlof and Kranton, lie two crucial factors: social exclusion and lack of economic opportunities.[4] Social exclusion derives from the well established sociological fact that dominant groups define themselves by differentiation and exclusion of others. This in turn creates a conflict for minority members: how to work within the dominant culture without betraying one's own. Such social differences may then open the possibility for adoption of oppositional identities by those in excluded groups. Lack of economic opportunity may also contribute to the adoption of an oppositional identity. For instance, it has been noted that the decline in well-paid, unskilled jobs could result in loss of self-respect by men who cannot support their families, and the rise in inner city crime and drug abuse (Wilson, 1996). Similarly, Liebow (1967) in a famous ethnographic work on 'corner street' men (i.e. street beggars and idlers) describes how the lack of decent-paying work leads these individuals towards the adoption of identities which severely inhibit the value of any labour market skill they may possess, in an attempt to avoid suffering the guilt of failing to provide for themselves and their families.

Motivated by these and other ethnographic accounts of oppositional identities in poor neighbourhoods in the USA and UK,[5] Akerlof and Kranton construct a model of identity formation where people

---

[4] A rapidly emerging economic literature on oppositional cultures includes, for instance, Ferguson (2001), Fryer (2004), Austen-Smith and Fryer (2005), Fryer and Torelli (2005), Battu et al. (2007), Battu and Zenou (2010), Darity et al. (2006), Pattacchini and Zenou (2006).

[5] See for instance MacLeod (1987) and Willis (1977).

belonging to poor and socially excluded communities can choose between two identities: the dominant culture or an oppositional identity which rejects it. Each identity is defined by a set of prescriptions on certain actions/decisions that ought to be taken. From the perspective of the dominant identity, the oppositional identity is perceived as inducing bad economic decisions, self-destructive behaviour (such as taking drugs, joining a gang, and becoming pregnant at a young age) which in turn can generate negative pecuniary externalities on the rest of the community. Also, the model accounts for important identity-based externalities: individuals adopting an oppositional identity may be angered by those who assimilate, because of their complicity with the dominant culture, while on the contrary those who assimilate may be angered by those individuals who oppose the dominant culture by breaking its prescriptions. Finally, social exclusion by the majority is modeled as a loss in identity that individuals from the minority will suffer if they choose to adopt the dominant culture. It represents the extent to which someone from the minority is not accepted by the dominant group in society. On the contrary, individuals who choose to adopt the oppositional identity do not suffer such a loss.

The model generates societies which in equilibrium display a prevalence of oppositional identities and 'anti-social' behaviour. Typically, an equilibrium with full assimilation of the dominant culture by the community is possible only when social exclusion from the dominant group is small enough. On the contrary, a positive level of social exclusion will always lead some people in the community to adopt an oppositional identity and some 'self-destructive' and 'anti-social' behaviour. Importantly, the 'self-destructive' behaviour is not the result of the individual's lack of rationality, but instead derives from lack of economic opportunity and a high degree of social exclusion. The model's implications lend themselves to suggest policies designed to reduce the effects of social exclusion. In particular, training programmes which take trainees out of their neighbourhoods may eliminate the negative effects of interacting with individuals sharing oppositional identities and therefore may reduce the likelihood of the emergence of such cultures. Moreover, being in a different location may also reduce a trainee's direct social exclusion loss from assimilation to the dominant culture as this loss may be both individual-specific and situational. Finally, the model also highlights issues in the affirmative action debate. In particular, the rhetoric and symbolism of affirmative action may affect the level of social exclusion by the dominant group. On the one hand, affirmative action may increase the perception of victimization of the minority community, therefore reinforcing social differentiation and exclusion from the dominant group (Loury, 1995). On the other hand, affirmative action may decrease social exclusion, to the extent it is seen as a form of acceptance of the minority into the dominant culture.

1.3.3 *Acculturation strategies*

One important element of the previous analyses is the fact that cultural identity formation is modeled as a simple binary choice: individuals with foreign backgrounds either choose to identify with the dominant culture or to their (e.g. ethnic) minority culture. Even when the model is extended to allow for oppositional identity, its scope and complexity is limited by assuming that a stronger identification to the culture of the majority necessarily implies a weaker identification to the ethnic minority. These views, however, have been criticized as too simplistic to capture the different possible patterns of cultural integration of minorities. Indeed, studies within cross-cultural psychology suggest a more complex model of identity formation,[6] treating the degree of identification with the culture of the majority as separate and independent from the degree of identification with the minority culture. Individuals may, for example, simultaneously feel a strong affinity for the majority and for a minority culture.

For instance, Berry (1997) actually considers four distinct acculturation strategies regarding how individuals relate to an original ethnic culture of the minority group and the dominant culture of the majority (see Figure 1.2). The first strategy, *integration*, implies a strong sense of identification to both the original and the majority culture. The second, *assimilation*, requires a strong relationship with the majority culture but a weak relationship with the original culture. The third, *separation*, is associated to a weak connection with the majority culture but a strong connection with the original culture. Finally, the fourth strategy, *marginalization*, involves a weak link with both the majority and the original culture.

While such an identity formation structure has been discussed empirically in several recent economic studies of migrants' cultural integration (see Constant *et al.*, 2006; Zimmermann *et al.*, 2007; Nekby and Rödin, 2007), little conceptual analysis has tried to disentangle the incentives of minority individuals to adopt a particular acculturation strategy in this framework. Consider, then, a specific minority or ethnic group that is part of the larger society. Each individual member derives

---

[6] See for instance (Berry, 1980, 1984, 1997; Phinney, 1990; Phinney *et al.*, 2001).

Majority group

	Strong	Weak
Strong	Integration	Separation
Weak	Assimilation	Marginalization

Minority group

Figure 1.2 Two-dimensional identity model (Berry, 1997).

utility from a general aggregate consumption good as well as from a group-specific good that effectively defines the identity of the group. Consumers allocate their time between ethnic and general activities that respectively enter as inputs in the household production function of the ethnic and general goods.

Individuals may as well invest in human capital, increasing the productivity of the household technology for the group-specific good and for the general good. More specifically, human capital can be distinguished along two types: *group-specific human capital*, that enhances the skills relevant for producing the group-specific good and *general shared human capital*. Group-specific or ethnic human capital is associated with skills and experiences that are useful only for members of that group, for example language, religion, or customs affecting family relationships. On the other hand, shared human capital develops skills that raise the household's productivity of the general good, like, for example, the mastery of a common language, and general skills useful in the labour market.

Group specific human capital accumulation, in the form, for example of 'ethnic education', begins with ethnic-specific parenting styles, family customs, cultural socialization, and group-specific training within the ethnic community. The key parameter in Chiswick's model is the degree of complementarity or substitutability between the accumulation processes for group-specific and general shared human capital. The types of acculturation strategies that emerge for members of the minority depend crucially on these complementarity and substitutability effects. The model is able, therefore, to successfully connect the pattern of investments in group specific and general human capital to the acculturation strategies that minority individuals may choose. More specifically, it suggests that strong complementarities between group-specific human capital and general human capital will favour the emergence of *cultural integration*, where individuals in the minority invest in the accumulation of both types of human capital, and consequently develop strong identification to both their original culture and the general dominant culture of society. On the contrary, substitutability in human capital accumulation promotes the occurrence of *cultural assimilation* or *cultural separation,* where individuals in the minority will only identify with one culture at the cost of the other. *Marginalization* will finally occur when substantial fixed costs dampen the accumulation of both types of human capital.

1.3.4 *Dynamic cultural adoption*

Cultural integration has an essential dynamic character across time and generations. Several recent economic approaches have tried to incorporate these features in their analyses. A dynamic approach to cultural assimilation is described by Konya (2005), who extends the static framework of Lazear (1999) to a dynamic context. Individual members of a small minority group may decide to assimilate with the dominant majority culture or not. Individuals live for one period and have exactly one child each. They are dynastic altruists in the sense that they are concerned with their own utility as well as the utility of their future 'dynasty'. As in Lazear (1999), assimilation strategies have a single dimension: minority individuals either assimilate completely into the culture of the majority or they do not, remaining as members of the minority group. Each child is born inheriting the culture adopted by his parent. Any child born inheriting the culture of the minority chooses in turn to either assimilate or not. Children of assimilated parents belong instead irreversibly to the dominant majority group. As in Lazear (1999), individuals are matched randomly in society and gains from trade obtain from the resulting social and economic interactions. A match between members of the same group generates a larger gain than a match between individuals of different groups. Belonging to the majority group is therefore relatively desirable because of scale effects. But assimilation is costly. Thus, when deciding about cultural assimilation, minority members weight the benefits and the costs. In contrast to the static approach, rational forward-looking altruistic individuals take into account the future expected benefits of assimilation accruing to their whole dynasty. An important feature of the dynamics is the fact that incentives for assimilation change for successive generations, according to changes in the population structure over time. The model highlights the crucial role of the initial size of the minority group. When the minority is initially small, the long-run outcome is full assimilation. When the minority is instead initially large, the unique long-run equilibrium is the initial distribution, that is, full cultural separation. Interestingly, for intermediate minority sizes, multiple long-run distributions are possible, including the full and no-assimilation ones.

The subtle interactions between the initial structure of the population and the role of expectations of population changes on the future gains of assimilation explain the dynamics of the distribution of the population across cultural groups. Suppose that the members of the minority expect the population structure to remain the same as initially and that in such an environment, assimilation is too costly for any individual. Then clearly there will not be cultural assimilation and the population distribution across cultural groups will replicate itself indefinitely, confirming the initial expectations of the members of the minority. On the other hand, suppose that minority individuals anticipate a drastic assimilation process of their own group with the majority and that, under such changing circumstances, the gains to assimilation are largely increased. Then, possibly, a fraction of minority individuals assimilate. This in turn might validate the expectations of assimilation. Depending on the initial beliefs shared inside the minority community, one may end up in two very different situations in the long run, everything else being equal.

From a normative perspective, the analysis points to two basic inefficiencies that characterize the dynamics of assimilation. First of all, the speed of assimilation may be too small as there are positive external effects of assimilation on the majority that are not internalized by minority members. Indeed, when interacting with minority members, majority members benefit from meeting an assimilated minority member, but the latter do not take this into account. This suggests a rationale for policies that tend to subsidize the assimilation strategy of minorities, as in the static case. The second source of inefficiency relates to the existence of multiple equilibrium paths of cultural assimilation. One such path might Pareto dominate another, while expectations coordinate on the second, along which society would end up converging to the stationary state.

At the heart of Konya's (2005) approach to cultural assimilation is the dynastic altruism assumption: parents weigh the dynamic socio-economic gains from cultural assimilation that they and their children will enjoy against the direct costs of assimilating. However, parents' decisions about cultural assimilation may also be motivated by a desire to transmit to their children their own (the parents') values, beliefs, and norms per se. Parents may be altruistic toward their kids, but in 'paternalistic' manner. Parents, in fact, are typically aware of the different traits children will be choosing to adopt and of the socio-economic choices they (the children) will make in their lifetime. Parents might then evaluate these choices through the filter of their own (the parents') subjective views, that is, they might not 'perfectly empathize' with their children. As a consequence of imperfect empathy, parents, while altruistic, might prefer to have their children sharing their own cultural trait. Imperfect empathy provides in fact a natural motivation for the observation that parents typically spend substantial time and resources to socialize their children to their own values and cultures. This obviously may have implications for the observed pattern of integration and identity formation of cultural minority groups.

1.3.5 *Cultural transmission*

Building on evolutionary models of cultural transmission (Boyd and Richerson, 1985), Bisin and Verdier (2000, 2001) incorporate parental socialization choices under imperfect empathy in their study of the dynamics of cultural transmission and integration patterns. In particular, Bisin and Verdier's model has relevant implications regarding the determinants of the persistence of different cultural traits in the population. Cultural transmission is modelled as the result of the interaction between purposeful socialization decisions inside the family ('direct vertical socialization') and indirect socialization processes like social imitation and learning ('oblique and horizontal socialization'). The persistence of cultural traits or, on the contrary, the cultural assimilation of minorities, is determined by the costs and benefits of various family decisions pertaining to the socialization of children in specific socio-economic environments, which in turn determine the children's opportunities for social imitation and learning.

More precisely, Bisin and Verdier (2001) consider the dynamics of a population with two possible cultural traits (A and B). Let q denote the fraction of the population with trait A, and $(1-q)$ the fraction with trait B. Families are composed of one parent and one child. All children are born without defined preferences or cultural traits, and are first exposed to their parent's trait, which they adopt with some probability d_i, for i = A or B. If a child from a family with trait i is not directly socialized, which occurs with probability $1-d_i$, he picks the trait of a role model chosen randomly in the population (i.e. he/picks trait A with probability q and trait B with probability $1-q$). The probability that a child of a parent of trait A also has trait A is therefore $\Pi_{AA} = d_A + (1-d_A)q$; while the probability that he has trait B is $\Pi_{AB} = (1-d_A)(1-q)$. The probabilities Π_{BB} and Π_{BA}, by symmetry, are $\Pi_{BB} = d_B + (1-d_B)(1-q)$ $\Pi_{BA} = (1-d_B)q$. The probability of family socialization d_i can be affected by the parent through various forms of costly effort. The benefits of socialization are instead due to imperfect empathy. For each parent, the chosen level of socialization effort will balance out the marginal cost of that effort against the marginal benefit of transmitting one's own culture.

In such a context, Bisin and Verdier (2001) analyse the resulting population dynamics of cultural traits, that is, the dynamics of the distribution of the population across cultural traits, with the objective of characterizing the conditions which give rise to persistence of cultural diversity in the long run. They show that the crucial factor determining the composition of the stationary distribution of the population consists in whether the socio-economic environment (oblique socialization) acts as a *substitute* or as a *complement* to direct vertical family socialization. More precisely, direct vertical socialization is viewed as a *cultural substitute* to oblique transmission whenever parents choose to socialize their children less when their cultural trait is more widely dominant in the population. This would be the case, intuitively, if parents belonging to the dominant majority tended to rely mostly on indirect 'oblique and horizontal' mechanisms to socialize their children, since such mechanisms are naturally more effective for cultural majorities than minorities. This property of the socialization mechanism promotes the persistence of cultural differences in the population. On the contrary, direct vertical transmission is a *cultural complement* to oblique transmission when parents socialize their children more intensely the more widely dominant their cultural trait is in the population. In such a case, the population dynamics converges to a culturally homogeneous cultural population. The complementarity between family and society in the process of intergenerational socialization gives a size advantage to the larger group (the majority) both in terms of direct vertical family socialization and in terms of indirect 'oblique and horizontal' socialization. This promotes the assimilation of the minority group and cultural homogeneity in the long run.

While Bisin and Verdier's (2001) model is stated in terms of general socialization mechanisms, specific choices contribute to direct family socialization and hence to cultural transmission. Prominent examples are, for example, education decision, family location decisions, and marriage.[7] The simple analytics of the model are obtained when the

---

[7] For instance, education choices have been studied by Pattacchini and Zenou (2004); marriage choices within ethnic and religious groups have been specifically discussed by Bisin-Verdier (2000) and Bisin et al. (2004). Other applications incorporating identity formation and oppositional cultures include Sáez-Martí and Zenou (2005) and Bisin et al. (2009). The role of horizontal socialization and peer effects is also discussed in Sáez-Martí and Sjögren (2005).

benefits of socialization are based on purely cultural motivations and are in particular independent of the distribution of the population. Many interesting analyses of cultural transmission require this assumption to be relaxed. Indeed, in many instances the adoption of a dominant cultural trait might provide a beneficial effect per se. An obvious example is Lazear (1999), where the adoption of the dominant language has beneficial effects in the labour market. In this case altruistic parents, even if paternalistic, might favour (or discourage less intensely) the cultural assimilation of their children. This trade-off between ethnic preferences and the disadvantage of minority traits in terms of economic opportunities may be central to the integration pattern of immigrants in the host country. Interestingly, when these elements are incorporated in cultural transmission models (Bisin and Verdier, 2000), they result in the existence of multiple equilibrium pattern of cultural assimilation and issues of coordination of beliefs across and within cultural groups.

In the previous sections, we reviewed some of the theoretical frameworks developed in the literature for the study of integration patterns of members of cultural minorities. These analyses stress three interesting components: structural socio-economic opportunities, complementarities and substitutabilities between the minority and the majority cultures, externalities and the role of expectations and beliefs. We discuss each of them in turn.

1.3.6 Socio-economic opportunities

As the structuralist approach in sociology, the economic analysis of cultural integration emphasizes the role of economic incentives and opportunities. Incentives and opportunities are in particular affected by the size of the minority group. Indeed, assimilation to the dominant culture is likely to provide scale benefits in terms of economic interactions. Therefore we should generally expect smaller minorities to culturally assimilate faster and more easily than bigger minorities. Also, the socio-economic gains of cultural assimilation depend importantly on several host country institutional factors as well as on the reactions of the dominant group to the pattern of integration of minorities. Specifically, supply factors such as forms of socio-economic exclusion by the dominant group may significantly reduce the demand for cultural assimilation by members of minorities and may stimulate, on the contrary, the adoption of strategies leading to cultural separation. In certain circumstances, socio-economic exclusion by the dominant group could even create the conditions for the emergence of oppositional cultures, as a sort of 'negative demand' for assimilation.

1.3.7 Complementarities and substitutabilities in human capital and socialization processes

Two dimensions of the degree of complementarities and substitutabilities between the minority culture and the majority culture appear relevant to understanding and explaining different integration patterns. First, as illustrated by Chiswick's human capital formation approach, complementarities in skill learning processes tend to favour similar and positively correlated patterns of human capital accumulation in different cultures. This leads to integration when associated with high levels of investments and marginalization when associated with low levels of investments. On the other hand, substitutabilities lead to negatively correlated human capital investments between minorities and the majority. Second, as suggested by Bisin and Verdier's cultural transmission framework, complementarities and substitutabilities between direct vertical family socialization and indirect oblique mechanisms of socialization may significantly affect the intensity with which minority members engage in cultural transmission to their children. Again, group size effects matter. When socialization mechanisms are characterized by complementarities in imitation processes and exposure to role models, minority parents tend to reduce their direct transmission efforts when they expect their children to be less exposed to cultural role models of their own group. On the contrary, when family and society are interacting as cultural substitutes in socialization, minority members try to compensate by their own socialization effort for the fact that their group's cultural influence is reduced.

Combining these two dimensions suggest conditions under which the four acculturation strategies of Berry's (1997) typology, as described in Figure 1.2, are likely to emerge. This is summarized in Figure 1.3. The horizontal dimension characterizes the degree of complementarity versus substitutability between group specific human capital and general human capital. The vertical dimension describes the degree of cultural complementarity versus substitutability between family and external cultural influences. Box 1 in Figure 1.3 represents the socialization environment characterized by substitutability along both dimensions. In this case minority groups are likely to socialize their children intensively with their own group specific values and skills. Because group specific human capital is a substitute for general human capital, this is likely to lead to *cultural separation* and significant cultural resilience of the

Human capitals

		Substitution effects	Complementarity effects
Socialization processes	Substitution effects	Box 1: **separation**	Box 2: **integration**
	Complementarity effects	Box 3: **assimilation**	Box 4: **marginalization**

Figure 1.3 Multi-dimensional models: a synthesis.

minority group. Box 2 in Figure 1.3 represents an environment where cultural transmission is characterized by cultural substitutability, while the two types of human capital are complements. In this case, minority group individuals again intensively transfer their values and traits to their children. At the same time, the complementarity between group specific skills and general skills implies also high levels of investments in general human capital. Hence *cultural integration*, where second-generation individuals are integrated with the majority group and still preserve many of their own distinctive characteristics, will tend to obtain. Alternatively, Box 3 in Figure 1.3 represents a socialization environment with cultural complementarities in socialization and substitutabilities between group specific and general skills. In this case, minority individuals weakly transmit their own cultural traits and, correspondingly, there is more investment in general human capital. This is likely to lead to a *cultural assimilation* across generations. Finally, the last configuration, in Box 4 in Figure 1.3, corresponds to an environment with complementarities along both dimensions. Minority group individuals provide weak socialization effort and low investment in general human capital. This induces *marginalization*, with little attachment to the original minority culture and also low integration with the majority group.

1.3.8 *Externalities and expectations*

All theoretical frameworks developed in the literature for the study of integration patterns we have discussed previously, highlight the fact that socialization and dynamic cultural evolution processes are characterized by several externalities. First of all, positive external effects of assimilation on the majority are by the choices of minority members, specifically when assimilation involves more efficient communication and coordination and therefore a larger surplus to be shared between minority and majority groups. A consequence of this externality is that cultural integration might proceed too slowly and would need subsidization. Second, individual socialization and assimilation choices are formed under certain sets of beliefs about the aggregate process of cultural dynamics itself. How such beliefs are formed and coordinated upon may affect the path of cultural integration. Again, this leaves scope for the emergence of collective institutions allowing individuals to coordinate their socialization and assimilation choices on a path that is socially efficient.

1.4 Measuring cultural integration

The integration process of an individual of a specific immigrant group into his host country is characterized by several dimensions, typically aggregated into four distinct but not mutually exclusive general categories: economic, legal, political, and social integration. The first category, economic integration, is associated with integration processes in 'market' relationships. These include integration in the labour market, in residential location, in education and training in skills which are valued in market interactions. The second category, legal integration, relates to the evolution of an immigrant's status and its implications for his (or her) conditions of stay. The third category is political integration. It connects to the public and political sphere, and to collective decision-making processes in the host country. Typically it includes interest in local political processes, participation in political organizations, voting, etc. Finally, cultural integration is the fourth category. It is associated with the social and cultural sphere and concerns cultural habits, values and beliefs, religion, and language. It involves dimensions which are not generally intermediated directly through markets or political processes. Measuring the cultural integration of minority groups implies, therefore, searching for indicators that essentially relate to all these categories.

1.4.1 *Behavioural data*

A first approach in measurement of integration consists in collecting empirical observations regarding the actual behaviour of minority individuals, and assessing how it differs from that of majority group members. Typical indicators include language spoken at home, religious practice, fertility patterns, educational achievement, gender gaps in education or labour market participation, prevalence of female labour supply, social participation, and marriage behaviour (intermarriage rates, marriage rates at age 25, cohabitation, divorce, partner age gaps, etc,).

One specific measure of objective behaviour that has attracted significant attention is intermarriage. It is generally considered as evidence of growing cultural 'integration'. A high rate of intermarriage signals reduced social distance between the groups involved and the fact that individuals of different ethnic backgrounds no longer perceive social and cultural differences significant enough to prevent mixing and marriage (Gordon, 1964; Kalmijn, 1998). There are several reasons why intermarriage may be an important indicator of integration. First, marriage is an important mechanism for the transmission of ethnically specific cultural values and practices to the next generation. Hence intermarriage, by changing the scope for socialization, may fundamentally affect the boundaries and distinctiveness of ethnic minority groups (Bisin and Verdier, 2000). Also, intermarriage at significant and sustained rates leads to major demographic changes in society, in particular to the emergence of 'mixed' children. This has important implications for the evolution of ethnic categorizations. Intermarriage is constrained by a variety of factors, such as the size of groups, segregation, and socioeconomic and cultural barriers. Among the variables often discussed as determinants, a major role is played by generational status (first versus second generation), educational attainment and socio-economic status, marriage pool structure of potential co-ethnic partners (group size, sex ratios at given socio-economic status), gender, religion, linguistic distances with majority group, residential integration, and spatial segregation (see, for instance, Furtado, 2006; Chiswick and Houseworth, 2008).

While it is generally assumed that intermarriage is a good indicator of immigrants' integration, a number of caveats should, however, be kept in mind. First, intermarriages measured as such may not give an adequate picture of interracial relationships as, for instance, they do not include dating or cohabitation. Second, there are difficulties related to the criteria by which a union is counted as intermarriage. The status of certain minority groups is not always clear, and what constitutes intermarriage may often depend on the specific data. As noted by Song (2009), for instance, the US Census Bureau does not regard a marriage between a Japanese American and an Indian (South Asian) American as intermarriage, but the same union would count as such in Britain. More generally, definitional questions on group boundaries (ethnic, racial, religious) may significantly affect the final picture regarding how inter-marriages are recorded. Collected data lack a standardization of methods in recording and describing patterns of intermarriage across countries. In particular, it is difficult to obtain comparable cross-national data about intermarriage in Europe. Indeed in many cases in European data, groups' boundaries are identified by the nationality or country of birth of marriage partners, rather than their ethnicity or race. More fundamentally, even if there is an observed correlation between inter-marriages and cultural integration, the nature of the relationship between the two variables remains unclear. In most cases, analysts talk of integration as the outcome of intermarriage. But in some cases, intermarriage is also seen itself as an outcome of cultural integration, as it may reflect social acceptance of mixed marriages. Taking another perspective, some scholars (e.g. ethnic competition theorists) have argued that while intermarriage may be associated with a form of inte-gration or of inclusion in some dimensions of the majority group, intermarried minority individuals are nonetheless not accepted in many mainstream social environments (Olneck, 1993). In particular, interracial partnerships do not automatically result in reduced prejudice within the couple, the family network, or society at large (Song, 2005).

1.4.2 *Survey data*

Rather than focusing on actual socio-economic behaviour, an alterna-tive approach to assess the pattern of integration of minority groups considers subjective perceptions and attitudes on various socio-eco-nomic dimensions, categorizations, and prescriptions, as collected in survey data. Again, the basic question is to see how these variables differ between minority members and the mainstream majority group and what the determinants are of such differences. Attitudes on gender roles, religious practices or political beliefs, and convictions are generally included in these analyses. One dimension also often investigated con-cerns the degree of cultural identification to some mainstream charac-teristics such as national identity (see for instance Constant *et al.*, 2006; Zimmermann *et al.*, 2007).

Subjective attitudes and perceptions are interesting as they directly connect to an individual's identification process. Some caveats, how-ever, need to be mentioned. First, as is well known, survey data suffer from problems with framing: the way survey questions are designed and the responses are collected may significantly affect the answers of the subjects investigated. More importantly, subjective attitudes are just expressive manifestations, reflecting what 'one does or intends to do' and one's expectations of 'what is socially acceptable to say in public'. Hence, subjective attitudes may only be partially related to the actual and objective behaviour of subjects, that is, immigrants in studies about cultural integration. Constant *et al.* (2006), for instance, recognize this problem in their analysis of immigrants' identity formation in Germany. Rather than limiting themselves only to subjective attitudes, they construct the indicator along five key elements, some of which include objective behaviour.[8] Using data from the German Socio-Economic Panel (GSOEP) on immigrants in the *guest worker* population, they follow the two-dimensional acculturation logic of Berry (1997) and present an *ethnosizer* indicator providing information on immigrants' attachment to both their original culture and the German culture. Looking at how individuals get classified across the four regimes of acculturation (integration, assimilation, separation, and marginalization), Constant *et al.* (2006) then find that the classification obtained by the direct measure of ethnic self-identification correlates only weakly with the one derived with their *ethnosizer* indicator. This suggests that there are limitations in how actual behaviour can be inferred from survey data on subjective perceptions.

As emphasized by the literature, a large part of the cultural integration process of immigrants' communities and minority groups goes through intergenerational shifts in behaviour and values. In order to assess such shifts, the literature focuses on how second-generation individuals compare to first-generation in terms of differences or similarities with respect to members of the majority group. For any given indicator, a convenient way to illustrate such dynamics is described in Figure 1.4. The vertical axis reflects the gap between first-generation immigrants and natives of the host country. This gap can be positive or negative. The horizontal axis reflects the gap between the second-generation immigrants and the natives of that same generation. The origin at 0 therefore is the point of perfect assimilation: immigrants do not show any difference with natives across either generation. A given point in that space shows how the first-generation gap compares with the second-generation gap. From this, one may uncover four different regimes describing the *relative* cultural dynamics between the immigrants or minority groups and natives or majority individuals. Quadrant I, in which both generations

---

[8] Those are: (1) language (speak German and/or the language of the origin country); (2) visible cultural elements (type of preferred food, media, and music); (3) ethnic self-identification; (4) ethnic networks structures (i.e. origins of closest friends); and (5) future citizenship and residency plans.

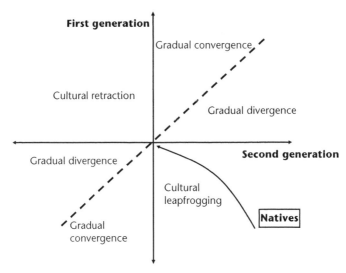

Figure 1.4 Intergenerational dynamics of cultural gaps between migrants/ natives.

have positive gaps with respect to the host country, is divided into two regions. Above the 45° line is a regime of *cultural convergence*, as the gap with natives is smaller for second generation than for first generation. Conversely, the region below the 45° line represents a regime of *cultural divergence* between the two groups. Similarly, the 45° line divides quadrant III, with both generations having negative gaps compared to the host culture. A *cultural convergence* region lies below the 45° line, as the second generation shows a less negative gap than the first generation. Conversely, there is a *cultural divergence* region above the line, with the second generation having a more negative gap than the first generation. Although they are presumably less likely to be observed, there are also two other regimes represented respectively by quadrant II and quadrant IV. In quadrant II, the first generation has a negative gap with the natives while the second generation a positive one. This is therefore a *'cultural leapfrogging'* regime, in which the immigrants overshoot the natives with respect to the indicator considered. Conversely, points in quadrant IV reflect the opposite situation of *'cultural retraction'*, in which the first generation has a positive gap while the second generation a negative one compared to the natives. This diagram captures in a condensed way the intergenerational dynamics of cultural integration of a given immigrant group compared to the natives. It can also be used to compare the relative cultural integration across different minority groups and may help to identify strategies of acculturation of specific groups in Berry's typology. For instance, regimes such as *'cultural divergence'* or *'cultural retraction'* are more likely to be consistent with *'separation'* or *'marginalization'* processes across generations, while on the contrary, regimes of *'cultural convergence'* and *'cultural leapfrogging'* may reveal processes of *'integration'* or *'assimilation'* of the minority.

1.5 The socio-economic impact of cultural integration and identity

Cultural integration phenomena interact in significant ways with how resources are allocated and redistributed in society. Integration patterns of immigrants may therefore have important implications for economic and political outcomes in society.

1.5.1 *Labour market*

Traditionally, economists have focused on how immigrants and minority groups directly integrate in the host economy through market transactions. For instance, a significant literature has investigated the impact that immigration has on the labour market in the host country, in terms of wages, employment, and income distribution for both natives and immigrants (see Kahanec and Zimmermann, 2008, for a survey of the literature). Typically, immigrants' economic integration has been viewed as the process by which the earnings of immigrants come closer to those of natives (Chiswick, 1978). The observed cross-sectional pattern generally indicates that initially immigrants have earnings which are significantly below those of natives, conditional on education, skills, and demographic factors. This is explained by the fact that upon arrival, immigrants lack certain unobservable skills and information specific to the host labour market, such as language, educational qualifications, or general information about how to behave in the host country. With time spent in the host country, however, immigrants will tend to acquire the missing skills and information and catch up with the natives. Eventually, because of positive selection bias in the immigration process (i.e. the fact that individuals with stronger economic prospects in the destination economy are more likely to migrate), immigrants may even outperform the natives. While cross-sectional data prima facie seem to support such view of economic integration, they may also hide important cohort effects (Borjas, 1985), for example if more recent immigrants have unobservable characteristics that make them less adapted to the labour market than the older cohorts. In this case, any immigrant group earning gaps with respect to natives are not so much because of slow economic integration but rather because of different cohort characteristics which cannot be identified by the statistical analysis of cross-sectional data.

Cultural integration patterns and identity formation are typically non-directly observable dimensions that may indeed interfere with the process of economic integration. A clear example of how cultural integration practices interact with economic integration is the generally observed labour market premium to intermarriage. A series of studies have found that immigrants married with natives or with spouses of a different ethnic group have higher earnings than immigrants in an ethnically homogamous marriage, after conditioning on the relevant earnings regressors (see Kantarevic, 2004; Meng and Gregory, 2005; Meng and Meurs, 2006; and Gevrek, 2009). The direction of causality is not always clear though. While Kantarevic (2004) fails to find a causal effect of intermarriage on earnings for the USA, Meng and Gregory (2005), Meng and Meurs (2006), and Gevrek (2009) suggest, on the contrary, that intermarriage has a causal effect on immigrants' earnings in Australia, France, and the Netherlands, respectively. Controlling for the endogeneity of the intermarriage decision more than doubles the estimate of this marginal effect. Several studies have also uncovered connections between subjective attitudes and identity and labour market outcomes for individuals with a foreign background. For instance, Constant et al. (2006) and Zimmermann et al. (2007) have studied the connection between Berry's categories of identity (integration, assimilation, separation, and marginalization) and the probability of being employed in Germany. While no systematic differences are found in labour market outcomes of integrated and assimilated men, integrated women seem to succeed better than assimilated ones. At the same time, for men and women alike, separated and marginalized individuals have a significantly lower probability of being employed than those who are assimilated. In other words, a strong minority identity does not seem to have any negative impact on labour market outcomes, provided that it is combined with a strong majority identity. In Sweden, Nekby and Rödin (2007) also find small differences in employment outcomes between individuals with an integrated identity and those with an assimilated identity. On the other hand, male individuals with a separated identity have considerably lower chances of being employed than those who are assimilated. There does not seem to be any systematic differences for women across the different cultural identities. Studying the effect of oppositional cultures on labour market outcomes, Battu and Zenou

(2008) show that for the UK, non-whites who are strongly opposed to the British identity have a significantly lower probability of being employed than non-whites who are not oppositional. Negative attitudes with respect to ethnically mixed marriages are also associated with a lower probability of being employed. There is, however, no 'penalty' in the labour market for individuals strongly identifying with their own cultural background per se.

In the end, the previous studies suggest that a strong identification with the dominant majority culture is the key element to succeed in the labour market. On the other hand, the degree of identification with the original cultural background seems less important.

1.5.2 Education

The level of education and the amount of ethnic group-specific versus general human capital of immigrants at arrival in a host country has significant implications on the pattern of cultural integration they will adopt. For instance, there is widespread evidence that more educated migrants have a higher propensity to intermarry with natives (see Lieberson and Waters, 1988; Schoen and Wooldredge, 1989; Sandefur and McKinnell, 1986; Meng and Gregory, 2005; Lichter and Qian, 2001; and Chiswick and Houseworth, 2008). Indeed Furtado (2006) proposes three mechanisms through which education could affect intermarriage: the cultural adaptability effect, the enclave effect and the assortative matching effect. The cultural adaptability effect captures the idea that educated people are better able to adapt to different customs and cultures. Therefore immigrants with higher human capital, having a better 'technology' for adapting, are more likely to marry natives. The enclave effect refers to the fact that educated immigrants are more likely to move out of their ethnic enclaves because they have better economic opportunities outside their group. They are, therefore, less likely to meet potential spouses of their own group and so, less likely to marry them. Finally the assortative matching effect reflects the fact that the gains from marriage are larger when the spouses' education levels are similar. Given a costly search process, educated immigrants will be more willing to substitute the benefits of ethnic homogamy for assortativeness on the education dimension. Using 1970 US Census data, Furtado (2006) finds that controlling for the enclave effect, assortative matching is more important than cultural adaptability in explaining marriage choices of second-generation immigrants, though the empirical evidence supports both the cultural adaptability and assortative matching effects.

Related to this, there are studies that have discussed the effect of education on identity formation. For instance, Zimmermann *et al.* (2006) study how human capital levels affect the ethnic self-identification of immigrants in Germany as well as their identification to the dominant majority culture. The results show that education acquired before immigration leads to a weaker identification with the dominant culture. On the other hand, human capital acquired after immigration does not affect the identification to the majority culture. Also, Constant *et al.* (2006) find that immigrants with higher education acquired prior to immigration are more likely to integrate than to assimilate, according to Berry's categorization. Cultural integration patterns may also in turn affect the process of human capital accumulation of immigrant groups, especially for second-generation immigrants. The economics literature on oppositional cultures suggests, for instance, a negative relationship between strong ethnic identity and school performance; more specifically a trade-off between ethnic, and often racial, cohesion and academic achievement (see Akerlof and Kranton, 2002; Austen-Smith and Fryer, 2005; Fryer and Torelli, 2005; Pattacchini and Zenou, 2006). It is posited that social discrimination lowers the returns to education for minority individuals, thereby triggering a response by which minority students view educational achievement as an indication of acceptance of the dominant culture, and hence reject it in order to be accepted by their peers. The mechanism has been well illustrated in the USA with respect to black student communities, in which at times those who invest in education are reportedly harassed for 'acting white' and rejected by their peer group (Fordham and Ogbu, 1986). As noticed by Nekby *et al.* (2007), however, the US context of racial relationships that motivated the 'oppositional culture' hypothesis may not replicate well in other western societies. Different types of host country educational systems may interact differently with the cultural identity formation process of immigrants and minority groups. Several studies in cross-cultural psychology indeed find that children from integrated immigrant families are more motivated and more successful at school than those from assimilated families (Olneck, 1993). In their study of the identity of students with foreign backgrounds in Sweden, Nekby *et al.* (2007) also find that, controlling for early educational outcomes which may influence both self-assessed identity and subsequent education levels, cultural integration is associated with significantly higher levels of education achievements than cultural assimilation. These results hold for both first and second-generation immigrants. Cultural marginalization on the other hand is found to be associated with significantly lower levels of education.

These results are consistent with the observation that rapid cultural assimilation of immigrants in certain dimensions serves to accelerate the process of human capital accumulation of children, while in other dimensions it may have the opposite effect. Indeed, for specific minority communities, strong attachment to traditional family values may well promote educational achievements. For instance, second-generation children may be more likely to live in households with both parents than their native counterparts (Jensen and Chitose, 1996) and a more stable family environment may in turn contribute to better academic achievements and to the economic success of the second generation. There are various ethnographic studies which support attributing the educational achievements of second-generation immigrants to close-knit family values. Waters (1996) describes, for instance, how, in New York City, the academic success of West-Indian teens differs from that of their Black American counterparts because of the more stable family structures of the former. Similar examples are reported for Vietnamese immigrants (Zhou and Bankston, 1996) or Punjabi Sikh communities (Portes and Zhou, 1994). On the other hand, it is also observed that immigrant households often have, on average, a larger number of children than do native households. This may delay the process of human capital investment of the second generation. As a matter of fact, immigrant family resources have to be spread over a larger number of individuals, creating a disadvantage for second-generation immigrants with respect to their native counterparts. In this respect, slower cultural integration along the fertility dimension leads to lower human capital accumulation of immigrant groups.

1.5.3 *Social capital*

Cultural integration patterns may also play an important role with regards to integration in other domains of public life, for example social relationships such as social networks, friendships, and local interactions with neighbours, between immigrants and natives, which are typically not mediated in markets. The socio-psychology literature on group conflict theory (Tajfel,1982) points out that these integration patterns might generate externality effects, typically negative. On the other hand, contact theory (Allport, 1954) emphasizes that these externalities may be positive, as repeated and multiple social interactions across group boundaries favour cultural integration.

The social capital literature suggests a link between cultural diversity and various measures of social capital. For instance, using individual-level data from US localities, Alesina and La Ferrara (2000, 2002) argue that racial diversity and fractionalization leads to lower levels of trust and participation in voluntary associations. Putnam (2007) also finds a strong negative effect of ethnic heterogeneity on generalized trust, as well as on other indicators of social capital, in the United States. Issues might be more complex though. As argued by Nannestad (2008) macro-level studies of the relationship between ethnic heterogeneity and generalized trust have not yet turned out robust results: the studies by Delhey and Newton (2005), Paxton (2002), and Bjørnskov (2007) display notable differences on the estimated relationship between ethnic heterogeneity and trust levels. Consistently, empirical results from within-country studies of ethnic heterogeneity and generalized trust span the whole range of possible outcomes (Stolle *et al.*, 2005; Pennant, 2005; and Anderson and Paskeviciute, 2006).

Uslaner (2006) argues that the level of local residential segregation across groups might be the most relevant dimension of cultural diversity which is negatively correlated with social capital. Using data from the Minorities at Risk (MAR) project of the Center for International Development and Conflict Management at University of Maryland, his analysis suggests that countries where minorities are most geographically isolated have the lowest levels of generalized trust.

From the point of view of immigrant integration patterns, however, these studies do not directly address the dynamics of social integration between groups which are initially culturally different. The study by De Palo *et al.* (2006) provides an indication of the determinants of immigrant social integration into the host country. This study relies on the European Community Household panel (ECHP), which provides data on the extent of social relations for both immigrants and natives, with particular information on the perceptions of immigrants regarding their own integration pattern rather than—as is typically the case in most opinion surveys—on natives' attitudes toward migrants. The analysis shows that immigrants from non-EU origin countries, even after controlling for several individual characteristics, such as age, education, family size, and employment status, tend to socialize less than natives. Importantly, education has a significant impact on the type of social activities that immigrants undertake. More educated immigrants tend to relate somewhat less with individuals from their close neighbourhood than with the broader community.

1.5.4 *Political economy*

Cultural integration of immigrants may also be important at the level of the public policy sphere through, for instance, the way they identify and participate in the host country political process. The importance of this issue is perhaps best illustrated by the recurrent debate on the viability and sustainability of multicultural welfare states in western societies (Banting, 1998; Banting and Kymlicka, 2003). In this respect, the comparison between the degree of redistribution in the American and the European political systems turns out to be central. While in the USA social expenditures reflect only about 15 per cent of GDP, they are about 25 per cent of GDP in most European countries. It has been argued that the lower redistributive character of the American political system is partly related to the fact that the American society is more culturally fragmented that the European ones (Alesina *et al.*, 2001). The current immigration flows into Europe might lead to a more intense cultural fragmentation, which in turn might result in the reduction of social redistribution in European countries.

At the heart of the debate on the dynamics of welfare state systems in culturally diverse societies is a political economy equilibrium linking cultural diversity with preferences for redistribution and for the provision of public goods. Several mechanisms may be at work. First, cultural diversity may affect the sentiments towards national community, sentiments which underlie the social consensus for redistribution. It may also divide coalitions rooted in socio-economic class that traditionally sustained the welfare state and change the pattern of political alliances and coalitions for social policies. More specifically, erosion of political support for universal social programmes could derive from the fact that cultural minorities prefer private or communal provision of public services that better fit their cultural preferences. The focus on group specific public goods may also divide pro-welfare coalitions. Support for affirmative action, group rights, or greater autonomy for the expression of cultural differences may weaken links with majority community members and therefore undermine their support for welfare policies. Furthermore, divisions among different minority groups may hurt coalition formation processes. Most importantly, cultural majorities might also reduce their preferences for redistribution due to cultural diversity. Indeed, in political environments in which minorities challenge the mainstream culture, majorities might tend to oppose programmes that channel resources to communities they do not recognize as their own. This effect may be magnified when socio-economic differences and cultural differences are highly correlated (i.e. when the poor are mostly minorities and the minorities are mostly poor). In this case, in fact, economic redistribution is closely associated with cultural redistribution and the decisive voter (who is likely to be from the majority group) may prefer a reduced size of the welfare state.

Cultural diversity may also weaken the mobilization of the working class and divide organized labour along ethnic and linguistic lines. This would reduce the political effectiveness and the organizational strength of trade unions, which, historically, have had a crucial role in the political support for welfare state institutions (Esping-Andersen, 1985 and 1990). Corroborating such a view, Stephens (1979) found, indeed, that during the expansion of the post-war welfare state, ethnic and linguistic diversity was strongly and negatively correlated with the effectiveness of labour organizations. Consistent with this discussion, the economic literature provides empirical evidence that cultural diversity (measured by ethnic or racial diversity) is associated with a reduced provision of public goods or redistribution, at the regional, city, or district level.[9] The study by Poterba (1997) on the provision of public education in USA states suggests that older citizens are less inclined to spend on public education benefiting younger generations when these generations belong disproportionately to a different race. Vigdor (2004) also finds that the greater a community's racial heterogeneity, the lower its rate of response to the 2000 Census form (this response is interpreted as a local public good, since the amount of federal funds allocated to the community depend on its response rate). While the conclusions from this literature cannot be applied directly to the question of support for European welfare state institutions, in particular because they relate mostly to racial rather than cultural diversity, they do suggest, however, that this issue is potentially important.

Shayo (2009) provides an interesting formal model of the endogenous interaction between social class or national identity formation and redistributive policies. The analysis builds on social psychology in exploiting the insight that an individual is more likely to identify with a group the more similar he is to that group and the higher the relative status of that group. The analysis highlights two interesting results: a relationship between national identification and income (the poor are more nationalist), and a link between preferences for redistribution and national identification (nationalists are for less redistribution, at a given income level). In turn the model implies that a more widespread sense of national identity is associated with less redistribution. Using data from the World Values Survey and the International Social Survey Program (ISSP 1995) for a large number of democracies, the paper provides some support for these implications and for the effect of within-class cultural

---

[9] Alesina and La Ferrara (2004) provide a good survey of this literature.

heterogeneity on the support for redistribution by the poor in European democracies.

An interesting recent literature addresses the specific issue of the preferences for redistribution of immigrants from the perspective of the observed persistence of cultural traits (Bisin and Verdier, 2010; Fernandez, 2010). For instance, using the separation and reunification of Germany as a natural experiment, Alesina and Fuchs-Schündeln (2007) find that those who lived in the former East Germany more strongly prefer redistribution after reunification. Similarly, Guiso *et al.* (2006) find that country-of-ancestry fixed effects are significant determinants of preferences for redistribution in the General Social Survey in the USA. Finally, Luttmer and Singhal (2008) use the three waves 2002/2003, 2004/2005, and 2006/2007 of the European Social Survey (ESS) to investigate how preferences for redistribution might have some purely cultural determinant. They find that the average preference for redistribution in an immigrant's country of birth has a large and significant effect on his own preference for redistribution. These analyses suggest that immigrants tend to 'export' to the host country the preferences for redistribution they formed in the origin country. Passed on to second generations through cultural transmission, these inherited cultural values are likely to shape the political support for redistribution in the host countries significantly, at least as long as they are effectively activated through civic and political participation.

It is therefore natural in this respect to ask what do we know about civic participation of immigrants and if there is a cultural component of such behaviour? Using information from the European Social Survey and the World Values Survey for immigrants from 54 origin countries, Aleksynska (2007) investigates the factors that determine civic participation of immigrants and explicitly considers the issue of cultural transmission and assimilation of migrants with respect to civic participation. Active civic participation is defined as membership in trade unions and political parties, unpaid work for a party or any other organization or association, the signing of petitions and boycotting of certain products, and participation in lawful demonstrations. Cultural transmission is identified by relating participation rates of non-migrants in origin countries to the participation rates of those who migrate in host countries. At the same time, cultural assimilation is identified by comparing immigrant and native civic participation in the same country.[10]

---

[10] The econometric issue with the possible selection of immigrants is somewhat accounted for by a procedure which matches immigrants to otherwise similar natives and compatriots who did not migrate.

The paper documents several interesting empirical regularities. First of all, limited evidence is found for the transmission of participation across borders. Typically, migrants originating from industrialized and culturally more homogeneous countries tend to participate more. Second, the culture of the host country matters most: higher participation patterns among natives tend to induce immigrants to participate more.

1.6 Conclusion: what this book does

This book compares the patterns of cultural and economic integration across European countries and the USA. We document two main questions: (1) how do European countries differ in their cultural integration process, between themselves and with respect to the USA? (2) how is the cultural integration process related to economic integration?

1.6.1 *Cultural and economic outcomes*

Because we aim at providing a comprehensive picture of the cultural and economic integration process in a cross-country perspective, we look at the same set of cultural and economic outcomes, and compatibly with available data. The list of indicators we construct is inspired by the literature we have reviewed above.

To measure cultural integration, we focus on both objective indicators and self-reported attitudes and values. The main objective indicators of cultural integration we look at in the country chapters are:

- Family arrangement: education gap between partners, age gap between partners;
- Marital status: early marriage, cohabitation, marital status, divorce rate;
- Interethnic marriage rate;
- Fertility rate.

The main self-reported attitudes and values we focus on are:

- Language spoken at home;
- Self-identity, measuring whether the immigrant self-identified mainly with the host country or the country of origin;
- Religious intensity, measured by the frequency of praying.

The main economic integration outcomes we report on include:

- Income;
- Educational attainment;
- Female labour force participation;
- Female and male employment rates.

1.6.2 Methodology to measure the integration process

In all country chapters, we propose two specifications to measure the integration process of immigrants.

Evolution of integration evolution between first and second-generation immigrants. This first specification compares the economic and cultural outcomes between the first and second generation of immigrants:

$$Outcome_i = \sum_j \beta_j CountryOrigin_j \times Immigrant\_FirstGeneration +$$

$$\sum_j \gamma_j CountryOrigin_j \times Immigrant\_SecondGeneration + \sum_k \theta_k Cohort_k + X_i'\alpha + \varepsilon_i$$

where β_j and γ_j measures the impact of being a first-generation immigrant and a second-generation immigrant from country j relative to natives.[11] *First-generation immigrant* and *second-generation immigrant* are dummies equal to 1 if the individual belongs to either group and zero otherwise. First-generation immigrants are defined as individuals who are foreign-born from country j and whose two parents are foreign-born. Second-generation immigrants are defined as immigrants who are born in the host country but whose parents are both foreign-born from country j. The reference group is represented by the natives in the host country, that is, individuals who are born in the country and whose both parents are also born in the country. The natives are always considered as the omitted group.

The comparison between β_j and γ_j thus measures whether the gaps in cultural and economic outcomes of immigrants relative to natives have evolved between first and second generation immigrants. This specification allows us to capture the integration process simply, as we have previously suggested in Figure 1.4. The origin at 0 represents the reference group of natives. The coefficient β_j on the vertical axis would reflect the gap between first generation immigrants and natives of the host

---

[11] Note that this specification assumes that the birth cohorts and other regressors have the same effect for all countries of origin.

country. The coefficient γ_j on the horizontal axis would measure the gap between second-generation immigrants and natives of the host country.

The country chapters report for each outcome the four potential integration processes suggested above: '*convergence*', '*divergence*', '*leap-frogging*', and '*retraction*'.

Evolution of integration evolution between younger and older cohorts of immigrants. This second specification allows us to explore further the integration process among cohorts. We use the same strategy as before but we distinguish the gap in cultural and economic outcomes between different birth cohorts within each wave of immigration.

$$Outcome_i = \sum_j \sum_k \beta_{j,k} CountryOrigin_j \times Cohort_k \times Immigrant$$
$$+ \sum_k \theta_k Cohort_k + X_i' \alpha + \varepsilon_i$$

where $\beta_{j,k}$ is the impact of being first-generation immigrant from country j and belonging to the birth cohort k, relative to the natives.

The country chapters distinguish mainly between two cohorts, those younger or older than 30-year-olds, and focus on the cohort evolution within the first-generation immigrants. This specification provides the same simple illustration of the integration process as in Figure 1.4 above, but where the horizontal axis represents gap between the natives and the younger cohort, and the vertical axis represents the gap between the natives and the older cohorts.

1.6.3 *Control variables*

The baseline controls are the dummies associated with the country of origin of first and second generation, or the cohorts of foreign born, with reference to the natives (omitted group). In addition, all the country chapters include a baseline vector X of controls, including gender, age, and education. Those are the co-variates available in all the country surveys. In addition to the baseline regressions, the country chapters explore further the role of additional controls, whenever available, such as the time spent in the host country or whether immigrants have been educated in the host country.

1.7 Caveats

The first caveat relates to the choice of the countries covered by the book. The selection of the European countries is based on two main criteria. The first is to gather European countries with sharp enough differences in their integration models and for which the question of cultural integration of immigration lies as the heart of the agenda. The second criterion is the availability of representative national databases combining information on both objective and subjective outcomes of cultural and economic integration. This book thus does not cover all the European countries. The conclusion will enlarge the cross-country comparison by using another database, the European Social Survey. We also document the results for the USA.

The second issue relates to the econometric specification. In order to gather descriptive data from heterogeneous national surveys, this book has to propose a simple econometric specification that can be replicated in all countries. This is a clear trade-off between providing in-depth analysis of endogeneity and omitted variables, but for a small set of countries, or enlarging the coverage of European countries with replicable estimations.

This book does not identify causal links between cultural and economic integration, and we are not aware of any research article that provides such a link so far. Besides, it might well be the case that identification is impossible due to the existence of potential multiple equilibria, as stated above. For instance, an increase in the number of immigrants can shift the preferences and shape institutions, say segregation at schools, which in turn affect the educational achievement of immigrants. But another equilibrium might appear. As the level of education of the country improves, so the perception of immigrants and institutions will change, with less segregation at schools, improving the educational achievement of immigrants. In this context, it is hopeless to identify a causality between institutions of cultural or economic integration of immigrants.

Yet, in the concluding chapter, we use the European Social Survey to check the robustness results of the country chapters. First, we can control for country of residence fixed effects that could drive the cultural and economic integration processes. Second, the information given by the country of origin fixed effects allows us to control partly for the sample composition of immigrants. Let's say, for instance, that we are interested in comparing the cultural integration of immigrants of Maghreb origin across European countries. This analysis is likely to be biased by the fact that all Maghreb immigrants do not come from the same country of origin, and the inherited specificities from the home country could determine the economic and cultural integration process of immigrants in their destination country. The cross-country dataset allows mitigating such biases.

1.8 Main results

We sum-up the main results of the different country chapters and of the cross-country comparison based on the European Social Survey.

1.8.1 *France*

The chapter on France estimates the integration process by combing three main surveys: the French Labour Force Survey 2005–2007, which provides for the first time the country of origin of the parents, the French Family Survey 1999, which report detailed data on the family structure of immigrants, and Histoire de Vie 2003 that reports attitudes and values of a representative sample of immigrants.

Those surveys provide a focus on the integration process of six main groups of immigrants coming from: Maghreb, Sub-Saharan Africa, Southern Europe, Northern and Eastern Europe, and Asia.

The chapter shows substantial heterogeneity in the cultural and economic indicators across first-generation immigrants. In particular, first-generation immigrants from Maghreb and Africa display significant cultural and economic gaps with natives regarding marriage at first age, age and education gap between spouses, or fertility rates. But we find evidence that in almost all dimensions and for all groups, there is a fast integration process between first and second-generation immigrants. The rate of cultural and economic integration is faster for some variables than others. It is religion, family arrangements, and endogamy that show the slowest rate of convergence, in particular among immigrants from Maghreb. Second-generation immigrants from Maghreb also display a persistent penalty in terms of employment. This seems a French particularity.

1.8.2 *Germany*

The analysis for Germany is based on the German Socio-Economic Panel (GSOEP) 2005–2007. This survey cover a representative sample of 20,000 individuals, with a wealth of information on cultural, social, and economic aspects of immigrants.

The main countries of origin of the immigrants covered in the survey are: Turkey, Ex-Yugoslavia, Greece, Italy, Spain, Poland, and Russia.

This chapter suggests an important heterogeneity in cultural outcomes for first-generation immigrants, but a steady convergence process among second-generation immigrants. For instance, fertility rates, age at first child and female labour force participation differ significantly between natives and first-generation immigrants, but differences vanish or at least diminish for later immigrant generations. Second-generation immigrants also report higher levels of language proficiency and of identification with Germany than members of their parental generation.

Regarding the particular case of the Turks, this analysis shows that comparison by generation is crucial when making statements about the integration process of ethnic groups. Turks differ in various ways from natives and also from other immigrant groups. They are more likely to be married in general, more often married at young ages, and often have more children than the average German person. They report the lowest level of political interest and lower levels of life satisfaction than other immigrant groups. But second-generation Turks show higher intermarriage rates, similar behaviour as natives in terms of age at first marriage, age at first child and number of children, and report better German language proficiency as well as greater identification with German identity.

1.8.3 *Italy*

The analysis is based on the Italian Labour Force Survey 2005–2007, which provided for the first time in 2005 onwards information on the country of birth of the parents. The six main origins of the immigrants are North Europe, South and East Europe, Africa, Asia, North and Central America, and South America.

This chapter suggests a more pronounced heterogeneity in cultural and economic integration among first-generation immigrants coming from: North and Central America, and from South America. But interestingly, second-generation immigrants from those countries no longer display significant differences with natives.

1.8.4 *Spain*

The analysis for Spain is based on two main databases: the 2007 Labour Force Survey ('Encuesta sobre la Población Activa' or LFS) and the 2007 National Immigration Survey ('Encuesta Nacional de Inmigrantes' or NIS), both conducted by the Spanish Statistical institute. The new National Immigration Survey sampled the foreign-born population residing in Spain in 2007 with the specific aim of providing insights on migrants' experiences in Spain.

Those surveys distinguish four main origins of immigration: Latin America, Morocco, other Maghrebian countries, and Eastern Europe.

This chapter shows that Latinos—the group with the shortest cultural distance to Spanish social norms—appear very similar to natives in most of the economic and cultural outcomes. In contrast, Moroccans and individuals from other Muslim countries still display large gaps along several dimensions. But the cultural and economic gaps for Moroccans and individuals from other Muslim countries is shrinking fast with the time spent in the host country.

1.8.5 *Sweden*

The data used for Sweden comes from the registered information at Statistics Sweden (SCB) on the entire working age population (16–65 years of age) residing in Sweden in 2005. Included in the data is rich individual information on personal and demographic characteristics, education, employment, and income. In addition, detailed information is available on country of birth and migration dates for the foreign-born portion of the population as well as parents' country of origin for the entire sample.

The survey distinguishes the following origins of immigration: Nordic, West Europe (non-Nordic), East Europe (non-Nordic,), South America, North/Central America, Asia, and Africa.

This chapter shows a large degree of social integration between natives and immigrants in terms of cultural and economic outcomes. The integration process is slower for the sample of second-generation immigrants with homogenous national backgrounds, in particular in terms of partnership patterns, female employment rates, and female education levels.

1.8.6 *Switzerland*

Data for Switzerland stems from the Swiss Census 2000 and the Swiss Household Panel (SHP) 2004–2005. The main origins of immigrants are: Western Europe, Southern Europe, Eastern Europe, Africa, Turkey-Maghreb, Latin America, Asia, and South-Central Asia.

The chapter shows that cultural integration processes, which are at work in various ways in the different groups, contribute to overall convergence. The most striking and lasting differences we can observe across groups do not relate to educational achievement, religious or political attitudes, but to gender-related attitudes and even more to gender-related behaviours. Differences are more pronounced in endogamous couples in general, specifically for women from South and Central Asia, from Turkey, the Middle East, and Maghreb.

1.8.7 *United Kingdom*

The analysis of integration in United Kingdom is mainly based on the Labour Force Survey (LFS) for the years 2000–2008 inclusive. The LFS contains information on country of birth, but no information on country of parental birth for the UK born. This means that it is impossible to identify second-generation immigrants. Instead, this chapter uses self-defined ethnicity as a measure of being a second (or subsequent) generation immigrant. The analysis of the descendants of immigrants is restricted to ethnic minorities.

The main immigrant groups in this chapter are: Indian, Pakistani, Bangladeshi, Black Caribbean, Black African, and Chinese.

The chapter finds significant differences across ethnic minorities in cultural and economic outcomes, but a striking common pattern that emerges is the extent to which the behaviour of UK-born ethnic minorities generally lies between that of white natives and the foreign-born from that community. This indicates a general pattern of cultural assimilation. The rate of cultural assimilation is faster for some variables than others—it is perhaps religion that shows the slowest rate. But overall there are very powerful forces that are acting to change the behaviour of immigrant communities once they are in United Kingdom.

1.8.8 *United States*

The analysis of the integration process in the United States draws on very detailed information from the Census, starting from 1900 onwards and covering all the countries of origin. The Census allows a unique look at the evolution of the integration process of different minorities since the early twentieth century.

The chapter shows that overall there has been little change in cultural immigration over the past century. But some important changes over time, and differences across groups, emerge. Members of the largest single immigrant group of the early twentieth century, those born in Italy, in general were much less assimilated upon arrival than members of the largest group of the early twenty-first century, those born in Mexico. Whereas one-third of newly arrived Mexicans spoke no English in recent years, nearly three-quarters of newly arrived Italians could not speak English in 1910. The rate of cultural integration over time has declined, however. The chapter shows that this decline in the rate of immigration is largely associated with the rise of the status of 'illegal immigrant' in the United States.

References

Akerlof, G.A. and Kranton, R.E. (2000) Economics of Identity. *Quarterly Journal of Economics*, 115, 715–753.

Akerlof, G.A. and Kranton, R.E. (2002) Identity and Schooling: Some lessons for the Economics of Education. *Journal of Economic Literature*, 40(4), 1167–1201.

Alba, R.D. (1985) *Italian Americans: Into the Twilight of Ethnicity.* Englewood Cliffs, NJ, Prentice-Hall.

Aleksynska, M. (2007) *Civic Participation of Immigrants: Culture Transmission and Assimilation.* MPRA Paper No. 7674.

Alesina, A. and LaFerrara, E. (2000) Participation in Heterogenous Communities. *Quarterly Journal of Economics*, 115, 847–904.

Alesina, A. and Fuchs-Schündeln, N. (2007) Good Bye Lenin (or Not?): The Effect of Communism on People's Preferences. *American Economic Review*, 97(4), 1507–1528.

Alesina A., Glaeser, E., and Sacerdote, B. (2001) Why Doesn't the United States Have a European-Style Welfare State? *Brookings Papers on Economic Activity*, 2, 1–70.

Alesina, A. and LaFerrara, E. (2002) Who Trusts Others? *Journal of Public Economics*, 85, 207–234.

Alesina, A. and LaFerrara, E. (2004) *Ethnic Diversity and Economic Performance.* NBER Working Paper 10313.

Allport, G. (1954) *The Nature of Prejudice.* Reading, MA, Addison-Wesley.

Anderson, C. and Paskeviciute, A. (2006) How Linguistic and Ethnic Heterogeneity Influences the Prospects for Civil Society. *The Journal of Politics*, 68(4), 783–802.

Austen-Smith, D. and Fryer, Jr, R.D. (2005) An Economic Analysis of 'Acting White'. *Quarterly Journal of Economics*, 120, 551–583.

Banting, K. (1998) The Multicultural Welfare State: Social Policy and the Politics of Ethno-Linguistic Diversity. Paper for the *Conference on Labour Market Institutions and Labour Market Outcomes*, Canadian International Labour Network, Burlington Ontario 27–28 September.

Banting, K. and Kymlicka, W. (2003) Do Multiculturalism Policies Erode the Welfare State? Paper presented at the Conference on *New Challenges for Welfare State Research*, RC 19 of the International Sociological Association, Toronto, Ontario, 21–24 August.

Battu, H. and Zenou, Y. (2008) *Do Oppositional Identities Reduce Employment for Ethnic Minorities? Evidence from Britain.* Working Paper, Stockholm University.

Battu, H. and Zenou, Y. (2010) Oppositional Identities and Employment for Ethnic Minorities: Evidence from England. *Economic Journal*, 120(542), F52–F71.

Becker, H.S. (1963) *Outsiders: Studies in the Sociology of Deviance.* New York, The Free Press.

Berry, J.W. (1980) Social and cultural change. In: H.C. Triandis and R. Brislin (eds), *Handbook* of *Cross-cultural Psychology*, 5, *Social*. Boston, Allyn & Bacon. pp. 211–279.

Berry, J.W. (1984) Multicultural Policy in Canada: A Social Psychological Analysis. *Canadian Journal of Behavioural Science*, 16, 353–370.

Berry, J.W. (1997) Immigration, Acculturation and Adaptation. *Applied Psychology International Review*, 46, 5–34.

Bisin, A. and Verdier, T. (2000) Beyond the Melting Pot: Cultural Transmission, Marriage and the Evolution of Ethnic and Religious traits. *Quarterly Journal of Economics*, 115, 955–988.

Bisin, A. and Verdier, T. (2001) The Economics of Cultural Transmission and the Dynamics of Preferences. *Journal of Economic Theory*, 97, 298–319.

Bisin, A. and Verdier, T. (2010) The Economics of Cultural Transmission and Socialization'. In: J. Benhabib, A. Bisin, and M. Jackson (eds) *Handbook of Social Economics*. Amsterdam, Elsevier.

Bisin, A., Topa, G., and Verdier, T. (2004) Religious Intermarriage and Socialization in the United States. *Journal of Political Economy*, 112(3), 615–664.

Bisin, A., Pattacchini, E, Verdier, T., and Zenou, Y. (2009) *Formation and Persistence of Oppositional Identities*. PSE and Stockholm University, Mimeo.

Bjørnskov, C. (2007) Determinants of Generalized trust: a Cross-country Comparison. *Public Choice*, 130, 1–21.

Blau, I. and Duncan, O.D. (1967) *The American Occupational Structure*. New York, Wiley.

Borjas, G. (1985) Assimilation, Changes in Cohort Quality and the Earnings of Immigrants. *Journal of Labor Economics*, 3(4), 463–489.

Boyd, R. and Richerson, P. (1985) *Culture and the Evolutionary Process*, Chicago, IL, University of Chicago Press.

Chiswick, B.R. (1978) The Effect of Americanization on the Earnings of Foreign-Born Men. *Journal of Political Economy*, 86 (October), 897–922.

Chiswick, B. and Houseworth, C. (2008) *Ethnic Intermarriage among Immigrants: Human Capital and Assortative Mating*. IZA DP No. 3740.

Constant, A., Gataullina, L., and Zimmermann, K.F. (2006) *Ethnosizing Immigrants*. IZA Discussion Paper No. 2040.

Darity, W. Jr, Mason, P.L., and Stewart, J.B. (2006) The Economics of Identity: The Origin and Persistence of Racial Identity Norms. *Journal of Economic Behavior and Organization*, 60, 283–305.

Delhey, J. and Newton, K. (2005) Predicting Cross-National Levels of Social Trust: Global Pattern or Nordic Exceptionalism? *European Sociological Review*, 21, 311–327.

De Palo, D., Faini, R., and Venturini, A. (2006) *The Social Assimilation of Immigrants*. FIERI and IZA Bonn Discussion Paper No. 2439.

Esping-Andersen, G. (1985) *Politics Against Markets: The Social Democratic Road to Power*. Princeton, NJ, Princeton University Press.

Esping-Andersen, G. (1990) *The Three Worlds of Welfare Capitalism*. Princeton, NJ, Princeton University Press.

Ferguson, R. (2001) A Diagnostic Analysis of Black-White GPA Disparities in Shaker Heights, Ohio. In: Ravitch, D. (ed.) *Brookings Papers on Education Policy 2001*, Washington, DC, Prookings Institution Press. pp. 347–414.

Fernandez, R. (2010) Does Culture Matter? In: J. Benhabib, A. Bisin, and M. Jackson (eds) *Handbook of Social Economics*. Amsterdam, Elsevier.

Fordham, S. and Ogbu, J.U. (1986) Black Students' School Success: Coping with the Burden of 'Acting' White. *The Urban Review*, 18(3), 176–206.

Fryer, R. (2004) An Economic Approach to Cultural Capital. Manuscript, Harvard University.

Fryer, R.G. and Torelli, P. (2005) *An Empirical Analysis of 'Acting White'*. NBER Working Paper No. 11334.

Furtado, D. (2006) *Human Capital and Interethnic Marriage Decisions*. IZA Discussion Paper Series No. 1989.

Gans, H.J. (1992) Second-Generation Decline: Scenarios for the Economic and Ethnic Futures of the Post-1 965 American Immigrants. *Ethnic and Racial Studies*, 15(2), 1734–2192.

Gevrek, E. (2009) *Interethnic Marriage and the Labor Market Integration of Immigrants*. Mimeo.

Glazer, N. and Moynihan, D.I. (1970) *Beyond the Melting Pot: The Negroes, Puerto Ricans, Jews, Italians, and Irish of New York City*, 2nd edn. Cambridge, MA, MIT Press.

Goffman, E. (1963) *Stigma; Notes on the Management of Spoiled Identity*. Englewood Cliffs, NJ, Prentice-Hall.

Gordon, M. M. (1964) *Assimilation in American Life: The Role of Race, Religion, and National Origins*. New York, Oxford University Press.

Guiso, L., Sapienza, P., and Zingales, L. (2006) Does Culture Affect Economic Outcomes? *Journal of Economic Perspectives*, 20(2), 23–48.

Handlin, O. (1973) *The Uprooted*, 2nd edn. Boston, MA, Little, Brown and Company.

Jensen, L. and Chitose, Y. (1996) Today's Second Generation: Evidence from the 1990 Census. In: A. Portes (ed.) *The New Second Generation*. New York, Russell Sage Foundation.

Kahanec, M. and Zimmermann, K.F. (2008) *International Migration: Ethnicity and Economic Inequality*. IZA Discussion papers 3450.

Kalmijn, M. (1998) Intermarriage and Homogamy: Causes, Patterns, Trends. *Annual Review of Sociology*, 24, 395–421.

Kantarevic, J. (2004) *Interethnic Marriages and Economic Assimilation of Immigrants*. IZA Discussion Paper Series No. 1142. Bonn.

Kao, G. and Tienda, M. (1995) Optimism and Achievement: The Educational Performance of Immigrant Youth. *Social Science Quarterly*, 76(1), 1–19.

Kónya, I. (2005) Minorities and Majorities: A Dynamic Model of Assimilation. *Canadian Journal of Economics*, 38(4), 1431–1452.

Landale, N.S. and Oropesa, R.S. (1995) *Immigrant Children and the Children of Immigrants: Inter- and Intra-Group Differences in the United States.* Research Paper 95–02. East Lansing, Population Research Group, Michigan State University.

Lazear, E. (1999) Culture and Language. *Journal of Political Economy,* 107(S6), S95–S126.

Lichter, D.T. and Qian, Z. (2001) Measuring Marital Assimilation: Intermarriage Among Natives and Immigrants. *Social Science Research,* 30, 289–312.

Lieberson, S. and Waters, M. (1988) *From Many Strands: Ethnic and Racial Groups in Contemporary America.* New York, Russell Sage Foundation.

Liebow, E. (1967) *Tally's Corner: A Study of Negro Streetcorner Men.* London, Rowman & Littlefield Publishers.

Loury, G. (1995) *One by One From the Inside Out: Essays and Reviews on Race and Responsibility in America,* 1st edn. New York, Free Press.

Luttmer, E. and Singhal, M. (2008) *Culture, Context, and the Taste for Redistribution.* Working paper John F. Kennedy School of Government—Harvard University, August.

MacLeod, J. (1987) *Ain't no Makin' it: Leveled Aspirations in a Low-Income Neighborhood.* Boulder, CO, Westview Press Inc.

Meng, X. and Gregory, R.R. (2005) Intermarriage and the Economic Assimilation of Immigrants. *Journal of Labor Economics,* 23, 135–175.

Meng, X. and Meurs, D. (2006) *Intermarriage, Language, and Economic Assimilation Process: A Case Study of France.* IZA Discussion Paper Series No. 2461, Bonn.

Nannestad, P. (2008) What Have We Learned About Generalized Trust, If Anything? *Annual Review of Political Sciences,* 11, 413–436.

Nekby, L. and Rödin, M. (2007) *Acculturation Identity and Labor Market Outcomes.* IZA Discussion Paper 2826.

Nekby L., Rödin, M., and Özcan, G. (2007) *Acculturation Identity and Educational Attainment.* Working Paper 2007: 6. University of Stockholm, Linnaeus Center for Integration Studies (SULCIS).

Olneck M. (1993) Terms of Inclusion: Has Multiculturalism Redefined Equality in American Education? *American Journal of Education,* 101, 234–260.

Pattacchini, E. and Zenou, Y. (2004) *Intergenerational education transmission: neighborhood quality and/or parents' involvement? Working Paper No. 631.* Stockholm, Research Institute of Industrial Economic.

Pattacchini, E. and Zenou, Y. (2006) *Racial Identity and Education.* CEPR Discussion paper 5607.

Paxton, P. (2002) Social Capital and Democracy: an Interdependent Relationship. *American. Sociological Review,* 67, 254–277.

Pennant, R. (2005) Diversity, Trust and Community Participation in England. *Findings,* 253, 1–6.

Perlmann, J. (1988) *Ethnic Differences: Schooling and Social Structure among the Irish, Jews, and Blacks in an American Ciq 1988–1935.* New York, Cambridge University Press.

Phinney, J.S. (1990) Ethnic Identity in Adolescents and Adults: Review of Research. *Psychological Bulletin*, 108, 499–514.

Phinney, J.S., Horenczyk, G., Liebkind, K., and Vedder, P. (2001) Ethnic identity, immigration, and well-being: An international perspective. *Journal of Social Issues*, 57, 493–510.

Poterba, J. (1997) Demographic Structure and the Political Economy of Public Education. *Journal of Policy Analysis and Management*, 16(1), 48–66.

Portes, A. and Borocz, J. (1989) Contemporary Immigration: Theoretical Perspectives on Its Determinants and Modes of Incorporation. *International Migration Review*, 23 (Autumn), 606–630.

Portes, A. and Zhou, M. (1994) Should Immigrants Assimilate? *Public Interest*, 116 (Summer), 1–17.

Putnam, R. D. (2007) E pluribus unum: diversity and community in the twenty-first century. The 2006 Johan Skytte Prize lecture. *Scandinavian. Political Studies*, 30, 137–174.

Rumbaut, R.G. and Ima, K. (1988) *The Adaptation of Southeast Asian Refugee Youth: A Comparative Study*. Washingon, DC, US Office of Refugee Resettlement.

Sáez-Martí, M. and Sjögren, A. (2005) *Peers and Culture*. Working paper 642. Research Institute of Industrial Economics.

Sáez-Martí, M. and Zenou, Y. (2005) *Cultural Transmission and Discrimination*. IZA Discussion Papers 1880. Institute for the Study of Labor (IZA).

Sandefur, G.D. and McKinnell, T. (1986) American Indian Intermarriage. *Social Science Research*, 347, 347–348.

Schoen, R. and Wooldredge, J. (1989) Marriage Choices in North Carolina and Virginia, 1969–1971 and 1979–1981. *Journal of Marriage and the Family*, 51, 465–481.

Shayo, M. (2009) A Model of Social Identity with an Application to Political Economy: Nation, Class and Redistribution. *American Political Science Review*, 103(2), 147–174.

Song, S. (2005) Majority Norms, Multiculturalism, and Gender Equality. *American Political Science Review*, 99(4), 473–489.

Stephens, J. (1979) *The Transition from Capitalism to Socialism*. Urbana, IL, University of Illinois Press.

Stolle, D., Soroka, S., and Johnston, R. (2005) *How Diversity Affects Attitudinal Social Capital. A US-Canada Comparison*. Presented at Workshop for Preliminary Presentations of Findings from the Citizenship, Involvement.

Suarez-Orozco, C. and Suarez-Orozco, M.M. (1995) *Transformations: Migration, Family Life, and Achievement Motivation among Ladno Adolescents*. Stanford, CA, Stanford University Press.

Tajfel, H. (1982) Social Psychology of Intergroup Relations. *Annual Review of Psychology*, 33, 1–39.

Uslaner, E. (2006) Does Diversity Drive Down Trust? *Working paper 69.2006*. Fondazione Eni Enrico Mattei.

Vigdor, J. (2004) Community Composition and Collective Action: Analyzing Initial Mail Response to the 2000 Census. *The Review of Economics and Statistics*, 86(1), 303–312.

Waters, M. (1996) Ethnic and Racial Identities of the Second Generation Black Immigrants in New York City. In: A. Portes (ed.) *The New Second Generation*. New York, Russell Sage Foundation.

Willis, P. (1977) *Learning to Labour: How Working Class Kids Get Working Class Jobs*. Farnborough, Saxon House.

Wilson, W.J. (1996) *When Work Disappears: The World of the New Urban Poor*. New York, Knopf.

Zhou, M. and Bankston, C.L. (1996) Social Capital and the Adaptation of the Second-Generation: The Case of Vietnamese Youth in New Orleans. In: A. Portes (ed.) *The New Second Generation*. New York, Russell Sage Foundation.

Zimmermann, L., Gataullina, L., Constant, A., and Zimmermann, K.F. (2006) *Human Capital and Ethnic Self-Identification of Migrants*. IZA Discussion Paper No. 2300.

Zimmermann, L., Zimmermann, K.F., and Constant, A. (2007) Ethnic Self-Identification of First-Generation Immigrants. *International Migration Review*, 41, 22–44.

2

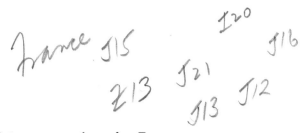

Cultural Integration in France

Yann Algan, Camille Landais, and Claudia Senik[1]

2.1 Introduction

Immigration has a very long history in France since the late nineteenth century (Noiriel, 1988). In the 1920s, France ranked second, just after USA, as the country with the highest share of immigrants, reaching seven per cent of total population. In the early 2000s, as many as 25 per cent of the population had some immigrant background, from the first, the second or the third generation.

Table 2.1 reports on the composition of the immigration population according to the most recent data set, the French Labour Force Survey, for the period 2005–2007. It distinguishes the sample proportions of native French, first-generation immigrants and second-generation immigrants. Around 90.2 per cent of the sample consists of natives, 6.5 per cent are first-generation immigrants and around 3.3 per cent are second-generation immigrants.

First-generation immigrants mostly come from Maghreb (44.1 per cent), Southern Europe (24.8 per cent), and Africa (11.3 per cent). These percentages are slightly modified for second-generation immigrants, the share of immigrants from Southern Europe is higher (37.4) and those from Africa (5.0) and Maghreb (40.7) is lower.

Table 2.1 also shows an evolution over time in the composition of the population of immigrants. During the first half of the twentieth century, immigration in France was mainly driven by inflows from Southern Europe, in particular from Italy and Spain, with some peaks, such as the inflows of Spanish immigrants during the Spanish Civil War.

[1] The authors would like to thank Vincent Tiberj (Sciences Po) for his helpful comments.

Table 2.1 Origins of immigrants in the French Labour Force Survey 2005–2007.

Country of origin	First generation	Second generation
Natives	90.2	
Immigrants of which (%)	6.5	3.3
Maghreb	44.1	40.7
Southern Europe	24.8	37.4
Africa	11.3	5.0
Northern Europe	6.6	3.7
Eastern Europe	5.9	7.5
Turkey	4.1	3.6
Asia	3.2	2.2

Note: Data source is the French Labour Force Survey (LFS) 2005–2007. Proportions are computed using individual sampling weights.

A second wave of immigration from Southern Europe took place in the 1960s and the 1970s, with ongoing inflows from Portugal now.

Immigration from Maghreb dates back to as early as the First World War, driven by the replacement of the labour force in farms and arms industry. But the main wave of immigration from this region took place after the Second World War. Immigration inflows come from three main countries: Algeria, Tunisia, and Morocco. Immigration from Algeria boomed after the Second World War until 1958 and the Algerian civil war. Immigration from Morocco and Tunisia took place later, during the 1970s.

Immigration from Sub-Saharan Africa is a more recent phenomenon. The immigrants from this region are mainly from the French ex-colonies: Cameroon, Ivory Coast, Mali, and Senegal. The most recent wave of immigration is from Eastern Europe and Turkey, with ongoing inflows from Turkey since the 1970s. The smallest group of immigrants come from Asia. Most of those immigrants originate from the ex-French colonies in South-East Asia: Cambodia, Laos, and Vietnam.

French immigration policy is rather pragmatic and dictated by the labour market conditions. First-generation immigrants are now accorded permits of various tenures ranging from one to ten years. Regarding citizenship, Weil (2002, 2005) documents that France is one of the most open countries in Europe. For second-generation immigrants, naturalization comes from the right of birth. Any immigrant born in France is granted French citizenship, but this right becomes effective mostly when children are older than 18 years.

Despite France's long immigration tradition, and the growing concerns about persistent cultural differences with immigrants from

Maghreb and Africa, very few studies have provided a quantitative assessment on the cultural integration path. Most studies have rather looked at economic outcomes. Silberman and Fournier (1999, 2007) look at job outcomes and show the persistent employment penalty for second-generation Maghrebis compared to French natives and other immigrant groups. Aeberhardt and Pouget (2007) estimate national wage origin differential by matching employer-employee data. They typically find that earning differentials mostly reflect differences in the type of jobs, suggesting the existence of occupational segregation rather than mere wage discrimination. Besides, it has been well documented that second-generation immigrants from Maghreb face the highest penalty on the French labour market among the different immigrant groups (see Algan *et al.*, 2010). Recent audit studies show that this labour market penalty is partly driven by pure cultural discrimination (Adida *et al.*, 2010).

In other social sciences a strong debate opposes the supporters of the Republican model, stressing that ethnic origin does not have to interfere with the public sphere (Schnapper, 1991) and those who call for a civil society are more open to multiculturalism (Wieviorka, 1996). But few economic studies have tried to quantify the evolution process of cultural attitudes by waves of immigration and birth cohorts. Yet, there is growing evidence of a strong interplay between cultural and economic integration in France. In particular, Algan *et al.* (2011) focus on the transmission of Arabic name versus non-Arabic name in the French society. They show that parents do take into account the expected economic cost that they inflict on their child by choosing a culturally distinctive name in order to maintain their cultural trait.

This chapter tries to fill this gap by providing a quantitative assessment of the path of cultural and economic integration of immigrants in France.

2.2 Data and methods

2.2.1 *Data*

We investigate the patterns of integration in France by using three main surveys. We measure labour market and educational outcomes with the French Labour Force Survey (FLFS), which cover the years 2005–2007. In addition to the traditional information on country of birth of the respondent, the FLFS has, since 2005, provided information on the country of birth of the parents. The FLFS contains information on country of birth for first-generation immigrants at a very detailed level. It distinguishes between 29 countries or regions.[2] The FLFS also reports the country of parental birth for the second generation but at a more aggregate level. There are nine categories: France, Northern Europe, Southern Europe, Eastern Europe, the Maghreb (Arab North Africa), Turkey (Middle East), (Sub-Saharan) Africa, Asia, and other countries. We exclude the last category as it comprises very heterogeneous populations. This leaves us with seven immigrant groups for our analysis. To facilitate the comparison of the results between first-generation and second-generation immigrants, we aggregate the more detailed countries of birth of first-generation immigrants into the seven broader immigrant categories. The native reference group consists of individuals who have lived in France for at least two generations, that is, those who are born in the country and whose two parents were also born in France. First-generation immigrants are individuals born abroad and whose parents were also born abroad and from the same country of origin. Second-generation immigrants are individuals who are born in France but whose parents were both born abroad. We exclude individuals born abroad with at least one parent born in France and individuals born in France with either one parent born in France and the other born abroad or both parents born abroad but in different countries.

We measure fertility rates based on the 1999 French Family Survey 'Enquete Histoire Familiale' (1999). This survey was conducted in parallel with the Population Census and aimed at analysing the evolution of family structures. It consists of a sub-sample of 380,000 adults, and the survey includes several questions about family status and family relationships, country of birth of the respondent, of his/her relatives (parents, husband/wife), language spoken at home, with children, with parents, etc. In particular this survey is extensively used to compute reliable completed fertility rates.

The French family survey displays three types of information concerning the origins of the respondent. It provides information on the respondent's country of birth: the recorded countries are broken down into 16 categories.[3] The survey also records the country of birth of the father, of the mother, and of the spouse. The countries that are recorded are exactly the same as for the survey respondent. The survey

---

[2] France, Algeria, Tunisia, Morocco, rest of Africa, Asia (including Vietnam, Laos, Cambodia), Italy, Germany, Belgium, Netherlands, Luxembourg, Ireland, Denmark, Great Britain, Greece, Spain, Portugal, Switzerland, Austria, Poland, Yugoslavia, Turkey, Norway, Sweden, Eastern Europe, United States or Canada, Latin America, and other countries.

[3] France, Algeria, Tunisia, Morocco, Africa, Vietnam, Laos, Cambodia, Italy, Spain, Portugal, other northern and eastern European countries, Turkey, other Asian countries, America, all other countries.

also gives information on the nationality (citizenship) of the respondent (at the time the survey was conducted, and at birth). The list of citizenship is exactly the same as the list of country of birth. To compute homogenous regions of origins, we cluster the countries: (1) France: France; (2) Northern and Eastern European Countries; (3) Southern Europe: Italy, Spain, Portugal; (4) Maghreb: Morocco, Algeria, Tunisia; (5) Africa: Sub-Saharian African countries; (6) Asia: Vietnam, Laos, Cambodia, and other Asian countries; (7) Others: mainly African countries. Contrary to the Labour Force Survey used for the analysis of economic integration, we cannot make a distinction here between individuals from Northern European countries and those from Eastern European countries.

In order to explore subjective attitudes of immigrants, we also a survey 'Histoires de Vies', conducted in 2003 by the French national statistical office (INSEE). The sample of the survey includes 8403 adults living in France, with a deliberate over-sampling of immigrants of the first and second generation. The survey includes many questions pertaining to subjective identity, gender issues and work values. It contains information about the country of birth of surveyed persons, their parents and their living partner (if any). Due to the small size of the sample, we only distinguish four main categories of ethnic origin, aggregating countries into large regions as follows: (1) France; (2) Southern Europe: Italy, Spain, Portugal; (3) North Africa or Maghreb: Algeria, Morocco, Tunisia; and (4) rest of the World (foreign country, but not Southern Europe or Maghreb). We chose to distinguish Maghreb and South Europe as these are the most important sources of immigration in France. For instance, in the 1999 French census, those two groups accounted for 62 per cent of foreign immigrants.

2.2.2 Specification

We compare the economic and cultural outcomes between first and second generation of immigrants by using the following specification:

$$Outcome_i - \sum_j \beta_j Country\,Origin_j \times Immigrant - First\,Generation +$$
$$\sum_j \gamma_j Country\,Origin_j \times Immigrant - Second\,Generation$$
$$+ \sum_k \theta_k Cohort_k + X_i'\alpha + \varepsilon_i$$

where β_j and γ_j measures the impact of being a first-generation immigrant and a second-generation immigrant from country j relative to natives.[4] First-generation immigrant and second-generation immigrant are dummies equal to 1 if the individual belongs to either group and 0 otherwise. First-generation immigrants are defined as individuals who are foreign-born from country j and whose two parents are foreign-born. Second-generation immigrants are defined as immigrants who are born in the host country France, but whose parents are both foreign-born from country j. The reference group is represented by the natives in the host country, that is individuals who are born in France and who have both parents also born in France. The natives are always considered as the omitted group.

2.3 Fertility and marriage

2.3.1 Fertility and age at first child

We look at two different outcomes in terms of fertility: completed fertility rates and age at first child.

To investigate the impact of ethnicity on completed fertility rates, we restricted the sample to women older than 40 to avoid censoring issues due to younger women not having completed their fertility. An alternative solution would have been to include all women regardless of their age and to include a polynomial in the age of the woman as explanatory variables.[5]

Table 2.2 reports the coefficient estimates associated with completed fertility rates of immigrants relative to natives. Positive coefficients on first-generation migrants in the first column of Table 2.2 mean that, regardless of their region of origin, immigrants have a greater completed fertility rate on average than native women. Among all immigrants, immigrants from Maghreb, Asia, and Africa exhibit the highest fertility rates. First-generation immigrant women from Maghreb have on average 0.56 more children than natives, and immigrants from Asia and Africa have 0.32 more children than natives. However, this discrepancy

---

[4] Note that this specification assumes that the birth cohorts and other regressors have the same effect for all country of origins.
[5] Each solution has its assets and its drawbacks. In the first case, we are compelled to look at older generations of immigrants, but we have a perfect picture of completed fertility rates. In the second case, we rely on functional form assumptions to control for the evolution of fertility with respect to age, but one can investigate more recent trends because of the inclusion of younger women. The reason we chose the first specification is that the EHF survey is specifically made for giving an accurate picture of completed fertility, whereas the use of Labour Force Surveys (such as in the UK study for instance) makes it difficult (not to say impossible) to observe completed fertility accurately.

Table 2.2 OLS estimates of completed fertility rates by country of origin and immigration generation.

Country of origin	First generation	Second generation
France	Reference	
Africa	0.328***	0.126
	(0.054)	(0.136)
Asia	0.329***	−0.065
	(0.053)	(0.111)
Europe	0.019	−0.036
	(0.030)	(0.025)
Southern Europe	0.043	−0.249***
	(0.024)	(0.023)
Maghreb	0.566***	0.166***
	(0.020)	(0.047)
Controls	Age, education, occupation	
N	135,025	
R^2	0.090	

Note: EHF 1999. The sample is for all women over 40. Specification is that of model (1). Standard errors clustered at the country of origin level. * Denotes statistical significance at the 10% level, ** at the 5% level, and *** at the 1% level.

seems to be greatly reduced for the second generation of immigrants. Second-generation women from Maghreb have only 0.16 more children during their lives than natives. For second-generation women from Asian origins, the difference with natives vanishes completely and is not significantly different from 0. Women born from parents from Southern Europe have 0.24 less children on average than French natives.

To estimate age at first child, we use all women aged 40 or younger and use a censored model to control for women without children at their current age.[6] Results are displayed in Table 2.3 and show that first-generation immigrants from Africa, Southern Europe, and Maghreb tend to have children earlier than natives. Median age at first birth is one year earlier for first-generation immigrants from Africa, and 0.23 years and 0.35 years earlier for women from Southern Europe and Maghreb, respectively. Note that these differences tend to persist among second-generation women from Africa and Maghreb who still have their first child 0.35 and 0.33 years earlier, respectively, than native women.

[6] In our cross-sectional setting, the censoring point varies across observations. To deal with this issue, we use a censored median regression described by Chernozukhov.

Table 2.3 Estimates of the age of the mother at first birth by country of origin and generation of immigration.

Country of origin	First generation	Second generation
France	Reference	
Africa	−1.082***	−0.351*
	(0.133)	(0.333)
Asia	0.921***	−0.249*
	(0.141)	(0.116)
Europe	0.329***	−0.332**
	(0.083)	(0.070)
Southern Europe	−0.232***	0.649***
	(0.065)	(0.062)
Maghreb	−0.351***	−0.329***
	(0.055)	(0.103)
Controls	Age, education, occupation	
N	88,449	
R^2	0.039	

Note: EHF 1999. Censored median regression estimates (Chernozukhov) to deal with censoring of women not having children at their current age. * Denotes statistical significance at the 10% level, ** at the 5% level, and *** at the 1% level.

2.3.2 Marriage and divorce rate

We next consider marriage patterns. We compare marriage rates at age 25[7] for natives and first and second-generation of immigrants. We restrict the sample to all men and women aged between 25 and 40. Table 2.4 displays the results for men and women, and then breaks down the results by gender. Marginal effects at the mean of a probability model of being or having been married at age 25 are reported.

Results show that first-generation immigrants tend to marry more and earlier than native individuals. This difference is especially large for individuals coming from Europe and Southern Europe, and for individuals coming from Maghreb. The probability of being married at age 25 is 7.9 percentage points higher for European immigrants, 7.2 percentage points higher for immigrants from Southern Europe and 1 percentage point higher for immigrants from Maghreb. This can be compared with an average probability of being married at age 25 of 27 per cent in our estimation sample. The difference between immigrants and natives is greatly reduced for the second generation. It is even reversed for second-generation immigrants from Maghreb, who have

---

[7] Marriage rate at age 25 is defined as the fraction of individuals being or having been married at age 25.

Table 2.4 Estimates of the probability of being married at age 25 by country of origin and generation of immigration.

Country of origin	All		Men		Women	
	First gen.	Second gen.	First gen.	Second gen.	First gen.	Second gen.
France			Reference			
Africa	−0.038**	−0.077***	−0.030	−0.093***	−0.044**	−0.063**
	(0.015)	(0.017)	(0.022)	(0.020)	(0.020)	(0.028)
Asia	−0.010	−0.059**	−0.055**	−0.063**	0.038	−0.054*
	(0.017)	(0.021)	(0.022)	(0.028)	(0.026)	(0.031)
Europe	0.079***	0.005	0.086***	0.008	0.070***	0.002
	(0.013)	(0.011)	(0.020)	(0.017)	(0.017)	(0.016)
Southern Europe	0.072***	0.009	0.084***	0.009	0.058***	0.011
	(0.014)	(0.007)	(0.021)	(0.010)	(0.017)	(0.010)
Maghreb	0.010	−0.025***	−0.003	−0.037***	0.026*	−0.010
	(0.010)	(0.006)	(0.014)	(0.008)	(0.014)	(0.008)
Controls			Age, education, occupation			
N	88,449		40,029		61,570	
R^2	0.095		0.059		0.086	

Note: EHF 1999. Logit estimates: marginal effects at the mean. Sample: individuals under 40. * Denotes statistical significance at the 10% level, ** at the 5% level, and *** at the 1% level.

a slightly smaller probability of being married at age 25 than native individuals (minus two percentage points). The next columns in Table 2.4 investigate the same probability model for men and women separately. The main result is that men and women from the same region of origin do not seem to differ significantly in their marriage behaviours. Both men and women migrating from Europe and Southern Europe have a higher probability of being married at age 25 than native French, but second-generation men and women from these same regions do not have significantly different marriage behaviours from native French.

Among immigrants from Maghreb, only women seem to be more likely to be married when they are young (with a higher probability of 2.6 percentage points), whereas men seem to marry later. This may reflect the different nature of immigration between men and women from Maghreb, men coming younger and for working purposes and women coming for family reasons along the policy of 'family gathering'.

Table 2.5 Estimates of the probability of being or having been divorced by country of origin and generation of immigration.

Country of origin	All		Men		Women	
	First gen.	Second gen.	First gen.	Second gen.	First gen.	Second gen.
France			Reference			
Africa	0.003	−0.0307	0.064*	−0.081***	−0.039**	0.000
	(0.017)	(0.021)	(0.035)	(0.009)	(0.016)	(0.031)
Asia	−0.044***	0.080**	−0.033**	0.095	−0.054***	0.067
	(0.014)	(0.039)	(0.024)	(0.068)	(0.017)	(0.044)
Europe	−0.009	0.042***	−0.001	0.032	−0.015	0.0476**
	(0.010)	(0.015)	(0.018)	(0.024)	(0.012)	(0.020)
Southern Europe	−0.000	0.006	0.005	0.010	−0.003	0.002
	(0.013)	(0.008)	(0.022)	(0.013)	(0.016)	(0.010)
Maghreb	−0.001	0.045***	0.005	0.049***	−0.010	0.041
	(0.010)	(0.008)	(0.015)	(0.015)	(0.013)	(0.010)
Controls			Age, education, occupation			
N	51,087		17,628		33,459	
R^2	0.032		0.026		0.038	

Note: EHF 1999. Logit estimates: marginal effects at the mean. Sample: all individuals being or having been married. * Denotes statistical significance at the 10% level, ** at the 5% level, and *** at the 1% level.

We then look at divorce patterns. We consider the fraction of individuals who got divorced.[8] Table 2.5 shows that divorce rates among first-generation immigrants are very close to that of natives. But interestingly, it seems that among second-generation individuals, divorce rates are greater than that of French natives. For second-generation immigrants from Magrheb, for instance, men have a 4.9 percentage point more probability of being divorced once married than native French, and this probability is 4.2 higher for women. Along with the evidence of high endogamy rates among second-generation immigrants from Maghreb, this may suggest the existence of some cultural tension in the marriage model of Maghrebian communities, with some conservative elements (high marriage and endogamy rates) being challenged by elements of high cultural integration (educational gap, etc.), which may explain higher divorce rates.

[8] Note that we therefore restrict the sample to individuals married or having been married. To control for possible censoring of younger individuals who may finally get divorced, we include a polynomial in age.

2.3.3 Inter-ethnic marriages

This section explores the frequency of inter-ethnic marriage. Table 2.6 reports the fraction of each community that is married to someone of a different immigration backgrounds. We distinguish three categories: a marriage with a native spouse, a marriage with a spouse who comes from the same country of origin, grouping together spouses from first and second generation, and marriages with non-native spouses coming from a different country of origin. We distinguish the exogamy rates among first and second-generation respondents.

The proportion of immigrants whose spouse or partner comes from the same country of origin (either first or second generation) is naturally higher for first-generation immigrants. The endogamy rates are equal to 74 per cent for first-generation Maghrebin, 69 per cent for first-generation African, 85 per cent for first-generation immigrants from Turkey or Middle East, and 79 per cent for first-generation immigrants from Asia. When we turn to immigrants from other European countries, the endogamous marriage rate is also higher than marriage rates with natives.

But as Table 2.6 shows, this endogamy is strongly reduced in the second generation: 23.4 per cent for South Europeans, 39.3 per cent

Table 2.6 Inter-ethnic marriages.

Country of origin	French native	Non-French Native—same origins	Non-French natives—different origins
First generation			
Maghreb	21.67	74.29	4.05
Africa	26.83	69.16	4.01
Southern Europe	30.34	65.84	3.82
Northern Europe	45.21	44.25	10.54
Eastern Europe	38.89	53.88	77.23
Turkey	9.72	85.35	4.92
Asia	18.63	78.59	2.78
Second generation			
Maghreb	41.06	53.40	5.54
Africa	52.40	39.35	8.24
Southern Europe	71.21	23.42	5.37
Northern Europe	85.27	6.16	8.57
Eastern Europe	72.48	16.16	11.36
Turkey	36.41	51.76	11.83

Note: Data source is the French Labour Force Survey (LFS) 2005–2007. Proportions are computed using individual sampling weights.

for Africans, 51 per cent for Turkish, and 53 per cent for Maghrebins. Maghrebin immigrants of the first and second generation remain particularly endogamous, as compared to other groups. This is confirmed by regression analysis controlling for the individual characteristics aforementioned.

2.3.4 Spousal age gap

Table 2.7 reports estimates for the age gap between the spouse, which could capture a gender inequality. Immigrant women of the first and second generations do not seem to get married younger than French natives. Their age at the first child is not significantly lower than that of French natives, except for the first-generation immigrants from Maghreb, where the age gap is on average 2 years older than for native couples; and up to 3.6 years higher when both spouses share the same origin. The age difference between spouses is statistically different for first-generation immigrants from Maghreb, but not for the second generation. However, when one distinguishes endogamous couples (where both spouses come from the same country) from exogamous ones, the difference is persistent and statistically significant, even for second-generation immigrants (the age difference is about two years older than for French native couples).

Table 2.7 OLS estimates of the age gap between husband and wife for all individuals by ethnicity and place of birth.

Country of origin	All		Spouses of same origin		Spouses of different origin	
	First gen.	Second gen.	First gen.	Second gen.	First gen.	Second gen.
France	Reference					
Southern Europe	−0.10	0.31	0.40	1.91	−0.80	−0.07
	(0.28)	(0.29)	(0.37)	(1.24)	(0.54)	(0.47)
Maghreb	1.88***	−0.07	3.55***	1.81**	0.18	−0.59
	(0.22)	(0.34)	(0.31)	(0.90)	(0.47)	(0.54)
Controls	Age, education, occupation					
N	5,905		4,212		1,690	
R^2	0.032		0.05		0.02	

Note: Histoire de Vie, INSEE 2003. * Denotes statistical significance at the 10% level, ** at the 5% level, and *** at the 1% level.

2.4 Educational attainment and gender gap in education

Another way immigrants are thought to be different from the French native is the level of education and the attitudes towards gender equality in education. We document these education patterns, focusing on the sample of individuals older than 26 years and who have left education. Table 2.8 reports education distribution and the gender gap in education for natives and immigrants.

2.4.1 *Educational attainment*

We first measure the gap in educational attainment of immigrants relative to French natives. We measure the evolution of this gap between different birth cohorts of immigrants and waves of immigration. We start by regressing the age they left full-time education on dummies for the country of origin of first and second generations. Native French are the reference group. The controls are a quadratic in year of birth, time dummies for the different waves of the survey, and region dummies.

Table 2.9 reports the educational gap for immigrant men relative to natives. The x-axis reports the coefficients for second-generation immigrants and the y-axis reports the coefficients for the first-generation immigrants. First-generation immigrant men from Africa, Northern Europe and Eastern Europe are one or two years older when leaving full-time education than their native counterparts, who themselves leave education when they are on average around 18.3 years old. First-generation immigrant men from Southern Europe and Turkey are on average three years and one year younger than native men, respectively, when they leave education, while immigrants from the Maghreb and Asia are of about the same age.

Table 2.8 Gender gap in age left full-time education.

Country of origin	Whole	First generation	Second generation
Natives	0.13		
Maghreb	0.73	1.2	−0.3
Africa	2.46	2.3	2.0
Southern Europe	0.41	0.3	0.4
Northern Europe	0.95	0.8	0.6
Eastern Europe	0.82	1.30	0.9
Turkey	1.61	1.60	1.2
Asia	2.61	2.72	−1.9

Note: Data source is the French Labour Force Survey (LFS) 2005–2007. Proportions are computed using individual sampling weights. * Denotes statistical significance at the 10% level, ** at the 5% level, and *** at the 1% level.

Table 2.9 Age left full-time education.

	Men		Women	
	First generation	Second generation	First generation	Second generation
Maghreb	−0.491***	−0.476***	−1.241***	−0.390***
	(0.103)	(0.161)	(0.106)	(0.145)
Southern Europe	−3.285***	−0.733***	−3.084***	−0.731***
	(0.128)	(0.134)	(0.119)	(0.128)
Africa	2.441***	3.252***	−0.443**	0.812
	(0.207)	(0.891)	(0.195)	(0.744)
Northern Europe	2.083***	−0.166	1.439***	−0.254***
	(0.248)	(0.454)	(0.210)	(0.380)
Eastern Europe	1.378***	−0.673**	0.066	−0.582**
	(0.299)	(0.303)	(0.224)	(0.255)
Turkey	−3.172***	−0.396	−3.579***	−0.680
	(0.311)	(0.586)	(0.325)	(0.567)
Asia	0.296	0.750	−0.905**	2.581*
	(0.365)	(1.016)	(0.359)	(1.052)
N	51,219	56,311	50,446	54,603

Note: Data source is the Labour Force Survey (LFS) 2005–2007, the sample is all individuals aged 26 and above. These are the coefficients on dummy variables in a censored linear regression. The outcome variable is age left full-time education. The other covariates included are a polynomial in year of birth, region dummies, and time dummies. Sample aged 16–64 including students for which the dependent variable is top-coded at the current age. Reported standard errors are robust. * Denotes statistical significance at the 10% level, ** at the 5% level, and *** at the 1% level.

From the first to the second generation, the gap in educational attainment relative to natives becomes negative for most immigrant groups. For instance, second-generation immigrants from Maghreb and Africa are 0.3 and 0.4 years younger when they leave the education system. Note, however, that the negative gap for Southern European men decreases from −2.9 years to −0.2 years from the first to the second generation.

Table 2.9 shows that only first-generation women from Northern and Eastern Europe are at least as old as native women when they complete their full-time education. All other groups are significantly younger than both native women and their male immigrant counterparts. Immigrants from Maghreb are almost one year younger, and immigrants from Southern Europe are three years younger. But there is an important improvement from the first to the second generation in terms of educational attainment, in particular among the groups which were the most disadvantaged in the first generation. Second-generation Asian women are performing outstandingly well, with an edge of 1.4 years of education relative to native French women. Second-generation women

Table 2.10 OLS estimates of the gender gap in age left continuous full-time education by country of origin, wave of immigration and birth cohort.

	Maghreb	Africa	Southern Europe	Northern Europe Caribbean	Eastern Europe	Turkey
French-born						
Born before 1970	−0.24	−2.27***	−0.20*	−0.38	−0.98***	−1.28
	(0.18)	(0.30)	(0.11)	(0.49)	(0.24)	(0.87)
Born after 1970	0.47***	−1.05***	0.50***	−0.14	0.90**	−0.27
	(0.18)	(0.39)	(0.18)	(1.68)	(0.43)	(0.95)
Foreign-born						
Born before 1970	−0.72***		−0.06***	−1.19***	−0.54***	−0.76*
	(0.099)		(0.08)	(0.21)	(0.25)	(0.40)
Born after 1970	−0.47***		0.64***	−0.82	1.81***	−0.72
	(0.30)		(0.24)	(0.57)	(0.83)	(0.49)
R^2	0.075		0.100	0.034	0.037	0.073
Observations	11,963	2,209	10,594	2,206	2,361	1,381

Note: Data source is the Labour Force Survey (LFS) 2005–2007, the sample is all individuals aged 26 and above. Clustered standard errors at the individual level in parentheses. * Denotes statistical significance at the 10% level, ** at the 5% level, and *** at the 1% level.

from Maghreb and Southern Europe also almost catch up their educational lag.

Table 2.10 provides a complementary picture of the evolution of the educational gap by distinguishing immigrants by birth cohorts. We focus on second-generation immigrants and compare the educational gap relative to natives among the young generation, born after 1970, and the old generation born before 1970. We run two separate regressions for the two different cohorts, taking the native as the reference group for each generation. Among natives, the average age they left full-time education is 20.67 years for the young generation against 17.83 years for the old generation, which represents a significant increase of almost three years between the two cohorts.

Relative to natives, the young second-generation immigrants are sometimes performing worse than the older cohort. Take the case of immigrants from Maghreb, who have an edge of 0.11 years among the old generation, and trail back by −0.45 years among the young generation. Naturally, this evolution does not mean that the younger cohort is less educated than the old one (in the particular case of immigrants from Maghreb, the younger cohort is educated for one year more than than the old one), but the gap relative to the natives has increased. The same is true for immigrants from Turkey. The evolution of the pattern of female education by birth cohort is slightly different to their male counterparts. In general, the gap narrows among the young cohort, or remains fairly similar.

2.5 Female employment

We now turn to the analysis of female employment rate. The sample is made up of prime-age women between 25 years and 59 years old. For almost all ethnic groups, the employment rate is much lower relative to the native women, whose employment rate reaches 74.4 per cent. The employment gap is the most significant for foreign-born women from Maghreb, Africa, and Turkey, whose employment rate is 43.0 per cent, 53.9 per cent, and 20.0 per cent respectively. The difference is greater among married women with children than with single women.

The female employment rate increases significantly from the first to the second generation of immigrants. The employment rate of second-generation women immigrants from Maghreb increases by 16.6 points relative to first-generation immigrants. With married women immigrants from Maghreb with dependent children, the employment rate increases by 20 points from the first to the second generation.

Table 2.11 shows the estimates for the evolution of the employment gap between first and second-generation immigrants, controlling for age and education. The coefficients are the marginal effects from probit estimates on employment. The regressions are run on the whole female prime-age population between 25 and 59 years old, where French-native women are taken as the reference group. Among the first-generation immigrant, there is a statistically significant employment gap of female immigrants relative to natives. The gap reaches around 23–24 percentage points for female immigrants from Africa and Maghreb, and 41.5 for female immigrants from Turkey. The female employment gap remains sizeable and statistically significant among the second-generation female immigrants from those countries of origin.

2.6 Values and beliefs

2.6.1 *National identity*

In the survey 'Histoire de Vies', a series of questions were asked concerning the elements of the respondents' identity. Table 2.12

Table 2.11 Estimates of the probability of being employed for women.

Country of origin	First generation	Second generation
France natives	Reference	
Maghreb	−0.232***	−0.172***
	(0.017)	(0.022)
Africa	−0.245***	−0.193***
	(0.030)	(0.106)
Southern Europe	0.026	0.023
	(0.018)	(0.022)
Northern Europe	−0.164***	−0.047
	(0.040)	(0.091)
Eastern Europe	−0.218***	−0.015
	(0.045)	(0.062)
Turkey	−0.415***	−0.334***
	(0.042)	(0.110)
Asia	−0.198***	−0.114
	(0.062)	(0.156)
Controls	Age, education	
N	86,059	

Note: Data source is the Labour Force Survey (LFS) 2005–2007. The sample is all female prime-age population between 25 and 59 years old. The coefficients are the marginal probit estimate, relative to native women. Clustered standard errors at the individual level in parentheses. * Denotes statistical significance at the 10% level, ** at the 5% level, and *** at the 1% level.

documents the result for national identity. If first-generation immigrants tend to have different attitudes and values, compared to French natives, this difference is largely attenuated for in second-generation immigrants. For example, the respondents are asked about their attachment to a particular country or continent: 'Overall, do you feel mostly: from a French region, French, European, from another country, from another continent?' Second-generation immigrants are more likely to declare that they feel French than the first generation. First-generation immigrants from Southern Europe are 50 per cent less likely to declare that they feel French than are French natives, controlling for age, gender, and education. This is particularly true of those who were born after 1970 (where the probability is reduced by 77 per cent). In the second generation, immigrants from Southern Europe are still 16 per cent less likely to declare that they feel French than native French. Those who were born after 1970 are three times less likely to declare that they feel French. By contrast, if first generation-immigrants from Maghreb are 28 per cent less likely to 'feel French', this effect is not statistically significant for second-generation immigrants from this region.

Table 2.12 Estimates of the feeling of French identity.

Country of origin	All		Born after 1970		Born before 1970	
	First gen.	Second gen.	First gen.	Second gen.	First gen.	Second gen.
France	Reference					
Southern Europe	0.133***	0.030	0.200	0.090**	0.127***	0.010
	(0.022)	(0.017)	(0.154)	(0.044)	(0.022)	(0.018)
Maghreb	0.129***	0.002	0.138***	0.010	0.128***	0.001
	(0.017)	(0.017)	(0.056)	(0.026)	(0.018)	(0.024)
Controls	Age, education, occupation					
N	8,403		1,626		6,777	

Note: Data source is Histoire de Vie, INSEE 2003. Marginal probit effects. Clustered standard errors at the individual level in parentheses. * Denotes statistical significance at the 10% level, ** at the 5% level, and *** at the 1% level.

2.6.2 Language and religion

Another key dimension of integration and identity is language. In the survey, the following question is asked: What language(s) did your parents usually speak when you were a child (around five years old)? The possible answers are: only French, another language, French and another language, two other languages. If the respondent answers that his parents spoke another language (including French), he is asked about this language, and whether he speaks in this language with his spouse, his children (who live in France), other adults living in the household and other adults living in the neighbourhood.

Table 2.13 shows the probit estimates of speaking in one's foreign mother tongue with their relatives, controlling for age, gender, and education. Even among the second-generation immigrants, around 30 per cent of immigrants declare that they speak in their foreign mother tongue with their spouse, children, family, or their neighbours. The differences shown in Table 2.12 remain statistically significant for all migrants from South Europe and Maghreb, of the two considered cohorts.

Immigrants attach a high importance to the transmission of religion to their children. This religious attachment does not decrease from the first to the second generation of Maghrebin immigrants. Surprisingly, this attachment to religious transmission is more pronounced in the younger cohort of Maghrebins born after 1970. The proportion of

Table 2.13 Estimates of the probability of speaking in one's foreign mother tongue with spouse, children, family or neighbours.

Country of origin	All		Born after 1970		Born before 1970	
	First gen.	Second gen.	First gen.	Second gen.	First gen.	Second gen.
France	Reference					
Southern Europe	0.672***	0.282***		0.485***	0.1653***	0.227***
	(0.019)	(0.027)		(0.024)	(0.020)	(0.030)
Maghreb	0.431***	0.250***	0.846***	0.413***	0.364***	0.117***
	(0.021)	(0.031)	(0.024)	(0.042)	(0.023)	(0.043)
Controls	Age, education, occupation					
N	8,403		1,626		6,777	

Note: Data source is Histoire de Vie, INSEE 2003. Marginal probit effects. Clustered standard errors at the individual level in parentheses. * Denotes statistical significance at the 10% level, ** at the 5% level, and *** at the 1% level.

immigrants of the first generation who declare that they have a religious practice is higher than that of French natives. This difference almost disappears for the second generation, except for Maghrebins, for whom this attitude remains statistically more pronounced, even in the younger generation of those born after 1970.

2.7 Conclusion

This chapter has compared a wide range of outcomes for immigrants relative to the natives in France. We have looked at fertility, marriage and divorce rates, inter-ethnic marriage, spousal age gaps, the gender gap in education, employment rates, national identity, religiosity, and language use. We find substantial heterogeneity across communities but also evidence that in almost all dimensions and for all groups, there is a fast integration process between first and second-generation immigrants. The rate of cultural and economic integration is faster for some variables than others. Religion, family arrangements, and endogamy show the slowest rate of convergence, in particular among immigrants from Maghreb. Second-generation immigrants from Maghreb also display a persistent employment penalty. Yet this slower assimilation process in religious and family arrangements does not go against a strong feeling of French identity among the second-generation immigrants from Maghreb.

References

Adida, C., Laitin, D., and Valfort, M.A. (2010) Identifying Barriers to Muslim Integration in France. *Proceedings of the National Academy of Sciences of the United States of America*, 107(52), 384–390.

Aeberhardt, R. and Pouget, R. (2007) National Origin Wage Differentials in France: Evidence from Matched Employer-Employee Data. Crest Working Paper.

Algan, Y., Dustmann, D., Glitz, A., and Manning, A. (2010) The Economic Situation of First and Second-Generation Immigrants in France, Germany and the United Kingdom. *Economic Journal. Royal Economic Society*, 120(542), 4–30.

Algan, Y., Mayer, T., and Thoenig, M. (2011) *The economic incentives of cultural transmission: Spatial Evidence from Naming Patterns across France*. Sciences Po Working Paper.

Noiriel, G. (1988) *Le Creuset Français: Histoire de l'immigration au XIX–XXème siècle*. Paris, Seuil.

Schnapper, D. (1991) *La France de l'intégration*. Paris, Editions Gallimard.

Silberman, R. and Fournier, I. (2007) Is French Society Truly Assimilative? Immigrant Parents and Offspring on the French Labor Market. In: A.F. Heath and S.Y. Cheung. *Unequal Chances Ethnic Minorities in Western Labour Markets*. Oxford, Oxford University Press.

Silberman, R. and Fournier, I. (1999) Les enfants d'immigrés sur le marché du travail: les mécanismes d'une discrimination sélective. *Formation et Emploi*, 65, 31–55.

Weil, P. (2005) *La République et sa diversité. Immigration, Intégration, Discriminations. La République des idées*. Paris,Seuil.

Weil, P. (2002) *Qu'est-ce qu'un immigré? Histoire de la Nationalité Française depuis la Révolution*. Paris, Grasset.

Wieviorka, M. (1996) Une société fragmentée: Le multiculturalisme en débat. Paris, La Découverte, pp. 11–60.

3

Cultural Integration in Germany

Amelie Constant, Olga Nottmeyer, and Klaus Zimmermann

3.1 Introduction

Immigration to Germany[1] began after the Second World War, when substantial inflows of Germans, refugees, and expellees from Eastern European territories immigrated to Western Germany. Immigrant labour was needed to rebuild a dilapidated Germany. In the late 1950s, under the auspices of the Federal Labour Institute and in cooperation with labour unions and local authorities, German employers actively recruited foreign workers. The German immigration system was, therefore, demand-driven and project-tied. Employers determined the number and the origin of the immigrant flow so that their industries would easily absorb them. Initially, it was Germans from East Germany who were a big number of these labourers. In addition, bilateral treaties for recruitment of blue collar workers were signed with Italy in 1955 and with Spain and Greece in 1960. After the erection of the Berlin Wall in 1961 the inflow of East Germans ended. Germany's massive shortage in labour supply, especially in low-qualified sectors, and its extraordinarily fast economic growth made the need for imported labour imperative. Germany signed additional treaties for low-skilled workers with Turkey in 1961, Morocco in 1963, Portugal in 1964, Tunisia in 1965, and Yugoslavia in 1968.

Recruited immigrant workers were called guest workers (*Gastarbeiter*), implying that they were invited to work in Germany under temporary

---

[1] Until 1990, when we say Germany we refer to the Federal Republic of Germany or FRG which was West Germany. After the unification of 1989, Germany means both East and West.

contracts and expected to return to their home countries after a set period of time. The largest inflow of immigrant workers was from Italy, Greece, Spain, Turkey, and Yugoslavia. These immigrants fostered the transformation of the southern regions, like Bavaria and Baden Wüerttemburg, from mostly agrarian into modernized industrial states and contributed to the well-known German economic miracle (*Deutsches Wirtschaftswunder*). By the late 1960s the German economy depended heavily on guest workers both economically and demographically. Unskilled immigrant workers were complements to skilled native workers. Complementarity of skills in the production process allowed for an upward economic and occupational mobility of native Germans. Besides native Germans, immigrants fared very well economically in terms of employment and wages. It is worth noting that during this era of the German economic miracle, West Germany had virtually no unemployment.

The first oil crisis in 1973 prompted the German government to change its immigration policy and stop the active recruitment of low-skilled workers by firms. While the November 1973 ban reduced the number of labour migrants, it led to an increase of the foreign population through family reunification and high fertility rates of immigrants.[2] Therefore, the immigrant composition shifted from brawny young males to women and children who arrived in Germany to join their husbands and fathers. As guest workers prolonged their residence in Germany and along with their families became permanent residents, the government offered them several lucrative options to return to their homelands, but had minimal success. Effectively, while Greek, Italian, and Spanish workers were fairly immobile even though their countries were part of the European Union labour market, immigration from countries with strong mobility constraints (Turkey, Yugoslavia) rose the strongest. This is a consequence of family re-unification, family formation (fertility), and minimal return migration to the homelands, caused by the impossibility or expected difficulties of returning to Germany again.[3]

Various geopolitical trends in the 1980s and 1990s played a significant part in bringing about a changing immigrant composition. During that time, immigration inflows in Germany were mainly shaped by asylum seekers[4] and 'ethnic' Germans. The latter, also called *Aussiedler*, came to

---

[2] This issue is further addressed in Zimmermann (1994).

[3] For further information see Zimmermann (1994).

[4] Mainly due to civil wars in Yugoslavia, conflicts in Kurdish territories of Turkey and northern Iraq. Iranians as well as Vietnamese and Chinese constitute a large percentage of asylum seekers.

Germany in the aftermath of the fall of the Iron Curtain, taking advantage of liberalized travel regulations.[5] Immigrant waves from Poland, Romania, and the former Soviet Union, 'flooded' Germany until a new more restrictive law was enforced in 1993 (Constant *et al.*, 2010a and 2010b). Most recently, during the process of EU East enlargement, it has been labour migrants from Poland and other Eastern European countries who constitute the dominant source of migration inflows to Germany (Brenke *et al.*, 2009).

In the 2000s, almost nine per cent of Germany's population was foreigners. Despite its long migration history, German policymakers refused for a long time to accept the status of an immigration country. However, taking a pioneering stance, the German government of Chancellor Schröder introduced the Immigration Act (*Zuwanderungsgesetz*) in 2001 to regulate immigration. Political compromise allowed only a reduced version to come into effect on 1 January 2005. The Act officially acknowledges Germany's status as an immigration country and addresses integration issues. Until today, the question of how to obtain a sufficient degree of economic and social coherence remains one of the most pressing topics in the current political debate.

Economists have completed many studies on the economic adaptation of migrants, either under the label of assimilation (or parity of immigrant and native earnings) or under integration (or progress without assimilation). Of less interest has been the issue of cultural or ethnic identity adaptation. However, recently the role of ethnic identity has come up as an important concept to study socio-economic integration and explain earnings disparities. This allows migration scholars to tackle the potential joint endogeneity of the processes of economic performance and social and cultural activities. Dealing with the role of an individual's identity, Akerlof and Kranton (2000) have provided a novel theoretical framework whereby the individual's self-identification is incorporated in the individual's utility maximization function as a powerful motivation for economic behaviour. The authors show that while achieving one's 'ideal self' and being comfortable with one's identity increases utility, one may not necessarily reach the neoclassical maximum but may end up at a suboptimal level of economic activity. Bénabou and Tirole (2011) model a broad class of beliefs of individuals including their identity, which people value and invest in. They also study endogenously arising, self-serving beliefs linked to pride, dignity, or wishful thinking. These emerging important contributions can also

---

[5] Immigrants who can prove that they are of German descent are by law German and are granted German citizenship almost immediately after arrival.

explain labour market performance. Accordingly, while some individuals have the drive and human capital to adapt and succeed in the labour market, they may not reach their goal because of behavioural norms and unfulfilled or confused self-identity images.[6]

Constant and Zimmermann (2008) and Constant *et al.* (2006 and 2009a) were the first to introduce a quantifiable measure of the multi-dimensional concept of ethnic identity in economics, employing literature from social psychology and other social sciences. They developed a framework of ethnic identity, constructed the quantifiable index 'ethnosizer' and tested it empirically with German data.[7] For the authors, ethnic identity is how individuals perceive themselves within an environment as they categorize and compare themselves to others of the same or different ethnicity. It is the closeness or distance immigrants feel from their own ethnicity or from other ethnicities, as they try to fit into the host society. Most importantly, ethnic identity can differ among migrants of the same origin and can be comparable among migrants of different ethnic backgrounds. In stark distinction to ethnicity, which indicates ethnic origin or home country and remains unaltered through time, ethnic identity measures how people perceive themselves in the new country rather than their ancestors. The authors allow for the individuality, personality, distinctiveness, and character of a person in an ethnic group to prevail, to differ from one person to another, and to alter and evolve in different directions over time. They define ethnic identity to be the balance between commitment to, affinity to, or self-identification with the culture, as well as norms and society of origin and commitment to or self-identification with the host culture and society.

The ethnic identity is composed of five essential elements: language ability, ethnic self-identification, visible cultural elements, ethnic interaction, and citizenship, as well as locational plans. That is, ethnic identity, whether it is with regards to the home or the host country, is formed by these elements. When considering both ethnic identities, the two-dimensional ethnosizer can be easily visualized in the positive Cartesian quadrant; it is formed by the horizontal axis measuring ethnic identity with regards to the home country and the vertical axis measuring ethnic identity with regards to the host country. In this quadrant, we can easily define four states or regimes of ethnic identity differentiated by the

---

[6] For further information on the topic, see Constant and Zimmermann (2011) who surveyed the literature and provided insights into the role of ethnic identity in economics.
[7] Constant and Zimmermann (2008, 2009); Constant *et al.* (2006, 2009b, 2009c, 2012); Zimmermann (2007a, 2007b); Zimmermann *et al.* (2007, 2008, 2009).

strength of cultural and social commitment to the home or host country. These four states are: (1) Assimilation, a pronounced identification with the host culture and society, coupled with a firm conformity to the norms, values, and codes of conduct of the host country. Self-identification with the country of origin is almost wiped out; (2) Integration, an achieved amalgam of both dedication to and identification with the origin and commitment and conformity to the host society. This is the case of a perfect bi-cultural state; (3) Marginalization, a strong detachment from both the host country culture and the culture of origin; and (4) Separation, an exclusive commitment to the culture of origin even after years of emigration, paired with weak involvement in the host culture and country realities.

This chapter focuses on the cultural integration of immigrants in Germany, which has the largest immigrant population in the EU and is a powerful player in the western developed world. The aim of this chapter is to study the current level of integration of immigrants in Germany. This is achieved by looking at educational gaps between partners, marriage and intermarriage rates, age at first marriage, age gaps between spouses, the number of children per woman, age at birth of first child; political interest, risk attitudes, overall life satisfaction, and female labour force participation. Additionally, we use a variation of the ethnosizer to determine the current degree of cultural integration of immigrant groups. We therefore compare immigrant groups with respect to their self-reported language abilities, their ethnic self-identification, and their religious beliefs. All these indicators are defined as deviations from natives and differentiated by ethnic origin and immigrant generation. Empirical findings are based on panel data from the German Socio-Economic Panel (SOEP) allowing for statements about development over time.

The structure of this chapter is as follows. The next section introduces the data and clarifies definitions, as well as remarking on the empirical methods used in this study. Section 3.3 presents the descriptive statistics and discusses the estimation results. The chapter concludes with a summary of findings from the analysis.

3.2 Data and definitions

The analysis of the cultural integration of immigrants in Germany is based on data from the German Socio Economic Panel (SOEP). The SOEP is a nationally representative longitudinal study that in 2007 contained information of roughly 20,000 individuals and 11,000 private households in Germany.[8] This unique data source provides a wealth of information about various social, cultural, political, and economic aspects of individuals living in Germany and allows the testing of corresponding social and economic theories. Due to its panel design and an over-sampling of immigrants it opens unique analytical possibilities, especially with regards to integration over time based on the behaviour of different immigrant generations. The descriptive statistics we present here refer to the period 2005–2007, or the most recent year for which information is available. The regressions are also estimated on data from the same time period in order to exploit the richness of the data.

A well acknowledged problem related to immigrant populations' research and international comparisons is the definition of who is an immigrant. Different countries have different definitions of who is a native and who is an immigrant. For example, in the US, the prevailing law is the Law of Soil (*jus soli*) that makes all individuals born in the US American citizens by default. Until recently, Germany recognized the *jus sanguinis* or bloodlines as the only law in recognizing a German citizen. With the new developments, Germany now allows, under certain exceptions in law, place of birth to determine citizenship as well. Accordingly, we define an immigrant to be a person who either (1) is not born in Germany or (2) is a person who is born in Germany but is not a German citizen or whose mother or father are not German born or have a non-German nationality. In those cases where both parents are not born in Germany but are also not born in the same country, the country of origin of the mother outweighs the country of origin of the father, assuming that cultural habits and norms are more likely to be transferred from the mother to the child than from the father.[9]

Distinctions between first and second-generation immigrants are based on the country of birth. By definition, individuals who are not born in Germany belong to the first generation of immigrants regardless of the age at which they immigrated to Germany. Individuals who were born in Germany but fulfil at least one of the criteria mentioned above[10] are considered second-generation immigrants. It is important to mention that the idiosyncrasies of the German law may often treat second or

---

[8] For further information about the survey see Wagner *et al.* (2007).

[9] This definition of immigrants defines *Aussiedler* as belonging to the group of immigrants. *Aussiedler* are not born in Germany but are eligible for German citizenship immediately after immigration due to their German bloodlines. *Aussiedler* are mostly born and raised in Eastern European countries, and will be treated as part of the immigrant population and do not take on an exceptional role in this analysis.

[10] Those that hold other than German citizenship, or one of the parents is not German born, or has a foreign nationality.

even third-generation immigrants as foreigners. Moreover, nationality may change over time and be related to a feeling of belonging and commitment to a specific country. Similar to ethnic identity,[11] nationality may be a dynamic feature expressing a certain degree of integration, assimilation, segregation or marginalization. In contrast, country of origin or ethnicity remains unchanged even after naturalization. Only in the case where there is no information available about the country of birth of the immigrant or the parents is nationality taken as the single criterion to determine immigrant status.

3.2.1 *Immigrant population in Germany*

According to the definition of immigrants given above, SOEP data show that 12.18 per cent of Germany's population have an immigration background either personally or induced by their parents (Table 3.1). Since the SOEP over-samples the foreign population in Germany there may be discrepancies between SOEP statistics and official statistics by the German Statistical Office. Since 2005, the German Statistical Office not only reported immigrant status defined by nationality but also introduced a new classification, which is supposed to account for migration background. Accordingly, individuals residing in Germany belong to the group of persons either with or without migration background. Previously, individuals holding other than German citizenship were counted as *Ausländer* (foreigners), completely ignoring country of birth and family background.

Depending on which definition is used, official data state that 8.8 per cent of Germany's population is of foreign nationality in contrast to almost 19 per cent of people with a migration background. Among these people with migration background, roughly 68 per cent belong to the group of people with their own migration experience (comparable to our definition of the first-generation immigrants) and

Table 3.1 Immigrant share on total population.

	Frequency	Percent
German	79,863	87.82
Immigrant	11,078	12.18
Total	90,941	100

Source: German Socio-Economic Panel (SOEP), unweighted sample, 2005–2007.

[11] See, for example, Phinney *et al.* (2001); Phinney (1992); Constant *et al.* (2009b).

32 per cent to the group of persons without migration experience (resembles the second-immigrant generation in this study).[12] Also in the SOEP data, the majority of the immigrants observed, namely 76.82 per cent, are classified as first-generation, whereas 23.18 per cent are second-generation immigrants (Table 3.2). This bias from official data might be related to the fact that the SOEP contains information mostly about individuals who are older than 16 years of age. This restriction possibly underestimates the share of younger immigrants in the total population and thus the share of second-generation immigrants in the sample. In total, the data used within this study include 11,078 observations for immigrants and 79,863 for Germans.[13]

Furthermore, immigrants are distinguished by country of origin. We concentrate on immigrants coming from one of the five sending countries during the guest worker period, namely Turkey, former Yugoslavia, Spain, Greece, and Italy.[14] Additionally, we include Polish and Russian immigrants since they are increasingly important ethnic groups in Germany. Table 3.2 shows the distribution of these ethnic groups living in Germany between 2005 and 2007. Turkish immigrants represent 21.13 per cent of the immigrant population and are therefore the biggest single ethnic group present in Germany. Even though Spanish immigrants made up a major part of the guest worker population coming to Germany during the 1950s and 1960s, immigrants who originate from Spain are currently a negligible part of the immigrant community, representing only 2.06 per cent of the

Table 3.2 Immigrant groups.

Ethnic origin	Frequency	Percent
Other	3,854	34.79
Turkey	2,341	21.13
Ex-Yugoslavia	1,263	11.4
Greece	517	4.67
Italy	1,049	9.47
Spain	228	2.06
Poland	1,057	9.54
Russia	769	6.94
Total	11,078	100

Source: German Socio-Economic Panel (SOEP), unweighted sample, 2005–2007.

[12] See Statistisches Bundesamt (2009).
[13] All numbers presented are not weighted.
[14] The category 'Former Yugoslavia' includes immigrants from Croatia, Bosnia and Herzegovina, Macedonia, Slovenia, and Kosovo-Albania.

immigrant population. Hence, results regarding this group need to be treated with caution. Findings reported in the tables might thus not be representative of Spanish immigrants. They are stated, nonetheless, mostly for reasons of completeness. The ethnic group labelled 'Other' refers to the immigrant population in Germany that originates from other countries than those explicitly mentioned above.

Considering the generational distribution of immigrants, Table 3.3 shows that within each immigrant group the majority of individuals belong to the first generation. This holds especially true for immigrants from Poland and Russia, who represent the most recent trends of immigration inflows to Germany. The share of first-generation immigrants from these countries lies at 86.66 per cent for Poles and even 94.93 per cent for Russians. Thus, statements regarding differences between first and second generation of these two ethnic groups must be treated carefully due to the small numbers of observations in the second generation. As a consequence, regressions that account for differences in behaviour by generation occasionally do not include Russian second-generation immigrants.

Comparing the ethnic distribution by generation, Table 3.4 shows that the share of Turkish, Italian, Greek, and Spanish immigrants, is greater in the second than in the first generation. First-generation Russians (8.58 per cent) and Poles (10.76 per cent) are also quite dominant ethnic groups, whereas the share of Poles and Russians in the second generation is relatively small. The share of immigrants from the countries of former Yugoslavia is almost identical in both generations.[15]

Table 3.3 Generational distribution.

Ethnic origin	First gen.	Second gen.
Other	81.27	18.73
Turkey	72.70	27.30
Ex-Yugoslavia	75.85	24.15
Greece	63.25	36.75
Italy	57.67	42.33
Spain	61.40	38.60
Poland	86.66	13.34
Russia	94.93	5.07
Total	76.82	23.18

Source: German Socio-Economic Panel (SOEP), unweighted sample, 2005–2007.

[15] The ethnic distribution by generation does not differ much by gender.

Table 3.4 Ethnic distribution by generation.

Ethnic origin	First gen.	Second gen.
Other	36.80	28.12
Turkey	20.00	24.88
Ex-Yugoslavia	11.26	11.88
Greece	3.84	7.40
Italy	7.11	17.29
Spain	1.65	3.43
Poland	10.76	5.49
Russia	8.58	1.52

Source: German Socio-Economic Panel (SOEP), unweighted sample, 2005–2007.

3.3 Integration indicators

We now turn to the cultural indicators that can provide insight to the integration process of immigrants in Germany. The estimation methods used to measure the effect of ethnic groups and generations on selected indicators are based on simple pooled OLS and Logit techniques run on data during the period 2005–2007.[16] Explanatory variables used in each model are dichotomous variables accounting for membership of one of the ethnic groups interacted with a dummy variable capturing information belonging to the first or second-generation immigrant. Additionally, three different birth cohorts are distinguished and included in the regression. The first cohort depicts immigrants born before 1942 who are older than 65 in 2007. The second birth group includes immigrants born between 1942 and 1967. In 2007 they are thus between 40 and 65. This group is set to be the base category in all estimations. Consequently, the last age group contains immigrants who are younger than 40 in 2007. The regression model includes years of schooling as an additional explanatory variable.[17] Native Germans are the ethnic reference group. Finally, each regression is run separately for men and women to account for possible gender peculiarities. The regression results are presented as tables within the text, figures visualizing these results are given in the Appendix at the end of the chapter.

3.3.1 *Education*

Table 3.5 shows the average years of schooling for each ethnic group, additionally differentiated by generation and gender. Accordingly, both

---

[16] In the cases where there is no information available for 2005 to 2007, the most recent year is considered instead.

[17] Except in the regression on the individual gender gap in education.

Table 3.5 Average years of schooling.

Ethnic origin	Women		Men	
	First gen.	Second gen.	First gen.	Second gen.
Other	11.83	11.93	12.22	12.36
Turkey	9.29	11.24	9.93	10.79
Ex-Yugoslavia	9.92	11.53	10.67	11.01
Greece	9.56	11.99	10.50	12.35
Italy	9.46	11.37	10.02	11.53
Spain	10.27	10.23	9.97	13.15
Poland	11.78	13.31	11.91	10.98
Russia	11.04	No obs.	10.85	13.07
Germany	12.11		12.55	

Source: German Socio-Economic Panel (SOEP), unweighted sample, 2005–2007.

male and female second-generation immigrants tend to have better education than first-generation immigrants.[18] The increase in education between generations is especially large (almost two additional years of schooling) for Greek immigrants. Still, even for Greek immigrants, average years of education are lower for immigrants regardless of gender compared to natives and this holds for the second generation as well. Turkish immigrants in particular have very low education levels, usually less than high school. That is, Turkish women have 9.29 years of schooling and men 9.93. In contrast, native women have, on average, 12.11 years of education and men 12.55 years. In general, immigrants from one of the guest worker countries have less education than more recent immigrant groups such as Poles or Russians, indicating different patterns in the educational composition of more recent migration inflows.

Comparisons by gender show that in almost every ethnic group first-generation men have more education than first-generation women. Interestingly, the opposite is true for the second generation, at least for Turks, ex-Yugoslavs, and Poles. Second-generation women from these ethnic groups have more years of schooling than second-generation men. For natives, gender differences in education can also be observed, showing higher levels of education for German men than for German women.

Next, we consider whether differences in education are not only present among ethnic groups in group averages, but if they also exist between spouses and thus on an individual level. Table 3.6 reports the average gap in education between partners differentiated by ethnic

[18] With the exception of Poles and Spaniards, as these numbers might not be representative due to small sample sizes.

Table 3.6 Educational gaps between spouses by sex and generation.

Ethnic origin	Women		Men	
	First gen.	Second gen.	First gen.	Second gen.
Other	−0.35	−0.39	0.45	0.69
Turkey	−0.63	0.55	0.31	0.13
Ex-Yugoslavia	−0.90	1.36	0.76	−1.22
Greece	−0.76	0.86	0.38	0.30
Italy	−0.73	0.25	0.20	0.78
Spain	−0.98	0.00	−0.97	−1.77
Poland	0.03	−0.18	0.05	−2.70
Russia	0.42	No obs	−0.16	3.00
Germany	−0.48		0.48	

Source: German Socio-Economic Panel (SOEP), unweighted sample, 2005–2007.

group and immigrant generation. Here we consider only individuals who report living with a partner in the same household. The question is whether educational diversity is more common among immigrants than among natives.

To that end we construct a variable of the difference of 'own years of education' minus 'years of education of the partner'. A negative difference, as is usually the case for most first-generation women, indicates that, on average, this gender group has less education than their partner. For first-generation immigrant men education differences are mainly positive, indicating more education for the husband compared to his wife.[19] Accordingly, first-generation Turkish men have on average 0.31 more years of education than their partner. Turkish women, who also belong to the first generation have an educational deficit of more than 0.63 years. In contrast, Turkish women who are born in Germany and are part of the second generation, have even more education than their partners (0.55 years). For their second-generation male counterparts the partner difference decreases compared to the parental generation to merely 0.13 more years of education, but it remains positive.[20]

In Table 3.7 we present the individual differences between spouses regarding the explanatory variables mentioned above[21] for men and women separately. Accordingly, the average difference in the education

[19] The numbers presented in Table 3.6 need not be identically reverse due to mixed marriages and different ethnic classifications for men and women.

[20] Please note that there is no information available on the gender gap in education of second-generation Russian immigrants. Please also keep in mind that results for Spanish immigrants might be misleading due to small observation numbers.

[21] Ethnic group dummies interacted with generation dummies and dichotomous variables accounting for three different birth cohorts, birth between 1942 and 1965 being the reference category.

Table 3.7 Estimated educational gaps between spouses by ethnicity and sex.

Ethnic origin	Women	Men
Other (first gen.)	0.0725	0.0001
	(0.0825)	(0.0888)
Other (second gen.)	−0.1557	0.4518
	(0.2950)	(0.2648)
Turkey (first gen.)	−0.3358**	−0.0068
	(0.1074)	(0.1026)
Turkey (second gen.)	0.6130*	0.1766
	(0.2616)	(0.2668)
Ex-Yugoslavia (first gen.)	−0.4806**	0.3445*
	(0.1552)	(0.1555)
Ex-Yugoslavia (second gen.)	1.5038***	−1.2416**
	(0.3564)	(0.4363)
Greece (first gen.)	−0.2315	−0.1730
	(0.2396)	(0.2293)
Greece (second gen.)	0.9074	0.2181
	(0.4662)	(0.5255)
Italy (first gen.)	−0.2621	−0.2156
	(0.2080)	(0.1689)
Italy (second gen.)	0.3495	0.6875
	(0.2957)	(0.3601)
Spain (first gen.)	−0.4252	−1.3976***
	(0.4828)	(0.3758)
Spain (second gen.)	0.2144	−1.8926*
	(0.9300)	(0.7424)
Poland (first gen.)	0.4233**	−0.3851*
	(0.1467)	(0.1640)
Poland (second gen.)	−0.1262	−2.6499*
	(0.5976)	(1.1012)
Russia (first gen.)	0.8640***	−0.5805**
	(0.1712)	(0.1790)
Russia (second gen.)	No obs	2.5827
		(1.4209)
Cohort 1	−0.6578***	0.5761***
	(0.0453)	(0.0415)
Cohort 3	0.3829***	−0.4674***
	(0.0419)	(0.0453)
Constant	−0.4332***	0.4173***
	(0.0241)	(0.0243)
N	20,459	20,461

OLS regressions; standard errors in parentheses; * $p <0.05$, ** $p <0.01$, *** $p <0.001$.
Source: SOEP, 2005–2007.

of native women who were born between 1942 and 1965 is negative, indicating that women of this generation have less schooling than their partners. The difference decreases for younger birth cohorts ('cohort 3') and increases for older generations ('cohort 1'). For Turkish women who were not born in Germany ('Turkey (first gen.)') the difference is greater and significantly different from native women, indicating greater disparities between husbands and wives in this ethnic group. In contrast, for second-generation Turkish women the difference becomes positive, implying better schooling levels for them compared to their partner. Similar patterns hold for female immigrants from ex-Yugoslavia. Polish and Russian women are an exception in that they show better educational skills for the wives compared to their husbands for the first generation; at least for immigrants born after 1942.[22]

For men the picture is slightly different. As expected, German men between 40 and 65 have on average more years of schooling than their partners. While this educational gap is even bigger for older birth cohorts, it decreases and reverses for the youngest age group. Turkish, Greek, and Italian men do not significantly differ from German men when it comes to educational differences within the partnership, whereas for the remaining immigrant groups the difference in education decreases for both immigrant generations. First-generation ex-Yugoslav men as well as second-generation Russian men are an exception. The decrease in the educational gap is even bigger for second-generation individuals, indicating more equality among partners in later immigrant generations.

Summing up, the educational advantage of men over women is present, and it is stronger for most first-generation immigrants compared to Germans. However, it declines and even reverses for second-generation immigrants. These findings indicate that second-generation women have, on average, better education in terms of years of schooling compared to their partners than women in their parental generation and hence converge towards more equal education levels within the partnership.

3.3.2 Marital behaviour

Table 3.8 shows that most first-generation immigrants are married and live in the same household as their partner, whereas most second-generation immigrants are single. This is not surprising, and is possibly due to the different age structures in the two generations, as can be seen from Table 3.9. On average, first-generation immigrants are slightly older than native Germans. Second-generation immigrants, however, are markedly younger.

---

[22] There is no information available for second-generation Russian women.

Table 3.8 Marital behaviour.

Women

Ethnic origin	First gen.		Second gen.	
	Single	Married	Single	Married
Other	39.83	60.17	73.62	26.38
Turkey	24.39	75.61	65.08	34.92
Ex-Yugoslavia	36.87	63.13	63.41	36.59
Greece	28.30	71.70	65.31	34.69
Italy	38.55	61.45	63.95	36.05
Spain	51.72	48.28	74.36	25.64
Poland	40.49	59.51	74.03	25.97
Russia	39.02	60.98	100.00	0.00
Germany	51.68	48.32		

Men

Ethnic origin	First gen.		Second gen.	
	Single	Married	Single	Married
Other	37.74	62.26	71.62	28.38
Turkey	24.26	75.74	67.59	32.41
Ex-Yugoslavia	36.60	63.40	75.18	24.82
Greece	23.81	76.19	71.74	28.26
Italy	27.99	72.01	72.99	27.01
Spain	40.24	59.76	57.14	42.86
Poland	36.36	63.64	92.19	7.81
Russia	39.65	60.35	86.36	13.64
Germany	50.56	49.44		

Source: German Socio-Economic Panel (SOEP), unweighted sample, 2005–2007.

Table 3.9 Average age.

Ethnic origin	Women		Men	
	First gen.	Second gen.	First gen.	Second gen.
Other	45.47	28.20	46.51	29.77
Turkey	44.56	25.08	45.49	24.55
Ex-Yugoslavia	48.94	28.85	48.81	27.15
Greece	54.99	28.44	54.23	28.79
Italy	52.27	28.82	51.79	28.12
Spain	53.48	26.97	52.13	30.35
Poland	43.69	23.26	46.50	20.58
Russia	46.22	19.18	44.57	24.00
Germany	41.44		40.06	

Source: German Socio-Economic Panel (SOEP), unweighted sample, 2005–2007.

Turning to the marital behaviour of the first generation we observe that it differs noticeably from that of the native population. Turkish immigrants, especially, show very high marriage rates. For example, among first-generation Turkish men, the share of those living with a partner is 75.74 per cent compared to a marriage rate of only 49.44 per cent for German men. First-generation women exhibit a similar marital behaviour to men of the same ethnic group, with marriage rates mostly at or above 60 per cent. In contrast, second-generation women have marriage rates only around 25 to 35 per cent. Differences are noticeably higher (between 34 and 37 per cent) for immigrants from the former guest worker countries. For second-generation men marriage rates are somewhat smaller especially for Poles and Russians. Only 32.41 per cent of Turkish men have similar marriage rates to their female counterparts. For natives, there are hardly any differences in the marital behaviour of men and women. The share of married Germans is almost 50 per cent, indicating a higher tendency of natives towards remaining single compared to immigrants.

In Table 3.10 we present the results of the multivariate regression. Regardless of their gender, first-generation immigrants tend to be more likely to be married than Germans, whereas second-generation immigrants seem to be less likely to be living with a partner. Polish women and Spanish men are the only groups whose marital behaviour does not differ from that of natives irrespective of generation. Second-generation Turks show no significant deviations from Germans with respect to marital behaviour.

3.3.3 *Intermarriage*

Analysing differences in marital behaviour even further, Table 3.11 shows that the type of marriage differs noticeably by immigrant generation and ethnic group. Intermarriage in this context is defined as the living partnership of an immigrant with a native German. A marriage between a Greek and a Turk, for example, is not considered intermarriage. This restrictive definition is based on the assumption that intermarriage is supposed to indicate integration to the German society. An immigrant who is living with a native partner possibly signals greater commitment to Germany than an immigrant who marries another immigrant or even marries within his or her own ethnic community.[23]

---

[23] For further research on intermarriage see, for example, Kalmijn (1998); Lievens (1998, 1999); Kantarevic (2004); Meng and Gregory (2005); Meng and Meurs (2006); Gonzáles-Ferrer (2006); Chiswick and Housworth (2011); Furtado and Theodoropoulos (2011); Furtado (2010).

Table 3.10 Marriage probability.

Ethnic origin	Women	Men
Other (first gen.) (d)	0.0552***	0.0831***
	(0.0119)	(0.0107)
Other (second gen.) (d)	−0.2490***	−0.1827***
	(0.0348)	(0.0331)
Turkey (first gen.) (d)	0.2047***	0.1888***
	(0.0106)	(0.0063)
Turkey (second gen.) (d)	−0.0375	0.0385
	(0.0341)	(0.0229)
Ex-Yugoslavia (first gen.) (d)	0.0643**	0.0893***
	(0.0217)	(0.0173)
Ex-Yugoslavia (Second gen.) (d)	−0.1517***	−0.1282*
	(0.0453)	(0.0503)
Greece (first gen.) (d)	0.1575***	0.0993***
	(0.0273)	(0.0281)
Greece (second gen.) (d)	−0.1987**	−0.1728**
	(0.0617)	(0.0627)
Italy (first gen.) (d)	0.0270	0.1268***
	(0.0326)	(0.0168)
Italy (second gen.) (d)	−0.1158**	−0.1082**
	(0.0391)	(0.0409)
Spain (first gen.) (d)	−0.1850*	−0.0388
	(0.0746)	(0.0551)
Spain (second gen.) (d)	−0.1515	0.0286
	(0.1132)	(0.0586)
Poland (first gen.) (d)	0.0348	0.0559*
	(0.0222)	(0.0217)
Poland (second gen.) (d)	−0.0733	−0.3785**
	(0.0761)	(0.1168)
Russia (first gen.) (d)	0.0745**	0.0599**
	(0.0233)	(0.0213)
Russia (second gen.) (d)	No obs	−0.2500
		(0.2119)
Cohort 1 (d)	−0.2617***	0.0069
	(0.0076)	(0.0072)
Cohort 3 (d)	−0.2223***	−0.3162***
	(0.0068)	(0.0067)
Years of schooling	0.0089***	0.0149***
	(0.0011)	(0.0010)
N	31,839	29,018

Logit regressions; marginal effects; standard errors in parentheses; (d) for discrete change of dummy variable from 0 to 1, * p <0:05, ** p <0:01, *** p <0:001.

Source: SOEP, 2005–2007.

Among those who are married, intermarriage rates are especially low for first-generation Turks, ranging between 1.94 per cent for first-generation women and 5.79 per cent for men. In contrast, Italian immigrants show comparably high intermarriage rates of 17.28 per cent for women and even 27.42 per cent for men already in the first generation,

Cultural Integration of Immigrants in Europe

Table 3.11 Intermarriage rates.

Ethnic origin		Women		
		Intermarriage	Intra-ethnic	No class.
Other	First gen.	45.39	51.41	3.20
	Second gen.	80.00	12.22	7.78
Turkey	First gen.	1.94	97.57	0.49
	Second gen.	3.43	95.47	1.10
Ex-Yugoslavia	First gen.	14.01	81.85	4.14
	Second gen.	33.90	59.32	6.78
Greece	First gen.	6.14	90.35	3.51
	Second gen.	6.06	84.85	9.09
Italy	First gen.	17.28	79.63	3.09
	Second gen.	33.72	61.63	4.65
Spain	First gen.	51.85	48.15	0.00
	Second gen.	36.36	36.36	27.27
Poland	First gen.	30.31	66.56	3.13
	Second gen.	90.00	10.00	0.00
Russia	First gen.	15.70	82.64	1.65
	Second gen.	15.70	82.64	1.65
Germany		3.89	91.59	4.52

Ethnic origin		Men		
		Intermarriage	Intra-ethnic	No class.
Other	First gen.	37.89	59.78	2.33
	Second gen.	74.77	16.82	8.41
Turkey	First gen.	5.79	93.92	0.30
	Second gen.	16.04	74.53	9.43
Ex-Yugoslavia	First gen.	13.44	85.90	0.66
	Second gen.	31.43	68.57	0.00
Greece	First gen.	15.27	80.92	3.82
	Second gen.	19.23	69.23	11.54
Italy	First gen.	27.42	71.77	0.81
	Second gen.	66.67	31.58	1.75
Spain	First gen.	63.27	34.69	2.04
	Second gen.	72.73	0.00	27.27
Poland	First gen.	21.03	77.38	1.59
	Second gen.	100.00	0.00	0.00
Russia	First gen.	3.29	96.24	0.47
	Second gen.	100.00	0.00	0.00
Germany		4.49	92.95	2.56

Source: German Socio-Economic Panel (SOEP), unweighted sample, 2005–2007, only persons who report a partner.

possibly indicating better integration of Italians compared to Turks. However, one should note that low intermarriage rates need not automatically indicate low integration ability, but are highly related to the availability of a partner within their own ethnic group. Thus, immigrants who belong to a dominant immigrant group, as do Turks, might simply face a bigger market of potential partners with the same ethnic background, which decreases the probability to intermarry. This argument is supported by the intermarriage rates of Germans—as the biggest ethnic group. German men only show intermarriage rates of 4.49 per cent and those of German women are even lower (3.89 per cent). Therefore, it is important to also look at differences by generation and thus behaviour over time.

Second-generation immigrants who were born in Germany and hence had the opportunity to socialize with natives all their lives, are expected to be more likely to intermarry than immigrants who migrated to Germany perhaps even after they were married to another immigrant. This assumption is supported by empirical findings for most immigrant groups. Only second-generation Greeks and Spaniards show lower intermarriage rates compared to the parental generation. For all remaining ethnic groups, second-generation immigrants are more likely to be married to a native than immigrants from their parental generation, indicating greater intermixing with the native population of the younger generations. Therefore, the increase of intermarriage rates between generations is especially big for Turkish men. In contrast, second-generation Greek women are as likely to intermarry as those in the first generation.

In Table 3.12 we present estimation results from logistic regressions on the probability of intermarrying. Comparing marital behaviour by ethnic group and generation with that of natives, immigrant men show a higher probability to intermarry than Germans. With the exception of Turkish and Greek women of either generation, this also holds for immigrant women. The likelihood of intermarrying is in general higher for second-generation immigrants. This suggests that immigrants born in the host country show more ability to integrate in the marriage market than members of their parental generation. The only exception is Turkish women, who behave just like Germans regardless of their generation.

3.3.4 *Age at first marriage*

There are not only differences by immigrant group regarding partner choice but also with respect to age at first marriage. Table 3.13 reports the share of individuals who are older than 25 but were first married before the age of 25. Our results show that first-generation immigrants are more likely to be married before the age of 25, regardless of gender,

Table 3.12 Intermarriage probability.

Ethnic origin	Women	Men
Other (first gen.) (d)	0.3285***	0.3024***
	(0.0138)	(0.0153)
Other (second gen.) (d)	0.3154***	0.3195***
	(0.0341)	(0.0327)
Turkey (first gen.) (d)	−0.0029	0.0385**
	(0.0084)	(0.0123)
Turkey (second gen.) (d)	0.0152	0.0995**
	(0.0189)	(0.0319)
Ex-Yugoslavia (first gen.) (d)	0.1199***	0.0857***
	(0.0212)	(0.0208)
Ex-Yugoslavia (second gen.) (d)	0.1756***	0.1316**
	(0.0409)	(0.0460)
Greece (first gen.) (d)	0.0476	0.1151***
	(0.0287)	(0.034)
Greece (second gen.) (d)	0.0042	0.0614
	(0.0252)	(0.0424)
Italy (first gen.) (d)	0.1465***	0.2774***
	(0.0319)	(0.0316)
Italy (second gen.) (d)	0.1971***	0.3182***
	(0.0371)	(0.0460)
Spain (first gen.) (d)	0.3356***	0.5140***
	(0.0747)	(0.0618)
Spain (second gen.) (d)	0.2334*	0.4839***
	(0.1094)	(0.0883)
Poland (first gen.) (d)	0.2251***	0.1404***
	(0.0230)	(0.0243)
Poland (second gen.) (d)	0.4929***	0.1893*
	(0.0833)	(0.0862)
Russia (first gen.) (d)	0.1174***	−0.0024
	(0.0230)	(0.0138)
Russia (second gen.) (d)	No obs	0.4410*
		(0.1929)
Cohort 1 (d)	−0.0105***	−0.0091***
	(0.0022)	(0.0025)
Cohort 3 (d)	−0.0045*	−0.0118***
	(0.0019)	(0.0023)
Years of schooling	0.0026***	0.0028***
	(0.0003)	(0.0004)
N	31,839	29,018

Logit regressions; marginal effects; standard errors in parentheses; (d) for discrete change of dummy variable from 0 to 1, * p <0:05, ** p <0:01, *** p <0:001.

Source: SOEP, 2005–2007, only persons who report a partner.

compared to individuals of later generations. Marriage rates at age 25 for that group are at or above 70 per cent for most immigrant groups and even higher for Turks. Accordingly, almost 89 per cent of first-generation Turkish women were married before the age of 25. This sharply contrasts with less than 57 per cent among native women. In general, the second

Table 3.13 Married before the age of 25.

Ethnic origin		Share of women	
		Not married before 25	Married before 25
Other	First gen.	37.47	62.53
	Second gen.	58.79	41.21
Turkey	First gen.	11.78	88.22
	Second gen.	30.61	69.39
Ex-Yugoslavia	First gen.	29.81	70.19
	Second gen.	63.30	36.70
Greece	First gen.	23.27	76.73
	Second gen.	63.49	36.51
Italy	First gen.	24.81	75.19
	Second gen.	51.80	48.20
Spain	First gen.	46.55	53.45
	Second gen.	58.82	41.18
Poland	First gen.	28.82	71.18
	Second gen.	68.97	31.03
Russia	First gen.	24.62	75.38
	Second gen.	24.62	75.38
Germany		43.22	56.78

Ethnic origin		Share of men	
		Not married before 25	Married before 25
Other	First gen.	55.45	44.55
	Second gen.	89.33	10.67
Turkey	First gen.	28.76	71.24
	Second gen.	54.88	45.12
Ex-Yugoslavia	First gen.	41.98	58.02
	Second gen.	87.91	12.09
Greece	First gen.	59.52	40.48
	Second gen.	78.18	21.82
Italy	First gen.	57.18	42.82
	Second gen.	76.42	23.58
Spain	First gen.	50.00	50.00
	Second gen.	75.68	24.32
Poland	First gen.	40.65	59.35
	Second gen.	100.00	00.00
Russia	First gen.	29.89	70.11
	Second gen.	30.63	69.37
Germany		61.78	38.22

Source: German Socio-Economic Panel (SOEP), unweighted sample, 2005–2007, only persons older 25.

generation shows lower shares of individuals who marry prior to their twenty-fifth birthday and a higher tendency towards marriage at later ages. The exceptions here are Spanish and Italian immigrants.[24]

[24] Please note that there is no information available about the marriage behaviour of second-generation Polish immigrants.

Compared to natives, estimates presented in Table 3.14 and the corresponding figures show that for women there is no statistically significant difference in the probability of being married before the age of 25 between Germans and second-generation immigrants, Turkish women being an exception. In contrast, first-generation immigrants seem to be more likely to be married young compared to natives. We

Table 3.14 Probability of being first married before age of 25.

Ethnic origin	Women	Men
Other (first gen.) (d)	0.0663***	0.0631***
	(0.0145)	(0.0172)
Other (second gen.) (d)	−0.0241	−0.2442***
	(0.0473)	(0.0339)
Turkey (first gen.) (d)	0.2578***	0.3288***
	(0.0156)	(0.0190)
Turkey (second gen.) (d)	0.2677***	0.3258***
	(0.0252)	(0.0376)
Ex-Yugoslavia (first gen.) (d)	0.0221	0.1578***
	(0.0286)	(0.0301)
Ex-Yugoslavia (second gen.) (d)	−0.0431	−0.2232***
	(0.0556)	(0.0637)
Greece (first gen.) (d)	0.1098*	−0.0846*
	(0.0450)	(0.0380)
Greece (second gen.) (d)	0.0131	0.0729
	(0.0720)	(0.0904)
Italy (first gen.) (d)	0.0497	−0.0568
	(0.0398)	(0.0295)
Italy (second gen.) (d)	0.0111	−0.0115
	(0.0491)	(0.0622)
Spain (first gen.) (d)	−0.2318**	−0.0003
	(0.0733)	(0.0616)
Spain (second gen.) (d)	−0.1338	−0.0018
	(0.1492)	(0.1184)
Poland (first gen.) (d)	0.1185***	0.1706***
	(0.0244)	(0.0316)
Poland (second gen.) (d)	0.0476	No obs
	(0.1016)	
Russia (first gen.) (d)	0.1736***	0.3001***
	(0.0262)	(0.0328)
Cohort 1 (d)	−0.0834***	−0.0132
	(0.0079)	(0.0074)
Cohort 3 (d)	−0.3057***	−0.2924***
	(0.0075)	(0.0065)
Years of schooling	−0.0489***	−0.0290***
	(0.0012)	(0.0012)
N	29,020	26,378

Logit regressions; marginal effects; standard errors in parentheses; (d) for discrete change of dummy variable from 0 to 1, * p <0:05, ** p <0:01, *** p <0:001.

Source: SOEP, 2005–2007, only persons older 25.

Table 3.15 Average age gap between spouses.

Ethnic origin	Women		Men	
	First gen.	Second gen.	First gen.	Second gen.
Other	−3.61	−2.65	2.68	1.57
Turkey	−2.80	−2.66	2.73	2.02
Ex-Yugoslavla	−3.49	−3.64	3.23	2.66
Greece	−3.97	−2.50	3.79	2.46
Italy	−3.81	−3.37	3.60	3.45
Spain	−0.63	5.63	2.69	1.31
Poland	−2.29	−2.90	2.23	−0.40
Russia	−2.00	No obs	1.20	3.00
Germany	−2.69		2.78	

Source: German Socio-Economic Panel (SOEP), unweighted sample, 2005–2007, only persons who report a partner.

find positive and significant effects for Turkish, Greek, Polish, and Russian women as well as for men from Turkey, ex-Yugoslavia, Greece, and Poland. While this confirms the different marriage behaviour of first-generation immigrants, there is no difference in marriage behaviour between Germans and the second generation.

3.3.5 Age gap between spouses

We now turn our attention to age disparities between partners, as partner constellations might be different also with respect to the age of the spouses. Immigrants living in a partnership where age differences between partners are about the same as for Germans might reflect greater adaption to German norms and marital habits and thus more social integration. Table 3.15 shows that the age gap between spouses differs moderately by generation and ethnic origin. For Germans, the average age gap between partners is about 2.7 years. For most first-generation immigrants from the guest worker countries the difference is slightly bigger, with a maximum average difference of four years for Greeks. Poles and Russians have a smaller marital age difference than natives. For second-generation immigrants the age difference between partners is smaller, except among Italian, Spanish, and Polish women.

Controlling for educational levels and birth cohorts, the estimation coefficients presented in Table 3.16 indicate that among first-generation Italian and Greek women the difference in the spouse's age widens, whereas it decreases for Spanish, Polish, and Russian women. This is partly confirmed by findings for men. Here, the difference increases for first-generation Turkish, ex-Yugoslav, Greek, and Italian men but

Table 3.16 Age gap between spouses.

Ethnic origin	Women	Men
Other (first gen.) (d)	−0.6688***	−0.0511
	(0.1481)	(0.1586)
Other (second gen.) (d)	0.5818	−0.6182
	(0.4969)	(0.4574)
Turkey (first gen.) (d)	0.2661	0.4047*
	(0.1989)	(0.1853)
Turkey (second gen.) (d)	1.3275**	0.4781
	(0.4645)	(0.4609)
Ex-Yugoslavia (first gen.) (d)	−0.4357	0.8790**
	(0.2674)	(0.2774)
Ex-Yugoslavia (second gen.) (d)	−0.4982	0.8539
	(0.6162)	(0.7646)
Greece (first gen.) (d)	−1.2288**	0.8434*
	(0.4342)	(0.4072)
Greece (second gen.) (d)	0.8562	0.4396
	(0.8396)	(0.9035)
Italy (first gen.) (d)	−1.1146**	1.1838***
	(0.3764)	(0.3015)
Italy (second gen.) (d)	−0.0572	1.3473*
	(0.5168)	(0.6157)
Spain (first gen.) (d)	1.9772*	−0.0066
	(0.8686)	(0.6594)
Spain (second gen.) (d)	10.9491***	−0.9010
	(1.7048)	(1.1650)
Poland (first gen.) (d)	0.6539*	−0.5186
	(0.2627)	(0.2962)
Poland (second gen.) (d)	0.5154	−1.9631
	(1.0102)	(2.0179)
Russia (first gen.) (d)	0.8405**	−1.4171***
	(0.3007)	(0.3212)
Russia (second gen.) (d)	No obs	0.1440
		(2.6037)
Cohort 1 (d)	1.0921***	0.8310***
	(0.0832)	(0.0748)
Cohort 3 (d)	−0.7485***	−1.1176***
	(0.0739)	(0.0806)
Years of schooling	0.0369**	0.0351**
	(0.0122)	(0.0112)
Constant	−3.1784***	2.3300***
	(0.1585)	(0.1518)
N	21,792	21,487

OLS regressions; standard errors in parentheses; (d) for discrete change of dummy variable from 0 to 1; * p <0:05, ** p <0:01, *** p <0:001.
Source: SOEP, 2005–2007, only persons who report a partner.

diminishes for first-generation Russians. There is hardly any difference between spousal age gaps of natives and second-generation individuals, second-generation Turkish women being an exception.

3.3.6 Number of children

In addition, we find that differences exist in the family structure, namely with respect to the number of children per woman. These differences emerge not only between natives and immigrants but also between different ethnic groups. As documented in Table 3.17, first-generation Turkish women have, on average, more children than women from any other country and in particular more children than natives.[25] The average number of children for German women is less than two, whereas for first-generation Turkish women it is more than three. The number of children per woman in the second generation is, in general, lower than in the first generation, and also often smaller than for natives. However, Turkish women have higher birth rates than natives even in the second generation. For Greek, Italian, and ex-Yugoslav the average number of children per women in later immigrant generations is noticeably smaller.

As can be seen from estimation results presented in Table 3.18 differences in the number of children are statistically significant for most first-generation immigrant women who consistently have more children than natives. This is especially true for first-generation Turkish women, who have on average one more child than German women. For second-generation Turkish women the effect is not significant.

Table 3.17 Average number of children per woman.

Ethnic origin	First gen.	Second gen.
Other	2.14	2.20
Turkey	3.17	2.00
Ex-Yugoslavia	2.26	0.70
Greece	2.04	1.00
Italy	2.80	1.23
Spain	1.87	2.57
Poland	2.01	No obs
Russia	2.56	No obs
Germany	1.84	

Source: German Socio-Economic Panel (SOEP), unweighted sample, 2005–2007, only women older 40.

[25] The numbers presented refer to women older than 40.

Table 3.18 Number of children.

Ethnic origin	Women older than 40
Other (first gen.) (d)	0.3026***
	(0.0437)
Other (second gen.) (d)	0.2717
	(0.2115)
Turkey (first gen.) (d)	1.0065***
	(0.0697)
Turkey (second gen.) (d)	0.1759
	(0.7114)
Ex-Yugoslavia (first gen.) (d)	0.2079**
	(0.0747)
Ex-Yugoslavia (second gen.) (d)	−1.2079**
	(0.3901)
Greece (first gen.) (d)	0.0912
	(0.1198)
Greece (second gen.) (d)	−0.8480
	(0.4660)
Italy (first gen.) (d)	0.5746***
	(0.0963)
Italy (second gen.) (d)	−0.5065
	(0.2629)
Spain (first gen.) (d)	−0.0874
	(0.1820)
Spain (second gen.) (d)	0.7790
	(0.5033)
Poland (first gen.) (d)	0.1686*
	(0.0766)
Poland (second gen.) (d)	No obs
Russia (first gen.) (d)	0.6729***
	(0.0899)
Russia (second gen.) (d)	No obs
Cohort 1 (d)	0.1576***
	(0.0189)
Cohort 3 (d)	−0.0773
	(0.0877)
Years of schooling	−0.0612***
	(0.0034)
Constant	2.5279***
	(0.0437)
N	21,029

OLS regressions; standard errors in parentheses; (d) for discrete change of dummy variable from 0 to 1; * $p < 0.05$, ** $p < 0.01$, *** $p < 0.001$.
Source: SOEP, 2005–2007, only women older 40.

Negative trends can be observed for second-generation immigrants from the former Yugoslavia. In general, for Spaniards, Greeks, and the second generation the number of children does not significantly differ from that of natives. This indicates that later immigrant generations integrate not only with respect to marriage behaviour, such as the age gap between spouses, age at marriage, and marriage probability, but also with regards to family structure, reflected in the number of children.

3.3.7 Age at first child

Apart from marital behaviour and family composition, birth behaviour might also give insight into the cultural adaptation and integration process. Table 3.19 shows the age at the birth of the first child. First-generation immigrant women seem to be only slightly younger when they give birth to their first child compared to natives, while second-generation women seem to be a little older. Again, Turkish women stand out, with a comparably young age at first child birth: on average 22.74 for the first generation. Interestingly, the age at first child birth is much higher for second-generation Turkish women (27 years of age). In comparison, German women give birth to their first child at the age of 25 on average. Results from a simple regression support the first impression of hardly any differences between immigrants and natives. The difference in age at the birth of the first child almost vanishes for all second-generation immigrants. It differs significantly from natives only for a few immigrants groups such as Spaniards (Table 3.20).

3.3.8 Religion

We now turn to religious aspects of immigrant integration. Table 3.21 shows the distribution of religious beliefs within each ethnic group differentiated by gender and generation. It is apparent from this table that no religious differences can be observed between men and women or between first and second-generation immigrants within a single

Table 3.19 Age at first child birth, ethnic origin compared with first and second generation.

Ethnic origin	First gen.	Second gen.
Other	25.33	26.03
Turkey	22.74	27.00
Ex-Yugoslavia	23.01	26.17
Greece	23.91	25.25
Italy	23.86	25.53
Spain	24.56	23.29
Poland	23.92	No obs
Russia	24.10	No obs
Germany	24.97	

Source: German Socio-Economic Panel (SOEP), unweighted sample, 2005–2007, only women older than 40.

Table 3.20 Age at first child birth, ethnic origin for women over 40.

Ethnic origin	Women older than 40
Other (first gen.) (d)	0.5174**
	(0.1713)
Other (second gen.) (d)	1.5093
	(0.8393)
Turkey (first gen.) (d)	−0.2487
	(0.2712)
Turkey (second gen.) (d)	2.6110
	(2.6516)
Ex-Yugoslavia (first gen.) (d)	−0.4985
	(0.2938)
Ex-Yugoslavia (second gen.) (d)	1.5441
	(1.8760)
Greece (first gen.) (d)	0.3218
	(0.4666)
Greece (second gen.) (d)	0.0025
	(2.2979)
Italy (first gen.) (d)	0.4211
	(0.3613)
Italy (second gen.) (d)	1.6586
	(1.1492)
Spain (first gen.) (d)	1.6142*
	(0.7372)
Spain (second gen.) (d)	−1.9351
	(1.8762)
Poland (first gen.) (d)	−0.4798
	(0.2917)
Poland (second gen.) (d)	No obs
Russia (first gen.) (d)	−0.2744
	(0.3482)
Russia (second gen.) (d)	No obs
Cohort 1 (d)	1.0951***
	(0.0746)
Cohort 3 (d)	1.4746***
	(0.3544)
Years of schooling	0.5598***
	(0.0138)
Constant	17.9516***
	(0.1762)
N	18,866

OLS regressions; standard errors in parentheses; (d) for discrete change of dummy variable from 0 to 1; * $p < 0.05$, ** $p < 0.01$, *** $p < 0.001$.

Source: SOEP, 2005–2007, only women older than 40.

ethnic group. That is, regardless of gender or generation, the majority of Turkish immigrants who report a religion are Muslims, most Italian, Spanish, and Polish immigrants are Catholics and the majority of Russian immigrants are Christian Orthodox. Among Germans, Protestants are a slight majority, closely followed by Catholics.

Table 3.21 Religious affiliation.

Ethnic origin		Women					
		Cathol.	Protest.	Other Christ.	Islam	Other Rel.	Un-denom.
Others	(first gen.)	32.75	35.81	9.17	3.28	2.18	16.81
	(second gen.)	33.71	41.57	2.25	3.37	0.00	19.10
Turkey	(first gen.)	0.47	0.00	2.37	87.20	1.42	8.53
	(second gen.)	0.00	1.37	2.74	84.93	1.37	9.59
Ex-Yugoslavia	(first gen.)	43.09	4.07	24.39	20.33	0.00	8.13
	(second gen.)	36.36	4.55	20.45	20.45	0.00	18.18
Greece	(first gen.)	0.00	0.00	92.31	5.13	0.00	2.56
	(second gen.)	8.33	12.50	75.00	0.00	0.00	4.17
Italy	(first gen.)	83.08	3.08	6.15	0.00	0.00	7.69
	(second gen.)	80.70	10.53	8.77	0.00	0.00	0.00
Spain	(first gen.)	93.33	6.67	0.00	0.00	0.00	0.00
	(second gen.)	100.00	0.00	0.00	0.00	0.00	0.00
Poland	(first gen.)	81.95	8.27	1.50	0.75	0.00	7.52
	(second gen.)	50.00	16.67	0.00	5.56	0.00	27.78
Russia	(first gen.)	19.23	51.92	17.31	0.00	2.88	8.65
	(second gen.)	0.00	100.00	0.00	0.00	0.00	0.00
German		28.99	39.40	1.23	0.08	0.05	30.25

Ethnic origin		Men					
		Cathol.	Protest.	Other Christ.	Islam	Other Rel.	Un-denom.
Others	(first gen.)	28.29	34.45	7.84	5.60	1.96	21.85
	(second gen.)	38.46	28.57	0.00	4.40	0.00	28.57
Turkey	(first gen.)	0.93	0.00	0.93	88.43	1.39	8.33
	(second gen.)	0.00	0.00	7.14	81.43	4.29	7.14
Ex-Yugoslavia	(first gen.)	29.36	1.83	25.69	32.11	0.00	11.01
	(second gen.)	43.75	9.38	18.75	21.88	0.00	6.25
Greece	(first gen.)	0.00	0.00	88.64	4.55	0.00	6.82
	(second gen.)	4.00	8.00	68.00	4.00	0.00	16.00
Italy	(first gen.)	90.24	2.44	2.44	0.00	0.00	4.88
	(second gen.)	81.25	8.33	4.17	0.00	0.00	6.25
Spain	(first gen.)	89.47	0.00	0.00	0.00	0.00	10.53
	(second gen.)	41.67	25.00	0.00	0.00	0.00	33.33
Poland	(first gen.)	75.26	6.19	3.09	0.00	0.00	15.46
	(second gen.)	53.85	15.38	0.00	7.69	0.00	23.08
Russia	(first gen.)	23.33	51.11	10.00	0.00	2.22	13.33
	(second gen.)	0.00	100.00	0.00	0.00	0.00	0.00
German		27.46	34.86	0.95	0.1	0.15	36.47

Source: German Socio-Economic Panel (SOEP), unweighted sample. 2005–2007.

3.3.9 *Language proficiency*

Proficiency in the language of the host country has been proven to be of paramount importance for social and economic integration. Using SOEP's subjective answers on language skills (both oral and written), we measure linguistic abilities on a scale from 1 to 5, where 1 denotes 'very good' language ability and 5 'very poor' skills. In general, reported written skills are worse than speaking abilities regardless of ethnic group and immigrant generation. These statistics are presented in Table 3.22. They are based on the 2005 wave, the most recent year for which information on language proficiency is available.

Table 3.22 Language proficiency.

Ethnic origin	German language				Language of home country			
	Women		Men		Women		Men	
	First gen.	Second gen.	First gen.	Second gen.	First gen.	Second gen.	First gen.	Second gen.
	Speaking				Speaking			
Other	1.77	1.14	1.82	1.15	1.68	2.20	1.80	2.35
Turkey	2.84	1.45	2.39	1.50	1.69	2.10	1.63	2.20
Ex-Yugoslavia	2.13	1.18	2.05	1.27	1.57	2.09	1.56	2.27
Greece	2.40	1.22	2.34	1.33	1.54	1.65	1.36	1.89
Italy	2.29	1.33	2.26	1.32	1.57	2.05	1.53	2.19
Spain	1.75	1.00	2.07	1.10	1.30	2.67	1.52	2.00
Poland	1.68	No obs	1.88	No obs	1.74	No obs	1.75	No obs
Russia	1.89	No obs	2.08	1.00	1.81	No obs	1.78	1.00

Ethnic origin	German language				Language of home country			
	Women		Men		Women		Men	
	First gen.	Second gen.	First gen.	Second gen.	First gen.	Second gen.	First gen.	Second gen.
	Writing				Writing			
Other	2.01	1.33	2.11	1.23	1.91	2.60	2.11	2.50
Turkey	3.38	1.64	3.04	1.74	2.15	2.47	1.94	2.71
Ex-Yugoslavia	2.86	1.31	2.57	1.39	1.83	2.73	1.77	3.12
Greece	3.05	1.39	2.85	1.41	1.89	2.22	1.66	2.41
Italy	3.23	1.55	3.12	1.62	2.05	2.56	1.90	2.94
Spain	2.75	1.33	3.07	1.20	1.65	2.67	1.83	3.10
Poland	1.91	No obs	2.20	No obs	2.10	No obs	2.19	No obs
Russia	2.21	No obs	2.45	1.00	1.99	No obs	2.05	1.00

Scale from 1 ('very good') to 5 ('none at all').

Source: German Socio-Economic Panel (SOEP), unweighted sample, 2005.

Second-generation immigrants should have better languages skills than first-generation immigrants since by definition immigrants who belong to the second generation were born in Germany and therefore mostly attended school and further education in Germany. As expected, their reported language abilities are higher in both the spoken and the written use of German, regardless of ethnic group. This implies a positive linguistic integration of second-generation immigrants.

Linguistic comparisons by ethnic groups show that Turks have the lowest German language proficiency among all ethnic groups. They seem to be the least integrated with respect to language. A possible explanation is related to the fact that language proficiency is self-reported, which might impose measurement errors and signal group specific characteristics. Some immigrant groups might overstate their abilities while other groups might continuously understate their skills. This might bias the results. Another explanation for the low language abilities of Turks might be by group size and enclave effects. Since Turks represent the largest single ethnic group in Germany, they are more likely to socialize predominantly within their ethnic community and do not need to put much effort into learning the German language in order to manage everyday life situations. Thus, poor language abilities might indeed signal less integration and more ethnic segregation among Turks.

Differencing by gender within each ethnic group indicates that, in particular, first-generation women of Spanish, Polish, and Russian origin have better German language skills than men from the same origin. In the other immigrant groups first-generation women report, on average, worse skills than men. For members of the second generation German language abilities seem to be mostly better for women regardless of ethnic group in both spoken and written use of language.

Examining the language of the country of origin we obtain opposite results. Here it is the first generation that reports better language abilities. This can be explained by a greater attachment of this generation to their home country, the fact that they were raised using this language, or the possibility that even though some of them are only a little bit literate in German, they still know how to speak their country of origin's language since it is much more difficult to learn a foreign language.[26]

---

[26] For further research on the impact of language on earnings see, for example, Chiswick and Miller (1995, 1998); Dustmann and van Soest (2002).

99

Table 3.23 Political interest, ethnic origin for women and men, first and second generation.

Ethnic origin	Women		Men	
	First gen.	Second gen.	First gen.	Second gen.
Other	3.00	3.11	2.64	2.59
Turkey	3.51	3.25	2.97	3.03
Ex-Yugoslavia	3.24	3.17	2.91	2.88
Greece	3.47	3.21	3.01	3.13
Italy	3.34	3.23	2.94	2.95
Spain	3.00	2.86	3.03	2.69
Poland	3.09	2.91	2.58	2.61
Russia	3.23	3.63	2.92	2.56
Germany	2.78		2.44	

Source: German Socio-Economic Panel (SOEP), unweighted sample, 2005. Scale from 1 ('very interested') to 4 ('not at all interested')

3.3.10 *Political interest*

The degree of political interest of a country's population can be extremely informative when we look at integration processes. Table 3.23 illustrates the immigrants' and Germans' political interest in 2005. It is measured on a scale from 1 to 4, where 1 refers to 'very interested' and 4 to 'completely uninterested'. Most immigrants show less interest in politics than natives. Turks, in particular, show a comparably low interest in politics regardless of immigrant generation, whereas Poles seem to be most interested in politics. Comparison across generations shows that the second generation tends to be more politically interested than the first, indicating again the greater commitment to Germany of later generations.

Running a simple regression on the degree of political interest (Table 3.24) confirms the picture given by the descriptive statistics. Accordingly, the index increases for almost all immigrant groups regardless of gender, implying lower political interest for most immigrant groups compared to natives. But since the increase is stronger for the first compared to the second generation within each ethnic group the assumption that second-generation immigrants are more interested in politics is supported by these results. Indeed, later generations exhibit greater concern in political and social processes in Germany, and immigrants born in Germany are thus better politically integrated.

Table 3.24 Political interest, ethnic origin for women and men.

Ethnic origin	Women	Men
Other (first gen.) (d)	0.1665***	0.1574***
	(0.0200)	(0.0244)
Other (second gen.) (d)	0.1477**	−0.0143
	(0.0482)	(0.0493)
Turkey (first gen.) (d)	0.3902***	0.2395***
	(0.0293)	(0.0302)
Turkey (second gen.) (d)	0.1691**	0.1645**
	(0.0555)	(0.0592)
Ex-Yugoslavia (first gen.) (d)	0.2439***	0.2884***
	(0.0368)	(0.0428)
Ex-Yugoslavia (second gen.) (d)	0.1038	0.1059
	(0.0654)	(0.0796)
Greece (first gen.) (d)	0.4988***	0.4061***
	(0.0623)	(0.0655)
Greece (second gen.) (d)	0.2796**	0.4980***
	(0.0867)	(0.0946)
Italy (first gen.) (d)	0.3296***	0.2803***
	(0.0514)	(0.0480)
Italy (second gen.) (d)	0.1791**	0.2597***
	(0.0577)	(0.0676)
Spain (first gen.) (d)	0.1210	0.3480***
	(0.1030)	(0.0953)
Spain (second gen.) (d)	−0.1284	0.2645
	(0.1636)	(0.1366)
Poland (first gen.) (d)	0.2323***	0.0787
	(0.0357)	(0.0455)
Poland (second gen.) (d)	−0.0090	−0.0467
	(0.1174)	(0.1412)
Russia (first gen.) (d)	0.3487***	0.3276***
	(0.0415)	(0.0482)
Russia (second gen.) (d)	No obs	−0.1803
		(0.2918)
Cohort 1 (d)	−0.1771***	−0.1603***
	(0.0105)	(0.0118)
Cohort 3 (d)	0.2400***	0.1926***
	(0.0095)	(0.0108)
Years of schooling	−0.0919***	−0.0997***
	(0.0016)	(0.0017)
Constant	3.8573***	3.6589***
	(0.0211)	(0.0227)
N	31,689	28,877

OLS Regressions; standard errors in parentheses; (d) for discrete change of dummy variable from 0 to 1; * p <0:05. ** p <0:01. *** p <0:001. Scale from 1 ('very interested') to 4 ('not at all interested').
Source: SOEP (2005).

Table 3.25 Identification with Germany.

Ethnic origin	Women		Men	
	First gen.	Second gen.	First gen.	Second gen.
Other	2.29	1.90	2.13	2.33
Turkey	3.89	3.25	3.60	2.97
Ex-Yugoslavia	3.29	2.76	3.32	2.67
Greece	3.85	3.04	3.72	2.70
Italy	3.54	2.81	3.59	2.84
Spain	3.38	3.13	3.42	2.54
Poland	2.03	No obs	1.93	No obs
Russia	1.65	No obs	1.60	No obs

Scale from 1 ('complete identification') to 5 ('no identification').
Source: German Socio-Economic Panel (SOEP), unweighted sample, 1999.

Table 3.26 Identification with country of origin.

Ethnic origin	Women		Men	
	First gen.	Second gen.	First gen.	Second gen.
Other	3.15	3.20	3.36	3.67
Turkey	2.18	2.90	2.26	2.76
Ex-Yugoslavia	2.33	2.59	2.29	3.03
Greece	1.84	2.29	1.82	2.82
Italy	2.02	2.54	1.95	2.47
Spain	1.77	3.13	1.68	2.38
Poland	3.15	No obs	3.22	No obs
Russia	3.16	No obs	3.53	No obs

Scale from 1 ('complete identification') to 5 ('no identification').
Source: German Socio-Economic Panel (SOEP), unweighted sample, 1999.

3.3.11 *Self-identification with Germany*

The fact that the second generation is more integrated also becomes visible from Tables 3.25 and 3.26, which report self-identification with Germany and with the country of origin. Identification is measured on a scale from 1 to 5, where 1 refers to 'complete identification' with either Germany or the country of ancestry and 5 refers to 'no identification' with the respective country. As depicted in these two tables the second generation has a clear tendency toward more identification with Germany and less identification with the country of the parents' origin. This tendency is noticeable for all immigrant groups. Considering ethnic groups separately, one can see that Poles and Russians, especially,

Table 3.27 Risk attitude, ethnic origin for women and men, first and second generation.

Ethnic origin	Women		Men	
	First gen.	Second gen.	First gen.	Second gen.
Other	3.56	4.81	4.63	5.71
Turkey	2.57	4.15	4.01	5.21
Ex-Yugoslavia	3.03	5.55	4.29	5.50
Greece	2.28	3.92	3.20	4.97
Italy	3.13	4.14	4.32	5.65
Spain	3.57	4.26	4.17	5.17
Poland	3.95	4.31	4.82	6.09
Russia	3.23	5.33	3.94	3.50
Germany	4.07		4.98	

Scale from 0 ('completely risk averse') to 10 ('completely risk loving').
Source: German Socio-Economic Panel (SOEP), unweighted sample, 2005.

show a great commitment to Germany, whereas Turks and Greeks still feel closely bound to their country of origin.[27]

3.3.12 *Risk behaviour*

Turning now to more general differences in characteristics between immigrants and Germans, Table 3.27 shows self-reported information about risk attitudes. Studies have shown that adaptation to the attitudes of the majority population closes the immigrant-native gap in risk proclivity, while stronger commitment to the home country preserves it (Bonin *et al.*, 2006, 2009). As risk attitudes are behaviourally relevant and vary by ethnic origin, these findings could help to explain differences in the socio-economic assimilation of immigrants. The risk-loving tendencies of people are measured on a scale from 0 to 10, where 0 refers to 'complete risk aversion' and 10 to 'complete risk affinity'. We find that second-generation immigrants seem to be more risk loving than their first-generation counterparts. This generational difference is especially pronounced for Turkish women. The average risk level of first-generation Turks is 2.57 and thus on the lower level of the scale, whereas the average value for second-generation Turkish women is 4.15 and therefore very close to the average value of native women (4.07). In general, first-generation immigrants seem to be more risk averse than

---

[27] The greater commitment of Poles and Russians might be due to the fact that most Polish and Russian immigrants belong to the group of *Aussiedler* and hence feel especially close to Germany.

Table 3.28 Risk attitude, ethnic origin for women and men.

Ethnic origin	Women	Men
Other (first gen.) (d)	−0.5979***	−0.4748***
	(0.0658)	(0.0741)
Other (second gen.) (d)	0.4696**	0.1367
	(0.1558)	(0.1454)
Turkey (first gen.) (d)	−1.2518***	−0.7447***
	(0.0936)	(0.0893)
Turkey (second gen.) (d)	−0.3704*	−0.2663
	(0.1816)	(0.1849)
Ex-Yugoslavia (first gen.) (d)	−0.7370***	−0.5969***
	(0.1177)	(0.1267)
Ex-Yugoslavia (second gen.) (d)	0.8736***	0.2534
	(0.2124)	(0.2417)
Greece (first gen.) (d)	−1.2250***	−1.2120***
	(0.1955)	(0.1946)
Greece (second gen.) (d)	−0.3524	−0.3650
	(0.2730)	(0.2847)
Italy (first gen.) (d)	−0.5345**	−0.2017
	(0.1635)	(0.1425)
Italy (second gen.) (d)	−0.1927	0.1156
	(0.1915)	(0.2072)
Spain (first gen.) (d)	−0.3151	−0.5418
	(0.3204)	(0.2800)
Spain (second gen.) (d)	0.1074	−0.4959
	(0.1154)	(0.4052)
Poland (first gen.) (d)	−0.3753**	−0.1191
	(0.1154)	(0.1367)
Poland (second gen.) (d)	−1.0322'**	0.8118
	(0.3885)	(0.4440)
Russia (first gen.) (d)	−0.8887***	−1.0461***
	(0.1371)	(0.1498)
Russia (second gen.) (d)	No obs	−2.2127*
		(0.9911)
Cohort 1 (d)	−0.8838***	−0.8800***
	(0.0340)	(0.0355)
Cohort 3 (d)	0.4113***	0.5992***
	(0.0315)	(0.0334)
Years of schooling	0.1145***	0.1048***
	(0.0053)	(0.0051)
Constant	2.7723***	3.6847***
	(0.0691)	(0.0693)
N	28,063	25,530

OLS regressions; standard errors in parentheses; (d) for discrete change of dummy variable from 0 to 1; * p <0:05. ** p <0:01. *** p <0:001. Scale from 0 ('completely risk averse') to 10 ('completely risk loving').
Source: SOEP (2005).

Germans, whereas second-generation immigrants tend to be as risk loving as natives or even more risk taking.

These raw statistics are supported by the estimation results presented in Table 3.28. The risk index is smaller for most first-generation women—except Spaniards—compared to natives, indicating more risk aversion. Among second-generation women only Turkish, Polish, and ex-Yugoslav women differ from natives. For men the picture is slightly different. Second-generation men seem not to differ at all from natives, while first-generation Turks, Greeks, ex-Yugoslav, and Russians tend to be more risk averse than German men. Men and women who belong to the first-generation Turks, Greeks, and Russians show especially high levels of risk aversion compared to natives. These results may clash with what was previously believed or with what intuition would predict, but are in line with previous studies. Bonin *et al.* (2009) confirm that first-generation immigrants have lower risk attitudes than natives, which only equalize in the second generation. One explanation could be related to the first-generation's insecurities in their social and economic situation in Germany. Yet, first-generation immigrants may have been more willing to take risks than their co-ethnics who never left their home county, but this risk level could subside once they arrived in the host country.

3.3.13 *Overall life satisfaction*

With respect to overall life satisfaction Table 3.29 shows that there is not much difference between immigrants and natives. Life satisfaction is also measured on a scale from 0 to 10, where 0 denotes 'complete dissatisfaction' and 10 'complete satisfaction'. Second-generation

Table 3.29 Overall life satisfaction, ethnic origin for women and men, first and second generation.

Ethnic origin	Women		Men	
	First gen.	Second gen.	First gen.	Second gen.
Other	7.07	7.20	7.03	7.00
Turkey	6.32	7.04	6.28	6.86
Ex-Yugoslavia	6.56	7.17	6.59	6.94
Greece	6.50	7.13	6.76	7.10
Italy	6.47	7.28	6.70	7.37
Spain	6.48	6.95	6.90	7.40
Poland	6.86	7.45	6.85	7.54
Russia	7.03	7.50	7.09	7.78
Germany	6.95		6.95	

Source: German Socio-Economic Panel (SOEP), unweighted sample (2005–2007). Scale from 0 ('completely dissatisfied') to 10 ('completely satisfied').

Table 3.30 Overall life satisfaction, ethnic origin for women and men.

Ethnic origin	Women	Men
Other (first gen.) (d)	0.1333**	0.1504**
	(0.0502)	(0.0559)
Other (second gen.) (d)	0.0116	−0.0549
	(0.1208)	(0.1126)
Turkey (first gen.) (d)	−0.3624***	−0.4075***
	(0.0735)	(0.0690)
Turkey (second gen.) (d)	−0.2061	−0.2548
	(0.1393)	(0.1355)
Ex-Yugoslavia (first gen.) (d)	−0.1542	−0.1946*
	(0.0923)	(0.0979)
Ex-Yugoslavia (second gen.) (d)	0.0545	−0.0343
	(0.1642)	(0.1823)
Greece (first gen.) (d)	−0.1553	0.1371
	(0.1569)	(0.1495)
Greece (second gen.) (d)	−0.0574	−0.1069
	(0.2191)	(0.2166)
Italy (first gen.) (d)	−0.1519	0.0545
	(0.1293)	(0.1100)
Italy (second gen.) (d)	0.3305*	0.2553
	(0.1442)	(0.1548)
Spain (first gen.) (d)	−0.2142	0.3408
	(0.2584)	(0.2181)
Spain (second gen.) (d)	0.1430	0.3804
	(0.4104)	(0.3128)
Poland (first gen.) (d)	−0.0644	0.0159
	(0.0894)	(0.1044)
Poland (second gen.) (d)	0.1510	0.3197
	(0.2945)	(0.3233)
Russia (first gen.) (d)	0.1478	0.3188**
	(0.1042)	(0.1106)
Russia (second gen.) (d)	No obs	0.3994
		(0.6680)
Cohort 1 (d)	0.0906***	0.2384***
	(0.0264)	(0.0270)
Cohort 3 (d)	0.2873***	0.3204***
	(0.0239)	(0.0247)
Years of schooling	0.0925***	0.1104***
	(0.0041)	(0.0039)
Constant	5.7082***	5.4029***
	(0.0529)	(0.0520)
N	31,686	28,874

OLS regressions; standard errors in parentheses; (d) for discrete change of dummy variable from 0 to 1; * $p < 0.05$. ** $p < 0.01$. *** $p < 0.001$ Scale from 0 ('completely dissatisfied') to 10 ('completely satisfied').

Source: SOEP, 2005–2007.

immigrants score, on average, greater values on that index (at or even above 7). Evidently, they tend to be more satisfied in life than their parents who were foreign-born. The life satisfaction values of natives lie between the values of first and second-generation immigrants. Estimation outputs in Table 3.30 imply hardly any significant deviation between immigrants and natives. Only for some groups, such as first-generation Turks and first-generation ex-Yugoslav men, does the index decrease, indicating a lower life satisfaction for these immigrants than for Germans. The deviation from natives is especially big for first-generation Turks of either gender. In contrast, second-generation Italian women and first-generation Russians seem to be more satisfied than natives. Overall, we find that immigrants integrate perfectly in terms of self-reported life satisfaction.

3.3.14 Female labour force participation

Finally, in Table 3.31 we consider one aspect of economic integration, namely female labour force participation by ethnic group and generation. The variable of interest equals 1 if the woman is working full or part-time and 0 if she is unemployed or irregularly working. Schooling and no information are coded as missing. The underlying sample is

Table 3.31 Female labour force participation, ethnic origin compared with unemployment, employment, and schooling.

Ethnic origin		Unempl. or irreg. empl.	Full or part-time empl.	School or no inform.
Other	First gen.	45.00	39.21	15.79
	Second gen.	34.43	40.57	25.00
Turkey	First gen.	65.00	21.11	13.89
	Second gen.	42.73	30.40	26.87
Ex-Yugoslavia	First gen.	44.52	37.53	17.95
	Second gen.	37.86	47.14	15.00
Greece	First gen.	31.45	54.03	14.52
	Second gen.	37.97	50.63	11.39
Italy	First gen.	37.38	45.33	17.29
	Second gen.	34.92	43.92	21.16
Spain	First gen.	46.94	32.65	20.41
	Second gen.	35.71	21.43	42.86
Poland	First gen.	31.40	50.78	17.82
	Second gen.	39.58	35.42	25.00
Russia	First gen.	38.64	43.05	18.31
	Second gen.	28.57	0.00	71.43
Germany		37.23	49.38	13.39

Source: German Socio-Economic Panel (SOEP), unweighted sample (2005–2007), women aged 20–65.

restricted to women older than 20 and younger than 65. The share of
women working full or part-time differs noticeably by immigrant group
and generation. Only 21.11 per cent of first-generation Turkish women
work full or part-time, whereas in later generations the share is about 10
percentage points higher, namely 30.40 per cent. Similar differences can
be observed for ex-Yugoslav women. Here the difference between first

Table 3.32 Female labour force participation.

Ethnic origin	Women
Other (first gen.) (d)	−0.0922***
	(0.0160)
Other (second gen.) (d)	−0.0025
	(0.0384)
Turkey (first gen.) (d)	−0.2088***
	(0.0229)
Turkey (second gen.) (d)	−0.1194**
	(0.0430)
Ex-Yugoslavia (first gen.) (d)	−0.0056
	(0.0282)
Ex-Yugoslavia (second gen.) (d)	0.0561
	(0.0479)
Greece (first gen.) (d)	0.2223***
	(0.0397)
Greece (second gen.) (d)	0.0024
	(0.0650)
Italy (first gen.) (d)	0.0847*
	(0.0372)
Italy (second gen.) (d)	0.0367
	(0.0421)
Spain (first gen.) (d)	−0.0517
	(0.0851)
Spain (second gen.) (d)	−0.0977
	(0.1318)
Poland (first gen.) (d)	0.0757**
	(0.0265)
Poland (second gen.) (d)	−0.1090
	(0.0894)
Russia (first gen.) (d)	−0.0126
	(0.0335)
Russia (second gen.) (d)	No obs
Cohort 1 (d)	−0.5108***
	(0.0105)
Cohort 3 (d)	−0.0490***
	(0.0070)
Years of schooling	0.0421***
	(0.0014)
N	24,244

Logit regression; marginal effects; standard errors in parentheses; (d) for discrete change of dummy
variable from 0 to 1; * p <0:05. ** p <0:01. *** p <0:001.
Source: SOEP (2005–2007), women aged 20–65.

and second generation also amounts to about 10 percentage points—even though on a higher level it is 37.53 and 47.14 per cent, respectively. Clearly, labour market participation is higher for second-generation immigrants from these groups. However, it is still much lower than the share of labour force participation of native women (about 50 per cent). The exception is Greek women, who have higher labour market participation than German women in both generations. Interestingly, first-generation Greek women participate more often in the labour market than later generations. Similarly, first-generation Italian women show very high participation rates of over 45 per cent.

Estimation results presented in Table 3.32 corroborate these raw statistics. Accordingly, first-generation Italian, Greek, and Polish women are more likely to work compared to native women. In contrast, Turkish women are less likely to work compared to Germans, regardless of generation. This indicates lower economic integration by some immigrant groups, but also very good labour market integration by others. In general, there are hardly any differences between second-generation immigrants and natives with respect to full or part-time work for those who are not enrolled in school and for whom information about their labour market status is available.

3.4 Conclusion

This chapter studies the cultural integration of immigrants in Germany. To gauge integration, we use natives as the 'gold standard' and refer to them every time we look at the cultural and general socio-economic and political progress of immigrants. We cover various social and economic aspects of the life of immigrants in Germany using data from the German Socio-Economic Panel (SOEP) for the period 2005–2007. Specifically, we study marital behaviour, family structure, soft skills such as risk attitudes and overall life satisfaction, German language proficiency, and self-identification, as well as economic characteristics such as female labour force participation. In order to capture trends and developments over time we analyse and study these indicators of socio-cultural and economic aspects for first and second-immigrant generations. Additionally, emphasis is put on differences between certain immigrant groups, in particular immigrants who originate from one of the former guest worker countries as well as immigrants from Poland and Russia, who represent more recent influences in immigrant inflows to Germany. We examine and present both raw statistics and estimation results on the above-mentioned indicators.

Considering marriage patterns is crucial in the integration process of immigrants since marriage and partner choice express individual commitment and attachment to the members of a host society at a very intimate level.[28] Convergence between immigrants and natives with respect to family behaviour signals to what extent immigrants adapt to German specific norms and embrace German habits.

Empirical results imply trends towards more remaining single among native Germans. This trend seems to be adopted by the second generation. Similar findings are observed regarding age at first marriage and age and educational gap between spouses. Accordingly, first-generation immigrants tend to get married more often and at younger ages than natives and the second generation. Clearly, they seem to cling to different role allocations and traditions from Germans and their offspring generation.[29] Age gaps and educational differences between partners are greater for older generations and mostly not different from natives for younger cohorts. Intermarriage rates depict an intimate link between immigrants and the native population. This can be seen as a special integration measure possibly even fostering economic integration. In general, the bigger the single ethnic group the less likely their members are to intermarry. This holds especially for Turks and members of the native population who show the lowest rate of intermarriage among all ethnic groups.

Furthermore, fertility rates, age at first child, and female labour force participation differ significantly between natives and first-generation immigrants, indicating different conceptions of gender roles and division of labour within the family between those groups. Differences vanish or, at least, diminish for later immigrant generations, implying greater adaption to German norms and perceptions for immigrants born in Germany. Comparing language and identification indexes among different ethnic groups, we observe noticeable discrepancies between generations. Accordingly, second-generation immigrants report higher levels of language proficiency than members of their parental generation, indicating better linguistic integration. Additionally, self-reported identification with Germany is stronger for immigrants born in Germany, expressing greater commitment to Germany and its society. All these findings fit the assumption that second-generation immigrants can enjoy a successful integration.

---

[28] For further research on the effect of marriage on economic success see, for example, Korenmann and Neumark (1991); Angrist (2002).

[29] See, for example, Baker and Benjamin (1997) for differences in the human capital accumulation of immigrants.

Finally, the underlying data provide information about soft characteristics, such as risk aversion, overall life satisfaction, and political interest, which also opens unique opportunities to compare immigrants and natives in the field of behavioural economics. Accordingly, immigrants and natives do not differ much with respect to life satisfaction. They do differ, though, regarding risk attitudes. Immigrants seem to be slightly less risk loving than natives. However, differences mainly disappear for later immigrant cohorts, indicating that, also from that perspective, younger immigrants converge towards native attitudes. Regarding political involvement, immigrants are in general less politically concerned than natives, but again the second-generation's political interest is more in line with that of natives, expressing better integration also in this dimension.

As a final remark, and referring to Turks as one immigrant group with pronounced differences, this analysis shows that comparison by generation is crucial when making statements about the integration process of ethnic groups in Germany. Turks differ in various ways from natives and also from other immigrant groups. They are more likely to be married in general, more often marry at young ages and often have more children than the average German woman. Their language abilities are worse compared to other immigrants, they report a lower identification with Germany and more commitment to their home country, and their religious beliefs are diverse from that of natives and co-immigrants. They report the lowest level of political interest and lower levels of life satisfaction than other immigrant groups. Finally, their labour force participation rates are comparably low.

All these findings indicate that Turks are the least integrated immigrant group with respect to the integration indicators considered in this study. But when studying Turkish immigrants by generation, it becomes clear that the second generation shows a tendency toward parity with native Germans. Second-generation Turks show higher intermarriage rates, similar behaviour to natives in terms of age at first marriage, age at first child, and number of children. They report better German language proficiency both regarding speaking and writing skills as well as greater identification with Germany and simultaneously less commitment to the country of ancestry. Hence, even if this group of immigrants often seems to be poorly integrated, trends over time need to be honoured and encouraged.

Appendix

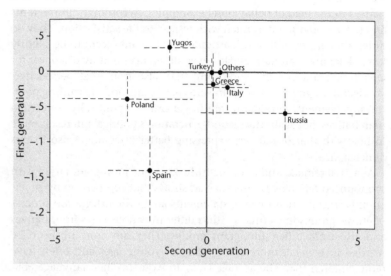

Figure 3.1 Individual gap in education between spouses—men.

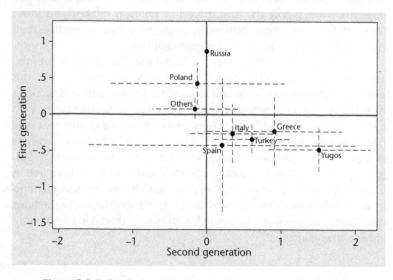

Figure 3.2 Individual gap in education between spouses—women.

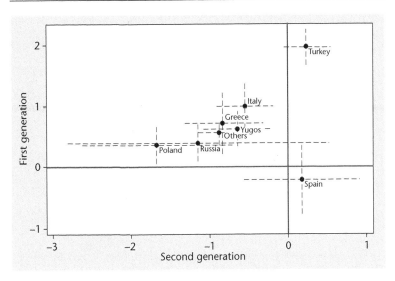

Figure 3.3 Marriage probability—men.

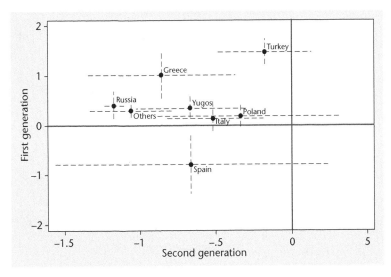

Figure 3.4 Marriage probability—women.

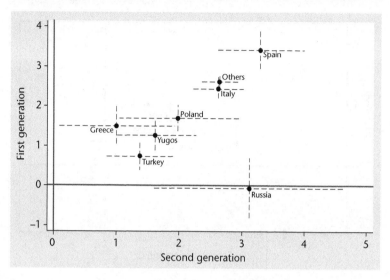

Figure 3.5 Intermarriage probability—men.

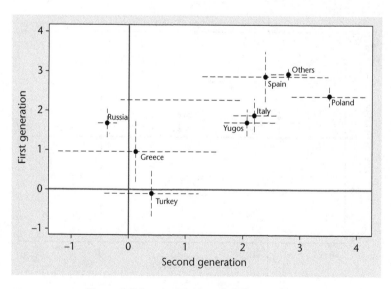

Figure 3.6 Intermarriage probability—women.

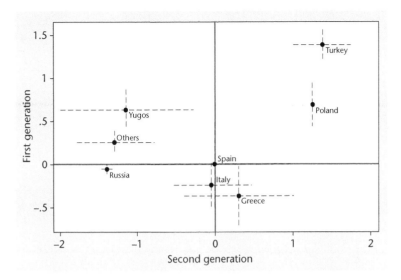

Figure 3.7 Probability of being first married before 25—men.

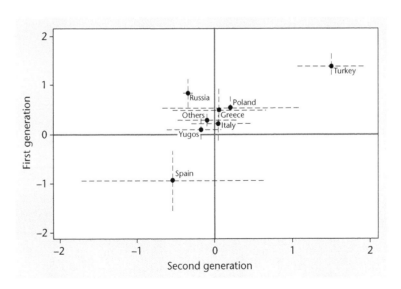

Figure 3.8 Probability of being first married before 25—women.

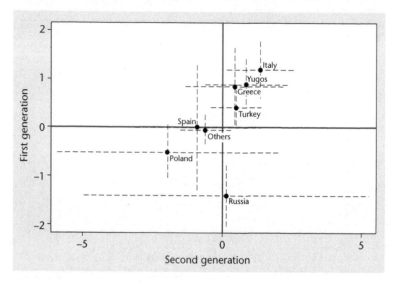

Figure 3.9 Age gap between spouses—men.

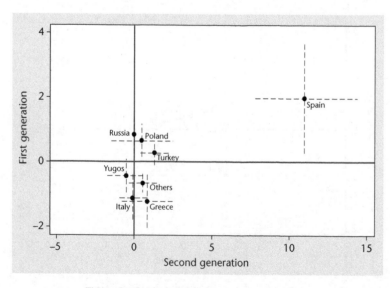

Figure 3.10 Age gap between spouses—women.

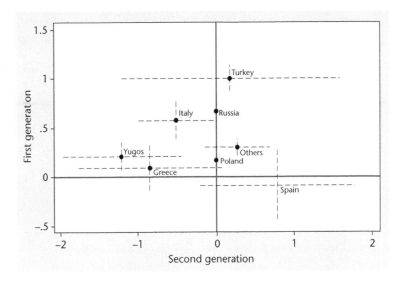

Figure 3.11 Number of children.

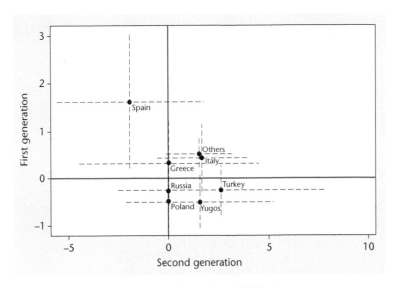

Figure 3.12 Age at first child birth.

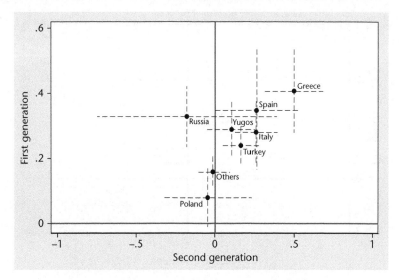

Figure 3.13 Political interest—men.

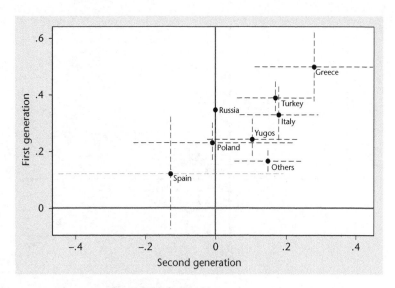

Figure 3.14 Political interest—women.

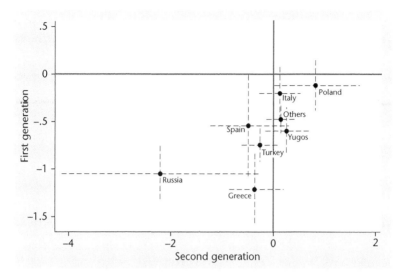

Figure 3.15 Risk attitude—men.

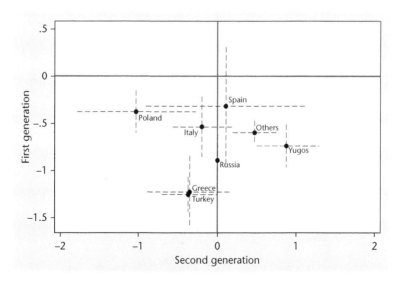

Figure 3.16 Risk attitude—women.

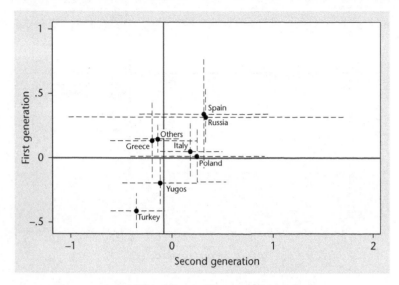

Figure 3.17 Overall life satisfaction—men.

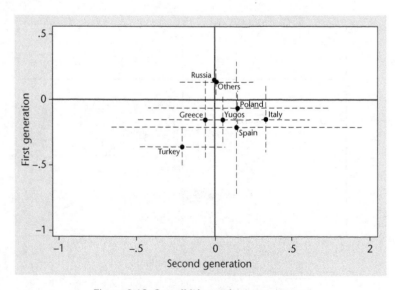

Figure 3.18 Overall life satisfaction—women.

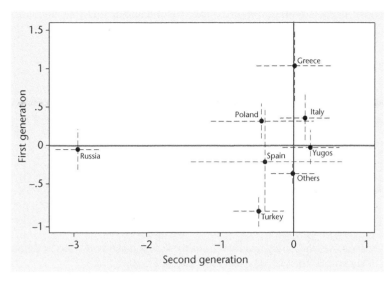

Figure 3.19 Female labour force participation.

References

Akerlof, G.A. and Kranton, R.E. (2000) Economics and Identity. *Quarterly Journal of Economics*, 115, 715–753.

Angrist, J.D. (2002) How do Sex Rations Affect Marriage and Labor Markets? Evidence from America's Second Generation. *Quarterly Journal of Economics*, 117(3), 997–1038.

Baker, M. and Benjamin, D. (1997) The Role of Family in Immigrant's Labor Market Activity: An Evaluation of Alternative Explanations. *American Economic Review*, 87(4), 705–727.

Bénabou, R. and Tirole, J. (2011) Identity, Morals and Taboos: Beliefs as Assets. *Quarterly Journal of Economics*,. 126, 805–855.

Bonin, H., Constant, A., Tatsiramos, K., and Zimmermann, K.F. (2006) *Ethnic Persistence, Assimilation and Risk Proclivity*. IZA DP, 2537.

Bonin, H., Constant, A., Tatsiramos, K., and Zimmermann, K.F. (2009) Native-migrant Differences in Risk Attitudes. *Applied Economics Letters*, 16, 1581–1586.

Brenke, K., Yuksel, M., and Zimmermann, K.F. (2009) EU Enlargement under Continued Mobility Restrictions: Consequences for the German Labor Market. In: M. Kahanec and K.F. Zimmermann (eds), *EU Labor Markets after Post-Enlargement Migration*. Berlin, Springer Verlag, pp. 111–129.

Chiswick, B.R. and Housworth, C.A. (2011) Ethnic Intermarriage among Immigrants: Human Capital and Assortative Mating. *Review of Economics of the Household*, 9(2), 149–80.

Chiswick, B.R. and Miller, P.W. (1995) The Endogeneity Between Language and Earnings: International Analysis. *Journal of Labor Economics*, 13(2), 245–287. Reprinted in K.F. Zimmermann and T.K. Bauer (eds) *The Economics of Migration*. Cheltenham, Edward Elgar Publishing, September 2002, Volume II, pp. 475–517. Volume in the series *The International Library of Critical Writing in Economics*, reprinted in D.M. Lamberton (ed.), *The Economics of Language*. Cheltenham,Edward Elgar Publishing, 2003, pp. 198–242 (volume in the series *The International Library of Critical Writing in Economics*).

Chiswick, B.R. and Miller, P.W. (1998) English Language Fluency Among Immigrants in the United States. *Research in Labor Economics*, 17, 151–200.

Constant, A.F. and Zimmermann, K.F. (2008) Measuring Ethnic Identity and Its Impact on Economic Behavior. *Journal of the European Economic Association*, 6(2–3), 424–433.

Constant, A.F. and Zimmermann, K.F. (2009) Work and Money: Payoffs by Ethnic Identity and Gender. *Research in Labor Economics*, 29, 3–30.

Constant, A.F. and Zimmermann, K.F. (2011) Migration, Ethnicity and Economic Integration. In: M.N. Jovanovic (ed.) *International Handbook on the Economics of Integration*, Vol. III. Cheltenham, Edward Elgar Publishing, pp. 145–168.

Constant, A.F., Gataullina, L., and Zimmermann, K.F. (2006) *The Clash of Cultures: Muslims and Christians in the Ethnosizing Process*. IZA DP No. 2350.

Constant, A.F., Gataullina, L., and Zimmermann, K.F. (2009a) Ethnosizing Immigrants. *Journal of Economic Behavior and Organization*, 69(3), 274–287.

Constant, A.F., Kahanec, M., and Zimmermann, K.F. (2009b) Attitudes towards Immigrants, other Integration Barriers and their Veracity. *International Journal of Manpower*, 30(1/2), 5–14.

Constant, A.F., Roberts, R., and Zimmermann, K.F. (2009c) Ethnic Identity and Immigrant Homeownership. *Urban Studies*, 46(9), 1879–1898.

Constant, A.F., Tien, B.N., and Xidous, A. (2010a) Germany: Labor Market Integration of Immigrants. In: A. Platonova and G. Urso (eds), *Migration, Employment and Labour Market Integration Policies in the European Union. Part 1: Migration and the Labour Markets in the European Union (2000–2009)*. International Migration for Migration. Belgium, IOM.

Constant, A.F., Tien, B.N., and Xidous, A. (2010b) Germany: Policies about the Labor Markets. In: A. Platonova and G. Urso (eds), *Migration, Employment and Labour Market Integration Policies in the European Union. Part 2: Labour Market Integration Policies in the European Union (2000–2009)*. International Migration for Migration. Belgium, IOM.

Constant, A.F., Zimmermann, L., and Zimmermann, K.F. (2012) *The Myth of Clash of Cultures: Muslims and Christians in the Ethnosizing Process*. Mimeo.

Dustmann, C. and van Soest, A. (2002) Language and Earnings of Immigrants. *Industrial and Labor Relations Review*, 55(3), 473–492.

Furtado, D. (2012) Human Capital and Interethnic Marriage Decision. *Economic Inquiry*, 50(1), 82–93. doi: 10.1111/j.1465-7295.2010.00345.x, 2010.

Furtado, D. and Theodoropoulos, N. (2011) Interethnic Marriage: A Choice between Ethnic and Educational Similarities. *Journal of Population Economics*, 24(4), 1257–1279.

Gonzáles-Ferrer, A. (2006) Who do Immigrants Marry? Partner Choice Among Single Immigrants in Germany. *European Sociological Review*, 22(2), 171–185.

Kalmijn, M. (1998) Intermarriage and Homogamy: Causes, Patterns and Trends. *Annual Review of Sociology*, 24, 395–421.

Kantarevic, J. (2004) *Interethnic Marriages and Economic Assimilation of Immigrants*. IZA DP, 1142.

Korenmann, S. and Neumark, D. (1991) Does Marriage Really Make Men More Productive? *The Journal of Human Resources*, 26(2), 282–307.

Lievens, J. (1998) Interethnic Marriage: Bringing in the Context through Multi-level Modeling. *European Journal of Population*, 14. 117–155.

Lievens, J. (1999) Family-Forming Migration from Turkey and Morocco to Belgium: The Demand for Marriage Partners from the Countries of Origin. *The International Migration Review*, 33(3), 717–744.

Meng, X. and Gregory, R.G. (2005) Intermarriage and the Economic Assimilation of Immigrants. *Journal of Labor Economics*, 23(1), 135–175.

Meng, X. and Meurs, D. (2006) Intermarriage, Language, and Economic Assimilation Process: A Case Study of France. *International Journal of Manpower*, 30(1/2), 127–144.

Phinney, J. S. (1992) The Multigroup Ethnic Identity Measure: A New Scale for Use with Diverse Groups. *Journal of Adolescent Research*, 7, 156–176.

Phinney, J.S., Horenczyk, G., Liebkind, K., and Vedder, P. (2001) Ethnic Identity, Immigration and Well-being: An International Perspective. *Journal of Social Issues*, 57, 493–510.

Statistisches Bundesamt (2009) *Statistisches Jahrbuch*, Wiesbaden, Statistisches Bundesamt (Federal Statistical Office).

Wagner, G.G., Frick, J., and Schupp J. (2007) *The German Socio-Economic Panel Study (SOEP)—Scope, Evolution and Enhancements*. Berlin, Schmollers Jahrbuch, 127(1), 139–169.

Zimmermann, K.F. (2002) European Migration: Push and Pull. Paper presented at the World Bank Annual Conference on Development Economics 1994. Supplement to *The World Bank Economic Review and the World Bank Research Observer* 10 (1995), 313–342. Reprinted in: *International Regional Science Review*, 19 (1996), 95–128, and K.F. Zimmermann and T. Bauer (eds) *The Economics of Migration*. Cheltenham, Edward Elgar Publishing Ltd. Vol. I, Part I, pp. 70–99.

Zimmermann, K.F. (2007a) Migrant Ethnic Identity: Concept and Policy Implications. *Ekonomia*, 10(1), 1–17.

Zimmermann, K.F. (2007b) The Economics of Migrant Ethnicity. *Journal of Population Economics*, 20(3), 487–494.

Zimmermann, K.F., Constant, A. F., and Gataullina, L. (2009) Naturalization Proclivities, Ethnicity and Integration. *International Journal of Manpower*, 30(1–2), 70–82.

Zimmermann, L., Zimmermann, K.F., and Constant, A.F. (2007) Ethnic Self-identification of First-generation Immigrants. *International Migration Review*, 41(3), 769–781.

Zimmermann, L., Gataullina, L., Constant, A.F., and Zimmermann, K.F. (2008) Human Capital and Ethnic Self-identification of Migrants. *Economics Letters*, 98(3), 235–239.

4

Cultural Integration in Italy

Alberto Bisin and Eleonora Patacchini

4.1 Introduction

While immigration is a recent issue for Italy, flows have been steadily increasing over time, with a significant increase during the last ten years. This has induced general concerns regarding, for example, increased ethnic and religious diversity. The integration pattern of immigrants is in fact often perceived by natives to be excessively slow and the persistence of ethnic identities is viewed as a threat. Such a perception is evident in the recent debate in the press and in the results of national elections, which have seen the success of anti-immigration platforms.

To ground this debate, it is important to have a better understanding of the economic and cultural integration patterns for different immigrant groups in Italy. The study of integration patterns in Italy, however, is severely limited by the availability of data. The existing studies have exploited dedicated data, for example those collected by Fondazione ISMU (Iniziative e Studi sulla Multietnicitá) and those collected by Caritas. Using ISMU data, Blangiardo and Baio (2010), for instance, have been able to construct an index of integration for specific groups of immigrants, with respect, for example, to education and religion; see also Golini *et al.* (2004). Finally, a government committee (Commissione per le politiche di integrazione degli immigrati) has produced two descriptive studies, the first and second reports 'Sull'integrazione degli immigrati in Italia' by Zincone (2001, 2005). They contain a thorough review of the various immigration policies in the last ten years in Italy and a discussion of their effects on legalization practices and procedures.

In this chapter we exploit available information from the revision of the Italian Labour Force Survey (ILFS) questionnaire in 2005. This data allows us to provide a first evaluation of the integration of immigrants in Italy. Specifically, we study immigrants by wave of immigration, gender, and cohort, in terms of education, employment, and female participation rates, and to a lesser extent in terms of marriage, divorce, inter-ethnic marriage, and completed fertility rates. Appropriate data on more detailed indicators of cultural integration of immigrants, such as attachment to ethnic and religious customs and traditions, political preferences, and attitudes towards natives are yet to be collected in Italy.

Our empirical analysis does not show evidence of slow integration patterns for immigrants into Italy, though inter-marriage rates between immigrants and natives are very low. For instance, while Asian and Africans immigrants have little education on average at immigration, the level of education increases substantially in their second generations, and particularly so for the younger cohort of African women. Similarly, second-generation immigrants do not seem to have female participation rates significantly different from Italians and they do not seem to show more traditional attitudes towards family formation nor appreciably higher fertility rates. First-generation immigrants show a probability to be employed which is only slightly lower than natives, while second-generation immigrants do not show a significantly different probability of finding a job compared to natives. We tentatively interpret these results as evidence that economic and cultural integration of immigrants does not seem to represent a particular issue in Italy.

Our results, however, need to be taken with more than some caution. First of all, as will be discussed below, an important peculiarity of the Italian immigration experience is the pervasive presence of illegal immigrants. The immigrants that we observe, the legal immigrants, are possibly the more integrated ones. In particular, legal immigrants are those who have 'emerged' from statistical obscurity because they are working. A recent survey of both legal and illegal immigrants, which was carried out between October and November 2009 in eight cities in Northern Italy documents the presence of a sizeable and non-random portion of illegal immigrants (see Boeri *et al.*, 2011).

Second, immigration being a relatively new phenomenon for Italy, most of our second-generation immigrant sample (72 per cent) are children (below 15 years old). An analysis of marriage and divorce rates, as well as about trends of inter-ethnic marriages can thus only be performed for first-generation immigrants. Finally, the ILFS does not directly report the country of origin of the respondent's partner (nor his or her citizenship) and the number of children is confidential (the answer is not reported in ILFS data files). We therefore impute this information from the household roster, merging data for the respondent and other family members. As a consequence, we cannot capture information on children or partners that live outside the household.

Our results are therefore far from being conclusive about patterns of integration of the immigrants in Italy. We interpret them as preliminary evidence, conditionally on data availability.

This study is organized as follows. We will first highlight some peculiar aspects of the immigration phenomenon in Italy, in Section 4.2. In Section 4.3 we introduce our data and describe our sample. The empirical model and the target outcome variables are detailed in Section 4.4, while in Section 4.5 we collect our main descriptive evidence and estimation results. Section 4.6 concludes.

4.2 Italian immigration in the European context

Immigration began relatively late in Italy, after the oil crisis of 1973–1984, when England, Germany, and especially the neighbouring France closed their frontiers to immigration. Since then, the flows have been steadily increasing over time, with a massive increase of the foreign population during the last ten years; see Calavita (2006) for more details on demographic trends. Notwithstanding the recent growth, the stock of immigrants remains relatively limited in Italy compared to the other European countries. As reported by the Italian Office of National Statistics (ISTAT), in 2007 immigrants scarcely reached 5 per cent of the resident population in Italy, compared to 8.8 per cent for Germany, 6.2 per cent for Spain, and 5.2 per cent for Great Britain. In France immigrants accounted for 5.9 per cent of the population in the 1999 Census. Such a national average in Italy hides, however, marked geographical differences. While in the centre-south the fraction of immigrants in the population is 1.6 per cent, in the north it reaches 6.8 per cent, making the north of Italy more similar to the European average (for further details see ISTAT, 2007).

The fraction of immigrants in the population reported by ISTAT, however, refers necessarily to registered immigrants, a subset of all the immigrants living in the territory, because of the pervasiveness of illegal immigration in Italy, which in turn is due to the difficulty of controlling the country's extensive borders and to its sizable informal economy. Immigrants seem to be particularly sought after in the markets for private care and domestic services as well as in the small family enterprises where unregistered labour can be easily employed. The pronounced territorial disparities in registered immigration shares might

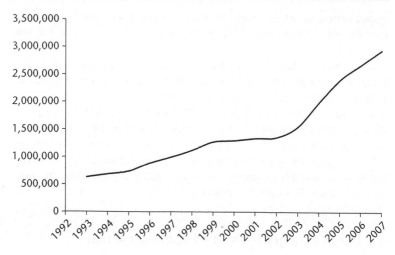

Figure 4.1 Immigration flows 1993–2007.

be due to the uneven distribution of the share of illegal immigrants by region, as the informal (underground) economy is particularly widespread in the south of Italy. Finally, the Italian immigration laws have exacerbated rather than contained illegal immigration. They have been mainly aimed at regularizing the status of those already illegally residing in Italy, rather than at regulating new legal entries. As a consequence, illegal immigration represents possibly the main viable form of immigration into Italy.

Figure 4.1 shows the pattern of Italian immigration since 1993, when the immigration flows started to be significant. The large increase after 2003 is only apparent, and it is due to a specific legislation allowing immigrants to regularize their status in 2002 (L.189/2002 and L.222/2002). More than 650,000 immigrants did so. Between 1995 and 2005, the increase in the immigrant population in Italy was about 300 per cent, doubling between 2001 and 2005. In 2007 the registered immigrants in Italy were 2,938,922 (ISTAT, 2007).

4.3 Description of data

We pooled data from the Italian Labour Force Survey (ILFS) for the years 2005–2007. Since 2005, such a survey contains information on each surveyed respondent's country of birth and citizenship. However, the Italian citizenship can be acquired in various ways, for example marrying an Italian citizen or after ten years of legal residence in Italy. We thus do not use citizenship to identify first and second-generation immigrants as well as natives. More specifically, we define first-generation immigrants on the basis of the country of birth, that is, as individuals born outside Italy. Consistently, we define second-generation immigrants using the country of birth of the parents, that is, as individuals with at least one parent born abroad. The native reference group consists of Italian citizens born in Italy whose parents were born in Italy. The ILFS contains information on country of birth of immigrants at a very detailed level, distinguishing between 162 countries. We adopt a categorization into six regions: Northern Europe, Southern and Eastern Europe, Africa, Asia, North and Central America, and South America. We do not include immigrants from Oceania due to small sample size, as well as immigrants from an unknown country of origin. Second-generation immigrants are assigned to a given area if at least one parent is from that specific area.

Table 4.1 reports the sample proportions for native Italians and for immigrants by generation and country of origin (in parentheses is the share of females in each group).

Around 94 per cent of our sample consists of natives, slightly more than 4 per cent are first-generation immigrants, and less than 2 per cent are second-generation immigrants. First-generation immigrants mainly come from Southern and Eastern Europe (33 per cent), Northern Europe (27 per cent), and Africa (17.50 per cent), this last group is predominantly from Maghreb. Female are slightly more numerous among first-generation immigrants, with the only exception of immigrants from Africa. As we noted, the low percentage of second-generation immigrants is due to the fact that immigration is a relatively new

Table 4.1 Immigrants by country of origin, generation, and gender.

Sample proportions in %

	First gen.	Second gen.
Natives	94.03 (52.01)	
Immigrants	5.97 (53.54)	
of which	4.19 (55.79)	1.78 (48.32)
Northern Europe	26.99 (58.89)	45.75 (48.80)
Southern and Eastern Europe	32.66 (58.72)	16.48 (48.08)
North and Central America	3.84 (67.06)	5.51 (47.45)
South America	9.84 (59.47)	10.07 (50.35)
Asia	9.26 (49.24)	6.63 (45.54)
Africa	17.41 (44.45)	16.54 (47.32)

We report in parentheses the share of females in each group.

Table 4.2 Immigrants by age and generation.

Sample proportions in %

Years	First gen.	Second gen.
0–14	8.89	72.08
15–24	11.10	19.75
25–34	22.78	6.09
35–44	28.36	1.32
45–54	15.17	0.40
55–64	6.15	0.25
65–74	4.19	0.11
75+	3.37	0.01

phenomenon for Italy. In fact, looking at Table 4.2, which reports the distribution of immigrants by age, it appears that most of our second-generation sample (roughly 72 per cent) are children below 15 years of age.

The inspection of our sample of immigrants by years since arrival in Italy (Table 4.3) reveals that most of them have stayed in Italy for either more than 11 years (53.21 per cent) or less than four years (22.21 per cent). Given the pervasive illegal nature of the Italian immigration, one possibility is that the question of the ILFS questionnaire on years of residence in Italy is perceived as asking the years of 'legal' permanence in Italy rather than the years of effective stay on the Italian territory. Under such hypothesis, our data are by and large capturing the share of the regularized immigration after the new laws in 2002 and the older wave of immigration after the oil crisis, in the 1990s. This is consistent with the fact that the largest share of first-generation immigrants that report a permanence in Italy of more than 11 years comes from Northern Europe (roughly 33 per cent).

Table 4.3 Immigrants by years since arrival and country of origin.

Sample proportions in %

Years	
Less than 4	22.21
More than 11	53.21
of which	
Northern Europe	33.12
Southern and Eastern Europe	20.33
North and Central America	3.61
South America	6.88
Asia	11.15
Africa	24.91

4.4 Empirical set-up

The differences of immigrants with respect to natives along various economic and cultural characteristics are estimated using a regression analysis on two model specifications. For each dependent variable representing a relevant economic or cultural characteristic, the first specification estimates differences with respect to natives for first and second-generation immigrants from different regions of origin. The second specification compares differences with respect to natives for two age cohorts (born before 1970 and after) for each immigrant generation and region of origin. Both specifications include as controls, when relevant, the level of education, and a quadratic function of age and time dummies. Each model is estimated separately for males and females, thus giving an evaluation of the immigrant to native gender gap for each of the economic and cultural indicators considered.

The economic and cultural indicators considered in the empirical analysis (dependent variables) are defined as follows:

- Education rates. The ILFS does not report at which age respondents left full-time education, but the level of qualification achieved. We then select respondents older than 19 and define a dummy variable, taking value 1 if the respondent has at least an high school diploma (i.e. a five-year secondary school degree) and 0 otherwise.

- Employment rates. We select respondents between 16 and 64 years of age and define a dummy variable taking value 1 if the respondent is employed and 0 otherwise.

- Female participation rates. We select female respondents between 16 and 64 years of age and define a dummy variable, taking value 1 if the female is employed or unemployed (i.e. searching a job) and 0 otherwise.

- Marriage rates. We select respondents older than 25 and define a dummy variable taking value 1 if the respondent is or has been married and 0 otherwise.

- Divorce rates. We keep the selection of respondents older than 25 that are or have been married and define a dummy variable taking value 1 if the respondent is no longer married (i.e. divorced) and 0 otherwise.

- Inter-ethnic marriage rates. The ILFS does not directly ask the respondents about the country of origin (nor the citizenship) of his or her partner. We obtain this information from the household roster, merging the information on the respondent and of the individual

Table 4.4 Summary data description (%).

	Natives	First gen.	Second gen.
Education rates	34.89	44.42	70.86
Employment rates	93.43	91.00	85.74
Female participation rates	48.22	55.31	33.16
Marriage rates	81.33	77.76	5.45
Divorce rates	1.78	3.64	—
Inter-ethnic marriage rates	19.76	61.88	—
Completed fertility rates	0.73	0.65	—

registered as wife/husband or partner of the respondent. Maintaining the selection of respondents older than 25 that are or have been married, we define a dummy variable taking value 1 if the respondent is or has been married to someone from the same country of origin and 0 otherwise.

- Completed fertility rates. The direct question on the number of children is confidential and the answer is not reported in ILFS data files. We once again obtain the information from the household roster, counting for each family the number of individuals registered as children. We then assign those children to the female which is registered as wife or partner in the same household roster. We consider only females older than 40 years. We exclude children from previous relationships so that we are sure to assign children to the correct mother, but we do not clearly capture children that live outside the household. Our results on completed fertility rates are thus only indicative and need to be taken with caution. Measurement errors can be large.

Table 4.4 shows the various rates for our sample of natives, first and second-generation immigrants. Such rates are further disaggregated (by gender and immigrant country of origin) and analysed in more detail in the following section.

4.5 Results

We summarize here the main results of our empirical analysis.

4.5.1 *Education rates*

Table 4.5 reports the level of education of natives, and of first and second-generation immigrants, by gender and region of origin. It reveals

Table 4.5 Education—descriptive statistics.

	% High school and above			
	male		female	
Natives				
	36.70		33.26	
Immigrants				
	First gen.	Second gen.	First gen.	Second gen.
of which	40.55	64.05	47.32	79.57
Northern Europe	46.82	63.25	48.81	78.15
Southern and Eastern Europe	40.32	66.03	51.25	78.21
North and Central America	61.03	81.58	59.66	75.00
South America	51.99	60.31	54.88	82.06
Asia	31.60	64.71	37.44	79.03
Africa	31.16	62.33	30.35	83.85

a rather high education level of first-generation immigrants and a remarkably higher education level of second-generation immigrants. As far as natives are concerned, about 37 per cent of men and 33 per cent of women have at least completed high school education. Looking at first-generation immigrants, three groups (Northern Europe, North and Central America, South America) show a higher degree of education compared to their native counterparts. Only immigrants from Asia and Africa seem to be significantly less educated than Italians. This evidence is true for both males and females. Immigrant women have on average a higher degree of education than immigrant men. They also appear to be more educated than their native counterparts, with the proportion with a high school diploma of roughly 60 and 55 per cent for those coming from North and Central America and South America, respectively. Also, the number with high school education is above 50 per cent for females from Southern and Eastern Europe. Second-generation immigrants are not only on average more educated than first-generation immigrants, but they are also more educated than natives, regardless of the region of origin. The difference in education between first and second generations is particularly marked for immigrants from Asia and Africa, that is, for immigrants with relatively low first-generation levels of education. For both males and females, the education rate of Asian immigrants in Italy roughly doubles between first and second generation and it more than doubles for African immigrants.

This descriptive evidence, however, is partly due to age differences between groups, as is revealed by our regression estimation results contained in Table 4.6. This table reports the estimation results of a probit regression analysis where the dependent variable is the probability of having a high school diploma, using the two model specifications

Table 4.6 Immigrants' education gap with respect to natives—all immigrants.

	All		Pre-70		Post-70	
	First gen.	Second gen.	First gen.	Second gen.	First gen.	Second gen.
Northern Europe	0.0435***	0.0669***	0.0815***	0.1150***	−0.0496***	0.0493***
	(0.0036)	(0.0106)	(0.0044)	(0.0287)	(0.0061)	(0.0113)
Southern and	−0.0098***	0.1150***	0.0951***	0.0566	−0.1416***	0.1217***
Eastern Europe	(0.0033)	(0.0188)	(0.0046)	(0.0412)	(0.0039)	(0.0211)
North and	0.1474***	0.2227***	0.2068***	0.2670***	0.0255	0.1952***
Central America	(0.0105)	(0.0400)	(0.0127)	(0.0738)	(0.0168)	(0.0472)
South America	0.0777***	0.0490**	0.1315***	0.2325***	−0.0430***	0.0270
	(0.0065)	(0.0209)	(0.0079)	(0.0855)	(0.0103)	(0.0212)
Asia	−0.1286***	0.0684	−0.0416***	0.5308***	−0.2350***	0.0146
	(0.0049)	(0.0423)	(0.0074)	(0.0987)	(0.0049)	(0.0418)
Africa	−0.1285***	0.1045***	−0.0589***	−0.0237	−0.2413***	0.1233***
	(0.0035)	(0.0189)	(0.0049)	(0.0415)	(0.0038)	(0.0212)
Observations	1,433,892		Observations 1,433,892			
Pseudo-R^2	0.136		Pseudo-R^2	0.138		

Marginal effects and standard errors (in parentheses) are reported; *** p <0.01, ** p <0.05, * p <0.1. Controls: quadratic in age, time dummies.

described in Section 4.4. Tables 4.7 and 4.8 collect the evidence for males and females separately. We show the marginal effects for each country of origin separately by males and females and generation of immigrants, with respect to their native counterparts, once the influence of (a quadratic function of) age and time effects is controlled for. Looking at Table 4.6, regarding first-generation immigrants, we find that not only those coming from Asia and Africa have a lower probability of being educated than natives, but also those coming from Southern and Eastern Europe. This latter result, however, is due to an age-cohort effect, which reveals that it is the younger first generation of immigrants for this area which has a substantially lower level of education than Italians. This tendency is true for all groups, with the exception of the younger first-generation immigrants from North America for whom the difference with Italians is not statistically significant. Interestingly, we also find a similar tendency for second-generation immigrants. Indeed, we find that it is the older second-generation immigrants that tend to have a much higher probability of having a high level of education than Italians. However, this is true for immigrants coming from Northern Europe, America, and Asia, whereas for those coming from Africa and Southern and Eastern Europe it is the younger second-generation cohort of immigrants that seems to be more educated than Italians.

Table 4.7 Immigrants' education gap with respect to natives. Probit estimation results—males.

	All		Pre-1970		Post -1970	
	First gen.	Second gen.	First gen.	Second gen.	First gen.	Second gen.
Northern Europe	0.0169***	0.0449***	0.0482***	0.0379	−0.0496***	0.0387***
	(0.0057)	(0.0138)	(0.0070)	(0.0365)	(0.0093)	(0.0148)
Southern and	−0.0670***	0.1071***	0.0331***	0.0617	−0.1877***	0.1152***
Eastern Europe	(0.0051)	(0.0240)	(0.0073)	(0.0495)	(0.0059)	(0.0274)
North and	0.1482***	0.2937***	0.2202***	0.1540	0.0245	0.3237***
Central America	(0.0188)	(0.0525)	(0.0233)	(0.1225)	(0.0290)	(0.0589)
South America	0.0584***	−0.0025	0.1181***	−0.0236	−0.0644***	−0.0084
	(0.0105)	(0.0265)	(0.0129)	(0.1139)	(0.0163)	(0.0270)
Asia	−0.1451***	0.0540	−0.0684***	0.3134	−0.2494***	0.0303
	(0.0071)	(0.0544)	(0.0104)	(0.2077)	(0.0079)	(0.0551)
Africa	−0.1222***	0.0468**	−0.0701***	−0.0648	−0.2451***	0.0655**
	(0.0051)	(0.0238)	(0.0065)	(0.0512)	(0.0066)	(0.0267)
Observations	675,451		Observations	675,451		
Pseudo-R^2	0.0870		Pseudo-R^2	0.0883		

Marginal effects and standard errors (in parentheses) are reported; *** $p <0.01$, ** $p <0.05$, * $p <0.1$. Controls: quadratic in age, time dummies.

The results by gender (Tables 4.7 and 4.8) reveal notable peculiarities. In particular, we find that, on average, first-generation women from Southern and Eastern Europe have an higher level of education than their Italian counterparts, whereas men from these regions exhibit a lower level of education, and this is due to the much lower level of education of younger first-generation men. We also find that the higher probability of second-generation immigrants from South America being highly educated with respect of natives depends entirely on women. While second-generation South American men do not show any significant difference with respect to Italians, second-generation women are much more educated, especially those from the first (older) cohort.

Taking the results as a whole, we can distinguish the first-generation immigrant from North and Central America as a particularly highly skilled immigrant group, followed by immigrants from Northern Europe; whereas Asian and Africans are the least educated, although their education increases substantially in their second generations and in particular for the younger cohort of African women (with 24 per cent higher probability of being more educated than Italians).

Table 4.8 Immigrants' education gap with respect to natives. Probit estimation results—females.

	All		Pre-1970		Post-1970	
	First gen.	Second gen.	First gen.	Secnd gen.	First gen.	Second gen.
Northern Europe	0.0651*** (0.0048)	0.1158*** (0.0174)	0.1106*** (0.0057)	0.2345*** (0.0457)	−0.0580*** (0.0077)	0.0822*** (0.0183)
Southern and Eastern Europe	0.0239*** (0.0043)	0.1414*** (0.0309)	0.1409*** (0.0060)	0.0496 (0.0752)	−0.1253*** (0.0049)	0.1464*** (0.0339)
North and Central America	0.1434*** (0.0126)	0.1489*** (0.0575)	0.2072*** (0.0153)	0.3397*** (0.0919)	0.0027 (0.0197)	0.0327 (0.0634)
South America	0.0882*** (0.0083)	0.1486*** (0.0364)	0.1447*** (0.0100)	0.5042*** (0.0931)	−0.0450*** (0.0128)	0.0997*** (0.0366)
Asia	−0.1136*** (0.0067)	0.1137 (0.0705)	−0.0120 (0.0106)	– –	−0.2241*** (0.0060)	0.0117 (0.0667)
Africa	−0.1379*** (0.0048)	0.2170*** (0.0328)	−0.0402*** (0.0078)	0.0560 (0.0731)	−0.2381*** (0.0041)	0.2408*** (0.0370)
Observations	758,441		Observations 758,434			
Pseudo-R^2	0.190		Pseudo-R^2 0.192			

Marginal effects and standard errors (in parentheses) are reported. *** $p<0.01$, ** $p<0.05$, * $p<0.1$
Controls: quadratic in age, time dummies.

4.5.2 Employment rates

Table 4.9 reports the employment rates of natives, and first and second-generation immigrants, by gender and region of origin. There are two notable facts here. First, first-generation immigrants show employment rates quite similar to Italians. Immigrant men from Southern and Eastern Europe and from Asia have higher employment rates than their native counterparts. Second, second-generation immigrants do not seem to enjoy higher rates of employment than first-generation immigrants.

The results of our regression analysis, controlling for education, (a quadratic of) age and time dummies, are contained in Table 4.10. In Tables 4.11 and 4.12 we report the evidence disaggregated by gender. Marginal effects for each region of origin are reported. First-generation immigrants show a probability of being employed which is only slightly lower than natives. First-generation Asians have even an higher probability of being employed than Italians, and this is due to the performance of the younger cohort, with roughly a two per cent higher probability for females and three per cent for males. Such evidence is in line with our descriptive statistics (Table 4.9). Second-generation immigrants do not seem to have a significantly different probability of

Table 4.9 Employment rate—descriptive statistics.

	Employment rates			
	Male		Female	
Natives				
	94.66		91.64	
Immigrants				
	First gen.	Second gen.	First gen.	Second gen.
of which	94.12	86.53	87.15	84.51
Northern Europe	93.37	86.82	88.59	86.79
Southern and Eastern Europe	95.14	89.08	86.84	87.39
North and Central America	93.84	73.81	88.93	88.00
South America	93.72	89.82	88.23	70.37
Asia	96.02	90.91	91.04	80.00
Africa	92.87	83.28	80.14	83.19

Table 4.10 Immigrants' employment gap with respect to natives—all immigrants.

	All		Pre-1970		Post-1970	
	First gen.	Second gen.	First gen.	Second gen.	First gen.	Second gen.
Northern Europe	−0.0204***	0.0089**	−0.0134***	0.0067	−0.0297***	0.0099**
	(0.0025)	(0.0039)	(0.0032)	(0.0163)	(0.0041)	(0.0039)
Southern and Eastern Europe	−0.0136***	−0.0047	−0.0484***	−0.0511	0.0101***	0.0017
	(0.0021)	(0.0083)	(0.0038)	(0.0319)	(0.0021)	(0.0083)
North and Central America	−0.0186***	−0.0403*	−0.0256**	−0.0060	−0.0122	−0.0427*
	(0.0066)	(0.0215)	(0.0100)	(0.0553)	(0.0087)	(0.0229)
South America	−0.0284***	−0.0058	−0.0512***	−0.1326	−0.0019	−0.0011
	(0.0043)	(0.0097)	(0.0065)	(0.0925)	(0.0052)	(0.0093)
Asia	0.0134***	0.0144	−0.0048	—	0.0279***	0.0143
	(0.0029)	(0.0140)	(0.0051)	—	(0.0031)	(0.0141)
Africa	−0.0339***	−0.0222**	−0.0446***	−0.0138	−0.0193***	−0.0219**
	(0.0032)	(0.0095)	(0.0044)	(0.0321)	(0.0045)	(0.0098)
Observations	675,942		Observations	675,933		
Pseudo-R^2	0.0751		Pseudo-R^2	0.0760		

Marginal effects and standard errors (in parentheses) are reported; *** $p <0.01$, ** $p <0.05$, * $p <0.1$. Controls: education, quadratic in age, time dummies.

being employed compared to natives. A slightly higher probability appears only for second-generation immigrants from Northern Europe, and such result is entirely due to the younger second-generation cohort of women which has a 2 per cent higher probability than their native counterparts of being employed. The distinction by gender shows

Table 4.11 Immigrants' employment gap with respect to natives—males.

	All		Pre-1970		Post-1970	
	First gen.	Second gen.	First gen.	Second gen.	First gen.	Second gen.
Northern Europe	−0.0102***	0.0007	0.0027	0.0026	−0.0246***	0.0014
	(0.0029)	(0.0046)	(0.0036)	(0.0193)	(0.0048)	(0.0047)
Southern and	0.0119***	−0.0173	−0.0167***	−0.0433	0.0263***	−0.0127
Eastern Europe	(0.0020)	(0.0110)	(0.0044)	(0.0348)	(0.0017)	(0.0113)
North and	−0.0015	−0.0769**	−0.0149	—	0.0078	−0.0834**
Central America	(0.0080)	(0.0305)	(0.0139)	—	(0.0091)	(0.0324)
South America	−0.0107**	0.0180***	−0.0287***	−0.0625	0.0076	0.0201***
	(0.0051)	(0.0070)	(0.0081)	(0.0961)	(0.0058)	(0.0066)
Asia	0.0166***	0.0233**	−0.0022	—	0.0291***	0.0236**
	(0.0029)	(0.0110)	(0.0057)	—	(0.0026)	(0.0108)
Africa	−0.0168***	−0.0286**	−0.0326***	0.0098	0.0043	−0.0305**
	(0.0032)	(0.0116)	(0.0046)	(0.0308)	(0.0039)	(0.0122)
Observations	398,445		Observations	398,433		
Pseudo-R^2	0.0807		Pseudo-R^2	0.0820		

Marginal effects and standard errors (in parentheses) are reported; *** p <0.01,** p <0.05,* p <0.1. Controls: education, quadratic in age, time dummies.

another exception in the younger cohort of second-generation immigrants from South America: while males seem to have higher probability of being employed than their parents and their native counterparts, females show the opposite evidence, with more than a 6 per cent decrease in the probability of being employed.

Such results are quite interesting if compared to our evidence in Tables 4.6, 4.7, and 4.8. Tables 4.6, 4.7, and 4.8 report on the education level of the immigrants in Italy, whereas Tables 4.10, 4.11, and 4.12 analyse their performance in the labour market, keeping constant the level of education. Immigrants from the two regions of origin with higher levels of education than natives, North and Central America and Northern Europe, do not perform equally well in terms of employment prospects, always showing a lower probability of being employed than Italians. Some improvement can be found only for the younger cohort of second-generation women from Northern Europe which shows approximately a 2 per cent higher probability of being employed with respect to its native counterpart. Also, the remarkably high skill level of second-generation women from South America does not seem to be correlated with employment prospects. Table 4.12 shows, respectively, a non-significant and a significantly negative difference (−6 per cent) in the probability of being employed with respect to native

Table 4.12 Immigrants' employment gap with respect to natives. Probit estimation results—females.

	All		Pre-1970		Post-1970	
	First gen.	Second gen.	First gen.	Second gen.	First gen.	Second gen.
Northern Europe	−0.0302*** (0.0043)	0.0217*** (0.0066)	−0.0274*** (0.0055)	0.0060 (0.0308)	−0.0347*** (0.0069)	0.0237*** (0.0066)
Southern and Eastern Europe	−0.0361*** (0.0036)	0.0109 (0.0129)	−0.0736*** (0.0061)	−0.0972 (0.0736)	−0.0059 (0.0041)	0.0201* (0.0122)
North and Central America	−0.0215** (0.0096)	0.0209 (0.0249)	−0.0225* (0.0136)	−0.0355 (0.0920)	−0.0203 (0.0136)	0.0305 (0.0234)
South America	−0.0375*** (0.0067)	−0.0733*** (0.0267)	−0.0654*** (0.0098)	−0.2635 (0.1736)	−0.0032 (0.0083)	−0.0634** (0.0261)
Asia	0.0040 (0.0061)	−0.0168 (0.0376)	−0.0119 (0.0095)	—	0.0195*** (0.0074)	−0.0209 (0.0397)
Africa	−0.0869*** (0.0077)	−0.0147 (0.0161)	−0.0954*** (0.0106)	−0.0456 (0.0624)	−0.0763*** (0.0112)	−0.0108 (0.0163)
Observations	277,497		Observations	277,490		
Pseudo-R^2	0.0782		Pseudo-R^2	0.0789		

Marginal effects and standard errors (in parentheses) are reported; *** $p < 0.01$, ** $p < 0.05$, * $p < 0.1$. Controls: education, quadratic in age, time dummies.

women. On the contrary, the only immigrant group with a higher probability of being employed than native Italians is Asians, which is one of the two least educated immigrant groups. Asians thus seem to have a higher probability of being employed than Italians, and this is true in particular for the younger first generation of immigrants which also show the highest education gap with respect to Italians.

4.5.3 Female participation rates

Table 4.13 reports the female participation rates of natives, first and second-generation immigrants, by gender and region of origin. It appears that first-generation immigrant women participate more in the labour market than their native counterparts (with the only exception being African women), whereas second-generation women participate less than their native counterparts. This picture, however, changes and acquires more nuances in our regression analysis.

Once differences in education, age, and time dummies are accounted for (Table 4.14), we find that second-generation immigrants do not seem to have female participation rates significantly different from those of their native counterparts. Only South American females seem to

Table 4.13 Female participation rate—descriptive statistics.

	Participation rates	
	female	
Natives		
	48.22	
Immigrants		
	First	Second
of which	55.31	33.16
Northern Europe	53.57	30.82
Southern and Eastern Europe	59.10	46.75
North and Central America	57.62	26.60
South America	59.79	25.29
Asia	53.22	25.64
Africa	46.16	41.70

participate less, and this evidence is mainly due to the younger cohort (that has an approximately 12 per cent lower probability of participating in the labour market than native females). It is worthwhile noting that South American females are a particularly highly skilled immigrant group. The remainder of the immigrants groups do not show any marked peculiarity by age cohort, signalling that this tendency might represent mainly a specific cultural attitude. First-generation immigrant females tend to participate less in the labour market when coming from Northern Europe, North and Central America, and Africa. They show a non-significant difference with respect to the native rate when coming from South America and Asia, whereas first-generation females from Southern and Eastern Europe tend to participate more than their native counterpart. This latter result is due to the higher probability of participation of the younger cohort. Also, the younger cohort of first-generation women from South America seems to be more active in the labour market than their Italian counterpart. The negative difference for women from North and Central America is due to the particularly lower probability of participation of the older first-generation cohort. The results for Northern Europe, Africa, and Asia (lower participation probability in the first two cases and a non-significant difference in the third one) remain qualitatively unchanged by age cohort, pointing also in this case towards cultural differences by wave of immigration and region of origin rather than by age cohort. Such cultural attitudes do not seem to attenuate in younger cohorts of women coming from these regions, given that their probability of participating decreases further with respect to their native counterpart.

Table 4.14 Immigrants' female participation gap with respect to natives. Probit estimation results—females.

	All		Pre-1970		Post-1970	
	First gen.	Second gen.	First gen.	Second gen.	First gen.	Second gen.
Northern Europe	−0.0586*** (0.0051)	0.0020 (0.0126)	−0.0564*** (0.0062)	0.0534 (0.0494)	−0.0635*** (0.0091)	−0.0014 (0.0130)
Southern and Eastern Europe	0.0176*** (0.0048)	0.0380 (0.0246)	−0.0016 (0.0065)	0.0782 (0.0907)	0.0408*** (0.0072)	0.0349 (0.0256)
North and Central America	−0.0603*** (0.0124)	−0.0451 (0.0412)	−0.0835*** (0.0154)	−0.0041 (0.0962)	−0.0215 (0.0207)	−0.0544 (0.0458)
South America	0.0138 (0.0086)	−0.1176*** (0.0249)	−0.0005 (0.0106)	−0.0748 (0.1410)	0.0406*** (0.0146)	−0.1188*** (0.0253)
Asia	0.0099 (0.0095)	−0.0326 (0.0473)	0.0188 (0.0126)	— —	−0.0020 (0.0146)	−0.0658 (0.0487)
Africa	−0.0830*** (0.0072)	−0.0170 (0.0237)	−0.0540*** (0.0097)	0.0115 (0.0776)	−0.1229*** (0.0108)	−0.0196 (0.0249)
Observations	571,770		Observations 571,763			
Pseudo-R^2	0.150		Pseudo-R^2 0.150			

Marginal effects and standard errors (in parentheses) are reported; *** $p < 0.01$, ** $p < 0.05$, * $p < 0.1$. Controls: education, quadratic in age, time dummies.

Table 4.15 Marriage and divorce—descriptive statistics.

	Marriage rates		Divorce rates	
	Male	Female	Male	Female
Natives	78.26	84.05	1.58	1.93
Immigrants (first gen.) of which	74.41	80.25	1.88	4.90
Northern Europe	68.16	80.51	0.76	4.01
Southern and Eastern Europe	79.84	78.90	2.45	6.83
North and Central America	69.56	79.04	3.27	2.90
South America	68.15	75.85	2.66	4.57
Asia	79.03	85.09	0.38	2.37
Africa	75.93	83.91	1.38	3.52

4.5.4 Marriage and divorce rates

As described in Section 4.1, second-generation immigrants in Italy are very young. Only 8.18 per cent of the sample is older than 25; not even six per cent of which is or has been married (less than 150 individuals).

Our analysis on marriage and divorce rates will thus concentrate on first-generation immigrants only. First, we collect in Table 4.15 some descriptive statistics. They seem to suggest that immigrants do not show a more traditional attitude towards family formation than Italians.

Table 4.16 Immigrants' marriage and divorce gap with respect to natives. Probit estimation results—first-generation immigrants.

	Marriage			Divorce		
	All	Pre-1970	Post-1970	All	Pre-1970	Post-1970
Northern Europe	−0.0153***	−0.0078	−0.0300***	0.0039**	0.0042**	−0.0002
	(0.0045)	(0.0054)	(0.0082)	(0.0019)	(0.0020)	(0.0065)
Southern and	0.0927***	0.0481***	0.1257***	0.0092***	0.0084***	0.0136**
Eastern Europe	(0.0027)	(0.0049)	(0.0026)	(0.0020)	(0.0022)	(0.0054)
North and	0.0242**	0.0079	0.0473***	0.0142*	0.0130*	0.0235
Central America	(0.0121)	(0.0166)	(0.0169)	(0.0073)	(0.0076)	(0.0241)
South America	−0.0213**	−0.0321***	0.0010	0.0064*	0.0064*	0.0065
	(0.0084)	(0.0105)	(0.0136)	(0.0035)	(0.0036)	(0.0133)
Asia	0.0960***	0.0801***	0.1121***	−0.0111***	−0.0108***	—
	(0.0043)	(0.0066)	(0.0052)	(0.0012)	(0.0014)	—
Africa	0.0321***	0.0203***	0.0582***	−0.0023	−0.0016	—
	(0.0042)	(0.0052)	(0.0066)	(0.0015)	(0.0016)	—
Observations	630,523	630,523	Observations	499,346	498,256	
Pseudo-R^2	0.267	0.267	Pseudo-R^2	0.0216	0.0213	

Marginal effects and standard errors (in parentheses) are reported; *** $p < 0.01$, ** $p < 0.05$, * $p < 0.1$. Controls: occupation, education, quadratic in age, time dummies.

Indeed, for both males and females, and for most immigrant groups marriage rates are lower than their native counterpart, whereas divorce rates are much higher, the only exceptions being Northern European and Asian men.

When controlling for age, education, (a quadratic in) age, and time dummies, however, we find that the immigrants have a higher probability of getting married. This evidence is contained in Tables 4.16, 4.17, and 4.18. They show the regression analysis results when using the probability to be married or the probability to be divorced as dependent variables, for all immigrants and for males and females separately. Only Northern Europeans and South Americans marry less than Italians. All the other groups show a higher probability to get married, and the tendency to marry more is particularly pronounced in the younger cohort. Turning our attention to divorce patterns, our estimation results confirm the suggestive evidence in Table 4.15. All immigrant groups have a higher propensity to divorce than Italians. Asians are the only exception in this regard, and their lower probability to divorce is entirely due to males. Interestingly we do not find any marked difference between age cohorts.

4.5.5 Inter-ethnic marriage rates

We start by presenting the endogamy rates of natives and immigrants by country of origin in Table 4.19. The proportion of respondents whose spouse or partner comes from the same country of origin is naturally highest for Italian natives, reaching more than 80 per cent. But is also almost 70 per cent for Asians. Endogamy rates are also high for immigrants coming from Southern and Eastern Europe and from Africa.

As explained above, we cannot appreciate the existence and extent of a process of cultural integration of immigrants on the basis of differences in endogamy rates between first and second generation because of the small sample size of married second-generation immigrant individuals. Nevertheless, we can estimate difference between age-cohorts in our sample of first-generation immigrants, distinguishing between region of origin and also gender. Our regression results are contained in Table 4.20. While Northern European immigrants and those coming from North and Central America seem to be more open toward marrying a spouse from a different country in the younger cohorts, none of the other groups show any tendency toward cultural integration in this respect. The evidence is not different by gender. The only notable

Table 4.17 Immigrants' marriage and divorce gap with respect to natives. Probit estimation results—males.

	Marriage			Divorce		
	All	Pre-1970	Post-1970	All	Pre-1970	Post-1970
Northern Europe	−0.0153***	−0.0078	−0.0300***	0.0039**	0.0042**	−0.0002
	(0.0045)	(0.0054)	(0.0082)	(0.0019)	(0.0020)	(0.0065)
Southern and	0.0927***	0.0481***	0.1257***	0.0092***	0.0084***	0.0136**
Eastern Europe	(0.0027)	(0.0049)	(0.0026)	(0.0020)	(0.0022)	(0.0054)
North and	0.0242**	0.0079	0.0473***	0.0142*	0.0130*	0.0235
Central America	(0.0121)	(0.0166)	(0.0169)	(0.0073)	(0.0076)	(0.0241)
South America	−0.0213**	−0.0321***	0.0010	0.0064*	0.0064*	0.0065
	(0.0084)	(0.0105)	(0.0136)	(0.0035)	(0.0036)	(0.0133)
Asia	0.0960***	0.0801***	0.1121***	−0.0111***	−0.0108***	—
	(0.0043)	(0.0066)	(0.0052)	(0.0012)	(0.0014)	—
Africa	0.0321***	0.0203***	0.0582***	−0.0023	−0.0016	—
	(0.0042)	(0.0052)	(0.0066)	(0.0015)	(0.0016)	—
Observations	630,523	630,523	Observations	499,346	498,256	
Pseudo-R²	0.267	0.267	Pseudo-R²	0.0216	0.0213	

Marginal effects and standard errors (in parentheses) are reported; *** p <0.01, ** p <0.05, * p <0.1.
Controls: occupation, education, quadratic in age, time dummies.

Table 4.18 Immigrants' marriage and divorce gap with respect to natives. Probit estimation results—females.

	Marriage			Divorce		
	All	Pre-1970	Post-1970	All	Pre-1970	Post-1970
Northern Europe	−0.0022	−0.0000	−0.0047	0.0157***	0.0169***	0.0012
	(0.0031)	(0.0037)	(0.0054)	(0.0018)	(0.0019)	(0.0047)
Southern and	0.0246***	−0.0266***	0.0733***	0.0399***	0.0399***	0.0404***
Eastern Europe	(0.0026)	(0.0043)	(0.0025)	(0.0023)	(0.0026)	(0.0055)
North and	0.0189***	−0.0094	0.0599***	0.0075*	0.0050	0.0235*
Central America	(0.0068)	(0.0097)	(0.0081)	(0.0039)	(0.0040)	(0.0138)
South America	−0.0166***	−0.0349***	0.0175**	0.0145***	0.0156***	0.0045
	(0.0056)	(0.0072)	(0.0081)	(0.0029)	(0.0032)	(0.0079)
Asia	0.0587***	0.0174**	0.0967***	0.0037	0.0036	0.0037
	(0.0043)	(0.0074)	(0.0037)	(0.0028)	(0.0030)	(0.0073)
Africa	0.0212***	−0.0432***	0.0824***	0.0195***	0.0217***	0.0073
	(0.0041)	(0.0069)	(0.0035)	(0.0030)	(0.0034)	(0.0063)
Observations	715,498	715,498	Observations	611,963	611,963	
Pseudo-R^2	0.162	0.164	Pseudo-R^2	0.0701	0.0702	

Marginal effects and standard errors (in parentheses) are reported; *** $p < 0.01$, ** $p < 0.05$, * $p < 0.1$. Controls: occupation, education, quadratic in age, time dummies.

Table 4.19 Proportion of marriages where the partner shares the same country of origin.

Natives	80.24
Immigrants (first gen.)	38.12
of which	
Northern Europe	6.84
Southern and Eastern Europe	54.70
North and Central America	5.00
South America	27.68
Asia	68.67
Africa	55.42

exception are the immigrants from South America, who seem to be more inclined towards exogamy, if females, and highly reluctant if males.

4.5.6 Completed fertility rates

Because of the young age of second-generation immigrants in Italy, second-generation women older than 40 years of age with children are almost non-existent in our sample (less than 0.2 per cent). Therefore also in this case we concentrate on first-generation immigrants only.

Table 4.20 Interethnic marriage. Probit estimation result—first-generation immigrants.

	All	Males	Females
	post-1970	post-1970	post-1970
Northern Europe	0.3359***	0.4100***	0.2742***
	(0.0057)	(0.0149)	(0.0052)
Southern and Eastern Europe	−0.1926***	−0.3584***	−0.0881***
	(0.0154)	(0.0178)	(0.0195)
North and Central America	0.3356***	0.4096***	0.2661***
	(0.0073)	(0.0284)	(0.0051)
South America	−0.0115	−0.2314***	0.0603***
	(0.0226)	(0.0385)	(0.0219)
Asia	−0.2869***	−0.2467***	−0.2853***
	(0.0199)	(0.0270)	(0.0286)
Africa	−0.2618***	0.0322	−0.3636***
	(0.0178)	(0.0287)	(0.0246)
Observations	45,588	18,464	27,124
Pseudo-R^2	0.148	0.114	0.204

Marginal effects and standard errors (in parentheses) are reported; *** $p < 0.01$, ** $p < 0.05$, * $p < 0.1$. Controls: occupation, education, quadratic in age, time dummies.

The results of our analysis are collected in Tables 4.21 and 4.22. Starting with some descriptive statistics (Table 4.21), it appears that immigrants in Italy have lower completed fertility rates than Italians. Only Northern Europeans show a higher fertility rate. When controlling for education, occupation, age, and time dummies, we find that all groups tend to have less children than Italians, with the exception of African women, whose fertility rate is not statistically different from that of Italian women. Such results, however, need to be taken with caution because of possibly large measurement errors in this variable due to the limitations of the ILFS data, as explained in this section.

Table 4.21 Completed fertility rates—descriptive statistics.

	Fertility rates
	Women older than 40 years
Natives	0.73
Immigrants (first gen.)	0.65
of which	
Northern Europe	0.93
Southern and Eastern Europe	0.42
North and Central America	0.52
South America	0.56
Asia	0.60
Africa	0.54

Table 4.22 Completed fertility rate—OLS estimation results. Immigrants' gap with respect to natives—females older than 40.

	First gen.
North Europe	−0.0839***
	(0.0096)
Southern and Eastern Europe	−0.4365***
	(0.0105)
North and Central America	−0.2011***
	(0.0265)
South America	−0.2367***
	(0.0166)
Asia	−0.2184***
	(0.0221)
Africa	−0.0183
	(0.0157)
Observations	520,371
R^2	0.605

Standard errors (in parentheses) are reported; *** $p < 0.01$, ** $p < 0.05$, * $p < 0.1$.
Controls: occupation, education, quadratic in age, time dummies.

4.6 Conclusion

Our empirical analysis of the cultural and economic patterns of integration of immigrants in Italy does not reveal a solid grounding in the data of the perception that integration is occurring at particularly slow rates. Severe data limitations suggest caution in the interpretation of these results.

References

Blangiardo, M. and Baio, G. (2010) *A Picture of Foreigners in Italy: Methodology and Experiences.* Mimeo, UCL. http://epc2006.princeton.edu/download.aspx?submissionId=60333.

Boeri, T., De Philippis, M., Patacchini, E., and Pellizzari, M. (2011) *Moving to Segregation: Evidence from 8 Italian Cities.* Working Papers from IGIER, no. 390.

Calavita, K. (2006) *Italy: Immigration, Economic Flexibility, and Integration.* Irvine, University of California.

Del Boca, D. and Venturini, A. (2005) Italian migration. In: K.F. Zimmermann (ed.), *European Migration: What we do now?* Oxford, Oxford University Press.

Golini, A., Strozza, S., Basili, M., Ribella, N., and Reginato, M. (2004) *L'immigrazione straniera: indicatori e misure di integrazione.* Technical report, FIERI—International and European Forum of Research on Immigration and

Department of Demographic Sciences, La Sapienza University of Rome, Italy. http://epc2006.princeton.edu/download.aspx?submissionId=60333.

Hassan, F. and Minale, L. (2010) *Immigrazione: Risorsa o Minaccia?* Mimeo, www.quattrogatti.info.

ISTAT (2007) *La popolazione straniera residente in Italia?* ISTAT. http://www3.istat.it/salastampa/comunicati/non_calendario/20071002_00/testointegrale2007 1002.pdf.

Zincone, G. (2001) *Primo rapporto sull'integrazione degli immigrati in Italia*, Commissione per le politiche di integrazione degli immigrati, Bologna, Il Mulino.

Zincone, G. (2005) *Secondo rapporto sull'integrazione degli immigrati in Italia*, Commissione per le politiche di integrazione degli immigrati, Bologna, Il Mulino.

5

Cultural Integration in Spain

Sara de la Rica[1] and Francesc Ortega[2]

5.1 Introduction

Since the early 1990s immigration flows into Spain have been on the rise. In particular, the decade between 1998 and 2008 has been characterized by one of the largest immigration episodes in recent history among OECD countries. Over this period, the foreign born share among the working age population in Spain has increased from below 3 per cent to almost 15 per cent.

Aside from the large size of the inflows, Spain's immigration experience is characterized by the large heterogeneity of these inflows, in terms of origin. In 2008 the largest ethnic groups among the foreign-born population are Latinos, Eastern Europeans, and Moroccans.[3] Interestingly, these groups differ substantially in their 'cultural distance' vis-à-vis the Spanish society. Presumably, Latino immigrants face the smallest cultural gap since Spanish is the mother tongue for the large majority of the population. Arguably, Eastern Europeans are the second

[1] The author acknowledges financial aid from the Spanish Ministry of Education and Science (ECO2009-10818).

[2] The author acknowledges financial aid from the Spanish Ministry of Science and Innovation (ECO2008-02779). Both authors are grateful to Javier Polavieja (IMDEA) for very helpful discussions.

[3] The next section provides a detailed description of the sizes of these groups and their composition in terms of countries of origin. See Sandell (2008) for a detailed description of the ethnic composition of Spain's foreign-born population, as well as their geographical distribution within Spain. Several recent papers have analysed the economic effects of immigration in Spain, such as Amuedo-Dorantes and De la Rica (2011, 2012), Farre *et al.* (2011), and Gonzalez and Ortega (2010), among many others. Bertoli *et al.* (2011) argue that for Ecuador, one of the main origin countries, Spain's immigration policy played a big role in determining the sizeable inflows from this country.

group regarding cultural distance vis-à-vis Spain. As shown later, the vast majority of Spain's immigrants from Eastern Europe are from Romania, a country with a Latin-based language (Romanian) and a traditionally Christian population (Eastern orthodox). Moreover, their education levels are high, roughly at Spanish levels. Finally, Moroccans face the largest cultural gap with today's Spanish society among the three large minority groups. Morocco is an eminently Muslim country with low average education levels relative to Spain.

Our goal is to examine the cultural and economic gaps of ethnic foreign-born minorities that differ in the cultural distance to the norms in their host society. In particular, we address the question of whether these gaps are increasing (or decreasing) in the cultural distance between natives and each minority ethnic group. Second, we examine the evolution of these gaps across cohorts, for each group.

We focus on the three main foreign-born ethnic groups: Latinos, Eastern Europeans, and Moroccans. Specifically, we study the following dimensions of cultural gaps: the gender gap in educational attainment, fertility rates, early marriage, inter-ethnic marriage, female employment, command of Spanish, and social participation. Methodologically, we use regression analysis to provide a comparison across ethnic groups that accounts for differences in observables. We also provide an analysis of the similarity between natives and immigrants along several socioeconomic dimensions, following Vigdor (2008).

Overall our results suggest that Latinos—the group with the shortest cultural distance to Spanish social norms, have assimilated the most. Moroccans have assimilated the least, although the main differences seem to reflect differences in education levels. Our results also suggest that years since migration and education are important determinants of economic and cultural gaps. Hence, it is important to control for differences in these two dimensions when comparing across ethnic groups. Furthermore, we find that education levels have risen rapidly for the younger cohorts of Morocco-born immigrants, which suggests a narrowing of the gaps over time.

The structure of the chapter is as follows. Section 5.2 introduces our datasets. Section 5.3 provides an overview of Spain's recent immigration experience and a descriptive summary by ethnic group. Section 5.4 analyses gender gaps in educational attainment. Section 5.5 is devoted to marriage and Section 5.6 to fertility. Section 5.7 studies female employment. Sections 5.8 and 5.9 explore the command of Spanish and social participation, respectively. Section 5.10 provides a measure of similarity between natives and immigrants and Section 5.11 concludes.

5.2 The data

Our two main data sources are the 2007 Labour Force Survey ('Encuesta sobre la Población Activa' or LFS) and the 2007 National Immigration Survey ('Encuesta Nacional de Inmigrantes' or NIS), both conducted by the Spanish Institute of Statistics.

The Spanish Labour Force Survey is well-known and standardized across all European countries. The new National Immigration Survey deserves some comments. This survey sampled the foreign-born population residing in Spain in 2007, with the goal of providing insights on migrants' experiences in transitioning from their home country into Spain, on their job history after arrival, and on their ties with the home country. The object of study was individuals born outside Spain, who were at least 16-years-old at the time of the survey, and had either been living in Spain for at least one year or intented to do so. The total size of completed questionnaires is around 15,000. Correspondingly, our definition of immigrant is a foreign born, adult individual who at the time of the interview (2007), had been living in Spain for at least one year. In most of our analysis we look at individuals age 16–60. When we report data on the native population we use the same age criterion. The next section provides a detailed overview of the foreign-born population in Spain.

5.3 Descriptive statistics

This section describes the main ethnic groups in terms of their size, demographics, years since migration, and educational attainment.

5.3.1 *Country of origin and ethnicity*

According to Registry data, in 1998 the foreign-born population in Spain was small (2.9 per cent of the total population) and originated mainly in Morocco (16 per cent), France (12 per cent), and Germany (10 per cent). However, during the period 1998–2008, the foreign-born population has increased sharply and there has been a dramatic change in the composition of the inflows by country of origin. By 2008, the foreign born share reached 13 per cent of the total population and the share of the immigrant population originating in Morocco, France, and Germany fell to 11 per cent, 2 per cent, and 3 per cent, respectively (2008 Registry). Let us now describe in a bit more detail the geographical

Table 5.1 Foreign-born population in Spain, by origin.

Continent	NIS 2007 Freq. thousands	NIS 2007 Rel. freq.	Registry 2008 Freq. thousands	Registry 2008 Rel. freq.
America	1,779	39.5	1,703	36.0
Ecuador	370	8.2	383	8.1
Colombia	299	6.6	268	5.7
Argentina	232	5.1	180	3.8
Europe	1,718	38.1	2,018	42.7
Romania	429	9.5	656	13.9
UK	269	6.0	315	6.7
France	203	4.5	88	1.9
Germany	160	3.5	158	3.3
Bulgaria	100	2.2	140	3.0
Africa	761	16.9	772	16.3
Morocco	534	11.8	539	11.4
Algeria	53	1.2	47	1.0
Senegal	30	0.7	42	0.9
Asia	207	4.6	230	4.9
China	54	1.2	107	2.3
Philippines	47	1.0	21	0.4
Pakistan	39	0.9	44	0.9
Total foreign born	4,508	100	4,725	100
Total Spain			46,064	

Source: NIS 2007, reference individuals. All Ages Registry 2008 (1 January).

origin of the foreign-born population in Spain by 2008 and its ethnic composition.

We start by examining the size of the immigrant population by geographical origin. Specifically, we use the 2007 NIS to classify the foreign-born population by country of birth. We also provide a comparison of this sample with the 2008 Registry data. The figures from the two sources are highly consistent. As Table 5.1 shows, according to the NIS almost 40 per cent of the foreign-born population originated in the American continent, with Ecuador, Colombia, and Argentina being the top three origin countries. Europe was the origin of 38 per cent of the foreign-born population, with Romania being the main country of origin, followed by the UK and France. According to the NIS, Romania accounted for 9.5 per cent of the foreign-born population in Spain in 2007. As the 2008 Registry shows, the number of Romanians residing in Spain increased sharply during 2007, reaching almost 14 per cent of the foreign-born population in 2008, and becoming the single main source country. Among the remaining immigrants, 17 per cent were born in African countries and slightly less than 5 per cent in Asia. The top three

151

Table 5.2 Main ethnic groups in Spain in 2007.

Ethnic group	Frequency thousands	Rel. frequency %
Latinos	1,746	38.7
Ecuador	370	0.21
Colombia	299	0.17
Argentina	232	0.13
Eastern Europe	720	16.0
Romania	429	0.60
Bulgaria	100	0.14
Ukraine	68	0.09
Moroccans	537	11.9
Rest	1,506	33.4
Total	4,509	100

Note 1: Source is NIS 2007, reference individuals. All ages.
Note 2: Relative frequency for ethnic groups is over total foreign-born population.
For each individual country, relative frequency is over the respective ethnic group.

African countries of origin were Morocco (11.8 per cent of the foreign-born population), Algeria (1.2 per cent), and Senegal (0.7 per cent). The top three Asian countries of origin were China (1.2 per cent), the Philippines (1 per cent), and Pakistan (0.9 per cent).

Next, we turn to the definition of the ethnic groups that we shall use throughout our analysis: Latinos, Eastern Europeans, and Moroccans. Respectively, these groups account for 38.7 per cent, 16 per cent, and 11.9 per cent of the foreign-born population in 2007 (Table 5.2). We use these groups for the following reasons: Latinos and Eastern Europeans account for the lion's share of the immigration flows into Spain over the last decade. Traditionally, Morocco has been the main source immigration country for Spain, and still represents a very large share of the foreign-born population. In addition, the vast majority of Moroccans are Muslim, which makes it a very interesting group to study the immigration and integration experience of Muslim immigrants into Western societies.

Table 5.2 reports the largest three countries of origin in each ethnic category and the share of each of those countries in the respective ethnic group. Latinos mainly originate from Ecuador (21 per cent), Colombia (17 per cent), and Argentina (13 per cent). By far, the main country of origin for Eastern Europe is Romania (60 per cent of the group), followed at a large distance by Bulgaria (14 per cent), and the Ukraine (9 per cent).

Table 5.3 Years since migration, by ethnic group (2007).

YSM	Latinos	Eastern Europe	Morocco
1	8.5	10.9	3.7
2	7.8	9.3	5.4
3	7.8	15.1	6.4
4	10.0	14.5	7.6
5	11.3	16.2	6.0
6	14.2	12.1	8.9
7	11.3	8.4	7.4
8	6.8	5.1	5.0
9	2.6	1.4	6.4
10	1.5	0.5	2.7
11–15	4.8	3.8	12.0
Over 15	13.6	2.8	28.5
All	100	100	100
Mean	8.8	5.1	14.0

Source: NIS 2007, main sample (reference individuals age 16–60).

5.3.2 *Years since arrival*

Table 5.3 reports the distribution of individuals in each ethnic group by years since migration. On average, Moroccans arrived in Spain 14 years ago. Latinos and, particularly, Eastern Europeans arrived in Spain much more recently: 8.8 and 5.0 years ago on average, respectively.

5.3.3 *Age and gender*

This section describes the distribution of immigrants by age and gender for each ethnic group. Clearly, differences across groups in these distributions are likely to affect the rates of overall and inter-ethnic marriage, which we shall analyse later. Table 5.4 reports the age distributions, separately for men and women. We also include the analogous data for the native population to provide a basis for comparison.

Two features stand out. First, the age distribution is roughly similar across all groups. For instance, the share of individuals below age 30 is roughly 30 per cent and the average age is 36 for immigrant males. Eastern Europeans are on average younger and Moroccans tend to be older. More dramatic differences appear when we look at the relative number of females in each age group, as illustrated by the third panel in Table 5.3. Consider women in the 16–29 and 30–49 age groups. Among Latinos and Eastern Europeans, the share of women is roughly 50 per cent. However, it is only 35 per cent for Moroccans,

Table 5.4 Age-gender distribution, by ethnic groups.

Only men Age	Latinos	Eastern Europe	Morocco	Natives
16–29	31.9	32.0	30.0	20.9
30–49	53.4	59.0	51.9	35.5
5–64	10.8	8.2	13.1	22.9
65–74	2.3	0.7	3.3	12.5
over 75	1.6	0.2	1.8	8.26
All	100	100	100	100
Mean	36.7	34.5	37.9	46.77

Only women Age	Latinos	Eastern Europe	Morocco	Natives
16–29	29.9	39.7	30.3	18.6
30–49	53.1	49.7	48.1	33.9
50–64	12.5	10.1	12.3	22.3
65–74	2.6	0.5	5.9	13.5
Over 75	2.0	0.1	3.3	11.7
All	100	100	100	100
Mean	37.7	34.1	39.1	48.94

Fraction of women Age	Latinos	Eastern Europe	Morocco	Natives
16–29	52.6	54.0	36.5	49.1
30–49	54.2	44.3	34.5	51.1
50–64	57.7	53.9	34.8	51.6
65–74	57.9	39.1	50.5	54.1
Over 75	58.9	29.2	51.9	60

Source: NIS 2007, main sample.

indicating that the supply of marriage-age women is shorter for the latter group.[4]

5.3.4 *Educational attainment*

We now turn to the distribution by schooling of each ethnic group. We define three groups: individuals that at most completed primary education, individuals that completed secondary education, and individuals with completed tertiary education.

---

[4] Cortina *et al.* (2008) report differences in sex ratios by country, within ethnic group. For instance, the female share among Ecuadorians is particularly high.

Table 5.5 Educational attainment of natives and immigrants.

Men	Latinos	Eastern Europe	Morocco	Natives
Primary or less	33.3	41.2	63.0	18.01
Secondary	45.2	48.5	26.6	56.35
Tertiary	21.5	10.4	10.4	25.64
Average years	11.1	10.6	7.6	11.42
Women	Latinos	Eastern Europe	Morocco	Natives
Primary or less	31.0	30.9	77.5	18.72
Secondary	43.2	45.5	15.0	52.83
Tertiary	25.8	23.6	7.5	28.45
Average years	11.1	11.2	5.7	11.61

Source: NIS for foreign born and LFS for natives. Ages 25–50. Completed education.

Table 5.5 reports the results, together with the education distribution of the native population. We restrict our sample to individuals aged 25–50 to make the comparisons across groups more informative. First, note that Moroccans have the lowest educational attainment. Average years of education are 7.4 for Moroccan men and 6.1 for Moroccan women. In contrast, Latinos and Eastern Europeans have on average 10–11 years of schooling, only slightly below natives. Next, we note that except for Moroccans, women are slightly more educated than men in all ethnic groups, including natives. The next section provides a more formal analysis of the gender gap in educational attainment.

5.4 Gender gaps in education

In many European countries, including Spain, there is public perception that Muslim minorities have markedly different attitudes regarding women's role in society. In this section, we provide a comparison of the gender gaps in education across ethnic groups and by birth cohort, which will be informative about the intensity of cultural assimilation for the different ethnic minorities.

Table 5.6 reports our estimates of the average gender gaps in years of education for different ethnic groups and birth cohorts using regression analysis. The dependent variable is years of education. The table reports the coefficient associated with a female dummy, which can be interpreted as the difference between the average years of education of women relative to men. We estimate a separate regression for each

Table 5.6 Gender gaps in years of education for different birth cohorts.

Age	Latinos	Eastern Europe	Morocco	Natives
Less than 30	0.194	0.558**	−0.593	0.821**
	(0.127)	(0.202)	(0.416)	(0.032)
31–40 years	0.191	0.490**	−2.466**	0.543**
	(0.142)	(0.186)	(0.459)	(0.045)
41–60 years	−0.315**	−0.155	−0.821*	−0.353**
	(0.165)	(0.316)	(0.455)	(0.038)

Note: The dependent variable is years of completed education; the coefficient reported is the impact of female on years of education from a linear probability model. There is a separate estimation for each ethnic group and for each birth cohort.

Source: NIS (2007) for foreign born and LFS (2007) for natives. ** significant at 5%, * significant at 10%. All regressions control for age and for years since migration (ysm). Standard errors are in parentheses.

ethnic group and cohort. Standard errors are in parentheses. Table 5.6 reveals important differences in gender gaps in education across ethnic groups, as well as across birth cohorts. Consider first individuals in age bracket 31–40. Point estimates are positive—that is, women have higher education than men—for all groups except for Morocco. The values range from –2.46 years (Morocco) to 0.49 (Eastern Europe). For earlier (older) cohorts, point estimates are negative—women have lower education—for all groups. Morocco displays the largest gender gap. Finally, among individuals younger than 30 we do not find a statistically significant gender gap for any group. Only Morocco displays a gender gap, although it is not statistically significant.

In sum, for the largest cohort (age 31–40), we find evidence of a sizeable gender gap only for Morocco. However, even for Moroccans, we find rapidly diminishing gender gaps across cohorts, possibly converging toward a situation with higher educational attainment for women.

5.5 Marriage

5.5.1 Early marriage

This section explores another interesting dimension along which behaviour may vary across ethnic groups. We quantify cultural differences in marriage habits. Specifically, we focus on differences in the frequency of early marriage and inter-ethnic marriage.

We focus on females and state that a woman 'married early' if she got married by age 25. Table 5.7 reports the distribution of early marriages

Table 5.7 Early marriage. Distribution and predicted probabilities by ethnicity, females ages 16–25.

	Latinos	Eastern Europe	Morocco	Natives
Proportion married	0.16	0.29	0.62	0.03
	(0.37)	(0.45)	(0.48)	(0.17)
Pred. prob. married, controls for	0.165	0.291	0.624	0.03
age and years since migr. (ysm)	(0.133)	(0.175)	(0.271)	(0.03)
Pred. prob. married, controls	0.165	0.291	0.624	0.03
age, ysm and education	(0.136)	(0.178)	(0.293)	(0.04)
No. observations	442	237	125	8,892

Note: The first row computes the proportion of marriages. Standard deviation in parentheses. In the second row, we compute the predicted probability of marriage evaluated at each ethnic group's average age, controlling for years since migration. For this prediction, the dependent variable is an indicator of marriage among all females between 16 and 25 years of age. A linear probability model is estimated, and there is a separate estimation for each ethnic group. The third row computes the predicted probability of an early marriage, as before, but controlling not only for years since migration but also for years of education. In rows 2 and 3, robust standard errors in parentheses.

Source: NIS (2007) for immigrants and LFS (2007) for natives. Sample consists of all females between 16 and 25 years of age.

by ethnicity, as well as predicted probabilities obtained from estimating linear probability models.[5] Predicted probabilities are evaluated for each group's average characteristics. The first row of Table 5.7 reveals that 16 per cent of Latino women married early. The figure is higher for Eastern European women (29 per cent), and much higher (62 per cent) among Moroccans. In comparison, only 2.9 per cent of native women married early.

The second and third rows report the predicted probability of an early marriage with and without controlling for schooling, while controlling for age in both cases. The comparison is interesting because it is often argued that differences in the probability of early marriage simply reflect differences in education. As seen in the third row of Table 5.7, significant differences across ethnic groups still remain. Moroccan females are much more likely to marry by age 25 than females from South and Central America (Latinos) or from Eastern Europe. Moreover, the result is not simply driven by lower educational attainment. We note that, relative to natives, early marriage is high for Latinas and Eastern European women as well.

[5] Our results do not vary much when we examine the distribution of early marriages for men, although males get married a bit older. We do not report the results for the sake of brevity.

5.5.2 *Inter-ethnic marriage*

This section explores the performance of the different ethnic groups along another important dimension of cultural integration, namely, the frequency of inter-ethnic marriages (Bisin and Verdier, 2000). We focus on foreign-born individuals who are married and classify them according to the country of birth of their spouse. We define three categories: the two spouses were born in the same country, the spouse was born in Spain, or the spouse was born in a third country (that is, neither Spain nor one's own country). For comparison we also report on inter-marriage rates for natives, defined as marriage with a foreign-born individual.[6]

Table 5.8 reports our findings for each ethnic group and birth cohort. Table 5.8a reports the distribution over the three types of marriage. Consider first, age bracket 31–40, the largest cohort. We note first that marrying someone from a third country is very rare (below 5 per cent for all foreign-born minorities). Interestingly, we only detect this behaviour in our data among Moroccans (1.82 per cent). Second, the fraction of inter-ethnic marriages with Spanish natives is highest among Latinos (33 per cent of all marriages), Moroccans (17 per cent), and Eastern Europeans (11 per cent). A proper interpretation of these figures requires accounting for differences in observables, such as years since migration, as well as taking into account differences in the age-gender distribution.

Table 5.8b estimates the probability of an inter-ethnic marriage for each group, defined as the probability of marrying a Spanish native or an individual from a third country of origin on the sample of married individuals. The dependent variable takes the value of 1 if the individual is married either to a Spanish native or to someone from a third country (not Spain and not the individual's own country of birth). The reference group is married individuals younger than 31. A linear probability model is estimated, separately for each group. The coefficient reported under age <31 is the constant of the estimation and the rest of the coefficients must be understood as the change in the probability of an inter-ethnic marriage with respect to the reference group. We control for years since migration and age. First, our results show that the probability of an inter-ethnic marriage increases with time since migration for all

---

[6] Cortina *et al.* (2008) study how inter-marriage affects the probability of employment for married women, using Spanish data. They find that foreign-born women married to Spanish-born natives have lower employment rates than those with foreign-born husbands. They also report that the type of partner does not have any effect on the probability of employment of native women.

Table 5.8 Inter-ethnic marriage.
Table 5.8a Conditional means by ethnic group and birth cohort.

	Latinos	Eastern Europe	Morocco	Natives
Aged less than 30				
% married	28	38	49	8.9
spouse from				
same country	68.6	80.6	90.9	79.3
Spain	31.0	19.1	9.1	
Third country	0.0	0.3	0.0	21.9
Aged 31–40 years				
% married	54	65	76	63.7
spouse from				
same country	66.7	88.6	80.9	89.6
Spain	32.9	11.4	17.3	
Third country	0.0	0.0	1.8	10.4
Aged 41–60 years				
% married	60	66	77	79.6
spouse from				
same country	55.0	87.9	61.7	95.3
Spain	45.0	12.2	38.0	
Third country	0.0	0.0	0.3	4.7

Note: The sample is composed of all married individuals between 16 and 60 years. Third country means a country different from one's birth country and from Spain. For natives, we have computed the percentage of all married individuals between 16 and 60 years married to a Spaniard (same country) or married to a foreign born.

Source: NIS (2007) for foreign born and LFS (2007) for natives.

Table 5.8b Probability of inter-ethnic marriage. Linear probability models.

	Latinos	Eastern Europe	Morocco	Natives
Aged <31 years	0.182**	0.081**	−0.027**	0.217**
	(0.020)	(0.023)	(0.019)	(0.012)
Aged 31–40	0.027	−0.109**	0.009	−0.113**
	(0.024)	(0.026)	(0.028)	(0.010)
Aged 41–60	0.094**	−0.150**	−0.067**	−0.169**
	(0.025)	(0.028)	(0.031)	(0.012)
Years since mig.	0.023**	0.025**	0.021**	—
	(0.002)	(0.002)	(0.001)	
Observations	2,624	1,181	1,064	48,707

Note: For foreign born, the dependent variable takes the value of 1 if the individual is married either to a Spanish native or to someone from a third country (not Spain and not the individual's own country of birth). For natives, the dependent variable equals 1 if married to a foreign born. The reference group is married individuals younger than 31. A linear probability model is estimated, and there is a separate regression for each ethnic group. The coefficient reported under age <31 is the constant of the estimation and the rest of the coefficients must be understood as the increase or decrease in the probability of an inter-ethnic marriage with respect to the reference group. ** significant at 5%, * significant at 10%.

Source: NIS (2007). The sample is composed of all married individuals between 16 and 60 years.

groups. When we focus on individuals aged 30 or younger, we find that 21 per cent of married Latinos are in an inter-ethnic marriage. The comparable figures for Eastern Europeans and Moroccans are, respectively, 19 per cent and 16 per cent. In comparison, 22 per cent of married natives age 30 or younger had a foreign-born spouse.

It is worth pointing out a striking feature that appeared in Table 5.4. Namely, the fraction of women of marriageable age is much lower among Moroccans (roughly, by 20–30 percentage points for ages 16–29 and 30–49). As a result, there is a large excess of demand for women in the 'marriage market' for this group. Thus, while it may be the case that Moroccans have a stronger preference for intra-group marriage, feasibility constraints in the marriage market push Moroccan men to marry outside their group. However, we find a probability of inter-ethnic marriage among Moroccans that lies only slightly below that of Latinos and Eastern Europeans, suggesting that there are a significant number of unmarried Moroccan women.

5.6 Fertility

This section examines fertility rates for each ethnic group. Following Georgiadis and Manning (2011), we focus on the sample of foreign-born women aged 18–45. For each of them we compute the total number of children alive. Unlike usual household surveys, our data include both children who are present in the household and children residing elsewhere (e.g. in the country of origin).

Table 5.9a reports the average number of children per woman for each of the ethnic groups considered in the study. Clearly, Moroccans have relatively more children on average, respectively, 1.72 and 1.95 children per woman. In comparison, Latino and Eastern European women have

Table 5.9a Average number of children by ethnic group.

	Latinos	Eastern Europe	Morocco	Average Spain*
Number of children	1.27	0.97	1.72	1.38
	(1.19)	(0.90)	(1.60)	
Average age Female	32.9	31.28	32.29	
	(6.86)	(6.72)	(7.18)	
Observations	2,628	1,063	548	

Source: NIS. The sample includes all females aged between 18 and 45 years of age. Standard deviations in parentheses. Data for average number of children in Spain is taken from the Spanish Institute of Statistics (Basic Demographic Indicators—2006, includes all native and immigrant women).

Table 5.9b Determinants of the average number of children.

Controls	Not controlling for education	Controlling for education
Eastern Europe	–0.18**	–0.20**
	(0.03)	(0.03)
Morocco	0.51**	0.03
	(0.06)	(0.06)
Years of education	—	–0.09**
		(0.005)
No. observations	4,239	4,239

Source: NIS. The sample includes all females aged between 18 and 45 years of age. The dependent variable is number of children and there is a joint regression for all ethnic groups. Reference is Latinos. A linear regression is estimated. Each reported coefficient measures the difference in the average number of children between Latinos and the other ethnic origins. Age and age squared, and years since migration and its square are also included in both regressions. Robust standard errors in parentheses. ** significant at 5%, * significant at 10%.

on average 1.27 and 0.97 children, respectively. The table also shows that the average age of women in the four ethnic groups is very similar.

We next provide a slightly more rigorous analysis in Table 5.9b. Specifically, we estimate a linear regression where the dependent variable is the total number of children on the sample of all foreign-born women in the age range 18–45. On the right-hand side we include ethnic group dummies (with Latinos being our reference group) and a quadratic polynomial in age. We present two sets of estimates. In the first estimation we do not control for years of education but we do so in the second set of estimates. In the former case, the results confirm the findings suggested by the descriptive statistics. Namely, Moroccan women have a significantly higher number of children than women from the other ethnic groups. Interestingly, the picture changes when we control for education levels. Now, Moroccan women have the same fertility as Latino women. In sum, controlling for age and education, Eastern European women have 0.2 fewer children than Latino and Moroccan women.

5.7 Female employment

We now turn to assimilation in the labour market. In particular, we are interested in comparing the employment rates of women across ethnic groups. It is traditionally believed that women from traditional Muslim societies are restricted in their ability to participate in the labour market.

Let us start by examining some descriptive statistics. Table 5.10a reports the average employment rates among females in the age bracket

Table 5.10a Female employment rates by ethnic group and for different demographic characteristics.

	Latinos	Eastern Europe	Morocco	Natives
All women	0.70	0.69	0.35	0.499
	(0.45)	(0.46)	(0.47)	(0.50)
Single women	0.76	0.71	0.65	0.527
	(0.43)	(0.45)	(0.48)	(0.499)
Married women	0.65	0.67	0.26	0.478
	(0.47)	(0.47)	(0.44)	(0.498)
Married women with children	0.65	0.66	0.24	0.438
	(0.48)	(0.47)	(0.43)	(0.499)

Source: NIS for foreign born and LFS for natives. The sample includes all females between aged 25 and 59 years.

Table 5.10b Conditional probability of employment—all women and for different demographic characteristics.

	Latinos	Eastern Europe	Morocco
All women	0.67**	0.58**	0.21**
	(0.02)	(0.05)	(0.05)
Single women	0.675**	0.61**	0.74**
	(0.04)	(0.10)	(0.13)
Married women	0.63**	0.64**	0.12**
	(0.03)	(0.06)	(0.05)
Married women with children	0.64**	0.62**	0.11**
	(0.04)	(0.06)	(0.05)

Note: A linear probability model is estimated separately for each ethnic group and for each group of women. All regressions control for age (three age categories (less 35, 36–45 and older than 45—less than 35 as reference), for years since migration and its square and for education (no education, primary, secondary and tertiary—reference: primary). Hence, the reported coefficients are the average employment rates for the reference female (<35 with primary education) for each ethnic group and for each family situation. Robust standard errors in parentheses.** significant at 5%, * significant at 10%.

Source: NIS. The sample includes all females between aged 25 and 59 years.

25–59 for each ethnic group. Each row represents a different set of women. We consider all women, single women, married women, and married women with children. When we compare the unconditional employment rates, we find striking differences. While almost 70 per cent of Latino and Eastern European women work, only 35 per cent of Moroccans do. In comparison, 50 per cent of native women work. Interestingly, when we focus on being single, the employment rates of all four groups are very similar (and larger than for natives). However, when Moroccan women get married or have children, their employment-population rates drop dramatically (30–40 percentage points). In contrast, the 'penalty' of getting married or having children is much smaller for native women as well as for Latino and Eastern European women. Respectively, their employment-population rates only decrease by 5, 10, and 4 percentage points.

Next, we estimate the conditional probability of being employed for each of the different ethnic groups and for each group of women, controlling for age and education. Table 5.10b displays the results. The estimates here confirm the findings suggested by the descriptive statistics above. Overall, Latino and Eastern European women are more likely to be employed. However, the marriage/children penalty is small for Latino and Eastern European women, while very large for women born in Morocco.[7]

5.8 Command of Spanish

The purpose of this section is to examine the knowledge of Spanish of the different ethnic groups. Language difficulties may clearly prevent immigrants from an adequate integration in the host country. Given that among our ethnic groups there is a wide disparity in the distance between their original languages and Spanish, it is interesting to examine the outcomes for each group.

We classify the foreign-born population in three levels of fluency. The highest level corresponds to individuals that report Spanish as their first language. The second level contains individuals that report understanding and speaking Spanish. Finally, the lowest level of fluency corresponds to individuals that declare that they understand Spanish but do not speak it.

Table 5.11a reports our results. First, we consider all individuals, regardless of their year of arrival. Naturally, the vast majority of Latinos appear as native Spanish speakers (95 per cent). The other group with a significant proportion of native Spanish speakers is Morocco (9.55 per cent), reflecting the fact that some individuals were brought by their parents when they were very young and report Spanish as their mother tongue. Eastern Europeans appear as the relatively less fluent group. However, even among this group the vast majority reports speaking and understanding the language.[8]

---

[7] It is worth noting that single Moroccan women have the highest employment-population rate.

[8] The high level of command of Spanish across all groups is a bit surprising, and may partly reflect the design of the NIS. Recall that only individuals living in Spain for at least one year (or that intend to stay) were interviewed.

Table 5.11 Fluency in Spanish by ethnic group.
Table 5.11a Means, main sample NIS.

	Latinos	Eastern Europe	Morocco
All individuals			
Native-speaker	94.9	0.5	9.6
Speaks and understands	4.9	96.7	87.3
Only understands	0.2	2.9	3.1
	100.0	100.0	100.0
Recent (ysm <3)			
Native-speaker	90.8	0.0	0.0
Speaks and understands	8.2	90.3	92.6
Only understands	0.9	9.7	7.3
	100.0	100.0	100.0

Table 5.11b Probability of speaking and understanding Spanish. Sample: non-Latino, non-native speakers, linear probability model.

Dependent variable	Speaks and understand
Constant	0.797
	(0.026)**
Eastern Europeans	0.027
	(0.012)**
Years since migration	0.000
	(0.000)
Age	−0.001
	(0.000)**
Years education	0.014
	(0.001)**
Female	−0.050
	(0.010)**
Observations	3,604
R^2	0.1

Robust standard errors in parentheses, ** significant at 5%.

The second part of the table reports on the command of Spanish of recent immigrants, defined as individuals that arrived one or two years prior to the survey. Clearly, the fraction of individuals that only understands Spanish increases for all groups, except for Latinos. The figures are 9.72 per cent for Eastern Europeans, and 7.32 per cent for Moroccans. Overall, these descriptive statistics suggest that immigrants learn Spanish very quickly after arrival.

Next, we turn to a regression analysis to investigate the determinants of language fluency and to provide a more rigorous comparison across groups. In our analysis, we drop Latinos and individuals that report Spanish as their mother tongue. Our dependent variable is an indicator for whether an individual speaks and understands Spanish. The right-hand side variables include dummy variables for being Eastern European. Thus, Morocco is the reference group in the regression. We also control for years since migration, age, and gender. We estimate a linear probability model.

Table 5.11b reports the results. The intercept of the regression takes the value 0.79, reflecting the very high proportion of individuals that speak and understand Spanish. Note that Eastern Europeans are significantly more likely to speak and understand Spanish than Moroccans (2.7 percentage points) when we control for age, years since migration, and years of education. Turning to the controls, we find the expected signs. The level of command of Spanish increases with education levels. Age and years since migration do not contribute to explain difference in the command of Spanish when comparing Moroccans and individuals from Eastern Europe. On the contrary, an extra year of education has a large effect on fluency for these individuals. Finally, our estimates suggest that women are less likely to be able to speak and understand Spanish.

In conclusion, the average level of Spanish is very high among all ethnic groups in our study, suggesting fast learning rates. However, we find significant differences across groups. Obviously, most Latinos are native Spanish speakers. More interestingly, we find that, after controlling for differences in observables, Eastern Europeans have better command of Spanish than Moroccans. Our results seem very reasonable, once we recall that the vast majority of Eastern Europeans in Spain are from Romania. Thus, their mother tongue is also Latin-based, which makes learning Spanish relatively easy.

5.9 Social participation

This section explores another dimension of integration, namely, the degree of participation in social activities. To address this issue we use two sets of questions posed to foreign-born individuals surveyed in the NIS. The first set asks about participation in clubs and associations specifically targeted to foreigners. More interesting for our purposes, the second set of questions is about participation in social activities that are not directly targeted to foreigners. In both cases, individuals are asked about participation in religious, cultural/educational activities, and sports clubs.

Table 5.12 Social participation in associations and clubs.
Table 5.12a Descriptive statistics.

	Latinos	Eastern Europe	Morocco
Targeted to foreigners			
Religious (1)	1.31	1.94	1.65
Cultural and educational	1.38	1.32	1.87
Sports	1.83	0.57	0.82
Non-targeted			
Religious (2)	3.03	1.63	1.32
Cultural and educational	3.57	1.54	2.31
Sports	4.88	2.07	2.86
Religious (1 + 2)	4.34	3.57	2.97

Source: NIS, main sample.

Table 5.12b Linear probability model.
Dependent variable: participation in either type of association not
targeted to foreigners.

Dep. var.	Participation
Constant	−0.013
	(0.007)*
Eastern Europeans	-0.010
	(0.003)**
Moroccans	−0.015
	(0.003)**
Female	0.008
	(0.003)**
Years since migration	0
	(0.000)
Age	0.001**
	(0.000)
Years of education	0.001
	(0.000)**
Observations	9,188
R^2	0.01

Omitted category is Latinos. Robust standard errors in parentheses, ** significant at 5%;
* significant at 10%

Table 5.12a presents some descriptive statistics. The first observation
is that take-up rates are relatively low (below 5 per cent for all groups and
activities). Sports clubs feature the highest participation, while religious
associations display the lowest. Second, Latinos seem to participate
in activities not targeted to foreigners more often than other ethnic
groups. Table 5.12b provides a regression analysis. The dependent
variable is an indicator for whether the individual participated in any

type of association not directly targeted to foreigners. The rest of the specification is very similar to the one used in the previous section. On the right-hand side we include dummies for ethnic groups Eastern Europe, and Morocco. The excluded category is Latinos. We control for age, gender, years since migration, and years of education.

Clearly, Latinos are the ethnic group that is more likely to participate in social activities not directly targeted to foreigners. Moroccans are the least likely group to participate, after controlling for observables. Age and education levels are conducive to larger social involvement, and women are less likely to participate.

5.10 Similarity between natives and immigrants

This section compares natives and immigrants along several socio-economic dimensions. Mainly, we focus on labour-market and family-formation outcomes. Our exercise follows Vigdor (2008),[9] who proposes the following thought experiment. Consider drawing an individual randomly from the population and asking what the probability is that he or she is foreign born. Clearly, if we do not control for any characteristics this is just the foreign-born share in the population. More interestingly, we can ask the question by focusing on relevant socio-economic outcomes after controlling for demographic characteristics.[10]

Specifically, we estimate a series of probit models for the probability of being foreign born. The outcomes of interest are employment, log mean wage in the current occupation (among natives), a dummy for being married or in cohabitation, the number of children, and an indicator for being married/cohabitating with a Spain-born (native) individual. We control for age, education, and gender.[11]

Table 5.13 presents the estimated marginal effects. The first column includes only the demographic controls and a dummy for being employed. Column 2 adds the average wage in the current occupation. Column 3 includes the variables concerning family formation (married,

[9] These estimates can be used to build 'assimilation' indices as in Vigdor (2008).

[10] To gain precision in our estimates, in this section we do not distinguish by ethnic origin.

[11] The data for the analysis in this section is from the 2007 Spanish Labour Force Survey. This dataset does not contain wage data. We compute median monthly wages by occupation for natives using the Wage Structure Survey and merge it into our dataset. We assign a zero wage to the non-employed. For a recent study showing that the task content of occupations affects natives' views over immigration see Ortega and Polavieja (2012).

Table 5.13 Similarity between native and foreign-born individuals. Dependent variable: probability of being foreign born. Probit model, marginal effects reported.

Variables	(1) FB = 1	(2) FB = 1	(3) FB = 1	(4) FB = 1
Employed	0.026**	0.050**	0.024**	0.019**
	(0.002)	(0.002)	(0.002)	(0.003)
Emp. *female				0.010**
				(0.004)
Avg. wage occupation (wocup)		−0.019**	−0.011**	−0.009**
		(0.001)	(0.001)	(0.001)
Wocup *female				−0.003*
				(0.002)
Married			0.216**	0.210**
			(0.004)	(0.005)
Married *female				0.010*
				(0.005)
Children			−0.041**	−0.043**
			(0.001)	(0.002)
Children *female				0.004*
				(0.002)
Spouse native			−0.353**	−0.345**
			(0.004)	(0.006)
Spouse native*female				−0.008*
				(0.005)
Edu2	−0.037**	−0.034**	−0.017**	−0.017**
	(0.002)	(0.002)	(0.002)	(0.002)
Edu3	−0.047**	−0.035**	−0.021**	−0.021**
	(0.002)	(0.002)	(0.002)	(0.002)
Female	0.013**	0.010**	0.010**	0.005
	(0.002)	(0.002)	(0.001)	(0.003)
Age	−0.002**	−0.002**	−0.001**	−0.001**
	(0.000)	(0.000)	(0.000)	(0.000)
Observations	101,530	101,530	101,530	101,530
Pseudo-R^2	0.019	0.023	0.290	0.290

Note: The dependent variable is an indicator for foreign born. We report marginal effects from a probit. Average monthly wages by occupation in thousands of euros. Standard errors in parentheses, ** significant at 5%, * significant at 10%.

number of children, inter-ethnic marriage). Finally, column 4 allows for different effects by gender of the respondent.

Several results stand out. First, compared to natives, immigrants are younger, less educated, and slightly more likely to be female. Among these, relatively lower education is the main predictor for being foreign born. Turning to economic differences, we note that foreign-born individuals are more likely to be employed than natives. However, immigrants are employed in lower quality occupations, as measured by mean wages. Based on the estimates in column 2, being employed increases the probability of being foreign born by five percentage points. Likewise, being employed in an occupation that pays, on average, one thousand euros more monthly, reduces the probability of being foreign born by 1.9 percentage points.

We now turn to the outcomes concerning family formation (column 3). Note that being married is a signal for being foreign born. However, as the number of children in the household increases the probability of being foreign born falls. This reflects the substantial number of recent immigrants that chose to leave their children in their respective origin countries. We also note that the marginal effects associated with these variables are substantially larger than the effects of differences in the labour-market characteristics. Not surprisingly, the largest predictor for being foreign born is being married (or cohabiting) with a Spain-born partner. It reduces the probability of being an immigrant by 35.3 percentage points. Finally, we note that most effects are very similar for men and women. Even though the interactions with the female dummy included in column 4 are often significant, the magnitudes are usually rather small. We find it interesting that being employed has a substantially larger effect on the probability of being foreign born for women (2.9 percentage points) than for men (1.9 percentage points).

Overall, these estimates suggest the following conclusions. First, young and low-educated individuals are much more likely to be foreign born. Second, high employment rates in low-paying occupations are an important distinction between the labour-market outcomes of natives and immigrants. However, the largest differences between natives and immigrants arise in their family organization. Controlling for age and education, immigrants are much more likely to be married (or in cohabitation) but much less likely to have a Spain-born partner or several children (in the household).

5.11 Conclusion

Our aim in this paper is to examine the cultural and economic gaps of ethnic foreign-born minorities that differ in the cultural distance to the norms in their host society. In particular, we address the question of whether these gaps are increasing (or decreasing) in the cultural distance between natives and each minority ethnic group living in Spain. Second, we examine the evolution of these gaps across cohorts, for each group.

Our results reveal large differences across ethnic groups in educational attainment, and in years since migration. Both variables are well known to be important determinants of integration. Moroccans arrived in Spain earlier and have substantially lower education levels. Eastern Europeans are the most recent arrivals and, together with Latinos, have schooling levels that are similar to those of natives. Second, we find that women are on average equally or more educated than men in all ethnic groups, except for Moroccans. Third, we also find large differences in marriage patterns across ethnic groups. Our results suggest that Latinos have the lowest rates of early marriage (and overall marriage) while Moroccans have the highest.

With respect to interethnic marriages, we find that the Latino group is the one with a higher fraction of marriages to Spanish natives (33 per cent), relative to the total number of marriages. This group is followed by Morocco, with a rate of 17 per cent of their married population having a Spanish-born spouse. At the other end, only 11 per cent of the married Eastern Europeans are married to Spanish natives. Our interpretation of these results is driven partly by cultural distance (which accounts for the high inter-ethnic marriage of Latinos) and partly by the imbalance in sex ratios faced by immigrants from Morocco. We also find that Moroccans have the highest fertility rates, while Eastern Europeans have the lowest. Our regression results show that low levels of education are largely responsible for the highest fertility of Moroccans.

Fifth, we find that among single women (without children), employment rates are high and very similar for all ethnic groups. However, while marriage and children impose only a small employment penalty on Latino and Eastern European women, Moroccan women's employment rates drop precipitously. The welfare implications are not obvious given that fertility rates are higher among women in these groups, which reduces the potential economic benefits of participating in the labour market.

Sixth, the command of Spanish is very high across all groups, although naturally the highest among Latinos. Among non-Latinos, our regression analysis reveals that Eastern Europeans are around three percentage points more likely to be fluent in Spanish than Moroccans, controlling for education and years since migration. Our analysis of social participation reveals that Latinos are more likely to participate in clubs and associations non-targeted to foreigners, compared to all other groups. Finally, we find substantial dissimilarity in the labour-market outcomes and family organization of natives and immigrants, after controlling for demographics and educational attainment.

Overall these results suggest that Latinos—the group with the shortest cultural distance to Spanish social norms—appear very similar to natives in most economic and cultural outcomes. Moroccans still display large gaps along several dimensions, which are largely explained by differences in educational attainment. Our results also show that these gaps shrink rapidly as time in Spain (since migration) rises and that native-immigrant gaps appear to be shrinking fast for the younger cohorts.

References

Amuedo-Dorantes, C. and De la Rica, S. (2011) Complements or substitutes? Task specialization by gender and nativity in Spain. *Labour Economics*, 18, doi: 10.1016/j.labeco.2011.02.002.

Amuedo-Dorantes, C. and De la Rica, S. (2012) Substitutability of Immigrant and Native Labor: Evidence from Spain. Forthcoming in *Empirical Economics*.

Bertoli, S., Fernandez-Huertas, J., and Ortega, F. (2011) Immigration Policies and the Ecuadorian Exodus. *The World Bank Economic Review*, doi: 10.1093/wber/lhr004.

Bisin, A. and Verdier, T. (2000) Beyond the Melting Pot: Cultural Transmission, Marriage, and the Evolution of Ethnic and Religious Traits. *Quarterly Journal of Economics*, CXV(3), 955–988.

Cortina, C., Esteve, A., and Domingo, A. (2008) Marriage Patterns of the Foreign-Born Population in a New Country of Immigration: The Case of Spain. *The International Migration Review*, 42(4), 877–902.

Farré, L., González, L., and Ortega, F. (2011) Immigration, Family Responsibilities and the Labor Supply of Skilled Native Women. *The B.E. Journal of Economic Analysis & Policy*, 11(1) (Contributions), Article 34. DOI: 10.2202/1935-1682.2875.

Georgiadis, A. and Manning, A. (2011) Change and continuity among minority communities in Britain. *Journal of Population Economics*, 24(2), 541–568. ISSN 0933–1433.

Gonzalez, L. and Ortega, F. (2010) How Do Very Open Economies Absorb Large Immigration Flows? Evidence from Spanish Regions. *Labour Economics*, 18 (2011) 57–70.

Ortega, F. and Polavieja, J.G. (2012) Labor-market Exposure as a Determinant of Attitudes toward Immigration. *Labour Economics*, 19), pp. 298–311. DOI information: 10.1016/j.labeco.2012.02.004.

Sandell, R. (2008) *A Social Network Approach to Spanish Immigration: An Analysis of Immigration into Spain 1998–2006*. FEDEA working paper 2008–33.

Vigdor, J.L. (2008) *Measuring Immigrant Assimilation in the United States*. Manhattan Institute Civic Report 53 (2008).

6

Cultural Integration in Sweden

Lena Nekby

6.1 Introduction

Negative attitudes towards immigration may stem less from the economic implications of immigration and more from the perceived threats of immigration to social and cultural institutions (Card *et al.*, 2005; Dustmann and Preston, 2007). In Sweden, as in many other European countries, there is an ongoing public debate that immigrants are not adapting to the social and cultural norms of the host country. The empirical evidence is, however, scant. In this chapter the process of cultural (or social) integration is studied in Sweden by comparing differences between immigrants and natives on a number of indicators, as well as across two generations of immigrants stemming from the same region of origin.

While economic integration is easily quantified by a number of commonly accepted measures, such as the development of wage, income, and employment gaps between natives and immigrants over time and/or across generations, cultural integration is not as readily definable. One reason for this is that what constitutes a social or cultural norm is inherently subjective and likely to be defined in relative terms. The cross-cultural psychology literature stresses the acculturation process, that is, the changes in social norms defined by attitudes, customs and values in *both* the majority and minority populations due to the contact brought about by immigration (Berry, 1997; Berry and Sam, 1997, 2006, Phinney 1989, 1990; Phinney *et al.*, 2001). The fluid nature of cultural norms implies that the choice of cultural indicators used to exemplify host country norms is likely to be, at least partially, defined relative to the predominant immigrant groups of the time. Religion is a case in point; if the dominant migrant groups have a similar religious affiliation to the majority population then religion is unlikely to be stressed as a defining cultural characteristic of the majority population. If, however, newly-arrived immigrant groups differ in terms of religious belonging or religiosity, then religion is more likely to be seen as a defining cultural characteristic.[1] Initial gaps in cultural indicators between various natives and immigrants are likely to be large precisely because it is this difference that defines the cultural norm of the majority population.

Although cultural integration is a process of adaptation in both the majority and minority groups, due to the asymmetry in size between the groups, the bulk of adaptation is likely to be on the side of immigrants. The majority population can, however, aid or inhibit this process through their attitudes and actions. If, for example, access to jobs is limited due to ethnic discrimination, some immigrant groups may never enter the social arenas necessary to forge contacts with natives which would in turn influence cultural indicators such as intermarriage propensities. Likewise, a preference for or against certain characteristics in partners implies that the likelihood of intermarriage is heavily influenced by the behaviour and attitudes of the much larger in size majority population.[2]

In order to examine the process of cultural integration between immigrants and natives it is therefore important to follow immigrant groups over time and preferably over several generations to see how a defined cultural gap at one time point develops due to changes in both the majority population and minority groups.[3] As data restrictions prevent an analysis of the intergenerational transmission of defined measures, this study instead analyses two generations of immigrants from the same region of origin at a given point in time, comparing natives and immigrants across these generations. For ease of interpretation, focus in this study is on immigrant groups defined broadly by region of origin (or, for second-generation immigrants, by parents' region of

---

[1] Recent focus on the cultural integration of Muslims in Europe in both the popular and academic debate is a case in point. Recent studies (and critiques) in economics on social or cultural integration with at least a partial focus on religion include Arai *et al.* (2009), Bisin *et al.* (2004, 2008), Bisin and Verdier (2000), Constant *et al.* (2006), de la Rica and Ortega (2009), Georgiadis and Manning (2008), and Manning and Roy (2009).

[2] Studies on inter-marriage patterns among immigrants include Angrist (2002), Chiswick and Houseworth (2011), Furtado (2006), Gilbertson *et al.* (1996), Kalmijn (1991a, 1991b, 1993, 1998), Kantarevic (2004), Lievens (1999), and Nielsen *et al.* (2009).

[3] Recent measures used to analyse social integration within the economics literature include marriage patterns, fertility norms, residential segregation, religious affiliation and religiosity, attitudes towards gender equality, and ethnic/national identity.

origin), although we recognize that there may be considerable hetero-geneity within these broadly-defined groups in the process of cultural integration.

Using Swedish register data from 2005, nine cultural measures are defined and analysed; within region gender gaps in education, marriage to a foreign born, marriage to a co-national, marriage rates at age 25, cohabitation, divorce, partner age gaps, as well as female employment rates and female education levels. In addition, survey data on identity (self-assessed affiliation to home and host cultures) is provided for a cohort of students with immigrant backgrounds. Throughout the ana-lysis, natives are defined as those born in Sweden with two Swedish born parents, first-generation immigrants as the foreign born (categorized by country of birth into seven regional groups), and second-generation immigrants as those born in Sweden with at least one foreign born parent. Region of origin for second-generation immigrants is categor-ized according to parents' region of birth. For comparative purposes, two samples of second-generation immigrants are used in estimation. Initi-ally, estimations are based on the minority of second-generation immi-grants with two parents born in the *same* non-Swedish country of origin. Thereafter, a second round of estimations is carried out based on all second-generation immigrants, including the majority with mixed backgrounds. Region of origin for those with mixed backgrounds is based on the mother's country of birth or, when the mother is born in Sweden, on the father's country of birth.

Results indicate the following. Within region gender gaps in educa-tion are positive or insignificant for all groups, implying that females have more years of education or insignificant differences to men from the same region of origin. Positive (or insignificant) gender gaps in education are found for both first and second-generation immigrants. In terms of the propensity to marry a foreign-born person, first-genera-tion immigrants indicate a larger likelihood than natives of partnering with a foreign born but differences are reduced in the second generation for all groups except for those with Asian and African backgrounds, when both parents stem from the same country of origin. When esti-mation is based on all second-generation immigrants, differences in this type of marriage are significantly and considerably reduced for all groups. Similar results are found when marriage to a co-national is considered; first-generation immigrants are less likely than natives to marry co-nationals and this difference increases for second-generation immigrants, implying a higher likelihood of marrying outside the national group across immigrant generations. This is true for all sec-ond-generation immigrants except those with North/Central American or African backgrounds when both parents stem from the same country of origin. Again, when estimation is based on the full sample of second-generation immigrants, including those with mixed backgrounds, the likelihood of marrying co-nationals is reduced in the second generation for all groups.

Indeed, when estimation is based on the full sample of second-generation immigrants, all cultural measures including cohabitation, divorce, partner age gaps, and female employment rates, suggest a clear pattern of increased cultural integration in the second generation in comparison to the first generation, regardless of region of origin. When female levels of education are considered, first-generation immigrants are found to have greater years of education than natives. This difference is smaller, insignificant, or negative for second-generation immigrants (full sample), implying a convergence across immigrant generations to native levels of education. Taken together results in this study suggest that a process of cultural integration between immigrants and natives is occurring as initial differences between first-generation immigrants and natives on all cultural indicators are, with few exceptions, smaller or non-existent for second-generation immigrants.

This chapter continues in Section 6.2 with a short history of migration to Sweden and an overview of previous Swedish studies on cultural integration. This is followed in Section 6.3 with a description of the data. Results are presented in Section 6.4 and concluding remarks in Section 6.5.

6.2 Migration to Sweden and previous studies

Sweden has a large immigrant population as approximately 15 per cent of the working age population (16–64) today is foreign-born. In addition, another 12 per cent of the population has a foreign background, defined as being born in Sweden with at least one foreign-born parent. Since the end of the Second World War, Sweden has been characterized by net immigration, with three main sources of immigration. First, many immigrants come from other Nordic countries, primarily Finland, due to the common Nordic labour market established in 1954. A second source of migration was labour migration stemming from Southern and Eastern European countries during the 1950s and 1960s, when migration legislation was non-restrictive and aimed at attracting foreign labour to the then expanding manufacturing sector. Refugee migration is the third source of post Second World War migration, and, together with immigration due to family reunification, the largest source of migration to Sweden today. Refugee migration to Sweden stemmed from Hungary in the late 1950s, former Czechoslovakia in the late 1960s, Latin America, the Middle East, and Africa in the 1970s, former Yugoslavia (mainly Bosnia-Herzegovina) in the 1990s, and Iraq in the early 2000s. In 2005, the five largest immigrant groups in Sweden originated from Finland (15 per cent of the foreign-born population), Iraq (7 per cent), Yugoslavia (6 per cent), Iran (5 per cent), and Bosnia-Herzegovina (5 per cent). Today there is an increasing inflow from other EU countries due to the EU enlargement of 2004, during which Sweden was one of few countries that did not impose temporary restrictions on labour mobility. This has led to a large inflow of especially Polish immigrants in the last few years.

Before the mid-1970s, the foreign born in Sweden had slightly higher average employment levels than natives and similar income levels. This was especially true for female immigrants who had considerably higher labour force participation rates than female natives at the time. Since the mid-1970s, relative employment rates have dropped and a widening immigrant-native employment and income gap have developed over time. Numerous explanations have been forwarded for this shift in relative employment rates. Among these are structural changes in the industrial sector, with a shift away from manufacturing jobs, the changing composition of immigrants, the changing underlying motivation for migration, skill-based technological change promoting soft skills such as language and communication, and discrimination of increasingly 'visible' immigrants from predominantly non-European countries. It is important to note, however, that the shift in immigration in the mid-1970s from predominately labour migration to predominately refugee migration also lead to a shift in the skill composition of the foreign born, from relatively unskilled labour migration to relatively skilled refugee migration. Today, the proportion with tertiary educations is approximately the same in the native and foreign-born population, at roughly 30 per cent.[4]

Although labour market gaps between immigrants and natives have been studied intensively within economics, fewer studies have analysed cultural integration. Swedish studies include Åslund et al. (2008) on the impact of age at migration for cultural integration as measured by exposure to the foreign born. Immigration at an older age is found to increase the probability of living among, marrying, and working with other foreign born individuals. Studies on the intermarriage patterns of

---

[4] See Schröder (2007) for an overview of immigrant-native labour market gaps and integration policy in Sweden.

immigrants find that intermarriage to natives is lower among groups with non-Western origin (Behtoui, 2009) and that assortative mating in terms of national background is lower among second-generation immigrants in comparison to first-generation immigrants (Çelikaksoy *et al.*, 2009). Andersson (2004) and Andersson and Scott (2005) studied the fertility patterns of foreign born females in Sweden and found that most immigrant groups display higher levels of childbearing after immigration but that the determinants of first births are similar to that of natives, with one exception. Foreign-born women, unlike their native counterparts, are *less* likely to have a child while on welfare. A recent study on second-generation immigrants finds even smaller differences from the majority population in fertility patterns (Scott and Stanfors, 2009). Finally, two studies examine how identity (to home and host cultures) influences subsequent investment in higher education and, respectively, employment rates (Nekby and Rödin 2007; Nekby *et al.*, 2009). Results from these studies show that integrated men, that is, men that identify with both home and host cultures, are associated with higher probabilities of completed tertiary educations and have similar employment levels to men that identify only with the majority culture (assimilated).

6.3 Data and empirical set-up

6.3.1 *Data*

The data used in estimation stems from registered information at Statistics Sweden (SCB) on the entire working age population (16–65 years of age) residing in Sweden in 2005.[5] Included in the data is rich individual information on personal and demographic characteristics, education, employment, and income. In addition, detailed information is available on country of birth and migration dates for the foreign-born portion of the population, as well as parents' country of origin for the entire sample. Due to partner identification numbers, it is also possible to link individuals in partnerships. As such, detailed information is available not only on the main individual but also on partners, provided that partners fall within the given age restrictions.[6] Partnership is

---

[5] The data (Statistics on Immigrants—STATIV) was initially created by the Swedish Integration Board.
[6] Due to the age restrictions of the data, information on partners above the age of 65 is not available. It is possible, however, to identify the civil status of those with older spouses due to registered information on civil status.

defined as marriage, registered partnership for same sex couples, or cohabitation in a household with common children. Data on partnerships stems from information on households. To date, Statistics Sweden does not track cohabitants without children.

The original data from 2005 consist of 5,880,793 individuals. After dropping observations due to missing information on variables of interest, the sample used in estimation consists of 4,221,597 natives (Swedish born with two Swedish born parents) and 818,148 first generation-immigrants (foreign born).[7] Two samples of second-generation immigrants are defined and used in estimation, both departing from a basic definition of second-generation immigrant status as someone born in Sweden with at least one foreign born parent. The first sample is restricted to the 128,808 second-generation immigrants with homogenous national backgrounds, that is, second-generation immigrants with two parents stemming from the same (foreign) *country* of origin (23 per cent of all second-generation immigrants). The second sample consists of all second-generation immigrants including those with mixed backgrounds, in total 549,156 individuals. The majority of second-generation immigrants in Sweden therefore have mixed backgrounds with either one foreign born and one Swedish born parent (68 per cent of all second-generation immigrants) or two foreign born parents stemming from different non-Swedish countries of origin (8 per cent of all second-generation immigrants).[8]

Region of origin is classified according to a Statistics Sweden categorization into eight regions: Sweden, (other) Nordic countries, Western Europe (non-Nordic EU15), Eastern Europe (non-Nordic, Non-EU15), North/Central America, South America, Asia, and Africa. Table 6.1 shows the distribution of region of origin (own or parents) for first and second-generation immigrants in Sweden. In parentheses is the average duration of residence, measured in years, for the foreign born population.[9]

---

[7] In the data 186,839 observations are dropped due to missing values on variables of interest such as country of origin. This includes 134,961 individuals classified as second-generation immigrants with one Swedish born parent and one foreign-born parent but where information on the country of origin of the foreign-born parent is missing (20 per cent of the originally defined population of second-generation immigrants). In addition, 2816 persons stemming from Oceania are dropped from estimation due to the small size of this immigrant group.

[8] Included in the group with mixed backgrounds are individuals with one foreign-born parent and missing information on the other parent (1.8 per cent of all second-generation immigrants).

[9] Duration of residence is measured based on latest year of immigration and may be underestimated for frequent (registered) migrants.

Table 6.1 Region of origin (and duration of residence)—second-generation immigrants with parents from the same country of origin.

Region of origin	Native	First generation (duration of residence)	Second generation: parents same origin	Second generation: full sample
Sweden	100	—	—	
Nordic	—	22.3 (28.5)	51.9	55.1
West Europe (EU15)	—	8.1 (20.8)	8.2	16.3
East Europe	—	24.0 (16.2)	20.0	14.3
North/Central America	—	2.1 (16.0)	0.1	2.8
South America	—	6.0 (18.2)	2.7	1.9
Asia	—	31.1 (14.6)	15.0	7.6
Africa	—	6.5 (13.6)	2.0	1.9
No. of observations	4,221,597	818,148	128,808	549,156

6.3.2 Empirical set-up

Differences in various measures of cultural integration (described further below) between natives and first or second-generation immigrants are estimated using two basic specifications. The first specification estimates differences between natives and first or second-generation immigrants from different regions of origin controlling, where relevant, for gender, level of education (six levels), and age (quadratic). The second specification, used in estimation of female employment rates and female education levels, compares differences between natives and two age cohorts of immigrants (younger than thirty and thirty plus) for each immigrant generation and region.

As the analysis is based on cross-section data for 2005, estimations provide a static picture of differences between natives and two generations of immigrants from the same region of origin. Note that first-generation immigrants today are likely to differ in many respects to the parents of second-generation immigrants today, for example concerning reasons for migration, the distribution of source countries, and the economic conditions in the host country at immigration, all of which may influence cultural integration. To fully capture the process of integration, it is necessary to study the intergenerational transmission of cultural measures or follow individuals over time. Such data is not available at present. Nonetheless, estimated differences between natives and immigrants can give an indication of the degree to which cultural integration has occurred today across immigrant generations in Sweden.

The measures used to exemplify social integration in this study are the following:

1. *Within-region gender gaps in education*—education is regressed on a female dummy variable for each region of origin and separately for natives, first-generation and second-generation immigrants. Two measures of education are used; 'age left full time education' and 'university graduate'. 'Age left full time education' is a proxy for years of education and is defined as the age at which individuals graduate from their highest registered level of education. There are two potential drawbacks with this measure. Information on year of graduation is missing for 29 per cent of the sample, partially due to fact that among first-generation immigrants educations may have been acquired prior to immigration.[10] The foreign born may also be forced to validate foreign degrees or comply with Swedish-specific educational requirements for certain occupations, implying more years of education but not necessarily higher levels of education. As such, the probability of being university educated is also estimated based on register information on highest completed level of education. University educated is defined as a dummy variable equal to 1 if an individual is registered as having completed a university education, and 0 otherwise.

2. *Marriage to a foreign born*—this type of marriage is defined as a dummy variable equal to 1 if an individual is partnered with, that is, married, in a registered partnership, or cohabitant with children in common, to a partner that is born abroad, and 0 otherwise.

3. *Marriage to a co-national*—this type of marriage is defined as a dummy variable equal to 1 if an individual is in a partnership with a co-national or a second-generation immigrant with the same national background, and 0 otherwise. For natives, this implies a partnership with someone born in Sweden with two Swedish-born parents. For the foreign born, marriage to a co-national is a partnership with a foreign-born individual from the same country of origin or to a second-generation immigrant with a parent from the same country of origin. For second-generation immigrants, this type of marriage is defined as a partnership with someone born in the same country of origin as a foreign born parent or a partnership with another second-generation immigrant with a similar (foreign) national background.

[10] Broken down by immigrant status, year of graduation is missing for 26 per cent of natives, 50 per cent of first-generation immigrants, and 15 per cent of second-generation immigrants (full sample).

4. *Young marriage*—young marriage is defined as a dummy variable equal to 1 if age at first marriage is less than or equal to 25, and 0 otherwise. Note that marriage dates are registered only for those who change their civil status in Sweden. This implies that there is no information on date of marriage for the foreign born who married prior to immigration. For these individuals, only subsequent changes of civil status, after immigration, are registered. As such, native-immigrant gaps in young marriage rates are considered only for natives and second-generation immigrants.

5. *Cohabitation rates*—cohabitation is defined as a dummy variable equal to 1 if a non-married individual is registered as living in the same household with a partner where there are children in common, that is, both partners are legal parents to at least one child in the household, and 0 otherwise. No information is available on cohabiting couples without children.

6. *Divorce rates*—divorce is defined as a dummy variable equal to 1 if the individual is registered as divorced in the year 2005, and 0 otherwise.

7. *Partner age gaps*—partner age gaps are defined as the absolute value of the age difference between partners (current unions).

8. *Female employment rates*—employment is defined as a dummy variable equal to 1 if individuals are registered as employed during a measurement week in November, and 0 otherwise.

9. *Female education levels*—education is defined as above using two measures, a proxy for years of education (age left full-time education) and university educated.

Descriptive statistics are shown in Table 6.2. Sample means suggest that differences between natives and especially second-generation immigrants on a number of cultural indicators such as young marriage, cohabitation, divorce, and partner age gaps are small or non-existent (regardless of which sample of second-generation immigrants is considered). For other indicators such as marriage to a foreign born and marriage to co-nationals, although differences between natives and second-generation immigrants remain pronounced, especially for those with homogenous national backgrounds, these gaps are considerably smaller than those found between natives and first-generation immigrants, suggesting a pattern of integration across immigrant generations. A higher proportion of individuals marrying a foreign-born person/co-national found for second-generation immigrants with

Table 6.2 Descriptive statistics by immigrant status (2005).

	Natives	First generation	Second generation— parents same origin	Second generation— full sample
Social indicators:				
Age left ft education	24.4 (F)	25.6 (F)	21.6 (F)	23.9 (F)
	22.4 (M)	24.5 (M)	20.6 (M)	22.1 (M)
Marriage to foreign born	2.7	24.5	7.2	3.8
	(5.7)	(46.9)	(19.9)	(9.4)
Marriage to a co-national	39.7	28.7	7.3	2.7
	(82.7)	(55.0)	(20.0)	(6.7)
Young marriage	13.7	—	14.2	13.0
Cohabitation	12.1	6.9	12.3	11.1
	(22.4)	(12.3)	(28.6)	(23.8)
Divorce	10.0	17.1	7.1	10.8
Partner age gap	3.3	5.0	3.5	3.5
Female employment rate	73.2	53.8	63.0	66.8
Economic indicators:				
Log income	7.35	7.06	7.09	7.23
Employment	74.8	55.4	63.8	67.7
Other characteristics:				
Level of education:				
Short compulsory	4.8	11.8	0.9	4.1
Compulsory	16.0	14.9	24.7	19.5
Secondary	47.6	41.2	49.4	47.6
Short tertiary	6.3	5.1	6.9	6.6
University	24.5	25.4	17.6	21.6
PhD	0.7	1.6	0.5	0.7
Female	49,0	51.2	48.7	49.0
Age	40.8	41.1	32.2	38.8
% ≥thirty (age)	74.1	77.8	55.0	62.9
Duration of residence (years)	—	18.8	—	—
No. of observations	4,221,597	818,148	128,808	674,732

Note: In parentheses, percentage of those in partnerships (married, cohabitation with children in common, registered partnerships).

homogenous backgrounds (parents from the same foreign country of origin) in comparison to second-generation immigrants with mixed backgrounds is consistent with theories suggesting a relatively stronger emphasis on ethnic (or national) group belonging as a basis for partnership choice in homogenous families, all else equal. This may be a consequence of higher social and psychological costs for children who marry outside the ethnic group in these families.

The economic indicators show that employment and income gaps between natives and second-generation immigrants are smaller in comparison to the gaps between natives and first-generation immigrants. Economic integration across immigrant generation is, however, weaker for second-generation immigrants with homogenous national backgrounds. Note that as mean age as well as the distribution of education and region of origin varies by immigrant status (first or second generation), it is important to control for these differences in estimation of cultural integration.

6.4 Results

6.4.1 *Within-region gender gaps in education*

Gender gaps in education are estimated separately by region, immigrant status, and age cohort (less than 30 and 30–65). Table 6.3 reports the estimated coefficient for the female dummy variable in each of these education equations, that is, the estimated differences in education for females in comparison to males within each region of origin and age group. Results show that females are more educated than men in all groups, with the exception of first-generation immigrants stemming from Africa (insignificant gender differences in education in both age cohorts) and, in the sample of second-generation immigrants with homogenous backgrounds, older second-generation immigrants from North/Central America, South America, and Africa (insignificant gender differences in education).[11] Significantly higher years of education for females are, however, found for all regions in the full sample of second-generation immigrants.

Gender gaps in education are re-estimated using a second measure of education, a dummy variable for completed university educations. Results shown in Table 6.4 largely confirm significantly higher levels of education for women in most groups. The exceptions are first-generation African women (both age cohorts) and Asian/Middle Eastern women (older cohort) where females are associated with significantly lower university probabilities than men. This pattern is reversed among second-generation immigrants. A significantly higher probability of females being university educated in comparison to men is found for all origin groups and both age cohorts in the full sample of second-generation immigrants.

Both measures of education therefore suggest that females are more highly educated than men from the same region of origin and age

---

[11] Note that sample sizes are small for older second-generation immigrants with homogenous national backgrounds. Only 30 individuals with North American backgrounds are 30 years or older and have parents stemming from the same country of origin and only 80 individuals with South American backgrounds.

183

Table 6.3 Within region gender gaps in age left full-time education, by region of origin and age cohort.

Age-cohort	Native	Nordic	West European	East European	North/Central America	South America	Asia	Africa
<30	0.433*** (0.005)	—	—	—	—	—	—	—
30–65	2.262*** (0.010)	—	—	—	—	—	—	—
First generation								
<30	—	0.760*** (0.059)	0.189*** (0.067)	0.501*** (0.024)	0.449*** (0.098)	0.386*** (0.049)	0.255*** (0.022)	0.048 (0.051)
30–65	—	2.681*** (0.056)	1.501*** (0.107)	1.587*** (0.068)	0.494*** (0.187)	0.362*** (0.116)	0.123** (0.059)	0.029 (0.136)
Second generation—parents from the same country of origin								
<30	—	0.530*** (0.022)	0.386*** (0.110)	0.349*** (0.048)	0.189*** (0.100)	0.261*** (0.073)	0.318*** (0.032)	0.283*** (0.078)
30–65	—	2.125*** (0.069)	1.757*** (0.174)	0.934*** (0.122)	-2.368 (3.059)	0.566 (1.202)	1.527*** (0.349)	1.174 (0.828)
Second generation—full sample								
<30	—	0.425*** (0.017)	0.399*** (0.033)	0.390*** (0.029)	0.337*** (0.069)	0.339*** (0.046)	0.285*** (0.024)	0.333*** (0.052)
30–65	—	2.275*** (0.036)	1.730*** (0.062)	1.425*** (0.070)	1.944*** (0.188)	0.777** (0.354)	1.654*** (0.163)	0.862*** (0.256)

Reported coefficients are for a female dummy variable in separate OLS estimation, within each age cohort and region of origin, on age left full-time education. Included in estimation are controls for age (quadratic). Robust standard errors in parentheses.

Table 6.4 Within region gender gaps in university education, by region of origin and age cohort.

Age-cohort	Native	Nordic	West European	East European	North/Central America	South America	Asia/Middle East	Africa
<30	0.061***	—	—	—	—	—	—	—
	(0.007)							
30–65	0.101***	—	—	—	—	—	—	—
	(0.001)							
First generation								
<30	—	0.107***	0.060***	0.094***	0.071***	0.052***	0.035***	-0.018***
		(0.007)	(0.009)	(0.003)	(0.013)	(0.006)	(0.003)	(0.005)
30–65	—	0.097***	0.042***	0.054***	0.016*	0.045***	-0.007***	-0.076***
		(0.002)	(0.004)	(0.002)	(0.009)	(0.005)	(0.002)	(0.005)
Second generation—parents from the same country of origin								
<30	—	0.060***	0.043***	0.047***	-0.034	0.020**	0.025***	0.036***
		(0.004)	(0.014)	(0.006)	(0.026)	(0.008)	(0.004)	(0.010)
30–65	—	0.101***	0.097***	0.056***	-0.076	0.107	0.071***	0.111*
		(0.004)	(0.010)	(0.008)	(0.204)	(0.111)	(0.019)	(0.063)
Second generation—full sample								
<30	—	0.052***	0.050***	0.047***	0.027***	0.034***	0.023***	0.039***
		(0.002)	(0.004)	(0.004)	(0.009)	(0.006)	(0.003)	(0.006)
30–65	—	0.100***	0.085***	0.074***	0.096***	0.059**	0.077***	0.088***
		(0.002)	(0.004)	(0.004)	(0.009)	(0.025)	(0.010)	(0.019)

Note: Reported coefficients are for a female dummy variable in separate estimations, for each age cohort and region of origin, on the probability of being university educated, based on register information on highest level of completed education. Included in estimation are controls for age (quadratic). Robust standard errors in parentheses.

group. Deviations from this pattern, for example in terms of relatively lower levels of higher education for Asian and African first-generation females, are reversed in the second generation and approach the native norm of positive gender gaps in education. Results therefore suggest that a process of cultural integration in gender norms concerning education is occurring.

6.4.2 Marriage patterns

The extent of assortative mating in society, based on immigrant status or national background, is an interesting measure of cultural integration as marriage markets reflect the degree of openness between social groups. If, for example, social or economic boundaries between ethnic or national groups are strong due to residential or workplace segregation, a high degree of assortative mating within ethnic/national groups may prevail, reinforcing social and economic differences between natives and immigrants across generations. As such, marriage gaps between natives and immigrants are analysed for a broad range of marriage patterns (marriage to a foreign born, marriage to a co-national, young marriage, cohabitation, divorce, and partner age gaps). Estimations of native-immigrant differences in marriage patterns are based on individuals thirty years or older in order to mitigate censoring problems or selection effects. With the exception of young marriage, estimations are also based on current unions. In general, parental pressure is thought to be lower in higher order partnerships implying, for example, that rates of intermarriage may be larger for those in second (or higher order) partnerships. Unfortunately, we are unable to control for this in estimation.

6.4.3 Marriage to a foreign born

Results of linear probability models estimating the probability of marrying or partnering with a foreign-born person are presented in Table 6.5. As expected, first-generation immigrants are significantly more likely than natives to be partnered with someone who is also born abroad. This is partially due to the fact that spouses immigrate together. Nearly 40 per cent of immigrants that have foreign-born partners migrated to Sweden within two years of each other, suggesting that they were married before immigration to Sweden. First-generation immigrants from the Nordic countries, West Europe, and North/Central America are associated with approximately 30–45 percentage point higher probabilities than natives of partnering with a foreign-born person, while

Table 6.5 International marriage (thirty plus age group).

	First generation	Second generation—parents same origin	Second generation—full sample
Native with native parents	Ref.	Ref.	Ref.
Nordic	0.315***	0.032***	0.015***
	(0.001)	(0.001)	(0.001)
West Europe	0.414***	0.048***	0.015***
	(0.002)	(0.003)	(0.001)
East Europe	0.186***	0.101***	0.040***
	(0.001)	(0.003)	(0.001)
North/Central America	0.459***	0.025	0.007***
	(0.004)	(0.046)	(0.002)
South America	0.234***	0.033	0.028***
	(0.002)	(0.030)	(0.006)
Asia	0.179***	0.230***	0.059***
	(0.001)	(0.010)	(0.003)
Africa	0.188***	0.180***	0.028***
	(0.002)	(0.028)	(0.005)
No. of observations		3,837,395	4,111,711
R^2		0.139	0.132
Controls		Age (quadratic), education, gender	

Note: Linear probability model estimating the probability of marrying a foreign born. Number of observations varies as estimation is done separately for two different samples of second generation together with the same sample of natives and first-generation immigrants. Robust standard errors in parentheses.

those from Eastern Europe, North/Central America, Asia, and Africa indicate a lower, but still positive probability at approximately 18 percentage points.

Differences between natives and second-generation immigrants in the probability of marrying a foreign born are generally smaller than those noted between natives and first-generation immigrants. This is true for all second-generation immigrants except those with homogenous national backgrounds stemming from Asian or African countries.[12] Results for these groups therefore suggest a lack of cultural integration to natives across immigrant generations as the likelihood of marrying a foreign born does not abate across generations. Note, however, that this result is heavily contingent on having a homogenous foreign national background.[13] When estimation is based on all second-generation

[12] Differences between natives and second-generation immigrants with homogenous backgrounds stemming from South and North/Central America are insignificant, but sample sizes are small.
[13] No reduction in the propensity to marry a foreign born between first and second-generation immigrants with homogenous backgrounds in comparison to natives is

Table 6.6 Intra-national marriage (thirty plus age group).

	First generation	Second generation— parents same origin	Second generation—full sample
Native with native parents	Ref.	Ref.	Ref.
Nordic	−0.299***	−0.426***	−0.464***
	(0.001)	(0.001)	(0.001)
West Europe	−0.362***	−0.458***	−0.496***
	(0.002)	(0.003)	(0.001)
East Europe	−0.088***	−0.397***	−0.469***
	(0.001)	(0.002)	(0.001)
North/Central America	−0.439***	−0.472***	−0.503***
	(0.002)	(0.003)	(0.001)
South America	−0.265***	−0.398***	−0.474***
	(0.002)	(0.035)	(0.004)
Asia	−0.048***	−0.252***	−0.447***
	(0.001)	(0.026)	(0.026)
Africa	−0.211***	−0.299***	−0.469***
	(0.002)	(0.010)	(0.003)
No. of observations		3,846,049	4,111,711
R^2		0.139	0.094
Controls		Age (quadratic), education, gender	

Note: Linear probability model estimating the probability of marrying co-nationals, defined as a partnership with someone from the same country of origin (own or parents). Number of observations varies as estimation is done separately for two different samples of second generation together with the same sample of natives and first-generation immigrants. Robust standard errors in parentheses.

immigrants, a clear reduction in the propensity to marry a foreign born is noted even for those with Asian and African backgrounds.

Results so far highlight the importance of considering not only the selected sample of second-generation immigrants with parents from the same country of origin, but also the majority of second-generation immigrants with mixed backgrounds. The few indications of a lack of cultural integration across immigrant generations found for some groups in the sub-sample of second-generation immigrants with homogenous backgrounds disappears when the full sample of second-generation immigrants is considered.

6.4.4 Marriage to a co-national

Results of linear probability models estimating the probability of marrying a co-national are shown in Table 6.6. As expected, due to the high propensity of natives to partner with other natives, both first and

consistent with theories suggesting a higher relative focus on ethnicity/nationality as a basis for marital choice in these families compared to families with mixed backgrounds.

second-generation immigrants are associated with significantly lower probabilities of marrying co-nationals than natives. Differences between natives and immigrants are generally larger for second-generation immigrants in comparison to first-generation immigrants, implying a significant decline in the propensity to marry co-nationals across immigrant generations. Differences between first-generation immigrants and second-generation immigrants with homogenous foreign backgrounds are insignificant for those stemming from North/Central America and Africa, but become large and significant in the full sample of second-generation immigrants. A significantly lower propensity to marry co-nationals in the second generation suggests that the social/cultural boundaries between ethnic groups in Sweden are declining across immigrant generations.

6.4.5 *Young marriages*

Another measure of cultural integration concerns the probability of marrying young, that is, before (or while) the age of 25. Date of marriage is registered only for those who change their civil status in Sweden. Date of first marriage for first-generation immigration is therefore missing for those that married prior to arrival in Sweden. The discussion here therefore focuses on differences in the propensity to marry young between natives and second-generation immigrants only.

Results from linear probability models on young marriage are reported in Table 6.7. Results for the selected sample of second-generation immigrants with homogenous backgrounds indicate that those with origins in Western Europe, Eastern Europe, Asia, and Africa are associated with higher probabilities of young marriage than natives. Differences are largest for those with Asian backgrounds, with a 15.6 percentage point higher relative probability of young marriage in comparison to natives. No gaps in young marriage probabilities are found between natives and second-generation immigrants with Nordic backgrounds and only weakly significant differences between natives and those with South and North/Central America backgrounds.

Results of estimation on the full sample of second-generation immigrants show that second-generation immigrants with a background in the Nordic countries, Western Europe, South America, and North/Central America are associated with similar or slight lower, but significant, young marriage probabilities in comparison to natives. Those with Asian and African backgrounds continue to show significantly higher relative probabilities of marrying young, but at considerably smaller levels than those reported for the selected sample of second-generation

Table 6.7 Young marriage (thirty plus age group).

	First generation	Second generation—parents same origin	Second generation—full sample
Native with native parents	Ref.	Ref.	Ref.
Nordic	NA	−0.002	−0.006***
		(0.002)	(0.001)
West Europe	NA	0.012***	−0.016***
		(0.004)	(0.001)
East Europe	NA	0.058***	0.009***
		(0.003)	(0.002)
North/Central America	NA	−0.087*	−0.001
		(0.045)	(0.004)
South America	NA	0.046*	−0.016*
		(0.028)	(0.008)
Asia/Middle East	NA	0.156***	0.025***
		(0.010)	(0.003)
Africa	NA	0.089***	0.013**
		(0.023)	(0.006)
No. of observations		3,200,474	3,474,663
R^2		0.058	0.057
Controls	Age (quadratic), education, gender		

Note: Linear probability model on young marriage defined as marriage before on or before the age of 25. Number of observations varies as estimation is done separately for two different samples of second generation together with the same sample of natives and first-generation immigrants. Robust standard errors in parentheses.

immigrants with homogenous backgrounds. In the full sample, second-generation immigrants with Asian backgrounds are associated with only a 2.5 percentage point higher probability of young marriage and those with African backgrounds with a 1.3 percentage point higher probability.

6.4.6 Cohabitation

Cohabitation without formal marriage is a relatively common phenomenon in Sweden. Eleven per cent of the working age population today is registered as cohabiting in comparison to 40 per cent who are registered as married. Registered information on cohabitation is based on household information and available only for those cohabitants that have children in common, meaning that we miss cohabitants without children. Nonetheless, cohabitation is a recognized legal union for couples that live together on a permanent basis even for those without children. Sweden and Denmark are often seen as the forerunners of this type of household constellation. Even in the early 1960s, cohabitation had become socially acceptable as a type of trial marriage. By 1975, the social

Table 6.8 Cohabitation (thirty plus age group).

	First generation	Second generation—parents same origin	Second generation—full sample
Native with native parents	Ref.	Ref.	Ref.
Nordic	−0.013***	−0.004***	−0.004***
	(0.001)	(0.002)	(0.001)
West Europe	−0.040***	−0.052***	−0.023***
	(0.001)	(0.004)	(0.001)
East Europe	−0.067***	−0.051***	−0.028***
	(0.001)	(0.003)	(0.002)
North/Central America	−0.069***	−0.133***	−0.022***
	(0.002)	(0.037)	(0.003)
South America	−0.033***	−0.102***	−0.040***
	(0.002)	(0.039)	(0.008)
Asia	−0.104***	−0.110***	−0.048***
	(0.001)	(0.006)	(0.003)
Africa	−0.094***	−0.153***	−0.071***
	(0.001)	(0.018)	(0.018)
No. of observations		3,837,395	4,111,711
R^2		0.058	0.056
Controls	Age (quadratic), education, gender		

Note: Linear probability model on cohabitation defined for cohabitants with children in common. No. of observations varies as estimation is done separately for two different samples of second generation together with the same sample of natives and first-generation immigrants. Robust standard errors in parentheses.

pressure for cohabiting couples to marry was relaxed and cohabitation became an accepted alternative to marriage. This family type is, however, less common in non-Nordic countries, especially for couples with children, suggesting that cohabitation can be an interesting measure of cultural integration between immigrants and natives in Sweden.

Results from linear probability models on cohabitation are shown in Table 6.8. Differences between natives and immigrants are surprisingly small for both first and second-generation immigrants. Among first-generation immigrants, this is partially a reflection of higher marriage propensities rather than cohabitation in comparison to natives.[14] The largest difference between natives and first-generation immigrants is found for those born in an Asian country (10.4 percentage point lower

[14] See Table 6.9 for an analysis of differences in marital status between natives and first and second-generation immigrants. A multinomial logit model on four civil status categories is estimated: single, married/registered partner, cohabitant, and divorced. With the exception of first-generation immigrants from the Nordic countries, all first-generation immigrants are more likely, in comparison to natives, to be married than single. These estimations also confirm lower relative propensities to cohabit among first-generation immigrants.

probability).[15] Second-generation immigrants are in some cases found to be even less likely than first-generation immigrants to cohabit (in comparison to natives) suggesting a lack of cultural integration across immigrant generations in this dimension. This is true for second-generation immigrants with homogenous national backgrounds stemming from countries in South and North/Central America, as well as Africa. For these two groups, lower propensities to cohabit do not stem from higher relative marriage propensities (as shown in Table 6.9).

When estimation is based on all second-generation immigrants, including those with mixed backgrounds, although point estimates continue to show significantly lower likelihoods of cohabitation for all region of origin groups in comparison to natives, coefficient estimates are smaller than those found for first-generation immigrants (with the exception of South Americans). Similar results are found when estimation takes into account numerous civil status categories via a multinomial logit analysis (see Table 6.9). Results suggest that a process of cultural integration in terms of cohabitation is occurring across immigrant generations for the majority of immigrants in Sweden.

6.4.7 Divorce

Based on registered information on current civil status, the probability of being divorced is estimated with linear probability models. Results, reported in Table 6.10, show that both first and second-generation immigrants are associated with higher divorce rates than natives.[16] Divorce gaps between natives and first-generation immigrants are highest for those stemming from countries in North/Central America and Africa (approximately 16 percentage points higher than natives).[17] Among second-generation immigrants, divorce gaps are highest for second-generation immigrants with homogeneous backgrounds stemming from an African country (9.7 percentage points higher). In the full sample of second-generation immigrants, differences between regions are small; a positive divorce gap of approximately two percentage points is found for all regions (except North/Central America). As differences between

---

[15] Asian first-generation immigrants also have the highest relative probability of being married rather than single in comparison to natives (see Table 6.9).

[16] Second-generation immigrants with backgrounds in a North/Central America country do not differ from natives in divorce propensities.

[17] Estimation allowing for different civil status states (see Table 6.9) confirms that first-generation immigrants are more likely to be divorced than single in comparison to natives, regardless of region of origin. This difference is smaller for second-generation immigrants, with the exception of second-generation immigrants with African backgrounds who have similar divorce propensities to first-generation immigrants stemming from African countries.

Table 6.9 Multinomial logit estimation of marital status (single, marriage, cohabitation, divorce), reference category: single.

	First generation	Second generation—parents same origin	Second generation—full sample
		Marriage	
Native with native parents	Ref.	Ref.	Ref.
Nordic	−0.217***	−0.236***	−0.230***
	(0.007)	(0.011)	(0.006)
	[−0.061]	[−0.056]	[−0.052]
West Europe	0.220***	−0.084***	−0.171***
	(0.011)	(0.027)	(0.010)
	[0.034]	[−0.007]	[−0.033]
East Europe	0.972***	−0.006	−0.181***
	(0.009)	(0.021)	(0.011)
	[0.111]	[0.002]	[−0.032]
South America	0.296***	−0.041	−0.080***
	(0.023)	(0.438)	(0.024)
	[0.017]	[0.008]	[−0.001]
North/Central America	0.197***	−0.893***	−0.368***
	(0.015)	(0.291)	(0.057)
	[−0.054]	[−0.210]	[−0.068]
Asia	1.260***	0.504***	−0.120***
	(0.008)	(0.061)	(0.023)
	[0.160]	[0.091]	[−0.016]
Africa	0.921***	0.045	−0.391***
	(0.015)	(0.154)	(0.043)
	[0.034]	[−0.078]	[−0.066]
		Cohabitation	
Native with native parents	Ref.	Ref.	Ref.
Nordic	−0.211***	−0.171***	−0.158***
	(0.010)	(0.014)	(0.007)
	[−0.010]	[−0.004]	[−0.003]
West Europe	−0.307***	−0.507***	−0.291***
	(0.018)	(0.040)	(0.013)
	[−0.036]	[−0.033]	[−0.016]
East Europe	−0.074***	−0.426***	−0.331***
	(0.013)	(0.029)	(0.015)
	[−0.057]	[−0.032]	[−0.018]
South America	−0.506***	−1.765*	−0.302***
	(0.037)	(1.060)	(0.039)
	[−0.052]	[−0.077]	[−0.019]
North/Central America	−0.057***	−0.863***	−0.462***
	(0.020)	(0.333)	(0.076)
	[−0.029]	[−0.034]	[−0.019]
Asia	−0.321***	−0.848***	−0.492***
	(0.013)	(0.099)	(0.033)
	[−0.074]	[−0.066]	[−0.032]
Africa	−0.254***	−1.142	−0.716
	(0.023)	(0.263)	(0.059)
	[−0.065]	[−0.069]	[−0.035]

(*continued*)

Table 6.9 Continued

	First generation	Second generation—parents same origin	Second generation—full sample
		Divorce	
Native with native parents	Ref.	Ref.	Ref.
Nordic	0.228***	0.072***	0.034***
	(0.008)	(0.017)	(0.008)
	[0.046]	[0.027]	[0.022]
West Europe	0.419***	0.108***	0.062***
	(0.015)	(0.041)	(0.015)
	[0.036]	[0.024]	[0.022]
East Europe	1.282***	0.199***	0.026
	(0.010)	(0.031)	(0.016)
	[0.076]	[0.028]	[0.019]
South America	0.822***	0.323	−0.068**
	(0.030)	(0.622)	(0.033)
	[0.090]	[0.056]	[0.001]
North/Central America	1.083***	0.288	−0.048
	(0.018)	(0.461)	(0.096)
	[0.143]	[0.125]	[0.025]
Asia	1.446***	0.652***	0.100***
	(0.010)	(0.090)	(0.034)
	[0.066]	[0.042]	[0.025]
Africa	1.732***	1.131***	−0.033
	(0.018)	(0.230)	(0.075)
	[0.166]	[0.188]	[0.031]
No. of observations		3,837,395	4,111,584
Pseudo R^2		0.070	0.070
Controls		Age, education, gender	

Note: Robust standard errors in parentheses. Marginal effects in square brackets.

natives and immigrants diminish across immigrant generations, results suggest that a process of cultural integration in divorce norms is occurring. See also Table 6.9.

6.4.8 Partner age gaps

On average, natives differ in age from their partners by 3.3 years, first-generation immigrants by 5 years and second-generation immigrants by 3.5 years. Results from OLS estimation on partner age gaps controlling for differences in age, education, and gender are shown in Table 6.11. As expected, first-generation immigrants tend to have larger age gaps between partners than natives, with as much as four years for those born in an African country. In the second generation, relative differences between natives and immigrants are much reduced for all groups

Table 6.10 Divorce (thirty plus age group).

	First generation	Second generation—parents same origin	Second generation—full sample
Native with native parents	Ref.	Ref.	Ref.
Nordic	0.059***	0.019***	0.020***
	(0.001)	(0.001)	(0.001)
West Europe	0.042***	0.020***	0.020***
	(0.002)	(0.004)	(0.001)
East Europe	0.092***	0.028***	0.020***
	(0.001)	(0.003)	(0.001)
North/Central America	0.088***	0.039	0.001
	(0.003)	(0.060)	(0.003)
South America	0.163***	0.043*	0.023***
	(0.002)	(0.026)	(0.007)
Asia	0.077***	0.040***	0.025***
	(0.001)	(0.008)	(0.003)
Africa	0.165***	0.097***	0.023***
	(0.002)	(0.023)	(0.005)
No. of observations		3,837,395	4,111,711
R^2		0.039	0.039
Controls	Age (quadratic), education, gender		

Note: Linear probability models on divorce. Number of observations varies as estimation is done separately for two different samples of second generation together with the same sample of natives and first-generation immigrants. Robust standard errors in parentheses.

in comparison to first-generation levels, especially when considering the full sample of second-generation immigrants.

6.4.9 Female employment rates

As noted earlier, unlike cultural integration, the economic integration of immigrants and natives in Sweden has been widely researched. The consensus in this literature is that employment gaps with natives are larger than wage gaps. Due to widespread unionization and collective agreements that also cover non-union members, the scope for wage discrimination in Sweden is relatively small. Another interesting fact is that native-immigrant wage gaps are smaller among females than males (le Grand and Szulkin, 2002). Any decline in employment gaps between native and immigrant females across immigrant generations should be interpreted as a sign of economic and cultural integration as female immigrants may have different initial norms concerning the trade-off between home and labour market production.[18]

[18] See also estimation of female, native-immigrant income gaps reported in Table 6.12.

Table 6.11 Partner age gaps (thirty plus age group).

	First generation	Second generation—parents same origin	Second generation—full sample
Native with native parents	Ref.	Ref.	Ref.
Nordic	0.391***	0.179***	0.198***
	(0.012)	(0.020)	(0.010)
West Europe	1.040 ***	0.382***	0.214***
	(0.022)	(0.052)	(0.018)
East Europe	1.369***	0.182***	0.140***
	(0.014)	(0.035)	(0.019)
North/Central America	1.254***	1.034*	0.080**
	(0.050)	(0.544)	(0.039)
South America	1.519***	0.208	0.123
	(0.035)	(0.569)	(0.108)
Asia	2.615***	0.248***	0.294***
	(0.014)	(0.091)	(0.043)
Africa	4.009***	1.306***	0.293***
	(0.040)	(0.350)	(0.087)
No. of observations		2,335,102	2,490,230
R^2		0.054	0.051
Controls		Age (quadratic), education, gender	

Note: OLS estimations on partner age gaps defined as the absolute value of partner age differences. Number of observations varies as estimation is done separately for two different samples of second generation together with the same sample of natives and first-generation immigrants. Robust standard errors in parentheses.

Results from linear probability models on employment comparing female natives with first and second-generation female immigrants are shown in Table 6.13. Three specifications are shown, for the entire sample as well as for two age cohorts of immigrants (younger than 30 and 30 plus). Throughout, the reference group is working age female natives (16–65). Results for the full sample (column 1), indicate that there is a significant employment gap between natives and immigrants (both generations). In comparison to first-generation immigrants, employment gaps for second-generation immigrants are significantly smaller, suggesting both cultural and economic integration across immigrant generations. A comparison of the two age cohorts of female immigrants shows that employment gaps are largest for first-generation immigrants in the older age group.

There are a number of potential explanations for larger employment gaps among older, female first-generation immigrants. First, older first-generation immigrants have a higher age at immigration. In the older age group the average age at arrival is 25 years, while in the younger age group the average age at arrival is 13 years. Numerous studies examining the impact of age at migration have shown that a higher age at arrival

Table 6.12 Female income levels (dependent variable: log income).

	All	Immigrants under thirty	Immigrants thirty plus
Natives with native parents (16–65)	Ref.	Ref.	Ref.
First generation			
Nordic	−0.073***	−0.010	0.081***
	(0.004)	(0.018)	(0.004)
West Europe	−0.240***	−0.213***	−0.247***
	(0.009)	(0.025)	(0.009)
East Europe	−0.304***	−0.185***	−0.341***
	(0.004)	(0.010)	(0.004)
South America	−0.367***	−0.342***	−0.377***
	(0.016)	(0.038)	(0.018)
North/Central America	−0.301***	−0.148***	−0.362***
	(0.009)	(0.018)	(0.010)
Asia	−0.499***	−0.300***	−0.593***
	(0.004)	(0.008)	(0.005)
Africa	−0.442***	−0.271***	−0.510***
	(0.010)	(0.019)	(0.011)
Second generation—parents from the same country of origin			
Nordic	−0.008	0.189***	−0.071***
	(0.006)	(0.013)	(0.006)
West Europe	−0.062***	0.006	−0.081***
	(0.016)	(0.041)	(0.017)
East Europe	−0.006	−0.023	0.014
	(0.016)	(0.020)	(0.012)
South America	−0.780***	−1.068***	0.065
	(0.197)	(0.247)	(0.161)
North/Central America	−0.310***	−0.292***	−0.077
	(0.039)	(0.040)	(0.191)
Asia	−0.182***	−0.182***	−0.038
	(0.017)	(0.018)	(0.036)
Africa	−0.317***	−0.309***	0.168
	(0.046)	(0.048)	(0.141)
No. of Observations	2,165,447	1,897,776	2,078,301
R^2	0.326	0.360	0.312
Second generation—full sample			
Nordic	−0.038***	0.089***	−0.078***
	(0.003)	(0.006)	(0.003)
West Europe	−0.052***	−0.001	−0.064***
	(0.005)	(0.012)	(0.006)
East Europe	−0.035***	−0.027**	−0.027***
	(0.006)	(0.012)	(0.006)
South America	−0.095***	−0.260***	−0.034***
	(0.013)	(0.031)	(0.014)
North/Central America	−0.213***	−0.213***	−0.072*
	(0.020)	(0.023)	(0.038)

(continued)

Table 6.12 Continued

	All	Immigrants under thirty	Immigrants thirty plus
Asia	−0.159***	−0.167***	−0.079***
	(0.010)	(0.013)	(0.014)
Africa	−0.181***	−0.212***	−0.031
	(0.019)	(0.023)	(0.029)
No. of observations	2,341,251	1,954,290	2,197,591
R^2	0.330	0.371	0.304
Controls	Age (quadratic), Education		

Note: OLS estimation on annual work income. Robust standard errors in parentheses.

decreases economic and cultural integration (see, for example, Åslund *et al.*, 2008). Second, the older group of first-generation female immigrants has a higher average duration of residence. In this age group, 25 per cent immigrated before the mid-1970s in comparison to less than one per cent in the younger group.[19] Higher duration of residence should arguably improve employment chances, but immigrants that arrived in Sweden prior to the mid-1970s were primarily labour immigrants recruited to work in the booming manufacturing sector. Female immigrants at the time had higher employment rates than natives, which subsequently led to higher rates of early retirement due to disabilities or for other health-related reasons.

6.4.10 *Female education gaps*

As a final measure of cultural and economic integration, female native-immigrant gaps in education are examined and results shown in Table 16.4.

Results for all females (Table 6.14, column 1) indicate that female first-generation immigrants have higher years of education than female natives. Female second-generation immigrants with homogenous national backgrounds are associated with significantly lower years of education than natives, regardless of region of origin. In the full sample of second-generation immigrants, education gaps again indicate lower years of education for those stemming from Nordic, South America, and Asian countries, but differences are smaller than those found between natives and second-generation immigrants with homogenous

[19] Note that duration of residence is based on latest year of immigration, which may underestimate duration of residence for frequent migrants.

Table 6.13 Female employment rates.

	All	Immigrants under thirty	Immigrants thirty plus
Natives with native parents (16–65)	Ref.	Ref.	Ref.
First generation			
Nordic	−0.098***	−0.132***	−0.098***
	(0.001)	(0.006)	(0.001)
West Europe	−0.189***	−0.208***	−0.188***
	(0.003)	(0.007)	(0.003)
East Europe	−0.206***	−0.141***	−0.228***
	(0.001)	(0.003)	(0.002)
North/Central America	−0.233***	−0.228***	−0.238***
	(0.005)	(0.011)	(0.006)
South America	−0.175***	−0.115***	−0.201***
	(0.003)	(0.006)	(0.004)
Asia	−0.284***	−0.208***	−0.323***
	(0.001)	(0.002)	(0.002)
Africa	−0.264***	−0.210***	−0.291***
	(0.006)	(0.005)	(0.004)
Second generation—parents from the same country of origin			
Nordic	−0.037***	0.006	−0.056***
	(0.002)	(0.005)	(0.003)
West Europe	−0.087***	−0.122***	−0.074***
	(0.006)	(0.013)	(0.007)
East Europe	−0.060***	−0.065***	−0.054***
	(0.004)	(0.006)	(0.005)
North/Central America	−0.171***	−0.170***	−0.132
	(0.037)	(0.039)	(0.101)
South America	−0.108***	−0.101***	−0.080
	(0.009)	(0.010)	(0.068)
Asia	−0.091***	−0.085***	−0.074***
	(0.004)	(0.004)	(0.014)
Africa	−0.132***	−0.122***	−0.150***
	(0.011)	(0.012)	(0.045)
No. of observations	2,548,710	2,188,280	2,427,294
R^2	0.221	0.237	0.208
Second generation—full sample			
Nordic	−0.035***	−0.005	−0.048***
	(0.001)	(0.002)	(0.001)
West Europe	−0.053***	−0.053***	−0.053***
	(0.002)	(0.004)	(0.002)
East Europe	−0.052***	−0.056***	−0.048***
	(0.002)	(0.004)	(0.003)
North/Central America	−0.034***	−0.090***	−0.012**
	(0.005)	(0.009)	(0.005)
South America	−0.081***	−0.076***	−0.063***
	(0.006)	(0.006)	(0.015)

(continued)

Table 6.13 Continued

	All	Immigrants under thirty	Immigrants thirty plus
Asia	−0.079***	−0.077***	−0.064***
	(0.003)	(0.003)	(0.005)
Africa	−0.096***	−0.093***	−0.085***
	(0.005)	(0.006)	(0.011)
No. of observations	2,753,867	2,259,718	2,561,013
R^2	0.222	0.244	0.203
Controls	Age (quadratic), Education		

Note: Linear probability models on employment. Robust standard errors in parentheses.

backgrounds. In the full sample of second-generation immigrants, those stemming from countries in Western European and North/Central American indicate higher years of education than natives, but differences are smaller than those found between natives and first-generation immigrants. Results therefore suggest a convergence between native and immigrant levels of education across immigrant generations. Note, however, that these results may also reflect selection effects, that is, the fact that second-generation immigrants today are to a large degree the descendents of relatively unskilled labour migrants, while first-generation immigrants today are more likely to be well-educated refugees or tied movers.

The probability of having a university degree is also estimated and results presented in Table 6.15. Results indicate greater heterogeneity in higher education gaps between natives and immigrants. First-generation female immigrants stemming from countries in Western Europe and North/Central America are associated with higher probabilities of being university educated in comparison to female natives, while first-generation immigrants from other regions have lower relative probabilities. In the full sample of second-generation immigrants, education gaps are smaller in comparison to first-generation levels, both positive and negative gaps are smaller. Similar to the pattern established throughout this study on the various cultural indicators, second-generation immigrants with homogenous backgrounds indicate a slower process of cultural integration across immigrant generations. Education gaps are negative and significant for all regions, often at similar levels to first-generation immigrants from the same region of origin.

Table 6.14 Female education (dependent variable: year of education as measured by 'age left full-time education').

	All	Immigrants under thirty	Immigrants thirty plus
Natives with native parents (16–65)	Ref.	Ref.	Ref.
First generation			
Nordic	1.376***	1.144***	1.430***
	(0.036)	(0.043)	(0.040)
West Europe	1.124***	1.145***	1.147***
	(0.067)	(0.056)	(0.083)
East Europe	0.254***	0.364***	0.215***
	(0.031)	(0.019)	(0.048)
North/Central America	1.440***	0.660***	1.822***
	(0.102)	(0.078)	(0.143)
South America	0.917***	0.048	1.533***
	(0.054)	(0.038)	(0.085)
Asia	0.781***	0.207***	1.342***
	(0.025)	(0.017)	(0.044)
Africa	1.041***	−0.299***	2.363***
	(0.061)	(0.039)	(0.111)
Second generation—parents from the same country of origin			
Nordic	−0.451***	−0.309***	−0.486***
	(0.037)	(0.029)	(0.055)
West Europe	−0.455***	0.095	−0.665***
	(0.099)	(0.081)	(0.140)
East Europe	−0.334***	−0.052	−0.597***
	(0.050)	(0.037)	(0.094)
North/Central America	−0.740***	−1.024***	0.817
	(0.286)	(0.187)	(1.596)
South America	−0.589***	−0.666***	2.078**
	(0.062)	(0.059)	(0.988)
Asia	−0.571***	−0.618***	−0.257
	(0.031)	(0.024)	(0.276)
Africa	−0.434***	−0.610***	1.470***
	(0.073)	(0.061)	(0.581)
No. of Observations	1,810,550	1,644,419	1,715,209
R^2	0.323	0.332	0.310
Second generation—full sample			
Nordic	−0.085***	−0.107***	−0.004
	(0.020)	(0.014)	(0.030)
West Europe	0.275***	0.341***	0.310***
	(0.032)	(0.025)	(0.048)
East Europe	0.013	0.171***	−0.051
	(0.031)	(0.023)	(0.053)
North/Central America	0.183**	0.070	0.290**
	(0.091)	(0.055)	(0.140)

(continued)

Table 6.14 Continued

	All	Immigrants under thirty	Immigrants thirty plus
South America	−0.109**	−0.267***	0.981***
	(0.046)	(0.038)	(0.263)
Asia	−0.157***	−0.375***	0.685***
	(0.029)	(0.019)	(0.115)
Africa	0.097**	−0.242***	1.356***
	(0.049)	(0.039)	(0.174)
No. of observations	1,976,128	1,713,377	1,811,829
R^2	0.325	0.435	0.302
Controls		Age (quadratic)	

Note: OLS estimation age left full time education. Robust standard errors in parentheses.

Table 6.15 Female education levels (dependent variable: university educated).

	All	Immigrants under thirty	Immigrants thirty plus
Natives with native parents (16–65)	Ref.	Ref.	Ref.
First generation			
Nordic	−0.049***	0.154***	−0.064***
	(0.001)	(0.006)	(0.001)
West Europe	0.110***	0.222***	0.091***
	(0.003)	(0.007)	(0.003)
East Europe	−0.015***	0.030***	−0.027***
	(0.001)	(0.003)	(0.002)
North/Central America	0.190***	0.124***	0.213***
	(0.006)	(0.003)	(0.007)
South America	−0.026***	−0.034***	−0.021***
	(0.003)	(0.004)	(0.004)
Asia	−0.045***	−0.015***	−0.055***
	(0.001)	(0.002)	(0.002)
Africa	−0.136***	−0.096***	−0.149***
	(0.003)	(0.004)	(0.003)
Second generation—parents from the same country of origin			
Nordic	−0.101***	−0.057***	−0.115***
	(0.002)	(0.003)	(0.003)
West Europe	−0.034***	0.004	−0.044***
	(0.006)	(0.011)	(0.008)
East Europe	−0.018***	−0.006	−0.019***
	(0.004)	(0.005)	(0.006)
North/Central America	−0.062**	−0.084***	0.089
	(0.026)	(0.015)	(0.118)
South America	−0.072***	−0.065***	0.070
	(0.006)	(0.006)	(0.081)
Asia	−0.064***	−0.055***	−0.056***
	(0.003)	(0.003)	(0.014)
Africa	−0.054***	−0.051***	0.032
	(0.008)	(0.008)	(0.047)

No. of observations	2,548,710	2,188,280	2,427,294
R^2	0.043	0.049	0.039
Second generation—full sample			
Nordic	−0.057***	−0.029***	−0.064***
	(0.001)	(0.002)	(0.002)
West Europe	0.012***	0.016***	0.015***
	(0.002)	(0.003)	(0.003)
East Europe	−0.003	0.006**	−0.002
	(0.002)	(0.003)	(0.003)
North/Central America	0.043***	−0.014***	0.070***
	(0.005)	(0.007)	(0.007)
South America	−0.034***	−0.040***	0.073***
	(0.004)	(0.004)	(0.018)
Asia	−0.025***	−0.035***	0.037***
	(0.002)	(0.002)	(0.007)
Africa	−0.006	−0.031***	0.104***
	(0.005)	(0.005)	(0.013)
No. of observations	2,753,781	2,259,695	2,560,950
R^2	0.045	0.053	0.037
Controls		Age (quadratic)	

Note: Linear probability models on the probability of having a university degree. Robust standard errors in parentheses.

6.4.11 *Subjective values—acculturation identity*

No information on subjective values is available in the register data used in the analysis above. Data on subjective values in Sweden comes from survey studies which tend to cover smaller, not always random, samples of the population. One such survey is the 1995 *Follow-up Surveys of Pupils* which follows a cohort of students that graduated from compulsory school in 1988.[20] The 1995 survey, conducted seven years after graduation from compulsory school, when the majority of respondents were 23 years of age, sampled the entire population of students with immigrant backgrounds, defined as having one or both parents born abroad (in total 4867 individuals). These individuals were asked a number of specific questions relating to their foreign background, including questions concerning identification to host and home cultures. Similar questions were not asked to respondents with Swedish backgrounds, prohibiting a comparison of identity between natives and immigrants. In addition, as the sample surveyed consists of a cohort of compulsory school graduates, immigrants in the sample are either born in Sweden with a foreign-born parent (second generation) or foreign born but immigrated before the age of sixteen (middle generation). As such, a

---

[20] Previous surveys on this cohort of students were conducted in 1990 and 1992.

comparison between first and second-generation immigrants is less relevant as the majority of the foreign born in the sample immigrated to Sweden before school start.

Nonetheless, this survey provides unique information on how a cohort of students with immigrant backgrounds identify with the majority society culture as well as background cultures. Respondents were asked the following questions: To what degree do you feel affinity to your original background culture? To what degree do you feel affinity to Swedish culture? Answers to these questions are coded into a four-level scale based on the answer options available (completely, partially, little, not at all). Departing from the acculturation framework developed in the cross-cultural psychology literature, individuals are coded into one of the four following categories (Berry, 1997; Berry and Sam, 1997; Berry *et al.*, 2006; Phinney 1989, 1990; Phinney *et al.*, 2001; Martinez and Dukes, 1997). The first, *integration*, implies a strong sense of belonging to the ethnic group together with a strong identification with the majority society. *Assimilation* implies a strong identification to Swedish culture but weakened ties to the culture of origin, while *separation* is the opposite, a strong affiliation to background cultures but weak ties to the majority culture. Finally, *marginalization* implies weak ties to both home and host cultures.

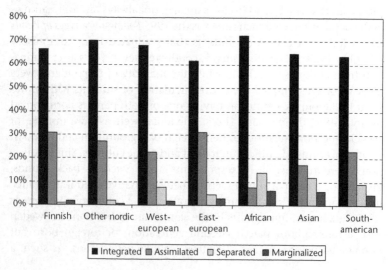

Figure 6.1 Distribution of acculturation identity (self-assessed), by region of origin.

The distribution of acculturation identity for respective region of origin is shown in Figure 6.1.[21] Within each region, the majority of respondents self-identify as integrated. Thereafter, the next largest proportion of respondents self-identify as assimilated. This implies that the vast majority in each region completely or partially feel an affinity to the Swedish majority culture. Those with non-European backgrounds (African, Asian, and South American) have the highest relative shares of separated and marginalized, but these groups also have the highest share of individuals born abroad. Ninety-three per cent of survey respondents with non-European backgrounds were born abroad, compared to approximately 30 per cent of those with Nordic or European backgrounds.[22]

6.5 Conclusion

Using data on the entire working age population of Sweden in 2005, this study has analysed differences between natives and immigrants on a number of cultural measures: within-region gender gaps in education, different types of marriage propensities, marriage rates at age 25, cohabitation, divorce, partner age gaps, female employment rates, female education levels, and, based on a follow-up survey of students, identification to home and host cultures. Cultural integration has throughout (with a few exceptions) been measured by differences between natives and immigrants across two immigrant generations from the same region of origin.

For comparative purposes, estimation on second-generation immigrants was based on two samples of second-generation immigrants. First, a selected sample of second-generation immigrants with parents from the same country of origin was considered. This group constitutes about 23 per cent of the population of second-generation immigrants (defined as individuals born in Sweden with at least one foreign-born parent). The majority of second-generation immigrants therefore have mixed backgrounds, of which 68 per cent have one foreign-born parent and one Swedish-born parent. A second round of estimation was

---

[21] Note that only a few respondents to the survey had North American backgrounds. This group is therefore not included in the comparison.
[22] Separate estimation by immigration status yields largely similar results for middle and second-generation immigrants. This is a likely consequence of the sample surveyed where the foreign born by definition have a low age at entry.

therefore based on the full sample of second-generation immigrants, including those with mixed backgrounds.

Results, across the board, suggest a large degree of cultural integration between natives and immigrants in Sweden. Estimation of within-region gender gaps in education indicated that females tend to be more educated than males in all groups, regardless of immigrant status, with the exception of first-generation immigrants stemming from African countries, where no gender differences in education were found. Younger second-generation immigrants with African backgrounds did, however, show a positive gender gap in education for women.

An analysis of marriage patterns (marriage to a foreign-born person, marriage to a co-national, divorce, cohabitation, and partner age gaps), suggests a high degree of cultural integration across immigrant generations. Deviations from this pattern, for example no reduction in the propensity to marry co-nationals across immigrant generations for some groups, was highly contingent on the selected sample of second-generation immigrants with homogenous backgrounds (both parents from the same country of origin). When estimation included the majority of second-generation immigrants with mixed backgrounds, differences between natives and immigrants in marriage patterns always diminished across immigrant generations.

Other indicators, such as female employment rates and female education levels, yield similar results. Female native-immigrant employment gaps are found to be negative and significant for both first and second-generation immigrants, but the employment gap is smaller for second-generation immigrants in comparison to first-generation immigrants. In terms of education, first-generation female immigrants are found to have higher levels of education than female natives, while second-generation immigrants (full sample) have similar or lower levels of education than natives.

A remaining question to answer is why cultural integration patterns appear to be weaker for the selected (and relatively small) sample of second-generation immigrants with homogenous national backgrounds. Results concerning partnership patterns are in line with theories stressing a higher relative emphasis on ethnic group belonging as a basis for marital choices in families with homogenous backgrounds. A lower degree of integration in terms of female employment rates and female education levels among this group of second-generation immigrants may also be due to a higher orientation towards origin countries, implying lower investment in host country skills and less interaction with the majority population (as well as other ethnic groups), which may sustain cultural and economic boundaries between groups in society across generations.

In conclusion, results from this study show that there is a process of cultural integration occurring between natives and immigrants in Sweden. Initial differences in the numerous cultural measures used in this analysis between natives and immigrants may be expected as it is precisely these differences which, at least partially, define the cultural norms of the majority population. Due to subsequent adaptations in both the majority and minority populations, initial differences are expected to diminish over time and across generations. This study provides empirical support that such a process of cultural integration is indeed occurring across immigrant generations in Sweden.

References

Andersson, G. (2004) Childbearing After Migration: Fertility Patterns of Foreign-Born Women in Sweden. *International Migration Review*, 38, 747–775.

Andersson, G. and Scott, K. (2005) Labour-market Status and First-time Parenthood: The Experience of Immigrant Women in Sweden, 1981–97. *Populations Studies*, 59, 21–38.

Angrist, J. (2002) How do Sex Ratios Affect Marriage and Labour Markets? Evidence from America's Second Generation. *Quarterly Journal of Economics*, 117(3), 997–1038.

Arai, M., Karlsson, J., and Lundholm, M. (2011) On Fragile Grounds: A Replication of 'Are Muslims Different in terms of Cultural Integration'. *Journal of European Economic Association*, 9(5), 1002–1011.

Åslund, O., Böhlmark, A., and Nordström Skans, O. (2008) *Age at Migration and Social Integration*. IZA Discussion Paper No. 4263.

Behtoui, A. (2010) Marriage Patterns of Immigrants in Sweden. *Journal of Comparative Family Studies*, 41(3), 415–435.

Berry, J.W. (1997) Immigration, Acculturation and Adaptation (Lead article). *Applied Psychology: An International Review*, 46(1), 5–34.

Berry, J.W., Phinney, J.S., Sam, D.L., and Vedder, P. (2006) Immigrant Youth: Acculturation, Identity, and Adaptation. *Applied Psychology*, 55(3), 303–332.

Berry, J.W. and Sam, D.L. (1997) Acculturation and adaptation. In: J.W. Berry, M.H. Segall, and C. Kagitcibasi (eds) *Handbook of Cross-Cultural Psychology*, Vol. 3: Social behaviour and applications (2nd ed.) (pp. 291–326). Boston: Allyn & Bacon.

Bisin, A., Patacchini, E., Verdier, T., and Zenou, Y. (2008) Are Muslim Immigrants Different in terms of Cultural Integration? *Journal of the European Economic Association*, 6, 445–456.

Bisin, A., Topa, G., and Verdier, T. (2004) An Empirical Analysis of Religious Homogamy and Socialization in the US. *Journal of Political Economy*, 112(3), 615–664.

Bisin, A. and Verdier, T. (2000) Beyond the Melting Pot: Cultural Transmission, Marriage and the Evolution of Ethnic and Religious Traits. *Quarterly Journal of Economics*, 115, 955–988.

Card, D., Dustmann, C., and Preston, I. (2005) *Understanding attitudes to immigration: The migration and minority module of the first European Social Survey.* Centre for Research and Analysis of Migration (CReAM) Discussion Paper Series, No. 03/05.

Çelikaksoy, A., Nekby, L., and Rashid, S. (2010) Assortative Mating by Ethnic Background and Education in Sweden: The Role of Parental Composition on Partner Choice. *Zeitschift für Familienforschung (Journal of Family Research)*, 1, 65–88.

Chiswick, B.R. and Houseworth, C.A. (2011) Ethnic Intermarriage among Immigrants: Human Capital and Assortative Mating. *Review of Economics of the Household*, 9(2): 149–180.

Constant, A., Gataullina, L., and Zimmermann K.F. (2006) *Clash of Cultures: Muslims and Christians in the Ethnosizing Process.* IZA Discussion Paper, No. 2350.

Dustmann, C. and Preston, I.P. (2007) Racial and Economic Factors in Attitudes to Immigration. *The B.E. Journal of Economic Analysis & Policy*, 7(1), Article 62, 1–41.

Furtado, D. (2006) Human Capital and Interethnic Marriage Decisions. IZA Discussion Paper No. 1989. Forthcoming in *Economic Enquiry.*

Georgiadis, A. and Manning, A. (2008) *Change and Continuity among Minority Communities in Britain.* Centre for Economic Performance, London School of Economics.

Gilbertson, G.A., Fitzpatrick, J.O., and Yang, L. (1996) Hispanic Intermarriage in New York City: New Evidence from 1991. *International Migration Review*, 30, 445–459.

Kalmijn, M. (1991a) Status Homogamy in the United States. *American Journal of Sociology*, 97, 496–523.

Kalmijn, M. (1991b) Shifting Boundaries: Trends in Religious and Educational Homogamy. *American Sociological Review*, 56, 786–800.

Kalmijn, M. (1993) Spouse Selection among the Children of European Immigrants: A comparison of Marriage Cohorts in the 1960 Census. *International Migration Review*, 27(1), 51–78.

Kalmijn, M. (1998) Intermarriage and Homogamy: Causes, Patterns, and Trends. *Annual Review of Sociology*, 24, 395–421.

Kantarevic, J. (2004) *Interethnic Marriages and Economic Assimilation of Immigrants.* IZA discussion paper series, No. 1142.

Le Grand, C. and Szulkin, R. (2002) Permanent Disadvantage or Gradual Integration: Explaining the Immigrant-Native Earnings Gap in Sweden. *Labour*, 16, 37–64.

Lievens, J. (1999) Family-Forming Migration from Turkey and Morocco to Belgium: The demand for Marriage Partners from the Countries of Origin. *The International Migration Review*, 33(3), 717–744.

Manning, A. and Roy, S. (2009) Culture Clash or Culture Club? The Identity and Attitudes of Immigrants in Britain. *The Economic Journal*, 120(542): F72–F100.

Martinez, R.O. and Dukes, R.L. (1997) The Effects of Ethnic Identity, Ethnicity, and gender on Adolescent Well-Being. *Journal of Youth and Adolescence*, 26(5), 503–516.

Nekby, L. and Rödin, M. (2007) Acculturation Identity and Employment among Second and Middle Generation Immigrants. *Journal of Economic Psychology*, 31(1), 2010, 35–50.

Nekby, L., Rödin, M., and Özcan, G., (2009) Acculturation Identity and Higher Education. Is There a Trade-off Between Ethnic Identity and Education? *International Migration Review*, 43(4), Winter, 938–973.

Nielsen, H.S., Smith, N., and Çelikaksoy, A. (2009) The Effect of Marriage on Education of Immigrants: Evidence from a Policy Reform Restricting Marriage Migration. *The Scandinavian Journal of Economics*, 111(3), 457–486.

Phinney, J.S. (1990) Ethnic Identity in Adolescents and Adults: Review of Research. *Psychological Bulletin*, 108, 499–514.

Phinney, J.S. (1989) Stages of Ethnic Identity in Minority Group Adolescents. *Journal of Early Adolescence*, 9, 34–49.

Phinney, J.S., Horenczyk, G., Liebkind, K., and Vedder, P. (2001) Ethnic identity, immigration, and well-being: An international perspective. *Journal of Social Issues* 57,493–510.

de la Rica, S. and Ortega, F. (2009) *Economic and Cultural Gaps among Foreign-born Minorities in Spain*. IZA Discussion Paper, No. 4115.

Schröder, L. (2007) From Problematic Objects to Resourceful Subjects: an Overview of Immigrant-Native Labour Market Gaps from a Policy Perspective. *Swedish Economic Policy Review*, 14(1), 7–40.

Scott, K. and Stanfors, M. (2009) Second Generation Mothers—Do the Children of Immigrants Adjust their Fertility to Host Country Norms? In: T. Salzmann, B. Edmonston, and J. Raymer (eds) *Demographic Aspects of Migration*. VS Verlag für Sozialwissenschaften, pp. 123–152.

7

Cultural Integration in Switzerland

Pierre Kohler

7.1 Introduction

Until the beginning of the Industrial Revolution, Switzerland was mainly an emigration country. Since the end of the nineteenth century, Switzerland and inflowing migrants have maintained a mutually beneficial relationship interspersed with difficult episodes.[1] Despite the impossibility of an accepted definition of (the Swiss) national identity, populist right-wing political parties recurrently attempt to instrumentalize successive migration waves to strengthen the fear that Switzerland may lose its identity to migrants unable to integrate culturally into society. The recent successes of popular anti-migrant initiatives stress the many open questions that remain concerning the handling of cultural integration issues in Switzerland (D'Amato, 2008).

Cultural integration can be defined as the evolution of behaviours, attitudes, daily life habits, beliefs, etc. (Wanner *et al.*, 2002). Different schools of thought exist in cultural integration literature. Assimilation theory assumes that cultural differences progressively level out, whereas multiculturalism insists on their persistence over time (Alba and Nee, 1997). Proponents of de-constructivism and system theories have criticized 'groupist' approaches, arguing that groups are a product of social processes or discourse and do not exist a priori. However, empirical observation tends to hint that none of these theories are adequate and that the relation between ethnicity, identity, behaviours, and attitudes is a complex multi-level evolutionary phenomenon (Wimmer, 2008). As an example, a study conducted in three migrant neighbourhoods in

---

[1] See next section for a brief review of migration history and policy in Switzerland.

Swiss cities shows that even if migrants do not primarily define themselves in ethnic terms, the majority of their social interactions occur within the group they belong to (Wimmer, 2004). Cultural integration may affect behaviours and attitudes in different ways. Furthermore, the cultural dimension of the integration process of migrant is influenced by economic factors as well as the social and political context in which the integration process is occurring. Wage and employment discrimination, legal incentives determining access to citizenship and host society culture are some of the factors influencing the cultural integration of migrants (Kohler, 2012). Such evidence calls for further research on the stability of group boundaries and their transformation, so as to better understand the evolutionary nature of group formation and how groups insert themselves in the host society. Qualitative studies have generated knowledge over the cultural integration patterns of specific communities residing in Switzerland. However, only few quantitative studies have been conducted on that subject.

This chapter contributes to this debate by specifically exploring the cultural integration paths of eight migrant groups from the first to the second generation. It traces the evolution of selected behaviours and attitudes, which are taken as indicative of cultural integration. Different perspectives are proposed to deepen the analysis. First, differences across cohorts are used to investigate change and continuity over time (Georgiadis and Manning, 2011) and to see if younger migrants depart from behaviours and attitudes of older migrants.[2] Second, to explore the role of intermarriage as a factor (and not only an outcome) of integration (Waldis, 2008), differences across individuals in endogamous and mixed couples are examined. Can significant patterns be identified? And what is the effect of education? These are some of the questions explored in this chapter. Special attention is given to migrant women, as they play a key role in the transmission of cultural traits and in the socialization process of the second generation on whom most policy efforts are targeted.

The remainder of this introduction proposes a short overview of migration history and policy in Switzerland since the mid-nineteenth century. Section 7.2 provides a review of related quantitative studies and Section 7.3 presents a snapshot of the migrant population in Switzerland as well as pertinent data. Section 7.4 defines the indicators of cultural integration and provides additional details pertaining to the common approach used in this book to investigate the cultural integration of migrants. Section 7.5 presents the results of the investigation of the evolution of migrants' behaviours by examining their performances at

---

[2] In this text, migrants born before 1970 are labelled as 'old' and those born after 1970 as 'young'.

school (educational achievement and gender education gap) as well as their position in the couple (marriage, intermarriage, age and education gap between partners, early marriage, cohabitation, fertility, divorce), and in the labour market (labour force participation). This section also covers their subjective attitudes by examining their use of national languages, their feelings towards Switzerland as well as their gender, religious and political attitudes. The last section concludes by summarizing key findings and proposes recommendations for future integration policies.

7.2 Migration history and policy: 'Ueberfremdung' and its shadow

For centuries, Switzerland was a country of emigration before becoming an immigration country. In 1850, migrants were almost non-existent in Switzerland except for the Huguenots (Henry *et al.*, 1995). The construction of infrastructure necessary for the unfolding Industrial Revolution created an excess demand for manpower. At that time, foreigners were welcome and perceived as indispensable. The Swiss government signed recruitment agreements with neighbouring countries, granting migrants the same rights as nationals. Two years of residence were sufficient to acquire Swiss citizenship. This policy was in line with the belief that naturalization was the most suitable way to assimilate migrants (Wicker, 2003). Figure 7.1 shows that the share of foreigners living in Switzerland progressively rose and reached 15 per cent in 1910, one of the highest rates in Europe.

The outbreak of the First World War signalled the beginning of a lasting change in the perception of migrants as a threat to Swiss culture. Conservative circles brought into the political debate the idea of *Ueberfremdung*, the fear that Swiss identity will be dissolved with the inflow of too many foreigners. In 1917, the Central Office for Aliens Police was created in order to better monitor the migrant population. In 1931, the Federal Law on the Settlement and Residence of Foreigners engraved in law the transmutation of 'migrants' into 'foreigners' (Wicker, 2003). It also made residence and naturalization more difficult. In the 1930s, a more malleable version of the *Ueberfremdung* idea, the *Geistige Landesverteidigung*, literally the spiritual national defence, insisted on the duty of individuals to defend typical Swiss values. With Nazi and fascist regimes at the border, liberal circles progressively rallied conservatives around the flag to promote 'Swiss' values such as cultural diversity, democracy, or technological progress. This episode of Swiss history is important because the national 'culture of threat' that developed in Switzerland and the representation of foreigners as a danger to Swiss identity had a lasting impact on Swiss

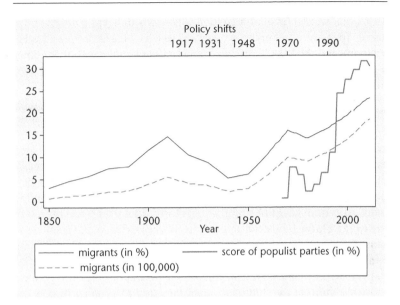

Figure 7.1 Migrant population and right wing populist parties in Switzerland (1850–2011).

Source: OFS and D'Amato (2008)

collective identity and immigration policy (Riano and Wastl-Walter, 2006). During that period, the proportion of migrant population dropped sharply and reached 5 per cent on the eve of the Second World War.

In the second half of the twentieth century, three successive waves of immigration brought different types of migrants to Switzerland. The defensive attitude inherited from the previous period still affected policy decisions. While the government attempted to provide cheap labour to the economy, it always had to pay attention to underlying xenophobic feelings likely to burst onto the political scene. Like other countries, Switzerland opted for a *Gastarbeiter* system. The first recruitment agreement was signed with Italy in 1948 and was followed by an inflow of Italian manpower. Spaniards came soon after. Despite a quota system, immigration kept rising. In 1970, the Schwarzenbach initiative, which proposed to expel one third of migrants and impose harsher quotas, was rejected only by 54 per cent in one of the highest poll turnouts in Swiss history. The federal government reacted by imposing more restrictive quotas, but it was mostly the non-renewal of permits that drove out migrants. This was also a convenient way for Switzerland to export its unemployment. During the economic crisis of the 1970s, 67 per cent of the 340,000 workers who lost their jobs were migrants (Mahnig and Piguet, 2003). As the economy recovered in the

1980s, the second wave of migration followed a different pattern. Portuguese, Yugoslav, and Turkish workers, as well as refugees from Sri Lanka, Vietnam, and the Middle East also brought their families with them. After a decline in the 1970s, migrant population again exceeded 15 per cent in 1990.

Pressure from European countries for the improvement of conditions for their nationals drove Swiss authorities to reconsider their immigration policy. The ideas of creating a point system or implementing a 'three circles' policy based on the concept of 'cultural distance' of migrants were debated as a means to satisfy Switzerland's neighbours without alienating xenophobic voters. In the 1990s, Switzerland started to apply a 'three circles' policy, defining an inner circle and outer circles, and creating a hierarchy favouring individuals from EU/EFTA countries over those from the US and the rest of the world. Through bilateral agreements, EU/EFTA citizens are granted the same living and working rights as the Swiss (Mahnig and Piguet, 2003), while, for other countries, immigration is restricted to highly-qualified individuals only. Beyond the pragmatism of Swiss authorities, this political move also hints at the shift of symbolic barriers and a change in how the Swiss define foreigners and themselves (Wicker, 2003). However, this new policy could not prevent unwanted migrants from coming to Switzerland. During this period, the third wave of migrants was mostly composed of refugees from former Yugoslavia, but also from Africa, as well as highly qualified workers, mainly from neighbouring countries (Piguet, 2009).

Despite different restrictive policies, the migrant population has kept rising and the proportion of foreigners officially reached 22.9 per cent in 2009 (OFS).[3] As it became obvious that many migrants will never return to their home countries, politicians could no longer escape the question of migrant integration. Some cantons had started to use their autonomy in matters of education, religious matters, and the attribution of local civic rights to deal with integration-related issues, but their practices are heterogeneous and resources very limited. The legal basis for a coherent federal policy was only set up in 1998 when the integration of migrants became an item on the Swiss political agenda and the Federal Law on the Settlement and Residence of Foreigners was once more amended to allow the government to subsidize the integration of 'foreigners'. In 2001, a budget of around ten million Swiss francs was accepted and has barely increased since (OFM, 2006). The previous year, an order of the government defined the objectives of integration and the tasks of the Federal Commission for Foreigners. The Central Office for Aliens' Police was changed into the Federal

---

[3] See www.bfs.admin.ch.

Migration Office (Wicker, 2003). For a majority of the Swiss population, Western and Southern European migrants may be considered as economic competitors, but not as a threat to the Swiss identity. This empathy, however, does not extend to 'non-European' migrants. In 2005, a new Federal Law on Foreigners was passed, defining in depth the objectives and principles of integration policy as well as the competence of the government (OFM, 2006). The fact that a conservative government has initiated such changes during a period where the populist right wing has risen to become the strongest political force in the federal parliament indicates that the design of an integration strategy is politically costly, but indispensable (D'Amato, 2008). As in other countries, many voters are caught between the fear that the country they know may change and the necessity of adapting to a globalizing economy and society.

7.3 Related literature

The findings of the few existing quantitative studies relevant for this investigation are briefly presented below, with some of the results referred to later, as necessary.[4] Qualitative studies are not presented here, but the results of some of them will be mentioned when interpreting the results.

Bauer and Riphahn (2005) investigated the performance of migrants at school through the study of intergenerational patterns of educational attainment. Fibbi *et al.* (2005) looked at statistical differences across gender and between naturalized and non-naturalized second-generation migrants. They also proposed an analysis of the probability to have a weak education level, to be in the labour force, to be unemployed, and to acquire Swiss citizenship, by regressing independent variables on a set of origin dummies (Germany, France, Italy, Spain, Portugal, Turkey, and six former Yugoslavian provinces) and other controls. Wanner *et al.* (2003, 2005b) prepared a comprehensive study on female labour force participation. Other reports proposed statistics only on socio-professional and household characteristics of migrants at large (Wanner, 2004), on migrants, the use of language and religion (OFS, 2005), or on migrant families, highlighting their specificity and understanding their role in the migration and integration process (Fibbi *et al.*, 2005b).

---

[4] International economic literature on cultural integration has rapidly grown in recent years and it is not possible to review all of them here. In Switzerland, sociologists and demographers were the first to conduct cultural integration studies based on larger datasets as they became available. By contrast, economists mainly focused on the economic integration of migrants in the labour market.

Quantitative studies on subjective attitudes of migrants are even less numerous, as surveys containing such data are costly to implement and usually have a small sample size. Wanner *et al.* (2002) investigate determinants of the values and beliefs of migrants based on data from the first two waves (1999 and 2000) of the Swiss Household Panel (SHP). They regressed many indicators on origin dummies (Swiss, Italian, Spanish/Portuguese, other European Economic Community/European Free Trade Association, other Europe, rest of the world) and controlled whether respondents have one or two parents of foreign origin.

This study is the first to systematically examine the evolution of the behaviours and attitudes of migrants to better understand their cultural integration paths from the first to the second generation. Previous articles either only focused on the second generation or attributed a common factor to the second generation when considering all migrants. It also differs from existing literature in the way migrant groups are defined. Although European migrants form the bulk of the migrant population in Switzerland, the focus is not on European national communities, but on a limited number of broadly defined migrant categories that are geographically more balanced.

7.4 Migrant population and data

7.4.1 *Migrant groups definition and composition*

Table 7.1 shows that in 2000 when the last census was conducted in Switzerland, 29 per cent of the population was of foreign descent and

Table 7.1 Migrants living in Switzerland in 2000 by region of origin and generation.[5]

Region of origin	All	First generation	Second generation
Natives (in %)	70.78		
Migrants (in %)	29.22	20.07	9.14
Of which (in %)			
WE	27.34	28.12	25.65
SE	34.79	28.62	48.35
EE	21.05	24.06	14.44
AF	2.03	2.51	0.98
TMM	6.84	6.99	6.49
SA	2.82	3.44	1.47
AS	2.52	3.29	0.8
SCA	2.61	2.98	1.82

Source: Swiss census, 2000.

[5] In all the regression tables, 'R^2' stands for 'R-squared'. When a probit estimator is used instead of an OLS estimator, a pseudo R-squared ('PR^2') is reported instead as well as a log likelihood statistics ('ll'). In all the figures, a value represents the average difference between a

more than 20 per cent were foreigners. As mentioned earlier, these proportions have slightly increased during the last decade. First-generation migrants are born abroad, whereas second-generation migrants are born in Switzerland, but are of foreign origin.[6] The proportion of second-generation compared to first-generation migrants is a rough indicator of the length of stay of a particular group in Switzerland.

Groups of migrants presented in Table 7.1 are based on an aggregated United Nations typology and correspond to broad regions of origin.[7] Besides natives, eight groups of migrants are formed: Western Europe and Anglo-Saxon countries (WE), Southern Europe (SE), Eastern Europe (EE), Africa (AF), Turkey, the Middle East and Maghreb (TMM), Latin Amercia (LA), Asia (AS), and South and Central Asia (SCA).[8] This classi-fication is arbitrary to some extent and can be the subject of a debate. Is it still relevant to distinguish between Southern, Western, and Central Europe? Should Turkey be considered part of Eastern Europe as Russia is? Should the focus be on national communities only? The implications of defining population groups and mapping differences across them can be problematic as it transmits information without explicitly addressing

migrant group and the natives. The dotted lines that are visible in some graphs represent standard deviations.

[6] More details on categorization issues can be found in Section 7.2.

[7] The SHP sample not displayed here is similar to the census sample, with two exceptions: (1) the sample of first-generation migrants is smaller; (2) the proportion of migrants from Eastern Europe is smaller.

[8] The categories include the following countries: (1) WE: Australia, Austria, Belgium, Canada, Denmark, Finland, France, Germany, Iceland, Ireland, Liechtenstein, Luxembourg, Monaco, New Zealand, Norway, Sweden, the Netherlands, United Kingdom, United States; (2) SE: Andorra, Greece, Italy, Malta, Portugal, San Marino, Spain, the Vatican; (3) EE: Albania, Belarus, Bosnia and Herzegovina, Bulgaria, Croatia, Czech Republic, Hungary, Macedonia, Moldova, Poland, Romania, Russia, Serbia and Montenegro, Slovakia, Slovenia, Ukraine; (4) AF: Angola, Benin, Botswana, Burkina Faso, Burundi, Cameroon, Cape Verde, Central African Republic, Chad, Comoros, Congo (Brazzaville), Congo (Kinshasa), Ivory Coast, Djibouti, Equatorial Guinea, Eritrea, Ethiopia, Gabon, Gambia, Ghana, Guinea, Guinea-Bissau, Kenya, Lesotho, Liberia, Madagascar, Malawi, Mali, Maurice, Mauritania, Mozambique, Namibia, Niger, Nigeria, Rwanda, Sao Tome and Principe, Senegal, Seychelles, Sierra Leone, Somalia, South Africa, Swaziland, Tanzania, Togo, Uganda, Zambia, Zimbabwe; (5) TMM: Algeria, Armenia, Azerbaijan, Bahrain, Cyprus, Egypt, Georgia, Iraq, Israel, Jordan, Kuwait, Lebanon, Libya, Morocco, Oman, Palestine, Qatar, Saudi Arabia, Sudan, Syria, Tunisia, Turkey, United Arab Emirates, Western Sahara, Yemen; (6) LA: Antigua and Barbuda, Argentina, Bahamas, Barbados, Belize, Bolivia, Brazil, Chile, Colombia, Costa Rica, Cuba, Dominican Republic, Dominique, Ecuador, El Salvador, Grenada, Guatemala, Guyana, Haiti, Honduras, Jamaica, Mexico, Nicaragua, Panama, Paraguay, Peru, Saint Kitts and Nevis, Saint Vincent and the Grenadines, St Lucia, Suriname, Trinidad and Tobago, Uruguay, Venezuela; (7) AS: Brunei Darussalam, Cambodia, China, China (Taiwan), Fiji, Indonesia, Japan, Korea (North), Korea (South), Laos, Malaysia, Mongolia, Myanmar, Papua New Guinea, Philip-pines, Samoa, Singapore, Solomon Islands, Thailand, Tonga, Vanuatu, Vietnam; (8) SCA: Afghanistan, Bangladesh, Bhutan, India, Iran, Kazakhstan, Kyrgyzstan, Maldives, Nepal, Pakistan, Sri Lanka, Tajikistan, Turkmenistan, Uzbekistan.

the assumptions that lie behind the classification (Winlow, 2006). In the present case, the main reason for lumping national communities into broad categories is that the Swiss political discourse is often articulated at such an aggregate level. It is however necessary to keep in mind the composition of the different groups when analysing results.

The first three groups are significantly larger than the five remaining ones and represent 83 per cent of the migrant population in Switzerland. The first group gathers Western and Northern Europeans as well as Anglo-Saxons. Three-quarters are from neighbouring Germany (37 per cent), France (26 per cent), and Austria (12 per cent), and are not part of any specific wave of migration. Italians dominate the Southern European group (65 per cent); Spaniards (19 per cent), and Portuguese (14 per cent) are also sizeable communities. The group of Eastern Europeans is largely dominated by former Yugoslavia (85 per cent), but remains heterogeneous. Migrants from this country first came as economic migrants in the 1980s, and then massively as refugees fleeing the civil war after 1991. The largest community comes from former Serbia-Montenegro (48 per cent), with half of them being Muslims from Kosovo. Bosnia and Herzegovina (13 per cent), Macedonia (12 per cent), and Croatia (9 per cent) follow in terms of size.

Immigration from Africa (excluding Maghreb) is more recent and very diverse. The three largest communities come from Angola (13 per cent), Congo (10 per cent), and Somalia (10 per cent). Many are political refugees. The Middle East generated a significant number of political refugees too, but most migrants of the sixth group are workers from Turkey (66 per cent) or Maghreb (20 per cent). Latin Americans mostly come from Brazil (29 per cent) and the Dominican Republic, Colombia, and Chile (10 per cent each). The Asian group is similarly heterogeneous, with economic migrants from Thailand (20 per cent), the Philippines (17 per cent), China (15 per cent), and Japan (10 per cent), and political refugees from Vietnam (19 per cent) and Cambodia (4 per cent). The final group of South and Central Asia is clearly dominated by political refugees from Sri-Lanka (59 per cent). Indians (17 per cent) and Iranians (12 per cent) are also sizeable communities.

7.4.2 *The Swiss census and the Swiss Household Panel*

Two surveys are used to investigate the patterns of migrant cultural integration in Switzerland: the 2000 Swiss census and the Swiss Household Panel (SHP). As mentioned in the introduction (see Table 7.1), the census covers the seven million individuals living in Switzerland in 2000. It provides information about the country of birth of an individual, his first and second nationality, and whether he is Swiss by birth or not. Individuals born in Switzerland and Swiss by birth are defined as natives. First-generation migrants are born abroad. A second-generation migrant is an individual born in Switzerland, but whose first or second nationality is foreign.[9]

The SHP started in 1999 with 7,799 individuals answering a detailed questionnaire. New observations from the European Survey on Income and Living Conditions (SILC) were added in 2004 and 2005 and increased the total number of observations by wave to 11,565. The SHP indicates whether an individual is born in Switzerland or not, and contains information on the first, second and even third nationality, as well as on the first and second nationality of both parents. An individual is defined as a second-generation migrant if he is born in Switzerland and one of his nationalities or one of his parents' nationalities is foreign. If parents are both of foreign origin, the nationality of the father prevails.

7.5 Cultural integration indicators and specifications

7.5.1 *List of cultural integration indicators*

The census conducted in 2000 and the SHP allow examining certain behaviours and attitudes, which are assumed to reflect the cultural dimension of integration. Integration processes cannot be localized geographically or institutionally, but some units of analysis are especially relevant. School is the first place where all second-generation migrants are exposed to natives and native culture, and school is an important integration mechanism. Secondly, as many adults spend most of their life in the couple (or family), it is of particular interest to observe behaviours in the couple, especially differing patterns of integration between individuals in endogamous couples and partners of mixed couples, where cultural accommodations and compromises are a necessity. Finally, the labour market is the most important mechanism stimulating contacts between natives and migrants outside the household. The list of selected indicators also includes information about the main language of migrants and their attitudes with respect to Switzerland, gender, religious, and political issues. Descriptive statistics

---

[9] A small fraction of second-generation migrants are included in the native group as some of them only have the Swiss nationality by birth. Those who are only Swiss, but are naturalized and are of unknown origin, are not included in either category.

Table 7.2 Descriptive statistics.

	Year	Natives		First generation		Second generation	
		Mean	Std Dev.	Mean	Std Dev.	Mean	Std Dev.
Census				Women			
Educational attainment	2000	11.71	2.34	11.26	3.38	11.58	2.68
Mixed couple	2000	0.12	0.32	0.34	0.47	0.38	0.49
Marriage	2000	0.55	0.5	0.72	0.45	0.42	0.49
Age gap	2000	−2.17	4.34	−2.71	5.1	−2.39	4.21
Education gap	2000	−3.13	6.87	−2.22	7.36	−0.94	7.34
Cohabitation	2000	0.13	0.34	0.06	0.24	0.16	0.37
Fertility	2000	1.83	1.26	1.84	1.21	1.68	1.2
Divorce	2000	0.13	0.33	0.1	0.3	0.1	0.29
Labour force participation	2000	0.76	0.43	0.73	0.44	0.85	0.36
Main language	2000	1	0.03	0.6	0.49	0.95	0.22
SHP							
Feelings (i)	1999–2007	0.5	0	0.75	0.44	0.57	0.5
Feelings (ii)	1999	2.4	1.26	2.07	1.18	2.33	1.2
Gender (i)	2002–2007	5.52	3.38	5.61	3.44	5.52	3.35
Religion (i)	1999–2007	0.33	0.47	0.32	0.47	0.35	0.48
Religion (ii)	1999–2007	0.4	0.49	0.37	0.48	0.41	0.49
Policy (i)	1999–2007	4.58	2.07	4.24	2.14	4.67	1.98
Policy (ii)	1999–2007	5.79	1.9	6	2.05	5.81	1.84
Census				Men			
Educational attainment	2000	12.64	2.72	11.6	3.52	11.93	2.91
Mixed couple	2000	0.16	0.36	0.24	0.43	0.46	0.5
Main language	2000	1	0.04	0.62	0.49	0.95	0.21
SHP							
Feelings (i)	1999–2007	0.63	0.48	0.8	0.4	0.64	0.48
Feelings (ii)	1999	2.27	1.22	2.11	1.16	2.22	1.17
Gender (ii)	2000–2007	5.08	2.65	4.98	3.02	5.17	2.65
Religion (i)	1999–2007	0.27	0.44	0.25	0.44	0.26	0.44
Religion (ii)	1999–2007	0.24	0.42	0.21	0.41	0.24	0.42
Policy (i)	1999–2007	5.06	2.18	4.39	2.22	4.97	2.14
Policy (ii)	1999–2007	6.03	2.01	6.38	2.18	6.19	1.93

Source: Swiss census, 2000; SHP, 1999–2007.

for natives, first-generation, and second-generation migrants are displayed in Table 7.2.

- Educational attainment: the number of years of education.[10] The sample is limited to individuals aged 25 years or more.

[10] In the census as well as in the SHP, the available educational variable is categorical. De Coulon *et al.* (2003) proposed a scale to compute the number of years of education.

- Marriage: a dummy equals 1 if an individual is married; the sample is composed of all women aged 18 years or more. Widows are excluded.

- Mixed couple: a dummy equals 1 if a Swiss individual has a partner from a different country of origin; the sample is limited to individuals in a couple, aged 18 years or more. Mixed couples where neither of the partners is Swiss are excluded.

- Age gap between partners: the age difference between the male and female partners; the sample is limited to individuals in a couple, aged 18 years or more.

- Education gap between partners: the difference in number of years of education between the male and female partners; the sample is limited to individuals in a couple, aged 18 years or more.

- Early marriage: a dummy equals 1 if an individual is married; the sample is limited to women aged between 18 and 25 years. Widows are excluded.

- Cohabitation: a dummy equals 1 if an individual lives in cohabitation; the sample is limited to individuals married or living in cohabitation.

- Fertility: the number of children of women aged 40 years or more.

- Divorce: a dummy equals 1 if an individual is divorced; the sample is composed of married and divorced women only, aged 18 years or more.

- Female labour force participation: a dummy equals 1 if a woman is in the labour force; the sample is limited to women aged between 25 and 62 years.

- Main language: a dummy equals 1 if an individual uses one of the four Swiss national languages (French, German, Italian, Romansh) as his main language.

- Feelings towards Switzerland: (1) In favour of more equality between Swiss and foreigners:[11] a dummy equals 1 if the respondent declares to be in favour of more equality. (2) In favour of opening Swiss traditions:[12] a dummy equals 1 if the respondent declares to be in favour of opening Swiss traditions to the world.

---

[11] Original question: Are you in favour of Switzerland offering foreigners the same opportunities as those offered to Swiss citizens, or in favour of Switzerland offering Swiss citizens better opportunities? Possible choices: in favour of equality of opportunities, neither, in favour of better opportunities for Swiss citizens.

[12] Orignal question: Are you in favour of Switzerland opening towards other countries, or in favour of Switzerland defending its traditions? Possible choices: opening towards other countries, neither, defending traditions.

- Gender attitudes: (1) Child suffers if mother is working:[13] 0 if the respondent does not agree at all with the statement, 10 if she totally agrees; the sample is limited to women. (2) Women penalized in general:[14] 0 if the respondent does not agree at all with the statement, 10 if he totally agrees; the sample is limited to men.

- Religious attitudes: (1) Participation in religious services:[15] a dummy equals 1 if the respondent declares she participates in religious services at least occasionally (not only on special occasions). (2) Prayers:[16] a dummy equals 1 if the respondent declares he prays at least occasionally.

- Political attitudes: (1) Political affiliation:[17] 0 if a respondent declares to have extreme left political views, 10 if extreme right. (2) Satisfaction with Swiss democracy:[18] 0 if a respondent does not agree at all with the statement, 10 if he totally agrees.

7.5.2 Specifications

The methodology used to investigate the evolution of migrants' objective behaviours and subjective attitudes is common to all chapters and presented in the introduction of this book. However, in addition to comparing outcomes between first and second-generation migrants, this chapter also looks at differences across birth cohorts (born before vs. born after 1970), across types of couples (endogamous vs. mixed couples) and across genders.

In addition to the regressors used in the specification common to all chapters, some additional controls are included to deal with specificities of Switzerland and of the datasets. With SHP data, the specification includes year dummies. With census data, the specification also controls for four linguistic regions, sixteen economic regions and four types of

---

[13] Original question: Please tell me how far you would agree with the statements I am going to read to you now, if 0 means 'I completely disagree' and 10 'I completely agree'. A pre-school child suffers, if his or her mother works for pay.

[14] Original question: Do you have the feeling that in Switzerland women are penalized compared with men in certain areas, if 0 means 'not at all penalized' and 10 'strongly penalized'?

[15] Original question: How frequently do you take part in religious services? In the beginning, no answer is proposed by the interviewer.

[16] Original question: How frequently do you pray apart from at church or within a religious community? In the beginning, no answer is proposed by the interviewer.

[17] Original question: When they talk about politics, people mention left and right. Personally, where do you position yourself, 0 means 'left' and 10 'right'?

[18] Original question: Overall, how satisfied are you with the way in which democracy works in our country, if 0 means 'not at all satisfied' and 10 'completely satisfied'?

communes. In order not to truncate the sample arbitrarily when looking at specific effects tied to intermarriage on a variable that is observable on individuals whether they are a couple or not (fertility, labour force participation, language), three civil status dummies are included to keep non-married individuals in the sample.[19] Finally, whereas a gender dummy is generally included in the analysis of attitudes, most regressions looking at behaviours focus strictly on women.

7.6 Results

This section first analyses how the behaviours of migrants have evolved in comparison to those of the natives in the three units of observations mentioned above: at school, in the couple, and in the labour market. It then turns to the subjective attitudes of migrants.

7.6.1 Objective behaviours

Integration processes cannot be localized geographically or institutionally, but some units of analysis are especially relevant. School is the first place where all second-generation migrants are exposed to natives and native culture, and attending school is an important integration mechanism. Second, couples are part of the private sphere. It is therefore of particular interest to observe differing patterns of integration between individuals in endogamous couples and partners of mixed couples, where cultural accommodations and compromises are a necessity. Finally, the labour market is another mechanism stimulating contacts between natives and migrants outside the household.

7.6.1.1 AT SCHOOL
According to recent studies, migrants fare rather well in the Swiss educational system. Focusing on a sample of second-generation Italian and Spanish migrants in the cantons of Geneva and Basel, Bolzman and Fibbi (2003) observe that their educational achievements are as good as those of natives. Using 2000 census data on 17-year-old individuals still in the parental household to analyse intergenerational transmission of educational attainment, Bauer and Riphahn (2007) found evidence of higher intergenerational mobility among second-generation migrants. They also found that their achievements or

---

[19] Married natives are the reference group.

Table 7.3 Group averages: educational attainment and the gender education gap (in years of education).

Origin	Years of education					Gender education gap		
	Women			Men		(Women–men)		
	Born	Born CH	(second–first)	Born abroad	Born CH	(second–first)	Born abroad	Born CH
Natives		11.56			12.85			−1.29
WE	12.67	12.99	0.32	14.34	13.83	−0.52	−1.67	−0.84
SE	9.63	12.03	2.40	10.23	12.70	2.47	−0.59	−0.66
EE	10.99	11.19	0.19	11.41	11.53	0.12	−0.42	−0.34
AF	11.10	12.77	1.67	12.33	13.15	0.82	−1.23	−0.38
TMM	10.36	11.51	1.15	11.39	11.65	0.26	−1.03	−0.14
SA	12.03	12.50	0.47	13.12	13.78	0.66	−1.10	−1.28
AS	11.62	11.24	−0.38	12.59	12.28	−0.30	−0.97	−1.04
SCA	11.17	11.26	0.10	11.14	10.62	−0.52	0.02	0.64
Total	11.28	12.29	1.00	11.85	12.95	1.10	−0.57	−0.67

Source: Swiss census, 2000.

failures are less dependent upon the level of education of their parents. Fibbi *et al.* (2005) observed that naturalized migrants are less likely to have a low education level, but this is not the case of non-naturalized first and second-generation migrants (except for Spaniards and Germans). How does the picture change if the scope of the analysis is enlarged to further include non-European migrants?

Table 7.3 shows the average number of years of education across migrant groups and the gender education gap. This table confirms the impressive educational success of second-generation migrants from Southern Europe that has been documented in previous studies. African women are in a similar situation. However, results also show that the educational achievements of 'Secundas' and 'Secundos'[20] are not characteristic of all second-generation migrants. Such an outcome might be partly explained by the fact that first-generation migrants are self-selected among the most motivated and capable individuals or by the lack of specific knowledge among migrant parents about the Swiss education system.

Despite the observed negative trend, the gender education gap common to all first-generation groups is reverted among second-generation migrants, with the exception of Western Europeans and Latin Americans, who have the highest average education levels, and Southern

---

[20] In reference to the title of the study of Bolzmann and Fibbi (2003) about second-generation migrants from Southern Europe.

Table 7.4 Educational attainment (I).

Origin	Women		Men	
	First gen.	Second gen.	First gen.	Second gen.
WE	0.928***	0.815***	1.235***	0.367***
	(0.006)	(0.014)	(0.007)	(0.015)
SE	−2.304***	−0.255***	−2.973***	0.856***
	(0.007)	(0.010)	(0.006)	(0.010)
EE	−1.041***	−1.076***	−1.796***	−1.902***
	(0.008)	(0.040)	(0.008)	(0.040)
AF	−1.266***	0.412***	−1.304***	−0.266*
	(0.024)	(0.141)	(0.025)	(0.160)
TMM	−1.855***	−0.828***	−2.036***	−1.910***
	(0.015)	(0.051)	(0.013)	(0.054)
LA	−0.311***	0.272**	−0.468***	0.473***
	(0.016)	(0.108)	(0.026)	(0.119)
AS	−0.607***	−1.031***	−0.844***	−1.171***
	(0.016)	(0.160)	(0.026)	(0.202)
SCA	−1.150***	−0.983***	−2.324***	−2.983***
	(0.025)	(0.132)	(0.020)	(0.147)
Observations	4,460,422			
R^2	0.18			

Source: Swiss census, 2000; standard errors in parentheses; *** p <0.01, ** p <0.05, * p <0.1.

European women, who make the largest progress from the first to the second generation.

Results in Table 7.4 (plotted in Figure 7.2) confirm that migrant women progress more at school than their male counterparts. It seems that second-generation men from South and Central Asia, Turkey, the Middle East, and Maghreb and Eastern Europe remain in a low education equilibrium. The better performance of Western Europeans is not very surprising given the very high education level of the first generation, but the impressive results of second-generation Latin Americans, Africans, and the tremendous progress of Southern Europeans support the idea that individuals with a mother tongue close to one of the Swiss national languages (in this case Latin languages) fare better at school.

Table 7.5 provides more detailed information about cohort effects for both genders (plotted in Figures 7.3 and 7.4). A striking result is that the educational level of first-generation migrants is generally declining. Another interesting trend is that second-generation men from Turkey, the Middle East, and Maghreb and Eastern Europe that are born after 1970 fare better than those born before 1970.

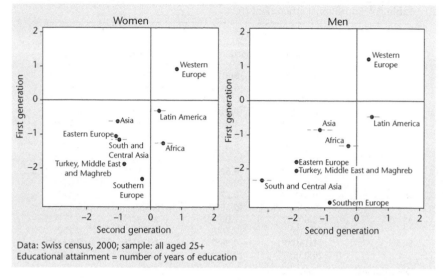

Data: Swiss census, 2000; sample: all aged 25+
Educational attainment = number of years of education

Figure 7.2 Educational attainment.

7.6.1.2 THE COUPLES

Previous studies (Wanner and Fibbi, 2002; Wanner *et al.*, 2005a) have looked at the role of the family in the migration and integration process. They observe that compared to natives, second-generation migrants tend to remain in the parental household for a longer period and get married after a much shorter cohabitation period with their partner. The overall marriage rate, however, is converging across migrant groups. In their qualitative study on binational couples, Ossipow and Waldis (2003) analyse the interests and strategies of both intermarried partners. Noticing that homogamy and heterogamy exist across many dimensions in any couple, they point to the existence of complementary exchanges in each couple.

In this chapter, the analysis is extended to examine the position of women in mixed as well as in endogamous couples. To what extent does origin matter in matching partners? Are women from some groups more likely to contract early marriage and have many children? It is often assumed that migrants from poorer countries are more inclined to form traditional unions with a clear distribution of roles within the household, but to what extent are these clichés supported by facts and do such behaviours persist among second-generation migrants? Also, if some

Table 7.5 Educational attainment (II).

Origin	Women				Men			
	Pre-1970		Post-1970		Pre-1970		Post-1970	
	First gen.	Second gen.	First gen.	Second gen.	First gen.	Second gen.	First gen.	Second gen.
WE	0.926***	0.716***	1.069***	0.533***	1.299***	0.621***	0.933***	0.294***
	(0.006)	(0.016)	(0.020)	(0.029)	(0.008)	(0.019)	(0.025)	(0.033)
SE	−2.330***	−0.424***	−2.458***	−0.555***	−2.948***	−0.621***	−2.876***	−0.801***
	(0.007)	(0.012)	(0.023)	(0.018)	(0.007)	(0.014)	(0.025)	(0.019)
EE	−0.979***	−1.822***	−1.771***	−0.676***	−1.592***	−2.196***	−2.569***	−1.110***
	(0.008)	(0.052)	(0.019)	(0.062)	(0.009)	(0.056)	(0.024)	(0.073)
AF	−1.274***	0.269*	−2.114***	0.163	−0.829***	−0.0861	−2.279***	−0.0242
	(0.025)	(0.158)	(0.050)	(0.277)	(0.029)	(0.203)	(0.062)	(0.346)
TMM	−1.905***	−0.840***	−2.424***	−1.347***	−1.820***	−2.018***	−2.515***	−1.440***
	(0.016)	(0.064)	(0.034)	(0.083)	(0.015)	(0.084)	(0.035)	(0.089)
LA	−0.208***	0.111	−1.541***	0.368*	−0.0217	0.678***	−1.472***	0.333
	(0.017)	(0.118)	(0.037)	(0.222)	(0.031)	(0.144)	(0.067)	(0.308)
AS	−0.611***	−1.263***	−1.325***	−0.998***	−0.705***	−1.607***	−0.889***	0.215
	(0.017)	(0.178)	(0.038)	(0.319)	(0.030)	(0.267)	(0.067)	(0.395)
SCA	−0.948***	−0.764***	−2.444***	−2.911***	−2.032***	−2.846***	−3.172***	−3.046***
	(0.027)	(0.136)	(0.050)	(0.344)	(0.023)	(0.191)	(0.051)	(0.294)
Observations	2,255,991				2,120,707			
R^2	0.17				0.13			

Source: Swiss census, 2000; standard errors in parentheses; *** $p < 0.01$, ** $p < 0.05$, * $p < 0.1$.

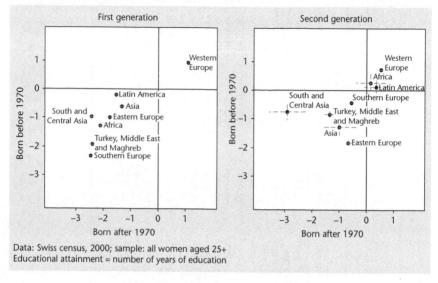

Data: Swiss census, 2000; sample: all women aged 25+
Educational attainment = number of years of education

Figure 7.3 Female educational attainment.

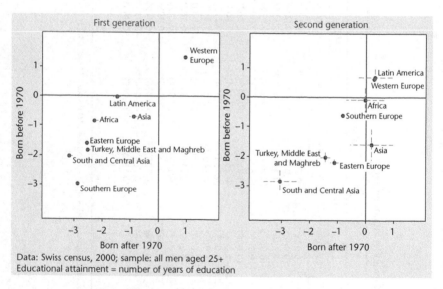

Data: Swiss census, 2000; sample: all men aged 25+
Educational attainment = number of years of education

Figure 7.4 Male educational attainment.

Table 7.6 Marriage and divorce.

Origin	Marriage		Divorce			
	All		Pre-1970		Post-1970	
	First gen.	Second gen.	First gen.	Second gen.	First gen.	Second gen.
WE	0.0573***	−0.0218***	0.00793***	−0.0504***	0.0196***	−0.0301***
	(0.001)	(0.002)	(0.001)	(0.002)	(0.002)	(0.005)
SE	0.195***	0.0825***	−0.0582***	−0.0677***	−0.0288***	−0.0342***
	(0.001)	(0.001)	(0.001)	(0.002)	(0.001)	(0.002)
EE	0.252***	0.127***	−0.0292***	−0.0730***	−0.0530***	−0.0343***
	(0.001)	(0.005)	(0.001)	(0.001)	(0.005)	(0.008)
AF	0.179***	0.102***	−0.00420	−0.0601***	−0.00989	−0.0859***
	(0.003)	(0.020)	(0.003)	(0.004)	(0.020)	(0.023)
TMM	0.253***	0.151***	−0.0347***	−0.0608***	−0.00561	−0.0101
	(0.001)	(0.005)	(0.001)	(0.002)	(0.008)	(0.010)
LA	0.230***	0.0532***	−0.0102***	−0.0567***	0.0271	−0.0469
	(0.001)	(0.016)	(0.002)	(0.003)	(0.017)	(0.030)
AS	0.201***	0.0680***	−0.0232***	−0.0627***	−0.0394**	−0.0722*
	(0.002)	(0.023)	(0.002)	(0.003)	(0.019)	(0.037)
SCA	0.274***	0.250***	−0.0721***	−0.0988***	−0.0894***	−0.0908***
	(0.002)	(0.012)	(0.002)	(0.002)	(0.007)	(0.01)
Education	−0.010***		−4.72e−05			
	(0.0001)		(0.0001)			
Observations	2,276,316		1,655,090			
PR^2	0.18		0.035			
ll	−1.217e+06		−585,480			

Source: SHP, 1999–2007; standard errors in parentheses; *** p <0.01, ** p <0.05, * p <0.1.

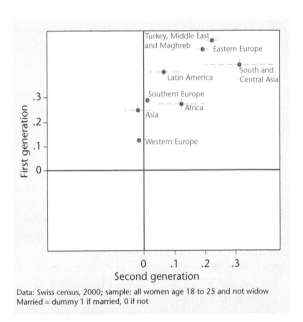

Data: Swiss census, 2000; sample: all women age 18 to 25 and not widow
Married = dummy 1 if married, 0 if not

Figure 7.5 Marriage.

behaviours seem more deeply rooted in specific communities, how do women of these communities behave in mixed couples?

Marriage: Results in Table 7.6 (plotted in Figure 7.5) show the marginal effect of origin dummies on the probability of getting married. First-generation women are much more likely to be married than natives. Differences among migrant groups hint at the existence of distinct cultural patterns. Western Europeans display the lowest propensity to be married. The decrease in the probability of second-generation women being married compared to the level of native women points to at least two possible hypotheses. Either cultural differences in the decision to marry disappear or there are other strong incentives (for example legal incentives) for first-generation migrants to get married, which do not exist for the second generation. Looking at differences across cohorts reveals that young first-generation migrants are more likely to get married compared to natives, whereas the opposite is true for the second generation. This might be due to more stringent legal conditions for entering Switzerland happening in parallel to a cultural trend to marry less that is not migrant-specific. This is true even for women of Central and South Asia, who remain in a very robust and much more traditional equilibrium characterized by a high probability of being married for first as well as second-generation migrants.

Mixed couples: Intermarriages differ from endogamous marriages because, through the partner and his social network, a migrant is exposed to the native culture in a way that is not possible in an endogamous relationship. Table 7.7 shows the distribution of endogamous and mixed couples across migrant groups. 'Other' couples are composed of partners from different origins, but none of them Swiss. First-generation women intermarry more than their male counterparts. Only women from Turkey, the Middle East, Maghreb, and South and Central Asia do not, and more surprisingly, this is accentuated for second-generation women belonging to these groups. The intermarriage rate of second-generation Western European, Latin American, and African women also decreases a lot, but from a very high initial level. Asian women remain in the highest equilibrium despite a slight decrease; Eastern and Southern European second-generation women are the only groups which enter mixed unions more than their mothers.

The marginal effect of origin dummies on the probability of being in a mixed couple reported in Table 7.8 (plotted in Figure 7.6) confirms the intuition conveyed by statistics in Table 7.7. First-generation migrant women from Latin America, Asia, Western Europe, and Africa are

Table 7.7 Group averages: mixed couples (in %).

Origin	Women						Men					
	Born abroad			(second–first)			Born abroad			(second–first)		
	Endo	Inter	Other	Endo	Inter	Other	Endo	Inter	Other	Endo	Inter	Other
Natives	90.8	9.2					86.76	13.24				
WE	36.6	53.6	9.8	9.6	−10.6	1	49.5	39.8	10.6	−2.5	0.4	2.1
SE	79.6	15.6	4.9	−13.1	10	3.1	76.5	15.6	7.9	−27.8	22.7	5.1
EE	82.1	12.2	5.8	−2.3	1.4	0.9	87	8	5	−2	1.7	0.3
AF	36.6	43.7	19.7	25.3	−18.7	−6.6	44.1	32.7	23.2	17.4	−7.2	−10.2
TMM	78.9	13.1	8	6.3	−5.3	−1	67	20.2	12.8	7.2	−6.9	−0.3
SA	19.9	57.6	22.6	18.4	−17	−1.4	38.8	37.4	23.8	20.2	−12.3	−7.9
AS	30.3	57	12.7	2.9	−5.6	2.7	73.8	16.4	9.8	−9.1	4.2	4.9
SCA	85.5	8.6	5.9	7.7	−4	−3.7	78.3	12.4	9.3	10.6	−5.9	−4.7
Total	61.5	30.4	8.2				70.6	20.5	8.9			

Source: Swiss census, 2000.

Table 7.8 Mixed couples.

Origin	All		Pre-1970		Post-1970	
	First gen.	Second gen.	First gen.	Second gen.	First gen.	Second gen.
WE	0.513***	0.389***	0.528***	0.376***	0.342***	0.555***
	(0.001)	(0.003)	(0.001)	(0.005)	(0.004)	(0.007)
SE	0.091***	0.176***	0.105***	−0.010***	0.167***	0.179***
	(0.001)	(0.002)	(0.001)	(0.003)	(0.002)	(0.004)
EE	0.049***	0.096***	0.066***	−0.005**	0.078***	0.095***
	(0.001)	(0.008)	(0.001)	(0.002)	(0.011)	(0.011)
AF	0.487***	0.186***	0.514***	0.388***	0.125***	0.302***
	(0.006)	(0.036)	(0.006)	(0.012)	(0.040)	(0.068)
TMM	0.060***	−0.023***	0.094***	−0.028***	−0.017	−0.039***
	(0.002)	(0.007)	(0.003)	(0.004)	(0.011)	(0.009)
LA	0.646***	0.423***	0.649***	0.622***	0.389***	0.521***
	(0.003)	(0.029)	(0.003)	(0.007)	(0.033)	(0.059)
AS	0.589***	0.574***	0.592***	0.560***	0.589***	0.507***
	(0.003)	(0.035)	(0.003)	(0.008)	(0.040)	(0.074)
SCA	−0.002	−0.061***	0.023***	−0.062***	−0.066***	−0.052
	(0.004)	(0.016)	(0.005)	(0.005)	(0.018)	(0.035)
Education	0.007***		0.007***			
	(0.001)		(0.001)			
Observations	1,492,037		1,492,037			
PR²	0.18		0.18			
ll	−548,027		−546,437			

Source: Swiss census, 2000; standard errors in parentheses; *** p <0.01, ** p <0.05, * p <0.1.

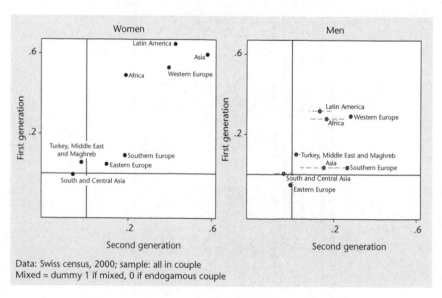

Data: Swiss census, 2000; sample: all in couple
Mixed = dummy 1 if mixed, 0 if endogamous couple

Figure 7.6 Mixed couples.

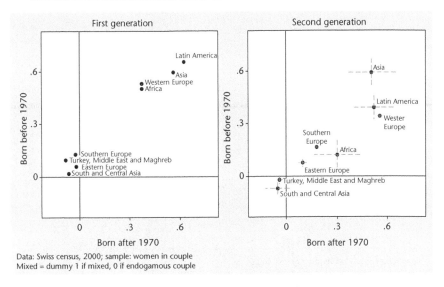

Figure 7.7 Women in mixed couples.

around 50 per cent more likely than natives to enter a mixed union. Asian women are more likely to choose a Swiss partner than their male counterpart. Women originating from South and Central Asia and Turkey, the Middle East and Maghreb are exceptions in this regard and, more surprisingly, the marginal effect for second-generation women of these groups is negative. Eastern and Southern European women also have a low probability of entering a mixed couple, but it increases for the second generation. It is also interesting to notice that whereas the propensity to choose a native partner rather decreases for second-generation women, it is less the case for men.

This trend also evolves slowly over time: young second-generation female migrants tend to have a lower probability of having a relationship with a native man compared to their mothers, but this probability is equal or higher for women born after 1970. The same is true for male migrants, and the magnitude of the change is even higher (Figures 7.7 and 7.8). The only exceptions are, again, women originating from South and Central Asia and Turkey, the Middle East, and Maghreb. It is surprising to see that their probability of intermarrying decreases for second-generation and younger migrants. This strong preference for endogamy contrasts with trends in other groups.

Different couples—early marriage vs. cohabitation: How do couples form? Early marriage is often associated with a traditional gender role

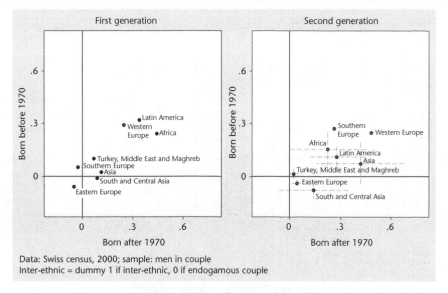

Data: Swiss census, 2000; sample: men in couple
Inter-ethnic = dummy 1 if inter-ethnic, 0 if endogamous couple

Figure 7.8 Men in mixed couples.

distribution between husband and wife, whereas cohabiting couples are supposedly more fragile, and consist of more independent partners. Table 7.9 shows that most migrant groups (across cohorts and types of couples) have a higher propensity for early marriage compared to natives, especially women from Eastern Europe, Turkey, the Middle East, Maghreb, and Central and South Asia. However, this tendency diminishes for all second-generation groups. It seems that migrant groups with the highest probability of getting married also do so at a younger age.

Cohabitation is a rather recent phenomenon that has developed as more women have started to become economically independent and politically empowered. It is not surprising that first-generation migrants are less likely to choose cohabitation over marriage. However, this propensity increases for the second generation, more so for women from Europe, Latin America, and Asia. The coefficients of the post-1970 cohort in Table 7.9 also clearly indicate that there is a cohort-specific change in behaviours concerning cohabitation. Whereas migrants born before 1970 behave more or less alike across generations, second-generation migrants born after 1970 converge to the native baseline, although less rapidly for women of Central and South Asia, Turkey, the Middle East, and Maghreb. Mixed couples are much more likely to

Table 7.9 Early marriage vs. cohabitation.

Origin	Early marriage		Cohabitation					
	All		All		Pre-1970		Post-1970	
	First gen.	Second gen.	First gen.	Second gen.	First gen.	Second gen.	First gen.	Second gen.
WE	0.124***	−0.0170***	−0.0240***	0.00376**	−0.0200***	−0.0125***	−0.0403***	0.0375***
	(0.004)	(0.002)	(0.001)	(0.001)	(0.0007)	(0.002)	(0.001)	(0.004)
SE	0.291***	0.046***	−0.060***	−0.034***	−0.054***	−0.041***	−0.072***	−0.030***
	(0.005)	(0.002)	(0.001)	(0.001)	(0.001)	(0.001)	(0.001)	(0.001)
EE	0.522***	0.191***	−0.079***	−0.055***	−0.065***	−0.054***	−0.083***	−0.059***
	(0.004)	(0.009)	(0.0003)	(0.001)	(0.001)	(0.003)	(0.0002)	(0.002)
AF	0.273***	0.123***	−0.060***	−0.063***	−0.052***	−0.075***	−0.071***	−0.052***
	(0.011)	(0.039)	(0.001)	(0.006)	(0.002)	(0.005)	(0.001)	(0.012)
TMM	0.532***	0.232***	−0.077***	−0.072***	−0.069***	−0.064***	−0.082***	−0.076***
	(0.007)	(0.011)	(0.0003)	(0.001)	(0.0007)	(0.003)	(0.0002)	(0.001)
LA	0.403***	0.064***	−0.066***	−0.045***	−0.058***	−0.044***	−0.075***	−0.052***
	(0.009)	(0.024)	(0.0006)	(0.007)	(0.001)	(0.010)	(0.0006)	(0.010)
AS	0.250***	−0.020	−0.062***	−0.049***	−0.055***	−0.072***	−0.074***	−0.011
	(0.009)	(0.023)	(0.0007)	(0.009)	(0.001)	(0.006)	(0.0007)	(0.024)
SCA	0.432***	0.313***	−0.077***	−0.075***	−0.074***	−0.077***	−0.079***	−0.076***
	(0.012)	(0.057)	(0.0004)	(0.002)	(0.0008)	(0.003)	(0.0004)	(0.003)
Education	−0.018***		0.002***		0.002***			
	(0.0002)		(9.92e-05)		(9.97e-05)			
Observations	281,477		1,531,937		1,531,937			
PR²	0.30		0.13		0.13			
ll	−79,229		−454,518		−452,617			

*Source: Swiss census, 2000; standard errors in parentheses; *** p <0.01, ** p <0.05, * p <0.1.*

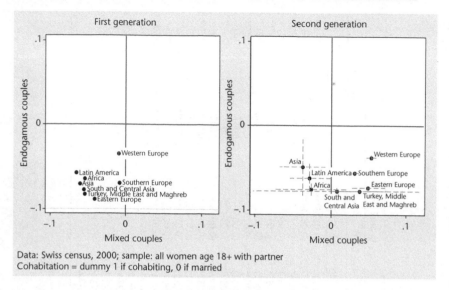

Figure 7.9 Cohabitation.

cohabit than endogamous couples (Figure 7.9). This supports the hypothesis that individuals living as mixed couples may be more liberal, but that legal incentives for first-generation migrants to improve their conditions of stay (or that of their partner) are strong enough to influence the decision to get married.

Partners' differences—age and education gap: Waldis (2008) stresses that heterogamy/homogamy in the couple is not limited to its ethnic dimension, and that complementary/symmetric exchanges happen at different levels in any couple. Table 7.10 shows three clear trends in relation to the role of age and education as matching factors in the couple. First, there seems to be a difference between European women, who are usually slightly younger than their partner, and non-European women, who display larger age gaps. More striking is the fact that non-European first-generation women born after 1970 are significantly younger than their partner (Figure 7.10). Age gaps might be explained by the fact that men who migrated alone only find a partner later on in their life. Some of them return home to choose a younger partner and then bring them back to Switzerland (Wanner *et al.*, 2005a). The age asymmetry is stronger among migrants born after 1970. However, age gaps in mixed couples are even larger for non-EU first-generation migrants, which supports the hypothesis that access to a permit or

Table 7.10 Age gap between partners.

Origin	All		Endo		Inter	
	First gen.	Second gen.	First gen.	Second gen.	First gen.	Second gen.
WE	−0.070***	0.101***	−0.152***	−0.123**	−0.073***	0.254***
	(0.015)	(0.038)	(0.024)	(0.055)	(0.020)	(0.057)
SE	0.118***	0.444***	0.060***	0.238***	0.695***	0.740***
	(0.017)	(0.026)	(0.019)	(0.031)	(0.039)	(0.049)
EE	−0.424***	0.301***	−0.026	0.321***	−2.102***	0.235
	(0.018)	(0.092)	(0.020)	(0.108)	(0.048)	(0.221)
AF	−2.645***	−0.174	−2.280***	1.465***	−3.648***	−3.991***
	(0.058)	(0.366)	(0.100)	(0.471)	(0.086)	(0.729)
TMM	−1.174***	0.099	−0.797***	0.335***	−2.618***	−1.410***
	(0.034)	(0.116)	(0.039)	(0.126)	(0.090)	(0.396)
LA	−1.334***	−0.676**	−0.115	−0.380	−1.734***	−0.892**
	(0.039)	(0.275)	(0.087)	(0.440)	(0.050)	(0.432)
AS	−1.799***	−1.547***	−0.704***	−0.223	−2.457***	−1.866***
	(0.039)	(0.380)	(0.072)	(0.695)	(0.051)	(0.510)
SCA	−1.559***	−1.485***	−1.597***	−1.662***	−1.359***	1.578
	(0.055)	(0.299)	(0.060)	(0.312)	(0.175)	(1.262)
Education	0.072***		0.077***			
	(0.001)		(0.001)			
Observations	1,532,692		1,532,692			
R^2	0.03		0.03			

Source: Swiss census, 2000; standard errors in parentheses; *** $p < 0.01$, ** $p < 0.05$, * $p < 0.1$.

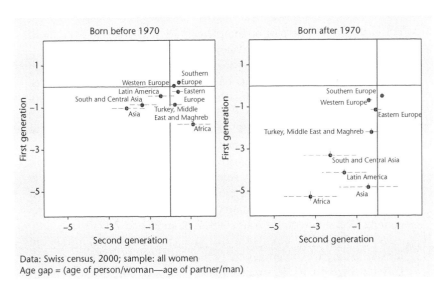

Data: Swiss census, 2000; sample: all women
Age gap = (age of person/woman—age of partner/man)

Figure 7.10 Age gap between partners.

237

Table 7.11 Education gap between partners.

Origin	Pre-1970		Post-1970		Endo	
	First gen.	Second gen.	First gen.	Second gen.	First gen.	Second gen.
WE	−0.213***	−0.260***	0.100***	0.062*	−0.728***	−0.381***
	(0.007)	(0.019)	(0.023)	(0.035)	(0.011)	(0.024)
SE	1.481***	0.870***	1.421***	0.889***	1.941***	1.285***
	(0.008)	(0.013)	(0.021)	(0.021)	(0.008)	(0.014)
EE	0.960***	1.079***	1.030***	0.888***	1.133***	1.312***
	(0.009)	(0.057)	(0.016)	(0.059)	(0.009)	(0.047)
AF	−0.076**	−0.027	−0.105**	1.138***	0.223***	0.514**
	(0.030)	(0.196)	(0.050)	(0.295)	(0.044)	(0.209)
TMM	1.066***	0.938***	1.042***	1.166***	1.405***	1.220***
	(0.018)	(0.073)	(0.029)	(0.072)	(0.017)	(0.056)
LA	0.077***	−0.054	−0.293***	−0.007	0.355***	−0.086
	(0.020)	(0.142)	(0.034)	(0.246)	(0.038)	(0.195)
AS	0.034*	0.443**	−0.307***	0.025	0.669***	1.070***
	(0.019)	(0.199)	(0.038)	(0.325)	(0.032)	(0.308)
SCA	0.968***	−0.005	1.572***	1.135***	1.467***	0.301**
	(0.030)	(0.150)	(0.043)	(0.291)	(0.026)	(0.138)
Education	0.425***				0.444***	
	(0.0008)				(0.0008)	
Observations	1,532,692				1,532,692	
R^2	0.17				0.18	

Source: Swiss census, 2000; standard errors in parentheses; *** $p <0.01$, ** $p <0.05$, * $p <0.1$.

citizenship might be part of complementary exchanges happening in mixed couples (Ossipow and Waldis, 2003).

However, the age asymmetry observed in mixed couples is balanced by the fact that partners have almost the same education level. Whereas education only seems to have a small impact on the probability of intermarrying, women who intermarry least (from South and Central Asia, Turkey, the Middle East, and Maghreb) also have the highest education gaps in endogamous couples. One likely reason for them to intermarry could be to live with a partner that has a similar level of education. In any case, it seems that having similar education levels is a factor in matching partners of different origins, and that education represents an important common ground between individuals coming from different horizons (Table 7.11 and Figure 7.11).

Fertility: Table 7.12 reports the marginal effect of origin dummies on fertility. Migrant women generally have more children than natives. Differences tend to be smaller for the second generation. Women from Switzerland, Western and Southern Europe, Latin America, and Asia have lower fertility rates than Eastern European women,

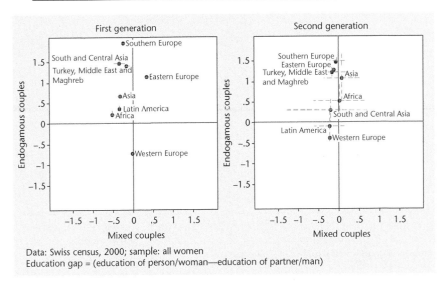

Data: Swiss census, 2000; sample: all women
Education gap = (education of person/woman—education of partner/man)

Figure 7.11 Education gap between partners.

Table 7.12 Completed fertility rate.

Origin	All		Endo		Inter	
	First gen.	Second gen.	First gen.	Second gen.	First gen.	Second gen.
WE	−0.122***	−0.056***	−0.180***	−0.074***	−0.195***	−0.047*
	(0.003)	(0.011)	(0.007)	(0.016)	(0.005)	(0.025)
SE	0.076***	0.061***	0.012**	−0.026**	−0.189***	−0.070**
	(0.004)	(0.010)	(0.005)	(0.012)	(0.011)	(0.027)
EE	0.200***	0.226***	0.273***	0.189***	−0.443***	−0.202
	(0.006)	(0.042)	(0.007)	(0.046)	(0.016)	(0.137)
AF	0.396***	0.325***	0.862***	0.219	−0.093***	−0.354
	(0.020)	(0.126)	(0.042)	(0.173)	(0.031)	(0.356)
TMM	0.560***	0.339***	0.702***	0.242***	−0.173***	−0.077
	(0.012)	(0.054)	(0.015)	(0.061)	(0.031)	(0.252)
LA	0.167***	0.088	0.271***	0.038	−0.200***	−0.091
	(0.013)	(0.085)	(0.032)	(0.136)	(0.019)	(0.175)
AS	0.031**	−0.183	0.375***	0.022	−0.417***	−0.432*
	(0.013)	(0.154)	(0.025)	(0.283)	(0.019)	(0.225)
SCA	0.410***	0.300***	0.351***	0.026	−0.193***	0.372
	(0.022)	(0.102)	(0.028)	(0.109)	(0.060)	(0.552)
Education	−0.058***		−0.041***			
	(0.0004)		(0.0004)			
Observations	1,512,842		1,512,842			
R^2	0.08		0.23			

Source: Swiss census, 2000; standard errors in parentheses; *** $p < 0.01$, ** $p < 0.05$, * $p < 0.1$..

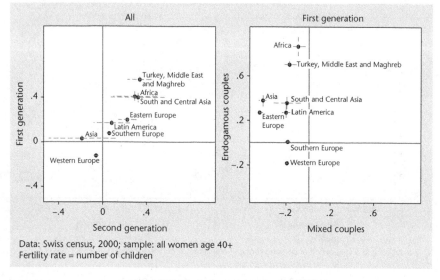

Data: Swiss census, 2000; sample: all women age 40+
Fertility rate = number of children

Figure 7.12 Completed fertility rate.

and women from Turkey, the Middle East, Maghreb, Africa, or South and Central Asia have the highest fertility rate. The coefficient of second-generation Asian women is not significant, but they seem to have a fertility pattern that is different from other non-European migrant groups. Second-generation women from the Middle East, Maghreb, and Turkey still display the largest differential, but the drop in their fertility rate is also the largest. As expected, the number of years of education has a negative and significant effect on the completed fertility rate.

Although coefficients of the second generation are not significant, columns 3–6 in Table 7.12 (Figure 7.12) indicate that the fertility rate of women in mixed couples is similar to that of natives. In endogamous couples, first-generation migrants from Africa, Turkey, the Middle East, and Maghreb have the most children.

Divorce: Differences in the probability of getting divorced vary across migrant groups, but the groups that tend to be more traditional in marriage also divorce less. Second-generation migrants have a higher divorce rate, but as was observed in cohabitation, it seems that the cultural trend facilitating divorce is not origin specific, but cohort specific (Table 7.5 and Figure 7.13).

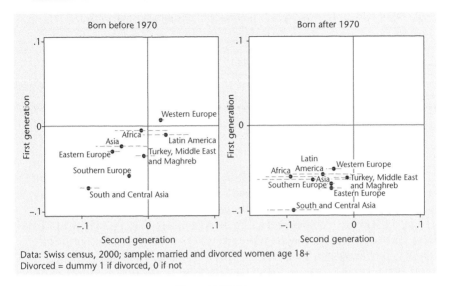

Data: Swiss census, 2000; sample: married and divorced women age 18+
Divorced = dummy 1 if divorced, 0 if not

Figure 7.13 Divorce.

7.6.1.3 IN THE LABOUR MARKET

Wanner *et al.* (2003) conducted a thorough analysis of factors impacting female labour force participation. They noticed that three factors specifically influence migrant women's behaviour in this regard: gender roles imported from the origin country, household income, and the fact that some permits are related to a pre-existing work contract. Although they are more likely to be active in the labour market compared to native women, migrant women originating from some countries display a significantly lower labour force participation rate. Fibbi *et al.* (2005) also propose an analysis of the probability of being out of the labour force, focusing on individuals aged 23–34 years. They do not find evidence of lower labour force participation of migrants compared to natives. Their results do not support the hypothesis that women from 'culturally distant' populations have a lower propensity to participate in the labour force. As mentioned before, their report focuses on European migrants, but how does the picture change when the scope of the analysis is enlarged to include non-European migrant women?

Table 7.13 shows that although there may be cultural differences among first-generation women that lead to varying labour force participation rates, second-generation women almost behave like natives.

Table 7.13 Group averages: female labour force participation (in %).

	Natives	WE	SE	EE	AF	TMM	SA	AS	SCA	Total
Born in Switzerland	75.4	81.9	84.1	82.1	82.6	82.9	78.3	71.4	77.5	76
Married	67	73.3	76.7	76.5	78.5	77.3	70.4	66	76.9	67.6
Single	88.7	90.6	93.3	90.9	89.1	90.8	88.2	78.7	81.3	89
Foreign born		72.1	74.6	74.8	75.1	69.3	70.6	68.8	70.3	73
Married		65.2	72.4	73	73.4	67.3	67.4	64.6	68.8	69.6
Single		86.1	83.2	83.2	78.8	78.1	82.1	83.2	77.5	83.8

Source: Swiss census, 2000.

Migrants from South and Central Asia, Turkey, the Middle East, and Maghreb as well as Asia, remain least likely to be active in the labour market, sticking to a more traditional gender role distribution.

Looking at cohorts reveals that women originating from Western and Southern Europe are more likely to enter the labour force, especially women born after 1970. This is partly due to the combination of better qualifications and lower fertility rates that were observed earlier. Regression results also show that first-generation women in mixed couples behave like natives in this regard (Table 7.14 and Figure 7.14).

7.6.2 Subjective attitudes

Besides influencing behaviours, integration processes also affect the daily habits, attitudes, values, and beliefs of migrants. This section explores the evolution of migrants' use of national languages, of their feelings towards Switzerland, and of their attitudes concerning gender, religious, and political issues. The SHP data (except for language) is used to investigate cultural integration paths in these subjective dimensions. The smaller sample size reduces the significance of the results obtained. The analysis is therefore mostly limited to the evolution from the first to the second generation. Gender differences are considered only when examining gender attitudes.

Language: Knowledge of one of the four national languages is fundamental not only to succeed at school and in the labour market, but also to understand native culture and develop enriching relationships in the host society. It is therefore not surprising that a substantial part of the federal budget devoted to cultural integration was spent on subsidizing organizations offering language courses for migrants (OFM, 2006), that mastering one of the national languages is often viewed as a prerequisite for naturalization, or that partners in mixed couples often consider it as a fundamental external sign of successful integration (Ossipow and Waldis, 2003).

Table 7.14 Female labour force participation.

Origin	Pre-1970		Post-1970		Endo		Inter	
	First gen.	Second gen.	First gen.	Second gen.	First gen.	Second gen.	First gen.	Second gen.
WE	-0.041***	0.010***	-0.009***	0.040***	-0.086***	0.029***	-0.020***	-0.015***
	(0.001)	(0.003)	(0.003)	(0.004)	(0.002)	(0.004)	(0.00˙)	(0.005)
SE	0.039***	0.019***	0.068***	0.086***	0.092***	0.064***	-0.008**	0.001
	(0.001)	(0.002)	(0.003)	(0.002)	(0.001)	(0.002)	(0.003)	(0.004)
EE	-0.007***	0.008	-0.043***	0.057***	0.048***	0.088***	-0.013***	0.003
	(0.001)	(0.009)	(0.002)	(0.008)	(0.001)	(0.006)	(0.003)	(0.019)
AF	-0.009**	0.036	-0.055***	-0.031	0.048***	0.080***	-0.013*	-0.138*
	(0.004)	(0.028)	(0.008)	(0.043)	(0.006)	(0.029)	(0.006)	(0.071)
TMM	-0.078***	-0.003	-0.075***	0.030***	-0.001	0.062***	-0.030***	0.046
	(0.003)	(0.012)	(0.005)	(0.010)	(0.002)	(0.008)	(0.007)	(0.031)
LA	-0.088***	-0.006	-0.143***	-0.026	0.004	0.012	-0.095***	-0.040
	(0.003)	(0.022)	(0.006)	(0.032)	(0.006)	(0.034)	(0.004)	(0.036)
AS	-0.095***	-0.127***	-0.187***	-0.124**	-0.011**	0.006	-0.107***	-0.108**
	(0.003)	(0.036)	(0.007)	(0.048)	(0.005)	(0.053)	(0.004)	(0.046)
SCA	-0.076***	-0.011	-0.151***	-0.008	-0.011**	0.043**	-0.091***	-0.033
	(0.005)	(0.025)	(0.008)	(0.052)	(0.004)	(0.021)	(0.016)	(0.112)
Education	0.017***				0.017***			
	(0.0001)				(0.0001)			
Observations	1,795,117				1,795,117			
PR²	0.05				0.09			
ll	-934,436				-888,678			

Source: Swiss census, 2000; standard errors in parentheses; *** p <0.01, ** p <0.05, * p <0.1.

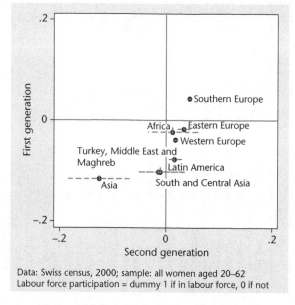

Data: Swiss census, 2000; sample: all women aged 20–62
Labour force participation = dummy 1 if in labour force, 0 if not

Figure 7.14 Female labour force participation.

Results in Table 7.15 (plotted in Figure 7.15) show that second-generation migrants are much more likely to declare one of the national languages as their main language. Surprisingly, young second-generation migrants do so more than those born before 1970, whereas no such trend is detectable among first-generation migrants. Different hypotheses could explain this. It might be that the methods to teach languages that are used at Swiss schools have become more effective or that younger second-generation migrants are more willing to adopt a national language as their own.

As expected, differences across migrant groups remain. Western and Southern Europeans are always more likely to adopt a national language of Switzerland as their own; Asians and South and Central Asians display lower probabilities to do so, but it is striking to observe a similarly low probability for Latin Americans, who seem to be much more attached to their mother tongue than Latin migrants from Southern Europe.[21]

First-generation migrants with a Swiss partner have a slightly higher probability of adopting a national language as their own than those in

---

[21] As Italian is a national language, the author tested this by keeping migrants of Italian origin out of the sample. Results are available upon request.

Table 7.15 Main language.

Origin	All		Pre-1970		Post-1970		Endo		Inter	
	First gen.	Second gen.	First gen.	Second gen.	First gen.	Second gen.	First gen.	Second gen.	First gen.	Second gen.
WE	-0.29***	-0.06***	-0.24***	-0.071	-0.34***	-0.046***	-0.10***	0.017***	-0.068***	0.024***
	(0.001)	(0.001)	(0.001)	(-0.001)	(-0.002)	(-0.001)	(0.0004)	(0.001)	(0.0004)	(0.001)
SE	-0.41***	-0.05***	-0.33***	-0.05***	-0.52***	-0.04***	-0.24***	0.01***	-0.13***	0.03***
	(0.001)	(0.0008)	(0.001)	(-0.001)	(-0.002)	(-0.001)	(0.001)	(0.0007)	(0.002)	(0.0004)
EE	-0.73***	-0.34***	-0.70***	-0.49***	-0.70***	-0.23***	-0.19***	-0.28***	-0.44***	-0.017**
	(0.001)	(0.004)	(0.001)	(-0.008)	(-0.002)	(-0.005)	(0.0004)	(0.006)	(0.003)	(0.007)
AF	-0.61***	-0.23***	-0.54***	-0.28***	-0.57***	-0.17***	-0.12***	-0.04**	-0.38***	-0.16***
	(0.003)	(0.018)	(0.003)	(-0.027)	(-0.005)	(-0.022)	(0.001)	(0.019)	(0.006)	(0.044)
TMM	-0.72***	-0.30***	-0.65***	-0.39***	-0.68***	-0.23***	-0.18***	-0.19***	-0.41***	-0.08***
	(0.001)	(0.005)	(0.002)	(-0.011)	(-0.003)	(-0.006)	(0.0007)	(0.007)	(0.005)	(0.016)
LA	-0.84***	-0.35***	-0.80***	-0.45***	-0.78***	-0.23***	-0.21***	-0.13***	-0.75***	-0.34***
	(0.001)	(0.013)	(0.002)	(-0.020)	(-0.003)	(-0.017)	(0.001)	(0.022)	(0.003)	(0.033)
AS	-0.84***	-0.37***	-0.80***	-0.60***	-0.77***	-0.17***	-0.20***	-0.32***	-0.74***	-0.43***
	(0.001)	(0.020)	(0.002)	(-0.029)	(-0.003)	(-0.022)	(0.001)	(0.048)	(0.003)	(0.045)
SCA	-0.83***	-0.45***	-0.78***	-0.49***	-0.78***	-0.37***	-0.21***	-0.30***	-0.60***	-0.19**
	(0.001)	(0.018)	(0.002)	(-0.023)	(-0.004)	(-0.028)	(0.001)	(0.023)	(0.009)	(0.0756)
Education	0.0004***		0.001***				0.004***			
	(8.30e-06)		(1.7e-05)				(3.25e-05)			
Obs	4,942,902		4,942,902				4,942,902			
PR²	0.53		0.53				0.33			
ll	-671,042		-668,672				-950,499			

Source: Swiss census, 2000; standard errors in parentheses; *** p <0.01, ** p <0.05, * p <0.1.

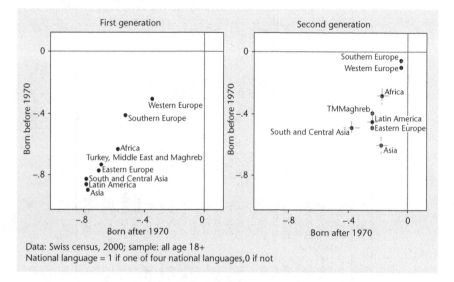

Figure 7.15 Main language.

endogamous couples. However, the picture is more blurred for second-generation migrants, as African and Latin American migrants are visibly rather keen to keep their mother tongue.

Feelings towards Switzerland: One could assume that in a non-discriminatory society, no one would request more equality between natives and foreigners. Table 7.16 shows that all migrants living in Switzerland are in favour of more equality compared to natives. This trend is stronger among first-generation than among second-generation migrants, except for those likely to have darker skin colour or those likely to be identified as Muslims (South and Central Asians, Africans and individuals originating from Turkey, the Middle East, and Maghreb), who feel that more could be done to facilitate their integration into Swiss society. Interestingly, migrants of the younger cohort have a more pronounced opinion than those born before 1970. When asked whether they are in favour of opening Swiss traditions to world influence, results look similar (Table 7.17 and Figure 7.16).

Gender attitudes: In relation to gender attitudes, it appears that more conservative behaviours of first-generation migrants are in line with their more conservative subjective attitudes. Results in Table 7.18 show how women internalize the traditional role of mothers. Compared to natives, migrant women are likely to believe children suffer when the mother is working. Western European women are the only exception. It might also be that as more migrant women live in precarious

Table 7.16 In favour of more equality between Swiss and foreigners.

Origin	All		Pre-1970		Post-1970	
	First gen.	Second gen.	First gen.	Second gen.	First gen.	Second gen.
WE	0.153***	0.055***	0.155***	0.036***	0.136***	0.086***
	(0.008)	(0.010)	(0.009)	(0.013)	(0.022)	(0.016)
SE	0.207***	0.103***	0.206***	0.103***	0.199***	0.102***
	(0.008)	(0.010)	(0.009)	(0.012)	(0.021)	(0.015)
EE	0.104***	0.087***	0.088***	0.014	0.133***	0.165***
	(0.019)	(0.029)	(0.024)	(0.044)	(0.030)	(0.037)
AF	0.023	0.069	−0.075	0.052	0.221***	0.107
	(0.053)	(0.086)	(0.068)	(0.104)	(0.065)	(0.153)
TMM	0.005	0.137***	−0.023	0.099**	0.060	0.174***
	(0.037)	(0.030)	(0.047)	(0.045)	(0.060)	(0.039)
LA	0.186***	0.031	0.193***	0.036	0.171***	0.022
	(0.027)	(0.054)	(0.032)	(0.068)	(0.047)	(0.091)
AS	0.050	−0.212*	0.011	−0.217*	0.130	−0.202
	(0.062)	(0.111)	(0.079)	(0.128)	(0.099)	(0.225)
SCA	0.027	0.104	0.044	0.065	−0.003	0.182
	(0.057)	(0.076)	(0.070)	(0.097)	(0.099)	(0.115)
Education	0.026***		0.026***			
	(0.001)		(0.001)			
Observations	40,692		40,692			
PR^2	0.038		0.039			
ll	−25,581		−25,568			

Source: SHP, 1999–2007; standard errors in parentheses; *** p <0.01, ** p <0.05, * p <0.1.

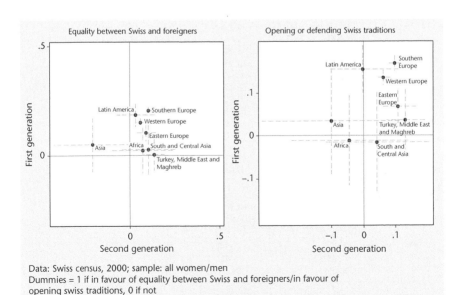

Data: Swiss census, 2000; sample: all women/men
Dummies = 1 if in favour of equality between Swiss and foreigners/in favour of opening swiss traditions, 0 if not

Figure 7.16 Feelings towards Switzerland.

Cultural Integration of Immigrants in Europe

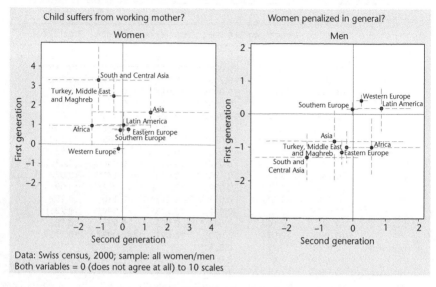

Data: Swiss census, 2000; sample: all women/men
Both variables = 0 (does not agree at all) to 10 scales

Figure 7.17 Gender attitudes.

Table 7.17 In favour of opening Swiss traditions.

Origin	All		Pre-1970		Post-1970	
	First gen.	Second gen.	First gen.	Second gen.	First gen.	Second gen.
WE	0.137***	0.063***	0.266***	0.032	−0.350***	−0.125*
	(0.009)	(0.010)	(0.045)	(0.056)	(0.103)	(0.071)
SE	0.170***	0.096***	0.073	−0.043	−0.665***	−0.214***
	(0.009)	(0.010)	(0.053)	(0.056)	(0.117)	(0.069)
EE	0.067***	0.109***	0.964***	0.095	0.975***	0.473***
	(0.020)	(0.028)	(0.107)	(0.177)	(0.144)	(0.183)
AF	−0.011	−0.043	0.953***	0.246	0.343	1.330**
	(0.053)	(0.093)	(0.258)	(0.438)	(0.343)	(0.636)
TMM	0.037	0.131***	1.188***	−0.057	0.516**	0.519***
	(0.036)	(0.030)	(0.188)	(0.201)	(0.249)	(0.195)
LA	0.155***	−0.0002	0.309*	0.549**	−0.559**	0.041
	(0.028)	(0.055)	(0.171)	(0.276)	(0.249)	(0.390)
AS	0.033	−0.101	0.656**	−0.141	0.489	−0.460
	(0.063)	(0.109)	(0.323)	(0.477)	(0.510)	(0.854)
SCA	−0.014	0.042	1.300***	0.047	0.955**	1.029
	(0.059)	(0.081)	(0.268)	(0.417)	(0.390)	(0.636)
Education	0.025***		0.071***			
	(0.0009)		(0.003)			
Observations	40,985		40,985			
PR^2	0.034		0.031			
ll	−25,598		−84,619			

Source: SHP, 1999–2007; standard errors in parentheses; *** p <0.01, ** p <0.05, * p <0.1.

248

Table 7.18 Child suffers from working mother.

Origin	All		Pre-1970		Post-1970	
	First gen.	Second gen.	First gen.	Second gen.	First gen.	Second gen.
WE	−0.215*	−0.189	−0.302**	−0.054	0.333	−0.367*
	(0.113)	(0.122)	(0.121)	(0.158)	(0.295)	(0.189)
SE	0.768***	−0.126	0.681***	−0.129	1.104***	−0.111
	(0.142)	(0.119)	(0.159)	(0.153)	(0.315)	(0.186)
EE	0.805***	0.238	0.773***	1.195**	0.872**	−0.796
	(0.223)	(0.394)	(0.280)	(0.544)	(0.365)	(0.569)
AF	0.981*	−1.392	1.551**	−0.998	0.355	−1.850
	(0.559)	(0.982)	(0.768)	(1.329)	(0.816)	(1.456)
TMM	2.495***	−0.421	2.364***	−0.807	2.719***	−0.101
	(0.492)	(0.333)	(0.627)	(0.498)	(0.791)	(0.446)
LA	1.019***	0.0389	0.324	−0.950	2.280***	1.041
	(0.336)	(0.617)	(0.418)	(0.871)	(0.560)	(0.872)
AS	1.686**	1.254	1.909***	1.031	0.561	1.490
	(0.665)	(1.329)	(0.729)	(1.879)	(1.627)	(1.879)
SCA	3.307***	−1.094	3.342***	−1.504	3.250**	−0.670
	(0.870)	(1.152)	(1.085)	(1.628)	(1.456)	(1.628)
Education	−0.229***		−0.231***			
	(0.0103)		(0.0103)			
Observations	15,482		15,482			
R^2	0.069		0.071			

Source: SHP, 1999–2007; standard errors in parentheses; *** $p < 0.01$, ** $p < 0.05$, * $p < 0.1$.

Table 7.19 Women penalized in general.

Origin	All		Pre-1970		Post-1970	
	First gen.	Second gen.	First gen.	Second gen.	First gen.	Second gen.
WE	0.405***	0.258***	0.454***	0.121	−0.314*	0.006
	(0.091)	(0.097)	(0.075)	(0.108)	(0.179)	(0.127)
SE	0.162	−0.017	−0.121	0.393***	0.037	0.284**
	(0.101)	(0.092)	(0.099)	(0.103)	(0.209)	(0.119)
EE	−1.145***	−0.346	−0.581***	0.564	−0.682***	−0.008
	(0.190)	(0.261)	(0.185)	(0.395)	(0.239)	(0.386)
AF	−0.982**	0.565	0.989*	−1.196	0.191	1.370
	(0.434)	(0.761)	(0.505)	(1.029)	(0.565)	(1.030)
TMM	−0.996***	−0.183	0.423	−0.034	−0.026	−0.513
	(0.249)	(0.370)	(0.415)	(0.344)	(0.505)	(0.315)
LA	0.192	0.869*	0.148	−0.456	−0.176	0.981
	(0.359)	(0.459)	(0.246)	(0.674)	(0.305)	(0.613)
AS	−0.818	−0.562	−0.693	1.479	1.113	2.900**
	(0.590)	(1.076)	(0.461)	(1.456)	(1.128)	(1.456)
SCA	−1.282***	−1.402*	−0.372	0.795	−0.015	−0.015
	(0.356)	(0.795)	(0.841)	(1.261)	(0.892)	(1.261)
Education	0.072***		0.101***			
	(0.007)		(0.006)			
Observations	19,449		19,449			
R^2	0.064		0.064			

Source: SHP, 1999–2007; standard errors in parentheses; *** $p < 0.01$, ** $p < 0.05$, * $p < 0.1$.

Table 7.20 Probability of participating in religious offices more than for special occasions.

Origin	All		Pre-1970		Post-1970	
	First gen.	Second gen.	First gen.	Second gen.	First gen.	Second gen.
WE	−0.110***	−0.031***	−0.086***	−0.012	−0.194***	−0.073***
	(0.009)	(0.011)	(0.010)	(0.014)	(0.019)	(0.016)
SE	0.042***	0.023*	0.060***	0.040***	−0.014	−0.006
	(0.013)	(0.012)	(0.013)	(0.015)	(0.030)	(0.017)
EE	0.079***	−0.033	0.036	−0.032	0.123***	−0.051
	(0.024)	(0.033)	(0.028)	(0.045)	(0.037)	(0.044)
AF	0.176***	0.006	0.224***	−0.059	0.064	0.239
	(0.054)	(0.096)	(0.063)	(0.111)	(0.079)	(0.151)
TMM	0.033	−0.145***	0.102*	−0.116***	−0.146***	−0.139***
	(0.039)	(0.029)	(0.045)	(0.044)	(0.049)	(0.038)
LA	0.112***	0.0135	0.158***	0.079	0.101*	−0.196***
	(0.038)	(0.063)	(0.044)	(0.078)	(0.060)	(0.073)
AS	0.084	−0.023	0.138*	0.068	0.002	
	(0.071)	(0.108)	(0.080)	(0.136)	(0.110)	
SCA	0.261***	0.044	0.328***	0.041	0.171*	0.018
	(0.057)	(0.092)	(0.062)	(0.106)	(0.092)	(0.180)
Education	−0.012***		−0.014***			
	(0.0009)		(0.0009)			
Observations	32,887		32,887			
PR²	0.034		0.033			
ll	−19,718		−22,640			

Source: SHP, 1999–2007; standard errors in parentheses; *** p <0.01, ** p <0.05, * p <0.1.

conditions, they feel strongly that working would harm their children (e.g. because they cannot afford to leave their children in a private day nursery). Results in Table 7.19 (plotted in Figure 7.17) show how sensitive men are to the specific discriminations women are suffering from. Male migrants from Western, Southern Europe, and Latin America are the only ones to be more sensitive to this issue than native men. Looking at the second generation, it is difficult to identify meaningful differences. It might be that attitudes of second-generation migrants concerning gender issues converge relatively fast with the Swiss average, while behaviours need more time to change.[22]

Religious attitudes: Religious attitudes are also losing their intensity over time. Table 7.20 shows that first-generation migrants are more likely to visit places of worship than natives. More assiduous attendance of religious offices could be explained by the fact that it is a social act

---

[22] See results on behaviours in the couple, and the findings of Wimmer (2004) that were cited above.

Table 7.21 Probability of praying at least occasionally.

Origin	All		Pre-1970		Post-1970	
	First gen.	Second gen.	First gen.	Second gen.	First gen.	Second gen.
WE	−0.123***	−0.041***	−0.088***	−0.031**	−0.197***	−0.064***
	(0.010)	(0.010)	(0.010)	(0.013)	(0.024)	(0.015)
SE	0.060***	0.050***	0.044***	0.037***	0.084***	0.060***
	(0.010)	(0.009)	(0.011)	(0.012)	(0.022)	(0.013)
EE	0.021	−0.068**	0.012	−0.035	0.063**	−0.103**
	(0.019)	(0.031)	(0.022)	(0.044)	(0.026)	(0.043)
AF	0.138***	−0.153	0.182***	−0.244**	0.084	0.011
	(0.036)	(0.097)	(0.038)	(0.118)	(0.058)	(0.137)
TMM	−0.052	−0.052	−0.072*	−0.010	−0.067	−0.029
	(0.035)	(0.034)	(0.042)	(0.048)	(0.056)	(0.042)
LA	0.098***	0.112***	0.143***	0.140***	0.123***	0.065
	(0.028)	(0.042)	(0.029)	(0.053)	(0.040)	(0.070)
AS	0.011	−0.070	−0.018	0.028	0.106	−0.216
	(0.059)	(0.105)	(0.072)	(0.113)	(0.071)	(0.179)
SCA	0.131***	0.100	0.161***	0.040	0.069	0.170*
	(0.038)	(0.068)	(0.041)	(0.098)	(0.071)	(0.090)
Education	−0.006***		−0.011***			
	(0.0008)		(0.0007)			
Observations	41,601		41,601			
PR^2	0.047		0.029			
ll	−24,118		−28,654			

Source: SHP, 1999–2007; Standard errors in parentheses; *** p <0.01, ** p <0.05, * p <0.1.

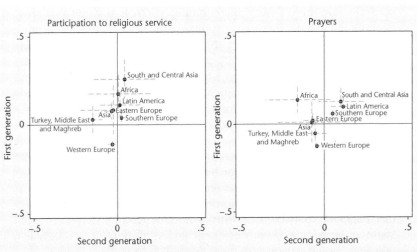

Data: Swiss census, 2000; sample: all women/men
Dummies = 1 if goes to religious offices not only on special occasions/prays at least occasionally, 0 if not

Figure 7.18 Religious attitudes.

Table 7.22 Political affiliation.

Origin	All		Pre-1970		Post-1970	
	First gen.	Second gen.	First gen.	Second gen.	First gen.	Second gen.
WE	−0.541***	−0.215***	−0.244***	−0.199***	−0.408***	−0.261***
	(0.073)	(0.048)	(0.048)	(0.063)	(0.107)	(0.079)
SE	−2.080***	−0.826***	−0.699***	−0.311***	−0.236	−0.696***
	(0.086)	(0.078)	(0.065)	(0.064)	(0.149)	(0.076)
EE	−1.875***	−0.281	−0.040	0.246	−0.859***	−0.766***
	(0.153)	(0.226)	(0.129)	(0.204)	(0.174)	(0.207)
AF	−2.546***	0.622	−1.400***	0.003	−1.421***	−0.067
	(0.366)	(0.641)	(0.310)	(0.496)	(0.448)	(0.665)
TMM	−1.193***	−0.584**	−0.023	−0.098	−1.091***	−0.841***
	(0.266)	(0.248)	(0.206)	(0.228)	(0.263)	(0.229)
LA	−1.716***	−0.830**	−0.868***	−0.450	−0.411	−1.206***
	(0.250)	(0.400)	(0.187)	(0.307)	(0.257)	(0.421)
AS	−1.212**	0.396	−0.290	0.0140	−1.118**	−0.600
	(0.484)	(0.740)	(0.355)	(0.543)	(0.510)	(0.940)
SCA	−2.182***	−0.298	−0.394	−0.068	0.257	−1.721**
	(0.392)	(0.619)	(0.355)	(0.482)	(0.448)	(0.701)
Education	0.092***		−0.054***			
	(0.006)		(0.003)			
Observations	40,985		40,985			
R^2	0.053		0.036			

Source: SHP, 1999–2007; standard errors in parentheses; *** $p < 0.01$, ** $p < 0.05$, * $p < 0.1$.

strengthening the cohesion of communities. The hypothesis that religion fulfils a social rather than a spiritual function in migrant communities is supported by the fact that migrants are not more inclined to pray than natives (Table 7.21 and Figure 7.18), and that second-generation migrants are not more religious than natives. Interestingly, migrants from Turkey, the Middle East, and Maghreb are very close to natives in terms of their propensity to attend religious offices or to pray. The qualitative study of Gianni *et al.* (2005) on Muslims in Switzerland draws similar conclusions.

Political attitudes: Finally, the analysis of political attitudes shows that all migrants are more leaning to the left than the more conservative Swiss majority, except for second-generation Asian and African migrants (Table 7.22). Their coefficients, however, are not significant. It also appears that migrants from countries with democratic traditions (Western and Southern Europeans, Latin Americans) are less likely to express satisfaction with the Swiss democracy than migrants coming from regions were political regimes are mostly undemocratic (Table 7.23 and Figure 7.19). Natives seem to be the most critical of their own political system.

Table 7.23 Satisfaction with Swiss democracy.

Origin	All		Pre-1970		Post-1970	
	First gen.	Second gen.	First gen.	Second gen.	First gen.	Second gen.
WE	0.168***	−0.017	0.266***	0.032	−0.350***	−0.125*
	(0.041)	(0.044)	(0.045)	(0.056)	(0.103)	(0.071)
SE	−0.053	0.102**	0.073	−0.043	−0.665***	−0.214***
	(0.048)	(0.044)	(0.053)	(0.056)	(0.117)	(0.069)
EE	0.975***	0.293**	0.964***	0.095	0.975***	0.473***
	(0.086)	(0.127)	(0.107)	(0.177)	(0.144)	(0.183)
AF	0.744***	0.598*	0.953***	0.246	0.343	1.330**
	(0.206)	(0.361)	(0.258)	(0.438)	(0.343)	(0.636)
TMM	0.950***	0.257*	1.188***	−0.057	0.516**	0.519***
	(0.150)	(0.140)	(0.188)	(0.201)	(0.249)	(0.195)
LA	0.038	0.390*	0.309*	0.549**	−0.559**	0.041
	(0.141)	(0.226)	(0.171)	(0.276)	(0.249)	(0.390)
AS	0.608**	−0.212	0.656**	−0.141	0.489	−0.460
	(0.273)	(0.417)	(0.323)	(0.477)	(0.510)	(0.854)
SCA	1.192***	0.348	1.300***	0.047	0.955**	1.029
	(0.221)	(0.349)	(0.268)	(0.417)	(0.390)	(0.636)
Education	0.069***		0.071***			
	(0.003)		(0.003)			
Observations	40,985		40,985			
R²	0.029		0.031			

Source: SHP, 1999–2007; standard errors in parentheses; *** p <0.01, ** p <0.05, * p <0.1.

7.7 Discussion

The main findings of this chapter can be summarized as follows:

- The evolution of selected indicators from the first to the second generation clearly shows that cultural integration processes are at work in all migrant communities. However, significant differences remain between behaviours and attitudes across migrant groups:
  - At school, men from South and Central Asia, Turkey, the Middle East, Maghreb, and Eastern Europe seem stuck in a low educational equilibrium. Young second-generation migrants, however, have improved their performances and the gender gap is declining, due to the progresses made by second-generation women. Differences across groups are especially obvious when looking at the position of women in the couple. Migrant women from South and Central Asia, Turkey, the Middle East, and Maghreb are least likely to intermarry, even less than their male counterparts, and they display more traditional behaviours in most of the indicators examined. In the labour market, migrant women are slightly

253

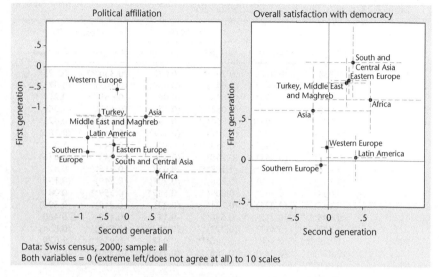

Data: Swiss census, 2000; sample: all
Both variables = 0 (extreme left/does not agree at all) to 10 scales

Figure 7.19 Political attitudes.

less likely to be active, but this difference disappears in the second generation, except for Asian migrants.

○ Patterns of migrants' subjective attitudes are more difficult to identify. Results show 'linguistically distant' migrants are less likely to declare one of the four national languages as their main language. Migrants' feelings toward Switzerland show that they perceive discriminations more strongly in comparison to natives, particularly migrants likely to have darker skin colour or those likely to be identified as Muslims. The more conservative behaviours of first-generation migrants in the couple are in line with their more conservative subjective gender attitudes. It might be that attitudes evolve more rapidly in a new social environment than behaviours do. Minor differences in religious attitudes vanish at the second generation, which supports the hypothesis that religious office attendance fulfils a social (and to some extent an economic) function rather than a spiritual function. Concerning political attitudes, migrants seem to be more satisfied with Swiss democracy, and they lean more to the left than natives.

• The general convergence pattern observed from the first to the second generation has no match across cohorts. Only a few cohort-specific cultural trends could be identified (see sections on cohabitation and divorce). It is therefore not possible to claim that younger migrants integrate better or worse than migrants born before 1970.

- Convergence is particularly at work in mixed couples, where first-generation women of all origins already adopt native behaviours (including women from South and Central Asia, from Turkey, the Middle East, and Maghreb), stressing the weakness of the 'cultural distance' argument. First and second-generation migrants in endogamous couples reproduce more traditional behaviours. Although it is not possible to capture individual traits that impact on the partner choice, this analysis leads to the conclusion that the interplay between household members, given the characteristics of individuals, of the household and of their social environment ('household dynamics') has an important role in integration processes.

- Education always has the expected significant effect on examined indicators. Its impact is non-negligible on fertility, but it is modest for most other indicators.

The review of the selected indicators reveals that cultural integration processes, which are at work in various ways in the different groups, contribute to overall convergence. The most striking and lasting differences that are observed across groups do not pertain to educational achievement, religious, or political attitudes, but to gender-related attitudes and even more to gender-related behaviours. Differences are more pronounced in endogamous couples in general, specifically for women from South and Central Asia, Turkey, the Middle East, and Maghreb.

As such, the decision to marry at an early age or to live in cohabitation, age and education gaps between partners, the preferred number of children, and opinions on gender issues are private matters. However, they also influence the position women have in the household and in society. Previous studies focused less on individuals in migration studies, and more on families, as they are key in socializing second-generation migrants on whom most policy efforts are targeted (Wanner and Fibbi, 2002). Others observed that some migrant groups are more inclined to reproduce traditional family structures and relationships (Moret *et al.*, 2007) and have very pronounced gender attitudes that may be exacerbated by the destabilizing effect of migration on families (Gianni *et al.*, 2005).

The findings presented in this chapter lead to the recommendation to take more account of migration-related gender issues and migration-specific 'household dynamics' in the design of future cultural integration policies. The term 'household dynamics' is used deliberately as it is preferred over 'family'. First, the term 'family' evokes the image of married couples with children, whereas a household is not associated with any particular structure (traditional or otherwise). Second, implicitly or explicitly insisting on the unity and intergenerational solidarity existing in (migrant) families conceals the fact that migrant households may be confronted by specific problems. Constraints imposed by migration require specific household arrangements, which facilitate the division of labour among household members and a clearer distribution of gender roles within the couple. Those constraints can intensify gender issues, which also exist, although to a different degree, among native couples. Education, labour market, and other policies can and should be used to influence the integration of migrants in Swiss society, but more targeted programmes (next to existing language courses, civic, and other programmes) and policies could be designed to address gender issues, which arise out of or are exacerbated by migration and migration-specific dynamics developing in migrant households.

Such programmes should not so much aim at informing migrants about what is considered to conform with Swiss values concerning gender or family, but about informing them of their individual rights. Moreover, programmes should support associations and organizations, which contribute to empower migrants in general (when confronted by the precariousness of their legal situation, the diminished job security, discrimination, etc.) and migrant women in particular (when confronted by situations of domestic violence, forced marriage, etc.) to exercise their rights. Given the ease with which extremist parties exploit such problems and the disproportionate emphasis cultural integration issues are given in the public debate, it is important that lawmakers grant decent financial support to actors involved in such work. Finally, the challenging situation that some migrant women face should not conceal that, although gender equality is claimed to be a fundamental value of Western societies, it is a relatively recent 'acquis', particularly in Switzerland,[23] and that much remains to be done.

---

[23] The emancipation of women is particularly recent in Switzerland. The fact that Switzerland was not militarily involved in either of the World Wars of the last century delayed the entry of women in the labour market and their access to economic independence compared to other industrialized countries. This and other factors in turn slowed down the acquisition of the voting rights for women, who obtained this political right only in 1971 at the federal level. In 1990, the Swiss federal court finally ruled that the exclusion of women in cantonal polls in Appenzell Inner Rhodes was unconstitutional.

References

Alba, R. and Nee, V. (1997) Rethinking Assimilation Theory for a New Era of Immigration. *International Migration Review*, 31, 826–874.

Bauer, P. and Riphahn, R. (2007) Heterogeneity in the Intergenerational Transmission of Educational Attainment: Evidence from Switzerland on Natives and Second-Generation Immigrants. *Population Economics*, 20, 121–148.

Bisin, A., Patacchini, E., Verdier, T., and Zenou, Y. (2008) Are Muslim Immigrants Different in Terms of Cultural Integration? *Journal of the European Economic Association*, MIT Press, 6(2–3), 445–456.

Bolzmann, C. and Fibbi, R. (2003) Secondas—Secondos: Le processus d'intégration des jeunes adultes issus de la migration espagnole et italienne en Suisse. In: H.-R. Wicker (ed.) *Les Migrations et la Suisse: Résultats du Programme National de Recherche 'Migrations et relations interculturelles'*. Zürich, Seismo.

D'Amato, G. (2008) *Mit dem Fremden politisieren. Rechtspopulismus und Migrationspolitik in der Schweiz seit den 1960er Jahren*. Zürich, Chronos Verlag.

De Coulon, A., Falter, J.-M., Flückiger, Y., and Ramirez, J. (2003) Analyses des différences de Salaires entre la Population Suisse et Étrangère. In: H.-R. Wicker *et al.* (ed.) *Les Migrations et la Suisse: Résultats du Programme National de Recherche 'Migrations et relations interculturelles'*. Zürich, Seismo, pp. 263–289.

Fibbi, R., Wanner, P., and Lerch, M. (2005) Processus de Naturalisation et Caractéristiques Socio-économiques des Jeunes Issus de la Migration. In: R. Fibbi *et al.* (ed.) *L'intégration des Populations Issues de l'immigration en Suisse: Personnes Naturalisées et Deucième Génération*. Neuchâtel, OFS, pp. 9–60.

Georgiadis, A. and Manning, A. (2011) Change and Continuity among Minority Communities in Britain. *Journal of Population Economics*, 24(2), 541–568.

Gianni, M., Schneuwly Purdie, M., Lathion, S., and Jenny, M. (2005) Vie Musulmane en Suisse'. Bern, Commission Fédérale des Étrangers.

Henry, P. and Gaudard, G., and Arbenz, P. (1995) *La Suisse, terre d'asile*. Bienne, Libertas Suisse.

Kohler, P. (2012) *Three Essays on the Economic and Cultural Integration of Migrants in Switzerland : Putting into Perspective the Influence of Economic Discrimination and of Host Society Culture*, Geneva: Graduate Institute of International and Development Studies, PhD thesis No. 940.

Mahnig, H. and Piguet, E. (2003) La Politique Suisse d'immigration de 1948 à 1998: Évolution et Effets. In: H.-R. Wicker *et al.* (ed.) *Les Migrations et la Suisse: Résultats du Programme National de Recherche 'Migrations et relations interculturelle'*. Zürich, Seismo. pp. 63–103.

Moret, J., Efi Onayi, D., and Stants, F. (2007) *Die Srilankische Diaspora in Der Schweiz*. Neuchâtel, SFM.

OFM, Office Fédéral des Migrations (2006) *Problèmes d'intégration des Eessortissants Étrangers en Suisse: Identification des Faits, des Causes, des Groupes à Risque, des Mesures Existantes Ainsi que des Mesures à Prendre en Matière de Politique d'intégration*. Bern, OFM.

OFS, Office Fédéral de la Statistique (2005) *Structure de la Population, Langue Principale et Religion*. Neuchâtel, OFS.

Ossipow, L. and Waldis, B. (2003) Couples Binationaux et Sociétés Multiculturelles. In: H.-R. Wicker *et al.* (ed.) *Les Migrations et la Suisse: Résultats du Programme National de Recherche 'Migrations et relations interculturelles'*. Zürich, Seismo, pp. 375–403.

Piguet, E. (2009) *L'immigration en Suisse: 60 Ans d'entrouverture*. Lausanne, Presses Polytechniques et Universitaires Romandes.

Riano, Y. and Wastl-Walter, D. (2006) Immigration Policies, State Discourses on Foreigners, and the Politics of Identity in Switzerland. *Environment and Planning*, 38, 1693–1713.

Waldis, B. (2008) Introduction: Marriage in an Era of Globalization. In: B. Waldis *et al.* (ed.) Migration and Marriage: Heterogamy and Homogamy in a Changing World. *Freiburger Sozialanthropologische Studien*, 1–20.

Wanner, P. (2004) *Migration et Intégration: Populations Étrangères en Suisse*. Neuchâtel, OFS.

Wanner, P. and Fibbi, R. (2002) Familles et Migration, Familles en Migration. In: P. Wanner *et al.* (ed.) *Etudes sur la Situation des Familles Migrantes et Recommandations de la Commission Fédérale de Coordination pour les Questions Familiales*. Bern, COFF, pp. 9–50.

Wanner, P., Gabadinho, A., and Ferrari, A. (2003) *La Participation des Femmes au Marché du Travail*. Bern, OFAS.

Wanner, P., Mathias, L., and Fibbi, R. (2005a) *Familles et Migration: le Rôle de la Famille sur les Flux Migratoires*. Neuchâtel, OFS.

Wanner, P., Neubauer, A., and Moret, J. (2002) *Caractéristiques de Vie et d'intégration des Populations Issues de l'immigration: une Analyse des Données du Panel Suisse des Ménages 1999–2000*. Neûchatel, SFM.

Wanner, P., Pecoraro, M., and Fibbi, R. (2005b) Femmes Étrangères et Marché du Travail. In: W. Haug *et al.* (ed.) *Migrants et Marché du Travail: Compétences et Insertion Professionnelle des Personnes d'origine Étrangère en Suisse*. Neuchâtel, OFS. pp. 17–38.

Wicker, H.-R. (2003) Introduction: Migration, Politique de Migration et Recherche sur la Migration. In: H.-R. Wicker *et al.* (ed.) *Les Migrations et la Suisse: Résultats du Programme National de Recherche 'Migrations et Relations Interculturelles'*. Zürich, Seismo, pp. 11–62.

Wicker, H.-R., Fibbi, R. and Haug, W. (2003) *Les Migrations et la Suisse: Résultats du Programme National de Recherche 'Migrations et Relations Interculturelles'*. Zürich, Seismo, pp. 11–62.

Wimmer, A. (2004) Does Ethnicity Matter? Everyday Group Formation in Three Swiss Immigrant Neighbourhoods. *Ethnic and Racial Studies*, 27, 1–36.

Wimmer, A. (2008) The Making and Unmaking of Ethnic Boundaries: A Multilevel Process Theory. *American Journal of Sociology*, 113, 970–1022.

Winlow, H. (2006) Mapping Moral Geographies: W. Z. Ripley's Races of Europe and the United States. *Annals of the Association of American Geographers*, 96(1), 119–141.

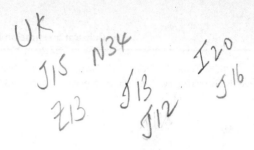

8

Cultural Integration in the United Kingdom

Alan Manning and Andreas Georgiadis[1]

8.1 Introduction

The UK has had a much longer history of large-scale immigration than many other European countries. For a long time there was a certain smug satisfaction that its generally tolerant and accommodating approach to cultural diversity had been relatively successful, although there is no doubt that problems of racism persisted. But this self-satisfaction has, in many quarters, now turned to alarm that some immigrant groups are not following the stereotypical immigrant path of economic and cultural integration into mainstream society. But, while views on this topic are often very strongly held, the evidence base is often weaker than one would like. That is what we seek to address in this chapter.

The plan of the chapter is as follows. The next section summarizes very briefly the history of immigration into the UK since 1945, the policy towards integration and the voluminous existing literature on the economic and social circumstances of ethnic minorities in Britain. The third section provides details about the data used in our analysis and presents some descriptive statistics as background for our findings in subsequent sections. The fourth section studies fertility, the fifth marriage and divorce, the sixth the gender gap in educational attainment, the seventh female employment, and the eighth values like national identity, religiosity, and language.

All in all, we find considerable heterogeneity across ethnic minority communities along the outcomes considered. However, we also find

[1] The authors would like to thank Andrew Clark (PSE) for his helpful comments.

evidence of a marked change in all these areas and this change is always in the direction of the behaviour of the indigenous British.

8.2 A brief history of immigration and integration policy in the UK since 1945

8.2.1 *Immigration*

Compared to many other European countries, the UK began to experience sizeable immigration much earlier, starting fairly soon after 1945. In the 1950s immigrants from the Caribbean and in the 1960s from the Indian sub-continent arrived, primarily as workers to help alleviate labour shortages. As the economy worsened in the 1970s, there were fewer economic migrants, though there was a steady trickle through family reunification and the 72,000 Ugandan Asians expelled by Idi Amin. However, as the economy improved again in the 1990s, there was a return of economic migration, with sizeable inflows from Eastern Europe (especially after the enlargement of the EU) and from Sub-Saharan Africa. In addition, the 1990s saw sizeable inflows of refugees. The proportion of immigrants in the UK population is now at its highest level since 1945 and the immigrant population is very diverse—for a summary of the ethnic minority population see Peach (1996).

8.2.2 *Integration policy*

By European standards, the UK began to wrestle with the question of how best to incorporate immigrant populations into society very early. What emerged as the dominant idea (essentially a form of 'multiculturalism') is well-summarized by the following quotation from the Home Secretary Roy Jenkins in 1966:

> I do not regard [integration] as meaning the loss, by immigrants, of their own national characteristics and culture. I do not think that we need in this country a 'melting pot', which will turn everybody out in a common mould, as one of a series of carbon copies of someone's misplaced vision of the stereotyped Englishman... I define integration, therefore, not as a flattening process of assimilation but as equal opportunity, accompanied by cultural diversity, in an atmosphere of mutual tolerance.

This led to early (by European standards), legislation against discrimination (the first law being the 1965 Race relations Act) and a generally sympathetic attitude to allowing cultural and religious exemptions to laws and practices, for example allowing Sikh motorcyclists to wear turbans instead of helmets and Muslim policewomen to wear the hijab on duty. There was a belief that if natives were hospitable to immigrants, the minorities would, in return, come to feel part of the wider community—just one big happy family. The reality was often far from this rosy picture, as there were riots in many British cities in the early 1980s and various organizations, notably the police, have been widely criticized for institutional racism.

But more recently there has been a feeling that this strategy of multiculturalism has failed to create a common core of values, primarily because it offered minorities more than it asked from them in return and that some communities chose not to integrate into the wider society. Events like the London bombings of 2005 have shocked people into thinking something has gone badly wrong. For example, the chairman of the Commission for Racial Equality (a non-departmental public body aimed to tackle racial discrimination and promote social equality, currently merged into the new Equality and Human Rights Commission) argued in a TV interview that multiculturalism was leading to segregation, saying that 'too many public authorities particularly [are] taking diversity to a point where they [are] saying, "actually we're going to reward you for being different, we are going to give you a community centre only if you are Pakistani or African Caribbean and so on, but we're not going to encourage you to be part of the community of our town"'. The reaction has included not just a wringing of hands but also substantive changes to policy—immigrants becoming citizens now have to pass a test on language, culture, and history designed to mould their values into those deemed appropriate.

8.2.3 *Existing literature on immigrants and ethnic minorities*

There is a vast amount of research on the ways in which the economic and social circumstances of ethnic minorities in Britain differs from that of the indigenous white population.[2] The earliest papers on economic outcomes (most commonly measured as earnings, employment, and unemployment) were probably Chiswick (1980) and Stewart (1983). Since then, there have been many studies, considering diversity in the ethnic minority experience (see Blackaby *et al.*, 1997; Modood *et al.*, 1997; Clark and Drinkwater, 2007; Elliott and Lindley, 2008 inter alia), the difference between first and second-generation immigrants (e.g.

---

[2] There is also an enormous literature, which we do not seek to summarize here, on other countries—see Adsera and Chiswick (2007) for an interesting comparison of European countries.

Blackaby *et al.*, 2002, 2005), the importance of language fluency (Leslie and Lindley, 2001; Lindley, 2002a; Dustmann and Fabbri, 2003), rates of integration (Bell, 1997; Clark and Lindley, 2006), the role of religion as opposed to ethnicity (Lindley, 2002b), and differences in time-use (Zaiceva and Zimmermann, 2007). These studies have given us excellent snapshots of the position of different ethnic minorities. In particular, earnings and employment penalties are typically found to be largest for the Pakistanis and Bangladeshis who are among the most economically disadvantaged groups in British society.

But, there is much less in the way of research into how this is changing over time. This is probably due to the fact that many ethnic minority populations in Britain are of relatively recent origin so that, until very recently, it has been hard to say anything very precise about trends. But there are a number of recent studies that do explicitly address the question of changes over time. Lindley *et al.* (2006) investigate how women's employment rates among ethnic minorities have been changing, paying particular attention to the changing role of education. Clark and Drinkwater (2007) compare data from the 1991 and 2001 censuses, looking at the way in which employment and unemployment rates have changed for different ethnic minorities. They find little change in the gap between the employment rates for Pakistanis and Bangladeshis on the one hand and whites on the other. Similar persistence in employment disadvantage is found in Berthoud and Blekesaune (2007) using General Household Survey data from 1974 to 2003 and in Dustmann and Theodoropoulos (2010), who, however, report more pronounced inter-generational improvements on educational achievement for ethnic minorities compared to white natives. Georgiadis and Manning (2011) look at how the behaviour of ethnic minority communities is changing over time, taking an approach somewhat similar to that used here but with a narrower range of variables.

The main contribution of our study is that we complement and extend the existing literature in two ways: (1) we present evidence on the differences between white natives and each of the main UK ethnic minorities for a wide range of outcomes, some of which haven't been considered by other studies and (2) we document patterns of change in the behaviour of ethnic minorities over time by comparing the outcomes for the foreign and UK born, with the evidence suggesting convergence of behaviour of all ethnic minorities towards that of white natives.

8.3 Data and background

The main data used in this chapter comes from the Labour Force Survey (LFS) for the years 2000–2008 inclusive. This is the main UK household survey for the collection of information on economic activity. It is an address-based household sample, with each household being interviewed for five successive quarters and one-fifth being replaced each quarter. The LFS contains information on country of birth but no information on country of parental birth for the UK born. This means that we cannot, strictly speaking, identify first-generation Britons, that is, the children of immigrants. This is different from every other chapter in this book. The standard practice in UK research, which we follow here, is to use self-defined ethnicity as a measure of being a first-generation Briton. Therefore, the analysis of the descendants of immigrants is restricted to ethnic minorities. For the sample period under analysis it is reasonable to assume that almost all of the non-white UK born have at least one immigrant parent, though this assumption will become less true in future years.[3]

Table 8.1 reports the sample proportions for natives, first-generation immigrants, and second-generation immigrants for the UK, using the current standard classification of ethnicity in UK surveys.[4] First-generation immigrants represent around 8.6 per cent of the sample, of which half (49.4 per cent) are of white ethnicity, 11 per cent are from India, 7.6 per cent Black African, and 6.5 per cent from Pakistan. The share of second-generation immigrants (those who are UK born but their ethnicity is not White British) in the sample is 6.6 per cent, of which the largest groups are 'other white' (27.4 per cent), Indian (14 per cent), Pakistani (13.2 per cent), and Black Caribbean (10.8 per cent).

The differences in the fraction of the ethnic minority communities who are UK born largely reflect the fact that they arrived in the UK at different times. Black Caribbean immigration into the UK began earliest (in the 1950s), followed by Pakistanis and Indians,[5] who began to arrive in

---

[3] Information on parental country of birth can be identified in the LFS for individuals who live in the same household as their parents. This is the case only for 40 per cent of adults (aged 16 and above), UK-born non-whites in the LFS 2000–2008 inclusive. However, among individuals in the latter group with information on parental country of birth, 80 per cent have at least one parent born outside the UK.

[4] There are 15 categories after 2001 and 13 beforehand, the extra two groups being two extra mixed ethnicity categories. Table 8.1 reports the 13 categories of the earlier classification.

[5] This is the case for adults only, whereas if one also considers children then Bangladeshis have the third highest proportion of UK-born.

Table 8.1 Ethnicity and place of birth composition of the Labour Force Survey 2000–2008.

Ethnic origin	Foreign born	UK born
White native	0	84.8
Other	8.6	6.6
of which (%)		
Other white	49.4	27.4
Black Caribbean	4	10.8
Black African	7.6	6.5
Other Black	0.3	1.5
Black mixed	0.6	7.6
Indian	11	14
Pakistani	6.5	13.2
Bangladeshi	2.9	4.4
Other Asian	4.8	2.4
Chinese	2.8	1.7
Other mixed	1.1	6.1
Other	8.7	4.1

Note: Data source is the Labour Force Survey (LFS) 2000–2008. Proportions are computed using individual sampling weights. The other white category also includes foreign-born white British.

large numbers in the 1960s. The Bangladeshi and Chinese communities are more recent, so have the lowest proportion of UK born among adults.

In the analysis that follows, we exclude some ethnic groups because the sample sizes are too small or because the groups are too heterogeneous for analysis to be reliable. We exclude the two mixed categories (that are mostly UK born), and the four 'other' categories (other white, other Asian, other black and other) as they are very heterogeneous. This leaves us with seven groups for our analysis—white natives, Indian, Pakistani, Black African, Black Caribbean, Bangladeshi, and Chinese.

8.4 Specifications

As in other chapters, the specification we are estimating is the following:

$$Outcome_i = \sum_j [\beta_j Ethnicity_{ij} * ForeignBorn_i + \gamma_j Ethnicity_{ij} * UKBorn_i]$$
$$+ \sum_k \theta_k BirthCohort_{ik} + X_i'\alpha + \varepsilon_i$$

Note that this specification assumes that birth cohort and other regressors (typically age and education) have the same effect on the outcome for all ethnicity and nativity groups. We do have evidence from other research (Georgiadis and Manning, 2009) that this is not true but we want to have a consistent specification across all country chapters.

Because white natives are the vast majority of all samples, the coefficients on birth cohort and other regressors are going to be mostly influenced by the white native coefficients. The coefficients on the ethnicity and nativity dummies will then be close to what one would get from an Oaxaca decomposition assuming white native coefficients.

8.5 Fertility and marriage

8.5.1 *Fertility and age at first child*

In this section we consider the two outcomes related to fertility—the number of children and age at first birth. The LFS is not ideal for investigating fertility, as it does not ask retrospective questions about the number of children a woman has had. The best we can do is to exploit its household-based structure to see the number of dependent children who are living with a woman. As children will tend to leave the family home at some point, older women will be seen to be living with fewer children just because their children are older. So, we restrict our sample to women aged between 18 and 40, to capture the youngest ages at which women are likely to have children and an age when few women's children will have left home. To capture the fact that, for many women in this age group, fertility will not be completed fertility, we include a polynomial in the age of the woman as explanatory variables (these coefficients are not reported). We also control for education (which has a negative effect on fertility). We include dummy variables for each of our ethnic groups, interacted with whether the individual is UK or foreign born. The results in Table 8.2 are reported relative to white UK-born women.

All ethnic minority groups, with the exception of the Chinese, have higher fertility rates than white native women. But it is also striking that, for all ethnic groups, fertility rates are lower among the UK born compared to the foreign born. For example, foreign-born Pakistani women have 0.83 more children than white natives but UK-born Pakistani women have 0.45 more. For Bangladeshis, the foreign born have 0.98 more children, but the gap falls to 0.31 for the UK born. For Black Africans, the foreign born have 0.4 more children but the gap falls to 0.18 for the UK born. For Indians, fertility among the UK born is not significantly different from the white natives.

Table 8.3 now considers age at first birth, which we compute by taking the current age of the woman minus the age of their oldest child in the household. There are similar problems with this measure as with our measure of number of children but it probably gives the right

Table 8.2 OLS estimates of the number of dependent children for females by ethnicity and place of birth.

Ethnicity	Foreign born	UK born
White native	Reference	
Indian	0.216***	0.043
	(0.023)	(0.023)
Pakistani	0.833***	0.447***
	(0.034)	(0.033)
Bangladeshi	0.984***	0.309***
	(0.045)	(0.065)
Black Caribbean	0.013	0.020
	(0.056)	(0.027)
Black African	0.399***	0.178***
	(0.029)	(0.056)
Chinese	−0.166***	−0.192***
	(0.035)	(0.062)
R^2	0.211	
Observations	541,234	

Note: Data source is the Labour Force Survey (LFS) 2000–2008, the sample is all women aged between 18 and 40 inclusive. Dependent children are all children below 16. Controls include age, age squared, and education, clustered standard errors at the individual level in parentheses, *** significant at 1%, ** significant at 5%.

Table 8.3 Estimates of the age of the mother at first birth by ethnicity and place of birth.

Ethnicity	Foreign born	UK born
White native	Reference	
Indian	−1.95***	−0.32
	(0.15)	(0.17)
Pakistani	−2.3***	−1.88***
	(0.16)	(0.17)
Bangladeshi	−4.2***	−1.93***
	(0.18)	(0.4)
Black Caribbean	−1.01**	−1.01***
	(0.4)	(0.2)
Black African	−1.58***	−1.28***
	(0.17)	(0.41)
Chinese	1.53***	1.47**
	(0.33)	(0.7)
R^2	0.211	
Observations	539,278	

Note: Data source is the Labour Force Survey (LFS) 2000–2008, the sample is all women aged between 18 and 40 inclusive. A censored regression model is estimated, controls include age, age squared, and education, clustered standard errors at the individual level in parentheses, *** significant at 1%, ** significant at 5%.

Table 8.4 Estimates of the probability of marriage/cohabitation for women by ethnicity and place of birth.

Ethnicity	Foreign born	UK born
White native	Reference	
Indian	0.330***	−0.113***
	(0.027)	(0.017)
Pakistani	0.412***	0.106***
	(0.020)	(0.020)
Bangladeshi	0.437***	0.045
	(0.023)	(0.038)
Black Caribbean	−0.110**	−0.229***
	(0.047)	(0.017)
Black African	−0.011	−0.248***
	(0.025)	(0.028)
Chinese	−0.004	−0.117
	(0.039)	(0.061)
R^2	0.113	
Observations	128,294	

Note: Data source is the Labour Force Survey (LFS) 2000–2008, the sample is all women aged between 18 and 40 inclusive. A linear probability model is estimated, controls include age, age squared, and education, clustered standard errors at the individual level in parentheses, *** significant at 1%, ** significant at 5%.

impression.[6] Table 8.3 reports the estimates and one sees a similar pattern to that seen in Table 8.2. With the exception of the Chinese, ethnic minority women are younger at first birth than white native women, but the difference is smaller for the UK born. On both these measures, fertility seems to be moving towards the white native pattern.

8.5.2 Marriage and divorce rates

We next consider marriage patterns (see Berthoud, 2005, for an existing analysis). In Table 8.4 we report estimates for the probability for currently being married or cohabiting. Our sample is women aged between 18 and 40 so our models can be thought of as estimating the difference in marriage rates across women in these age groups. We control, as before, for age and education. For the foreign born, Table 8.4 shows that all those from South Asian communities are very much more likely to be married than white native women. However, this gap falls dramatically for the UK born, even becoming negative for UK-born Indians and only remaining significantly positive for Pakistanis. Black Caribbean

---

[6] One could use a censored regression model for those women who, when observed, have not given birth.

Table 8.5 Estimates of the probability of divorce/separation for women by ethnicity and place of birth.

Ethnicity	Foreign born	UK born
White native	Reference	
Indian	−0.051***	0.013
	(0.004)	(0.010)
Pakistani	−0.014**	0.071***
	(0.007)	(0.012)
Bangladeshi	−0.025**	−0.0001
	(0.010)	(0.026)
Black Caribbean	0.167***	0.129***
	(0.015)	(0.016)
Black African	0.209***	0.113***
	(0.010)	(0.028)
Chinese	−0.007	−0.021
	(0.010)	(0.025)
R^2	0.019	
Observations	916,963	

Note: Data source is the Labour Force Survey (LFS) 2000–2008, the sample is all non-single women aged between 18 and 40 inclusive. A linear probability model is estimated, controls include age, age squared, and education, clustered standard errors at the individual level in parentheses, *** significant at 1%, ** significant at 5%.

women are less likely to be married than white women, especially for the UK born, where the differential is 23 per cent. One also notes that UK-born Black African women have much lower marriage rates than white natives.

These differences in marriage rates may indicate different propensities to marry (or cohabit) in the first place, or differences in divorce and separation rates. To investigate the latter, Table 8.5 considers the fraction of ever-married women who are currently divorced or separated. As the married category includes those who have divorced and remarried, this will be an under-estimate of those who have ever divorced but probably gives the right picture. For the foreign born, those from the South Asian communities are significantly less likely to be divorced, whereas the Chinese are as likely to be divorced as white natives. But Black Caribbeans and Black Africans are significantly more likely to be divorced, by more than 15 percentage points for both ethnic groups. However, among the UK born significant differences in divorce/separation rate appear for the Pakistanis, Black Caribbeans, and Black Africans, who are more likely than white women to be divorced. The observation for Pakistanis is particularly interesting but does chime with some who have written that the practice of taking a spouse from Pakistan—which remains very common—results in marriages that do not last.

Table 8.6 Proportion of exogamous individuals by gender, ethnicity, and place of birth.

Ethnicity	Men			Women		
	White native spouse	Non-white native spouse	Total	White native spouse	Non-white native spouse	Total
White native	0	3.6	3.6	0	3	3
Foreign born						
Indian	5.4	4.6	10	4.7	4.7	9.4
Pakistani	3.4	4	7.4	2.3	3.8	6.1
Bangladeshi	1.7	3.4	5.1	1	3.4	4.4
Black Caribbean	22.8	10.1	32.9	14.7	9.7	24.4
Black African	10	12.8	22.8	9	8	17
Chinese	9.8	6.2	16	28.6	8.8	37.4
UK born						
Indian	14.4	5.8	20.2	15.7	7.2	22.9
Pakistani	7.8	7.3	15.1	3.7	6.8	10.5
Bangladeshi	8.3	20.8	29.1	6.7	1.7	7.4
Black Caribbean	46.7	15.8	62.5	30.4	14	44.4
Black African	22.5	16	38.5	10.6	19	29.6
Chinese	53.6	13.1	66.7	70.4	7.6	78

Note: Data source is the Labour Force Survey (LFS) 2000–2008. Proportions are computed using individual sampling weights.

These marriage patterns suggest, in line with other evidence, that the South Asian communities are relatively conservative in their marital patterns, with women typically marrying relatively young and divorce being relatively rare, while Black Caribbeans have been much less conservative. One would also see this pattern if one differentiated between cohabitation and marriage—cohabitation would be rare among South Asians and much more common among Black Caribbeans. However, as for fertility, there is a clear indication that differences in behaviour are falling.

8.5.3 Inter-ethnic marriage

Perhaps the most striking way in which communities can converge culturally is by marrying outside their own ethnic group (see also Coleman, 1994). Table 8.6 reports the fraction of each community that is married to someone of a different ethnicity. We also report the fraction of individuals who are married to white natives. We report exogamy rates separately for men and women as there are some interesting differences.

Table 8.7 Estimates of probability of exogamy by ethnicity and gender.

Ethnicity	Men		Women	
	Foreign born	UK born	Foreign born	UK born
White native	Reference		Reference	
Indian	0.0105*	0.0826***	0.0191***	0.117***
	(0.00438)	(0.0124)	(0.00477)	(0.0127)
Pakistani	−0.000780	0.0500***	−0.000671	0.0177
	(0.00530)	(0.0128)	(0.00573)	(0.00982)
Bangladeshi	−0.0169*	0.165**	−0.0198**	0.00777
	(0.00721)	(0.0555)	(0.00723)	(0.0243)
Black Caribbean	0.362***	0.556***	0.253***	0.372***
	(0.0206)	(0.0203)	(0.0203)	(0.0221)
Black African	0.103***	0.255***	0.0598***	0.149***
	(0.0105)	(0.0376)	(0.00944)	(0.0326)
Chinese	0.0595***	0.545***	0.253***	0.634***
	(0.0138)	(0.0591)	(0.0173)	(0.0535)
R^2	0.053		0.052	
Observations	834,571		817,757	

Note: Data source is the Labour Force Survey (LFS) 2000–2008, the sample is all married individuals. A probit model is estimated, estimates presented are marginal effects, controls include education, age, and age squared, clustered standard errors at the individual level in parentheses, *** significant at 1%, ** significant at 5%.

Exogamy rates are lowest for white natives (about 3 per cent), but vary very considerably across ethnic minority communities. Among the foreign born, exogamy rates are lowest for the South Asian communities, but extremely high among the Black groups and the Chinese. For all groups, exogamy rates are much higher among the UK born. Among the South Asians, there is some indication that exogamy with white natives is higher for Indians than the Pakistanis and Bangladeshis (where religion may be more of an obstacle). Exogamy rates for some groups are extremely high—78 per cent of UK-born Chinese women are exogamous, as are 66.7 per cent of UK-born Chinese men, and 62.5 per cent of UK-born Black Caribbean men.

There is a lot of information in Table 8.6 which also does not control for age and education. Table 8.7 reports regression estimates—the patterns are very similar to those reported for Table 8.6.

8.5.4 *Spousal age gaps*

Table 8.8a reports estimates for the age gap between wives and their husbands, which could perhaps be interpreted as a measure of gender relations, with a larger age gap reflecting greater gender inequality. For the foreign born, all ethnic minority groups have a significantly

Table 8.8a OLS estimates of the age gap between husband and wife for all individuals by ethnicity and place of birth.

Ethnicity	Foreign born	UK born
White native	Reference	
Indian	1.413***	−0.221
	(0.078)	(0.133)
Pakistani	1.628***	−0.149
	(0.123)	(0.142)
Bangladeshi	4.230***	1.894***
	(0.203)	(0.401)
Black Caribbean	1.703***	−0.762***
	(0.328)	(0.202)
Black African	3.188***	0.247
	(0.186)	(0.346)
Chinese	1.294***	0.596
	(0.209)	(0.492)
R^2	0.023	
Observations	759,733	

Note: Data source is the Labour Force Survey (LFS) 2000–2008, the sample is all non-single women aged between 18 and 40 inclusive. Controls include age, age squared, and education, clustered standard errors at the individual level in parentheses, *** significant at 1%, ** significant at 5%.

Table 8.8b OLS estimates of the age gap between husband and wife for endogamous and exogamous individuals by ethnicity and place of birth.

Ethnicity	Endogamous		Exogamous	
	Foreign born	UK born	Foreign born	UK born
White native	Reference		Reference	
Indian	1.430***	−0.374***	1.423***	0.471
	(0.078)	(0.122)	(0.354)	(0.432)
Pakistani	1.560***	−0.275	2.886***	0.494
	(0.127)	(0.148)	(0.582)	(0.516)
Bangladeshi	4.281***	2.019***	4.128***	−1.304
	(0.207)	(0.400)	(1.223)	(1.460)
Black Caribbean	2.333***	−0.468	0.994	−0.832**
	(0.403)	(0.252)	(0.630)	(0.344)
Black African	2.841***	0.435	5.415***	−0.347
	(0.185)	(0.322)	(0.680)	(0.912)
Chinese	0.993***	0.229	1.761***	0.612
	(0.228)	(0.548)	(0.426)	(0.577)
R^2	0.022		0.016	
Observations	751,708		724,190	

Note: Data source is the Labour Force Survey (LFS) 2000–2008, the sample is all married individuals. Controls include age, age squared, and education, clustered standard errors at the individual level in parentheses, *** significant at 1%, ** significant at 5%.

greater spousal age gap than white native women, it being largest among Bangladeshis (4.2 years) and Black Africans (3.2 years), and smallest among the Chinese (1.3 years). However, it is striking that, among the UK born it is only for the Bangladeshis who have a significantly different spousal age gap and even that is much reduced. UK-born Black Caribbeans have a significantly lower spousal age gap than white native women.

One possibility is that this is driven by the higher rates of exogamy among the UK born that we saw in Table 8.6. However, Table 8.8b shows that this is generally not the case. In Table 8.8b we estimate separate spousal age gap equations for endogamous and exogamous groups with the reference group, in both cases, being all white native women. Although there are some significant differences in spousal age gaps between exogamous and endogamous couples (though sample sizes are small for the exogamous group), it is clear that the declining gaps are present among endogamous couples.

8.6 Educational attainment and the gender gap in education

It is of very considerable interest how the level of education of ethnic minorities compares with that of natives (see Briggs *et al.*, 2005; Modood, 2005, for other research on the educational attainment of ethnic minorities). The gender gap in education is also a good way of looking for evidence of gender equality. Table 8.9 shows the average age left full-

Table 8.9 Average age left continuous full-time education and proportion left full-time education by the age of thirteen for men and women by ethnicity.

Ethnicity	Average age left full-time education		Proportion of people who left continuous full-time education by the age of thirteen	
	Men	Women	Men	Women
White native	17.2	17.1	0.19	0.15
Indian	19.6	18.6	2.14	4.46
Pakistani	18.3	16.2	4.68	15.2
Bangladeshi	17.5	15.7	8.4	19
Black Caribbean	17.2	17.5	1.5	0.7
Black African	20.6	19	1.8	5.8
Chinese	20	19.4	3.7	4

Note: Data source is the Labour Force Survey (LFS) 2000–2008. Proportions are computed using individual sampling weights.

time education for different ethnic groups. This measure of education is not ideal as a given age left full-time education may reflect very different types and quality of education, especially when comparing the foreign and UK born. But, unfortunately, the UK LFS does not adequately code foreign qualifications so the measure we use here is the best available.

Table 8.9 shows that, for men, it is white natives who, on average, left full-time education at the youngest age. The Black Africans, Chinese, and Indians are the best-educated. Among women, Pakistanis and Bangladeshis have lower levels of education than white natives, clearly indicating a gender gap in education for these groups. A smaller gender gap is found among the Indians and Chinese.

However, these figures on average age left full-time education hide a lot of variation. The last two columns look at the fraction of communities who left full-time education by the age of 13, that is, who have a very low level of education. This should be impossible for those born and brought up in the UK and one sees essentially zero rates among white natives. The fractions are higher for all ethnic minority communities—and very high for some groups. Most strikingly, 19 per cent of Bangladeshi women and 15.2 per cent of Pakistani women have completed education by the age of 13, so levels of education are low for these groups.

Table 8.10 OLS estimates of the gender gap in age left continuous full-time education by ethnicity, place of birth, and birth cohort.

	Indian	Pakistani	Bangladeshi	Black Caribbean	Black African	Chinese
UK born						
Born before 1970	0.760***	1.277***	3.198	−0.181	0.497	−1.089**
	(0.203)	(0.331)	(1.713)	(0.102)	(0.364)	(0.549)
Born after 1970	0.546***	0.875***	0.951	−0.139	−0.065	0.337
	(0.156)	(0.207)	(0.572)	(0.203)	(0.393)	(0.456)
Foreign born						
Born before 1970	1.382***	2.907***	2.422***	−0.294**	2.084***	0.799***
	(0.099)	(0.171)	(0.300)	(0.120)	(0.166)	(0.250)
Born after 1970	0.903***	1.719***	1.457***	−0.452	1.278***	0.814**
	(0.162)	(0.207)	(0.247)	(0.325)	(0.199)	(0.369)
R^2	0.075	0.116	0.100	0.034	0.037	0.073
Observations	38,202	21,614	7,145	19,709	18,163	7,245

Note: Data source is the Labour Force Survey (LFS) 2000–2008, the sample is all individuals aged 26 and above. Clustered standard errors at the individual level in parentheses, *** significant at 1%, ** significant at 5%.

Table 8.10 reports regression estimates for the gender gap in education. In these regressions we also interact the ethnicity and foreign-born dummies with a cohort dummy for whether the respondent was born before or after 1970. The reported coefficients are gender gaps. For all the foreign-born groups except the Black Caribbeans there is a significantly larger gender gap in education than among white natives. However, this gender gap is smaller for later birth cohorts. Among the UK born, the gender gaps are lower and, within this group, lower for those born after 1970 (although small sample sizes make it hard to draw precise conclusions on this).

To summarize: the gender gap in educational attainment is larger among Pakistani and Banglasdeshi communities than for the other main ethnic minorities. In large part, this is the result of enormous past differences in the educational attainment of men and women in the countries of origin. But there is marked change, driven in part by changes among both the UK and foreign born,[7] and in part because of the change in the share of the communities who are UK born. Our conclusions here are consistent with those of more qualitative studies (e.g. Ahmad *et al.*, 2003) who conclude that cultures often portrayed as opposed to the education and employment of women seem to be producing growing cohorts of highly motivated young women.

8.7 Female employment

We now turn to an analysis of female employment. For white natives the last 60 years have seen a large growth in female employment rates, though there is some evidence that the growth is now slowing or even stopping. But many of the ethnic minorities come from cultures in which female employment is lower, so female employment is an interesting indicator of cultural change. It may, of course, also reflect economic opportunities.

Table 8.11 reports female employment rates, by ethnicity, place of birth and—because it is so important—marital status and the presence of dependent children. The first row reports employment rates for all women. These are highest for white natives, though Black Caribbeans are only slightly behind. However, the exceedingly low rates for Pakistani (25 per cent) and Bangladeshi (17 per cent) women are quite

---

[7] Changes among the foreign born might be the result of the changes in the source countries discussed above, but another factor that might be important is the changing selection of immigrants into the UK.

Table 8.11 Female employment rates by ethnicity, place of birth, marital status, and presence of dependent children.

	White Native	Indian	Pakistani	Bangladeshi	Black Caribbean	Black African	Chinese
All Women	0.74	0.64	0.25	0.17	0.71	0.59	0.63
UK born							
All	0.74	0.75	0.45	0.46	0.73	0.73	0.77
Single	0.7	0.81	0.72	0.7	0.67	0.7	0.78
Married	0.78	0.88	0.72	0.8	0.91	0.92	0.82
Married with dependent children	0.74	0.68	0.33	0.31	0.76	0.71	0.73
Foreign born							
All		0.61	0.18	0.14	0.7	0.56	0.6
Single		0.76	0.3	0.54	0.66	0.54	0.64
Married		0.61	0.25	0.22	0.72	0.72	0.6
Married—with dependent children under 16		0.6	0.15	0.11	0.7	0.53	0.57

Note: Data source is the Labour Force Survey (LFS) 2000–2008, the sample is all women aged between 25 and 59 inclusive.

Table 8.12 Estimates of employment probability for women by ethnicity and place of birth.

Ethnicity	Foreign born	UK born
White native	Reference	
Indian	−0.185*** (0.00815)	−0.0421** (0.0129)
Pakistani	−0.555*** (0.00848)	−0.322*** (0.0167)
Bangladeshi	−0.587*** (0.0122)	−0.298*** (0.0416)
Black Caribbean	−0.0543*** (0.0134)	−0.0619*** (0.0115)
Black African	−0.255*** (0.0102)	−0.0959*** (0.0256)
Chinese	−0.210*** (0.0161)	−0.0343 (0.0373)
R^2	0.053	
Observations	948,814	

Note: Data source is the Labour Force Survey (LFS) 2000–2008, the sample is all women aged between 25 and 59 inclusive. A probit model is estimated, estimates presented are marginal effects, controls include education, age, and age squared, clustered standard errors at the individual level in parentheses, *** significant at 1%, ** significant at 5%.

striking. This is well known (see, for example, Cabinet Office, 2003, Berthoud and Blekesaune (2007) and Clark and Drinkwater (2007)). The Equalities Review went so far as to say that the gap in employment rates between Pakistani/Bangladeshi and white women would never be eliminated (Cabinet Office, 2007). However, one can also see in Table 8.11 that there is a very large difference in employment rates between the foreign and UK born. For example, UK-born Pakistani women have an employment rate of 45 per cent—still low, but much higher than the rate of 18 per cent for foreign-born Pakistani women. For Bangladeshi women, the figures are 46 per cent and 14 per cent, respectively. There is also some indication that UK-born women from these communities are no longer stopping employment on marriage but waiting until they have children.

The employment rates of Table 8.11 do not control for age or education. Table 8.12 reports estimates from specifications that control for education. For the foreign born, women from all ethnic minorities are significantly less likely to be in employment than white native women, with the largest gaps being for Pakistanis and Bangladeshis. But, these gaps are much reduced among the UK born.

Again, we see evidence of convergence in behaviour. The quantitative conclusions we have drawn here mesh well with the more qualitative studies of Ahmad *et al.* (2003) and Aston *et al.* (2007).

8.8 Values and beliefs

8.8.1 *National identity*

Since spring 2001 the LFS has asked about the national identity of respondents (though not in Northern Ireland), a question motivated by concern that some immigrant groups did not think of themselves as British. The specific question asked is 'What do you consider your national identity to be? Please choose as many or as few as apply'. There are six possible responses: British, English, Scottish, Welsh, Irish, and Other. The order in which these responses are listed depends on the country of residence so English is the first option in England, Scottish in Scotland and Welsh in Wales. For the purposes of this chapter we group British, English, Scottish and Welsh into a single 'British' category and we will use the term British to refer to any of these answers in what follows.

Table 8.13 reports estimates from a probit equation—the coefficients are differences from white natives. In line with Manning and Roy (2010), and Georgiadis and Manning (2009) we find that all ethnic minorities are less likely to report a British national identity than white natives but

Table 8.13 Estimates of the probability of reporting British national identity by ethnicity and place of birth.

Ethnicity	Foreign born	UK born
White native	Reference	
Indian	−0.406***	−0.0819***
	(0.00582)	(0.00528)
Pakistani	−0.340***	−0.0692***
	(0.00707)	(0.00555)
Bangladeshi	−0.346***	−0.0497***
	(0.0111)	(0.0110)
Black Caribbean	−0.374***	−0.0764***
	(0.0108)	(0.00512)
Black African	−0.629***	−0.0802***
	(0.00725)	(0.01000)
Chinese	−0.580***	−0.0962***
	(0.0119)	(0.0156)
R^2	0.474	
Observations	1,944,169	

Note: Data source is the Labour Force Survey (LFS) 2001–2008, the sample is all individuals aged 16 and above. A probit model is estimated, estimates presented are marginal effects, controls include education, age, and age squared, clustered standard errors at the individual level in parentheses, *** significant at 1%, ** significant at 5%.

the gap is very much smaller for the UK born (in the 5–10 percentage point range) than among the foreign born (where it is in the 30–60 percentage point range). In line with other studies, it is worth pointing out that the Muslim groups (the Pakistanis and Bangladeshis) whose loyalty to Britain is often questioned are the ethnic minorities who are most likely to report a British national identity.

8.8.2 Religion

Since 2002, the Labour Force Survey has collected data on religion and Table 8.14 documents the proportions of different ethnicities describing themselves as of different religions. We also report the fraction with no religion and the fraction who report that they are practising their religion. The groups from the Indian sub-continent and Black Africans remain very religious, as very few report having no religion compared, for example, to the 56.6 per cent share of individuals reporting no religion among the Chinese. The most religious are the Pakistanis and Bangladeshis who are overwhelmingly Muslim.[8] These groups are also much more likely to be practising their religion.

---

[8] It is hard to know from this data whether the non-Muslims have converted or were brought up that way, as there are small religious minorities in both countries.

Table 8.14 Reported religion and whether practising religion by ethnicity.

Religion	White Native	Indian	Pakistani	Bangladeshi	Black Caribbean	Black African	Chinese
Christian	82.5	7.9	1.3	0.24	84	76.7	25.4
Buddhist	0.14	0.3	0.02	0.05	0.2	0.1	14.5
Hindu	0.01	46.1	0.18	1.07	0.24	0.27	0.17
Jewish	0.43	0.1	0.02	0.03	0.12	0.04	0
Muslim	0.07	13.3	96.5	97	0.62	18	0.2
Sikh	0.01	27.6	0.11	0.1	0.01	0.04	0
Other religion	0.7	1.95	1.22	0.28	2.3	0.93	3
No religion	16.2	2.6	0.66	1.21	12.5	3.9	56.6
% practising religion	17	64	80	82	33	65	6

Note: Data source is the Labour Force Survey (LFS) 2002–2008 for religious denomination and LFS 2002–03 for whether practising religion, the sample is all individuals aged 16 and above.

Table 8.15 reports estimates for the differences in the proportions who are practising their religion. In line with Table 8.14, all the South Asian and Black groups are more religious than white natives, with the Pakistanis and Bangladeshis standing out as being the most religious. There is evidence of less religiosity among the UK born than the foreign born, although the decline is noticeably less marked for Pakistanis.

What this suggests is that, while there is some evidence of a trend towards lower rates of religiosity among all the ethnic minorities studied here, the trend is less marked for Pakistanis than for other groups. This is perhaps consistent with the evidence in Bisin *et al.* (2007) that Muslims are more serious about their faith than adherents to other religions, although the Muslim Bangladeshis do show a marked decline in religiosity for the UK born.

8.8.3 *Language*

If one has problems with the English language, it is likely to be very hard to assimilate into British culture and one is very likely to remain economically disadvantaged. The LFS asks[9] whether English is the first language at home and, if some other language other than English, Welsh, Gaelic, or Ullans is spoken, whether the respondent has language difficulties with work and education. We code an individual as reporting

[9] This is only for one quarter every three years, so sample sizes are much reduced for the analysis that follows.

Table 8.15 Estimates of the probability of whether practising religion by ethnicity and place of birth.

Ethnicity	Foreign born	UK born
White native	Reference	
Indian	0.604***	0.448***
	(0.0130)	(0.0200)
Pakistani	0.748***	0.679***
	(0.0130)	(0.0197)
Bangladeshi	0.805***	0.609***
	(0.0121)	(0.0559)
Black Caribbean	0.266***	0.161***
	(0.0201)	(0.0147)
Black African	0.627***	0.389***
	(0.0140)	(0.0376)
Chinese	−0.0592***	−0.0286
	(0.00860)	(0.0247)
R^2	0.087	
Observations	315,866	

Note: Data source is the Labour Force Survey (LFS) 2002–2003, the sample is all individuals aged 16 and above. A probit model is estimated, estimates presented are marginal effects, controls include a dummy for whether the individual is female, education, age, and age squared, clustered standard errors at the individual level in parentheses, *** significant at 1%, ** significant at 5%.

language difficulties if they report problems with either work or education.

In our analysis we assume that no white natives have language problems.[10] We also assume the same for Black Caribbeans, the vast majority of whom come from English-speaking islands. Table 8.16 reports rates of using English at home for the other groups. Only 11 per cent of foreign-born Bangladeshis and 19 per cent of foreign-born Pakistanis use English at home, compared to 30 per cent of foreign-born Indians and Chinese and 47 per cent of Black Africans. For all ethnic minorities the proportions rise very markedly for the UK born, though a sizeable minority continue to use a language other than English at home.

Table 8.17 presents estimates of the proportions reporting difficulties with English. Among the foreign born, 22 per cent of Bangladeshis, 16 per cent of Pakistanis, 15 per cent of Chinese, and 10 per cent of Indians and Black Africans report difficulties. In many ways these differences reflect differences in educational attainment reported earlier in the chapter in Table 8.9. Among the UK born these proportions become

[10] In doing this we ignore the fact that a non-negligible fraction of the white native population do have literacy problems. However, we have little choice as the LFS does not ask the language difficulty question to those who report using English, Welsh, Gaelic, or Ullans at home.

Table 8.16 Estimates of the proportion with English as the first language at home by ethnicity and place of birth.

Ethnicity	Foreign born	UK born
Indian	0.294***	0.620***
	(0.0109)	(0.0184)
Pakistani	0.189***	0.509***
	(0.0112)	(0.0216)
Bangladeshi	0.114***	0.546***
	(0.0133)	(0.0517)
Black African	0.466***	0.865***
	(0.0151)	(0.0236)
Chinese	0.284***	0.784***
	(0.0216)	(0.0374)
R^2	0.48	
Observations	8,257	

Note: Data source is the Labour Force Survey (LFS) 2002 second quarter, 2003 second quarter, and 2006 third quarter, the sample is all individuals aged 16 or above who are not white natives or Black Caribbeans, as all individuals with either ethnicity speak English at home. A linear probability model is estimated, the constant term is not included in estimation, controls include education, age, and age squared, clustered standard errors at the individual level in parentheses, *** significant at 1%, ** significant at 5%.

Table 8.17 Estimates of the proportion reporting that English language difficulties are causing problems in finding a job or in education.

Ethnicity	Foreign born	UK born
Indian	0.0912***	0.0191**
	(0.00653)	(0.00726)
Pakistani	0.165***	0.0160
	(0.0105)	(0.00884)
Bangladeshi	0.220***	0.0263
	(0.0175)	(0.0187)
Black African	0.101***	0.0157**
	(0.00901)	(0.00579)
Chinese	0.155***	0.0561**
	(0.0155)	(0.0182)
R^2	0.14	
Observations	8,257	

Note: Data source is the Labour Force Survey (LFS) 2002 second quarter, 2003 second quarter, and 2006 third quarter, the sample is all individuals aged 16 and above who are not white natives or Black Caribbeans, as all individuals with either ethnicity speak English at home. A linear probability model is estimated, the constant term is not included in estimation, controls include education, age, and age squared, clustered standard errors at the individual level in parentheses, *** significant at 1%, ** significant at 5%.

dramatically smaller, even though, as Table 8.16 shows, a large fraction do not use English as a first language at home. However, this perhaps comes as no surprise given that education is in English.

8.9 Conclusion

This chapter has compared the behaviours of the largest ethnic minorities in Britain with white natives across a wide, though not exhaustive, range of indicators. In all these dimensions there are significant differences across ethnic minorities some of which are well-established in the literature, as, for example, the strikingly low employment rates for Pakistani and Bangladeshi women but there are other differences less well-documented. An example of the latter is the finding that the Muslim minorities (the Pakistanis and Bangladeshis) are more likely to report a British National identity compared to other ethnic minority communities both among the foreign and UK born. Moreover, another striking common pattern that emerges is the extent to which differences in behaviours between ethnic minorities and white natives tend to be less pronounced for the UK than the foreign born. This indicates a general pattern of cultural integration, something perhaps not surprising to those who study the topic but not the impression one might gain from public discourse on the subject. The rate of cultural integration is faster for some variables than others—it is probably religion that shows the slowest rate. This has the implication that within religions, behaviours are changing so that what it means to be a good Christian or Muslim or Hindu is changing over time.

It is an important question whether, in future years, this process of convergence will continue until behaviours are the same or whether permanent differences will remain. Statistical analysis of data inevitably can only tell us about the past. But it is clear that there are very powerful forces that are acting to change the behaviour of immigrant communities once they are in the UK and it is not unreasonable to guess that these will continue into the future.

References

Adsera, A. and Chiswick, B. (2007) Are There Gender and Country of Origin Differences in Immigrant Labor Market Outcomes Across European Destinations? *Journal of Population Economics*, 20, 495–526.

Ahmad, F., Lissenburgh, S., and Modood, T. (2003) *South Asian Women and Employment in Britain: The Interaction of Gender and Ethnicity.* London, Policy Studies Institute.

Aston, J., Hooker, H., Page, R., and Willison, R. (2007) *Pakistani and Bangladeshi Women's Attitudes to Work and Family.* Department for Work and Pensions Research Report, No. 458.

Bell, B.D. (1997) The Performance of Immigrants in the United Kingdom: Evidence from the GHS. *Economic Journal*, 107, 333–344.

Berthoud, R. (2005) Family formation in multi-cultural Britain: diversity and change. In: G. Lowry, T. Modood, and S. Teles (eds) *Ethnicity, Social Mobility and Public Policy.* Cambridge, Cambridge University Press.

Berthoud, R. and Blekesaune, M. (2007) *Persistent Employment Disadvantage.* Department for Work and Pensions research Report No. 416.

Bisin, A., Patacchini, E., Verdier, T., and Zenou, Y. (2007) *Are Muslim Immigrants Different in Terms of Cultural Integration?* CEPR Discussion Papers 6453.

Blackaby, D.H., Drinkwater, S., Leslie, D.G., and Murphy, P. (1997) 'A Picture of Male and Female Unemployment Among Britain's Ethnic Minorities. *Scottish Journal of Political Economy*, 44, 182–197.

Blackaby, D.H., Leslie, D. G., Murphy, P.D., and O'Leary, N.C. (2002) White/Ethnic Minority Earnings and Employment Differentials in Britain: Evidence from the LFS. *Oxford Economic Papers*, 54, 270–297.

Blackaby, D.H., Leslie, D.G., Murphy, P.D., and O'Leary, N.C. (2005) Born in Britain: How are Native Ethnic Minorities Faring in the British Labour Market. *Economic Letters*, 88, 370–5.

Briggs, A., Burgess, S., and Wilson, D. (2005) *The Dynamics of School Attainment of England's Ethnic Minorities.* CMPO Working Paper 05/130, Bristol University.

Cabinet Office (2003) *Ethnic Minorities and the Labour Market: Final Report.* London, Cabinet Office.

Cabinet Office (2007) *Fairness and freedom: The Final report of the Equalities Review.* http://webarchive.nationalarchives.gov.uk/20100807034701/http:/archive. cabinetoffice.gov.uk/equalitiesreview/upload/assets/www.theequalitiesreview. org.uk/equality_review.pdf.

Chiswick, B.R. (1980) The Earnings of White and Coloured Male Immigrants in Britain. *Economica*, 47, 81–87.

Clark, K. and Drinkwater, S. (2007) *Ethnic minorities in the Labour Market: Dynamics and Diversity.* York, Joseph Rowntree Foundation.

Clark, K. and Lindley, J. (2006) *Immigrant Labour Market Assimilation and Arrival Effects: Evidence from the UK Labour Force Survey.* IZA Discussion Paper No. 2228.

Coleman, D. (1994) Trends in Fertility and Intermarriage Among Immigrant Populations in Western Europe as Measures of Integration. *Journal of Biosocial Science*, 26, 107–136.

Dustmann, C. and Fabbri, F. (2003) Language Proficiency and Labour Market Performance of Immigrants in the UK. *Economic Journal*, 113, 695–717.

Dustmann, C. and Theodoropoulos, N. (2010) Ethnic Minority Immigrants and their Children in Britain. *Oxford Economic Papers*, 62, 209–233.

Elliott, R.J.R. and Lindley, J.K. (2008) Immigrant Wage Differentials, Ethnicity and Occupational Segregation. *Journal of the Royal Statistical Society, Series A*, 171, 645–671.

Georgiadis, A. and Manning, A. (2009) *One Nation Under a Groove? Identity and Multiculturalism in Britain*. CEP Discussion Paper No. 944.

Georgiadis, A. and Manning, A. (2011) Change and Continuity Among Minority Communities in Britain. *Journal of Population Economics*, 24, 541–568.

Leslie, D. and Lindley, J.K. (2001) The Impact of Language Ability on Employment and Earnings of Britain's Ethnic Communities. *Economica*, 68, 587–606.

Lindley, J.K. (2002a) The English Language Fluency and Earnings of Ethnic Minorities in Britain. *Scottish Journal of Political Economy*, 49 (4), 467–487.

Lindley, J.K. (2002b) Race or religion? The Impact of Religion on the Employment and Earnings of Britain's Ethnic Communities. *Journal of Ethnic and Migration Studies*, 28(3), 427–442.

Lindley, J.K., Dale, A., and Dex, S. (2006) *Ethnic Differences in Women's Employment: The Changing Role of Qualifications*. Oxford Economic Papers, 58, 351–378.

Manning, A. and Sanchari, R. (2010) Culture Clash or Culture Club? National Identity in Britain. *Economic Journal Features*, 120, F72–F100.

Modood, T. (2005) The Educational Attainments of Ethnic Minorities in Britain. In: G.C. Loury, T. Modood, and S.M. Teles (eds) *Ethnicity, Social Mobility and Public Policy: Comparing the US and UK*. Cambridge, Cambridge University Press.

Modood, T., Berthoud, R., Lakey, J., *et al.* (1997) *Ethnic Minorities in Britain Diversity and Disadvantage*. London, Policy Studies Institute.

Peach, C. (1996) *Ethnicity in the 1991 Census, Volume 2: the Ethnic Minority Populations of Great Britain*. London, HMSO.

Stewart, M.B. (1983) Racial Discrimination and Occupational Attainment in Britain. *Economic Journal*, 93, 521–541.

Zaiceva, A. and Zimmermann, K.F. (2007) *Children, Kitchen, Church: Does Ethnicity Matter?* IZA Discussion Paper No. 3070.

9

Cultural Integration in the United States

Jacob Vigdor

9.1 Introduction

Immigration figures prominently in the social and political history of the United States. At the time of the nation's founding in the late eighteenth century, concerns about the cultural integration of foreign-born aliens were already widespread. Writing in 1751, a quarter of a century before the Declaration of Independence, Benjamin Franklin wrote a treatise expressing grave concerns about the presence of non-Anglo-Saxon residents. A hundred years later, the rapid arrival of Catholic immigrants from Germany and Ireland inspired the brief but intense 'Know-nothing' movement, which soon divided itself over the issue of slavery in the lead-up to the nation's civil war. Half a century after that, a new wave of immigration from the nations of Southern and Eastern Europe inspired a series of legislative interventions intended to preserve the nation's dominant culture against perceived threats—first by encouraging immigrants to assimilate, later by excluding them from the nation entirely.

Between the 1920s and the 1960s, legal restrictions on immigration all but eliminated the flow of permanent settlers into the nation. Since 1965, a partial relaxation of those restrictions has led to a new wave of immigration in the United States, this time composed predominantly of migrants from Asia and Latin America. Recently, roughly one million new immigrants have legally entered the United States every year, while hundreds of thousands more enter without legal authorization to reside or work in the country. In a nation of some 300 million residents, 40 million are foreign born. While the density of immigrants in the population was higher in the early twentieth century, the sheer number of foreign-born residents in the United States is unprecedented.

The post-1965 wave of immigration has inspired a litany of concerns. It has coincided with a prolonged period of stagnation or decline in the earnings of low-skilled workers; the work of George Borjas has argued that these two coincident trends are in fact causally linked (Borjas, 2003). In more recent years, immigration has been viewed as a national security issue, and the loyalty of foreign-born residents to their host nation is a common subject of concern. Beyond these issues, just as in earlier eras, there are frequently-voiced concerns that new immigrants are failing to integrate into the native culture. Unlike earlier eras, where immigrants came from many nations and spoke a number of languages, one-third of contemporary immigrants come from a single country, Mexico, and about half are native Spanish speakers. Thus, while the lessons of earlier eras would indicate that linguistic minorities quickly disperse into the mainstream population, there are credible reasons to think that this migration wave is substantively different.

This chapter will review the evidence of the cultural integration of immigrants in the United States, both past and present. Two methods of measuring cultural integration will be reviewed. First, a number of individual indicators will be combined into a univariate measure. Second, individual indicators of cultural integration, including the ability to speak English, residential location, and intermarriage will be reviewed. Using both measures, a common story emerges. In all, the rate of cultural integration among modern immigrants to the United States is quite similar to the rate observed a century ago, during the last great wave of European immigration. The overall rate, however, masks important forms of heterogeneity across immigrant groups. In particular, immigrants from Mexico and nearby parts of Latin America exhibit slow rates of cultural integration over time. Immigrants from other regions of the world, by contrast, are integrating quite rapidly by historical standards.

The chapter concludes with a discussion of the factors that might explain the substantial heterogeneity in the experiences of modern immigrants. The lack of legal status, which influences an immigrant's incentive to invest in cultural capital, is a clear impediment to assimilation. Proximity between host and origin countries is also a factor; the greater the likelihood of return to one's home country, the weaker the incentive to invest in cultural capital. Finally, advances in communication technology have increased the ability of even relatively small linguistic minorities to function in a host society.

9.2 An index measure of integration in the United States

9.2.1 *Methodology*

Vigdor (2008) describes a method of deriving a unidimensional index measure of immigrant assimilation from multidimensional data on the characteristics of native and foreign-born residents of a nation. Using a dataset with an equal number of observations in each group, the method begins by estimating a probit regression, with nativity status serving as the dependent variable. A series of characteristics, including economic, cultural, and civic indicators, serve as predictors. Intuitively, the degree of assimilation or integration increases as the probit model's predictive power decreases. In the limit, when the distribution of predictive characteristics is identical in both groups, they can be considered fully integrated with one another.

To quantitatively express the degree of integration between groups, the probit regression model is used to compute a predicted probability of foreign nativity for each member of the sample, based on the observed characteristics included on the right hand side.[1] Because the probit model is estimated on a sample divided evenly between foreign and native born, when no characteristics predict nativity all sample members will be assigned a 50 per cent likelihood of being foreign born. At the other extreme, a perfectly predictive model (which is in fact not estimable in a maximum-likelihood framework, but should be considered as a theoretical possibility) would yield predicted likelihoods of 100 per cent for the foreign-born and 0 per cent for the native born. As a summary measure, then, the mean predicted probability p can be computed for the entire foreign-born population, or subsets thereof, and converted to an index according to the formula:

(1) index = $2^*(100-p)$,

which returns a value of 100 when p is 50 per cent, and converges to 0 as p approaches 100 per cent. On occasion, when computed for a subset of the immigrant population, the index may exceed 100 per cent. This occurs when a particular subset of immigrants, such as those born in a neighbouring country, exhibit characteristics that are in fact more typically associated with natives than immigrants. In such cases, the index is truncated to the value of 100.

---

[1] Probit regression results are not reported in this chapter. Sample results for various years can be found in Vigdor (2008).

9.2.2 Data

In the United States, detailed individual-level data identifying birthplace as well as social characteristics including language ability, household structure, and residential location has been collected systematically since the Census of 1900. Given the paucity of newly arrived immigrants in the years between 1920 and 1965, the assimilation index is most meaningfully computed using data from the Census enumerations of 1900 through 1930, and then again from 1980 to the present. In the years since 2000, annual information of comparable quality and quantity has been collected through the American Community Survey (ACS). These data can be used to generate four predictive indicators to be used to form a consistent measure of cultural integration from 1900 to 2007, the most recent years' worth of data.

Ability to speak English: Although the United States does not have an official language, the rate at which immigrants acquire the ability to speak English has typically been a widely monitored indicator of cultural integration. In the early twentieth century, English ability was assessed using a simple binary coding by in-person enumerators who canvassed each residential address nationwide. In later years, respondents have self-reported their English-speaking ability using a multivalued scale. For purposes of analysis, this variable is recoded as a binary indicator, separating those who have any English ability whatsoever from those who have none. Even with this recoding, however, it remains possible that observed changes in English ability over long periods of time might reflect changes in reporting rather than an actual difference in mastery. This caveat should be kept in mind for the duration of the analysis below.

Marital status: Marital status is coded consistently throughout the sample period, with the exception that the category 'separated' was not an option in the early years. Individuals who report being separated in later years are recoded as 'married, spouse absent' for purposes of consistency.

Intermarriage: Data permit the identification of spouse's birthplace in those situations where both husband and wife reside at the same address. The actual indicator used to code intermarriage is not whether a respondent's spouse belongs to a different nativity group. Given random mating in the population, such a measure would indicate higher rates of intermarriage among members of rarer groups. Instead, the intermarriage measure indicates whether a respondent's spouse is native born. In a situation of random mating, all groups should have an equal probability of having a native born spouse, regardless of the representation of natives in the population.

Number of children present in the household: The Census and ACS provide a complete record of individuals residing at a given address, as well as their relationship to other individuals living in the same household.

Residential location: The Census records detailed geographic location information for each household. This information is not consistently available in the public use microdata records used to compute the assimilation index, however. As such, this factor will not be incorporated into the index. Trends in the residential integration of the native and foreign born will be examined in the section on supplemental analyses below.

9.2.3 Other dimensions of assimilation

Beyond measuring cultural integration, this methodology can also be used to examine the degree of distinction between immigrants and natives along more purely economic dimensions, or along civic indicators, including citizenship and military service. This task is complicated in earlier Census samples by the absence of many economic and civic indicators. In addition to the cultural assimilation index, this chapter will report information on a more comprehensive assimilation index that incorporates information on citizenship, home ownership, labour force participation, and a basic socio-economic status indicator based on respondents' reported occupations and the average earnings of individuals employed in those occupations in 1950.

9.2.4 Results

Table 9.1 presents two versions of the assimilation index: one focusing purely on cultural factors, the other incorporating some economic and civic indicators as well, for selected years between 1900 and 2007. Cultural integration, as measured by the index, varies only slightly across these dates, from a low value of 59 in 1910 to a high value of 67 in 1980. The indices are not reported for the years between 1930 and 1980, when the flow of new migrants to the United States was minimal and most foreign-born residents had lived in the country for several decades. Presumably during this interval the assimilation index was relatively high.

There are two periods of noteworthy decline in cultural assimilation: between 1900 and 1910, and again between 1980 and 1990. The earlier period coincides with a decade of rapid arrival rates for non-English

Table 9.1 Assimilation indices for the United States, 1900–2007.

Year	Cultural assimilation index	Composite assimilation index
1900	64	54
1910	59	48
1920	60	41
1930	62	45
1980	67	46
1990	61	29
2000	61	28
2007	62	29

Source: US Census (1900–2000) and American Community Survey (2007), author's calculations. The cultural assimilation index summarizes the distinctiveness between the native and foreign-born population on the basis of ability to speak English, marital status, likelihood of marriage to a native-born spouse, and number of children present in the household. The composite index adds information on citizenship, labour force participation, and an occupation-based measure of imputed income.

speaking migrants in the United States. As assimilation is a process that takes time, the assimilation index will naturally decline as the ratio of newly arrived immigrants to longer-term foreign-born residents rises. In light of this, it is perhaps surprising that the cultural assimilation index fails to decline in the period after 1990, when rapid immigration to the United States continued. This pattern will be explored in greater depth.

The composite assimilation index is generally lower than the cultural version, as any algorithm for distinguishing two groups of people will make more accurate predictions when it considers more information. The index begins at a relatively high value of 54 in 1900, then declines through 1920, before ticking upwards as immigration nearly halted in the 1920s. Between 1930 and 1980, there is virtually no change in the index. Like the cultural version, the composite index declines in the 1980s before stabilizing over the past two decades.

As noted above, the assimilation index can be computed for subsets of the immigrant population. Table 9.2 exploits this feature to illustrate the process of assimilation over time, as well as variation in assimilation across groups. The table focuses on immigrants of three nationalities drawn from three time periods. The first two rows examine the experience of Italian immigrants who arrived in the United States between 1906 and 1910, around the peak of immigration from that origin country. Observed shortly after arrival, this group is very close to perfectly distinct from the native population when civic and economic factors are considered alongside cultural ones. Along the cultural dimension alone, the index stands at 19, substantially below the overall average for that year.

Table 9.2 Assimilation of specific immigrant cohorts at varying points in time.

Country of birth	Arrival in USA	Year observed	Cultural	Composite
Italy	1906–1910	1910	19	4
		1930	43	29
Mexico	1975–1980	1980	39	8
		2007	55	28
Vietnam	1975–1980	1980	48	6
		2007	58	56
Mexico	2001–2007	2007	43	3
Vietnam	2001–2007	2007	44	8

Source: US Census (1910–1980), American Community Survey (2007), author's calculations.

Twenty years later, this cohort of Italian immigrants had exhibited substantial progress. The cultural assimilation index had increased from 19 to 43, reflecting a combination of English language learning and other factors, including intermarriage. The composite index had increased to 29, thanks to these processes as well as economic advances and naturalization. Even after 20 or more years in the United States, though, Italian immigarnts were far below the overall average in terms of cultural and overall integration. In the early twentieth century, a substantial proportion of immigrants were from nations such as the United Kingdom, Germany, Ireland, and Canada. With fewer cultural and ethnic barriers to cross, these groups undoubtedly experienced more instantaneous assimilation along many dimensions.

In more recent years, Mexico and Vietnam have been two of the most prominent origin countries. Table 9.2 shows that since 1980, recently arrived immigrants from these nations have been poorly assimilated overall, though not as noteworthy in the cultural dimension. Cultural assimilation upon arrival ranges from 39 among Mexican immigrants in 1980 to 48 among Vietnamese immigrants in that same year. This reflects a combination of better language skills and, for Mexican immigrants at least, a higher likelihood of intermarriage, as defined for purposes of the assimilation index. The overall assimilation index, measured shortly after arrival, is in the single digits for all groups, dragged down in particular by low rates of naturalization.

Cohorts arriving in the late 1970s had posted substantial improvements in integration by 2007. The improvements are most noteworthy among Mexican immigrants, who close two-thirds of the initial gap with the Vietnamese. As in an earlier era, cultural integration is achieved primarily through improvements in English skills and intermarriage. As will be documented below, intermarriage is a relatively important part of the story for Mexican immigrants, but also a controversial one. The vast majority of marriages pairing a Mexican and American-born spouse involve individuals of Mexican heritage.

In terms of composite assimilation, the progress evinced by Vietnamese immigrants far outstrips that of their Mexican counterparts. This in large part reflects important background differences between the groups. Mexican immigrants, who come from an adjacent country, migrate primarily for economic reasons. Many lack legal status, which prohibits them from taking important steps toward assimilation. Vietnamese immigrants, by contrast, come from a distant country, with more political motives for migration. As such, both their incentives and opportunities to assimilate are stronger. This theme will be extended in the concluding discussion below.

9.3 Examining individual indicators of integration

The assimilation index is a useful summary measure of the degree of similarity between two groups; however, by necessity it has the potential to obscure important details regarding specific attributes. For example, the seeming improvement in cultural assimilation among Mexican immigrants might lead one to believe that this group enjoys substantial improvements in language skills; in actuality intermarriage explains a large portion of the increase. This section summarizes some of the findings of Vigdor (2009), who more closely examines three attributes: immigrants' English-speaking ability, their proclivity to intermarry, and their residential integration with the native-born population.

9.3.1 *English ability*

Table 9.3 shows the trends in the English language ability of non-Anglophone immigrants in the United States between 1980 and 2007.[2] There is very little trend in English ability over time. Over this period of nearly three decades, the proportion of immigrants speaking no English remained steady at around 10 per cent. The proportion of immigrants speaking English either exclusively or 'very well' held steady around 50 per cent. To the extent that any trend exists, it occurred during the 1980s, when English language skills declined somewhat in the immigrant population overall. This is consistent with the trends present in

---

[2] Non-anglophone immigrants are here defined as those born in a country where fewer than half of US immigrants report speaking exclusively English at home. The excluded nations include the United Kingdom, Ireland, Canada, various former British possessions in the Caribbean, South Africa, Australia, and New Zealand.

Table 9.3 Immigrant English ability, 1980–2007.

Year	Does not speak English	Speaks English, but not well	Speaks English well	Speaks English very well	Speaks English at home
1980	8.7	16.6	24.9	31.0	18.8
1990	9.7	19.6	24.0	35.3	11.4
2000	8.7	19.2	24.3	37.1	10.8
2007	10.7	20.1	23.8	35.8	9.7

Source: US Census (1980–2000), American Community Survey (2007), author's calculations.

Table 9.4 Immigrant English ability, 1900–1930.

Year	Proportion of immigrants that do not speak English
1900	18.8
1910	31.9
1920	16.5
1930	11.0

Source: US Census, author's calculations.

index data above, which also show a decline in assimilation during the 1980s.

Table 9.4 presents comparable information drawn from the period between 1900 and 1930. Recall that in this earlier era, Census enumerators coded only whether a respondent could or could not speak English. The proportion of non-English speakers in this earlier era is consistently at or above more recent levels; at the peak of immigration in 1910 about three in ten foreign-born residents of the United States could not speak English. As the flow of newly arrived immigrants slowed after 1920, the recorded English ability of the foreign-born population improved.

Stratifying immigrants in each year by their point of arrival, it becomes clear that the English skills of newly arrived immigrants in the United States, as recorded in the Census, were very poor in the early twentieth century, and had improved substantially by the latter part of the century. Defining newly arrived immigrants as those arriving in the five years immediately before a Census enumeration, Table 9.5 shows that the proportion of new arrivals who could not speak English stood at levels between 50 and 63 per cent in the first part of the twentieth century, but had declined to levels around 20 per cent by the century's end. The general improvement in English ability in the immigrant population, then, can be attributed largely to increased ability upon

Table 9.5 English ability of newly arrived immigrants.

Year	Proportion of immigrants from non-Anglophone nations arriving in previous five years who could not speak English
1900	54.8
1910	63.4
1920	50.0
1980	17.0
1990	18.2
2000	20.8
2007	20.0

Source: US Census (1900–2000), American Community Survey (2007), author's calculations.

arrival, rather than any increased rate of language acquisition among non-speakers.[3]

Just as the degree of overall assimilation varies by immigrant group, English speaking ability differs substantially. Fully one-third of newly arrived Mexican immigrants in 2007, for example, report speaking no English; another third report speaking English 'not well'. By contrast, among newly arrived Vietnamese immigrants in 2007, only 16 per cent reported not speaking English at all. A more substantial 42 per cent of this group reported speaking 'not well'.

The high rate of cultural assimilation exhibited by Mexican immigrants in Table 9.2, visible as the increase in the assimilation index for individuals arriving in the late 1970s when evaluated in 1980 and 2007, might lead one to believe that English languages skills improve rapidly for this group. In fact, the rate of progress is modest. In 1980, Mexican immigrants arriving in the previous five years had a one-third chance of speaking no English, and another one-third chance of speaking English 'not well'—a pattern identical to that exhibited by their counterparts arriving two decades later. By 2007, 15 per cent of this cohort continued to report speaking no English, and another 28 per cent reported speaking 'not well'. Assuming no selective return migration, the likelihood of transitioning from poor English skills to a higher level of English skills was only 36 per cent over this 27-year period.[4]

Vietnamese immigrants arriving in the same time period had better language skills to begin with: while one-third spoke English 'not well',

---

[3] In fact, Vigdor (2009) shows that the rate of English language learning for non-speakers actually declines over the course of the twentieth century.

[4] Espinosa and Massey (1997) use a unique data source to assess whether selective return migration yields a skewed picture of linguistic progress among Mexican immigrants in the United States. They conclude that real linguistic progress does occur. The effect of return migration should be more modest in the Vietnamese and Italian immigrant populations.

only 9 per cent reported no English ability in 1980. By 2007, the proportion of this cohort with no English skills had dropped to 3 per cent, and the proportion with poor English skills stood at 19 per cent. Again, assuming no selective return migration, the transition probability to a higher level of English skills among those who started at a low level was closer to 50 per cent.

For the purposes of historical comparison, about three-quarters of newly arrived Italian immigrants in 1910 were coded as speaking no English. By 1930, this proportion had dropped to 14 per cent. Making the same assumption about return migration, the likelihood of English skill improvement in this group was over 80 per cent. This rapid language acquisition explains why the cultural assimilation index for this group rises so rapidly compared to more recent cohorts.

If Mexican immigrants exhibit only a modest tendency to improve their English skills over time, by historical and contemporary standards, why does their cultural assimilation index rise so much more than that of, say, Vietnamese immigrants? Intermarriage patterns explain much of the difference.

9.3.2 Intermarriage

First-generation immigrants have traditionally intermarried at extremely low rates. An early study based on marriages in New York City between 1908 and 1912 showed that even among immigrant men who elected to marry after arrival in the United States, fewer than one in ten married a woman born in the United States to native-born parents (Drachsler, 1920). More recent work examining both historical and contemporary records confirms these findings (Pagnini and Morgan, 1990; Qian and Lichter, 2001). In more recent years, however, the tendency toward homogamy has not been universal. Among immigrants from developed countries, in particular, tendencies toward intermarriage are quite strong by historical comparison.

Table 9.6 summarizes the marital patterns for immigrants of specific nationalities at varying points in time. Data on spouse nativity is available in the US Census for years predating 1900, so information on Irish immigrants in 1880 appears on the list as well. For this group, as well as for Italian immigrants in 1910, marriage to a native-born spouse of native parentage was very uncommon: 1 in 25 adult males born in Ireland had intermarried in 1880, and only 1 in 100 Italians had done so in 1910.

In later years, the distinction across immigrant groups is summarized in the comparison between immigrants from Vietnam and Canada. The

Table 9.6 Spouse's nativity for foreign-born adult males.

Year	Respondent's country of birth	Per Cent unmarried	Per Cent with spouse born in:			
			same foreign country	different foreign country*	US	
					to co-ethnic parents	to native parents
1880	Ireland	36.4%	48.9%	2.8%	8.0%	3.9%
1910	Italy	55.3%	40.0%	1.4%	2.4%	0.9%
2007	Vietnam	36.7%	55.5%	5.0%	2.7%**	
2007	Canada	32.2%	19.1%	6.3%	42.4%**	

* In 1880 and 1910, the 'different foreign country' category includes native-born spouses with parents born abroad in a different country. ** In 2007, parents' birthplace is not reported.

marital patterns of Vietnamese men are quite similar to their predecessors, with roughly one in 40 adults married to a native-born spouse. This statistic likely overstates the amount of intermarriage, as in recent data parental birthplace is no longer recorded systematically. Among Canadian immigrants, by contrast, the rate of intermarriage is significantly higher. For every Canadian-born adult male married to another Canadian, there are more than two married to an American-born spouse.

Not depicted here are statistics for the nation's largest single immigrant group. Intermarriage statistics for Mexican-born adults are skewed by the presence of co-ethnic spouses of second or higher generation. Vigdor (2009) reports that 94.3 per cent of native-born spouses of Mexican-born adults claim Mexican ancestry; another 3.4 per cent claim non-Mexican but Hispanic ancestry. Thus, even restricting attention to those Mexican immigrants married to native-born spouses, only 2.3 per cent have married outside their broad ethnic category.

9.3.3 Residential integration

Residential segregation is typically measured using segregation indices, which describe the distribution of a group across neighbourhoods on a scale from perfect integration (where the group forms an equal share of the population in all neighbourhoods) to perfect segregation (where the group is restricted to a subset of neighbourhoods where they are the only residents).[5] Using these measures, the segregation of immigrants

---

[5] The dissimilarity and isolation indices vary in their treatment of intermediate levels of segregation. Dissimilarity tends to be high when a group is found in only a handful of

Table 9.7 Residential isolation of immigrants, 1900–2000.

Arrival cohort	Average per cent foreign born in neighbourhood after:	
	0–5 years	10–15 years
1896–1900	38.3	36.5
1906–1910	40.1	32.4
1986–1990	28.8	30.6
1996–2000	28.5	—

Note: Neighbourhood is defined as a city ward for the first two cohorts, and as a census tract for the last two.

Source: US Census (1900–2000), author's calculations.

from the native majority declined over the first half of the twentieth century, as immigration itself waned, then rose again in the period after 1965 (Cutler *et al.*, 2008).

Segregation tends to track the arrival of new immigrants because newly arrived migrants are generally the most likely to live in ethnic enclaves. Table 9.7 presents summary statistics of the average neighbourhood-level, foreign-born concentration experienced by four separate immigrant arrival cohorts, from the end of the ninetheenth century to the end of the twentieth. The table shows both the average concentration experienced by a cohort after 0–5 years in the United States and after 10–15 years in the United States. Several patterns are apparent here. As asserted above, immigrants find themselves in increasingly integrated neighbourhoods as they spend more time in the United States. The exception to this pattern occurs in more recent data; immigrants arriving in the late 1980s were more segregated in 2000 than they were in 1990—in 2000, they were in fact more segregated than the typical immigrant of the late 1990s. Note also that neighbourhood concentration is lower in more recent data. This trend is observed in spite of the fact that the Census definition of 'neighbourhood' became a geographically more compact area at mid-century.[6] Immigrants are thus more integrated upon arrival now than they were a century ago, but show less evidence of increasing integration

neighbourhoods, even if it forms only a small proportion of the population in those neighbourhoods. Isolation, by contrast, tends to be high when a group forms a high share of the population in the neighbourhoods it occupies. For a complete discussion of segregation indices and their properties, see Massey and Denton (1988) and Cutler *et al.* (1999).

[6] In the early data, city wards are used as neighbourhoods. These are political subdivisions of cities that contain varying numbers of people. In later data, the census tract becomes the neighbourhood construct of reference. Tracts are defined consistently across cities, and tend to be smaller than wards. For a more complete discussion of census geography and its implications for the measurement of segregation, see Cutler *et al.* (1999).

over time. This pattern is entirely consistent with the language patterns described above, which are in turn consistent with a bifurcated view of the immigrant population: one subset of immigrants is highly integrated even upon entry, the second shows very little sign of integrating even after a decade or more.

9.4 Discussion: what explains the variation in integration?

On a very basic level, there has been little change in cultural immigration over the past century, as measured by the cultural assimilation index. The index takes the exact same value in 1930 and 2007, and never deviates by more than five points from that value. The composite index, which incorporates a wider array of information, shows a substantial change in only two decades: the 1900s and the 1980s, both decades of relatively rapid migration to the United States.

Beneath this seemingly placid surface, however, more important changes over time, and differences across groups, emerge. Members of the largest single immigrant group of the early twentieth century, those born in Italy, in general were much less assimilated upon arrival than members of the largest group of the early twenty-first century, those born in Mexico. Whereas one-third of newly arrived Mexicans spoke no English in the early twenty-first century, nearly three-quarters of newly arrived Italians could not speak English in 1910. The rate of cultural integration over time has declined, however. Moreover, conclusions about the integration of Mexican immigrants are sensitive to the definition of intermarriage. Not every modern group shares the trajectory of Mexican immigrants, however; migrants from Vietnam show signs of assimilating rapidly along multiple dimensions.

While several factors can potentially explain the differences in immigrant experiences over time and across groups, legal status is almost certainly the most important. In the early twentieth century, the concept of an 'illegal immigrant', or at least an illegal European immigrant, did not exist.[7] The combination of restrictions on the number of immigrants legally permitted in the country, coupled with the relative ease of entry—whether through illegal border crossings or overstayed legal visas—created a substantial disconnect between policy and reality. Illegal immigrants are prohibited from integrating into the mainstream in some respects: many employers will not hire them; they ordinarily have

---

[7] The Chinese Exclusion Act of 1882 and subsequent legislation placed restrictions on immigration from Asia.

no hope of becoming citizens. Along other dimensions, their incentive to invest in cultural capital is weakened by the prospect of deportation. The decision to learn English, for example, is an investment where up-front costs must be balanced against anticipated future returns. These anticipated returns are necessarily lower under a threat of removal from the host society.

The rise of illegal immigration is not the only explanation for across-group and time period variation in cultural integration. Immigrants' initial motivation for migrating and cost of return migration matter as well. Migrants from Italy and Mexico share a common underlying narrative: they moved from nations with low living standards to high living standards to exploit earnings differentials. Migrants from Vietnam are distinct. Although an economic incentive to move existed for this group, in many cases their decisions flowed directly from the mid-1970s regime change in South Vietnam, in the aftermath of war. Politically motivated migrants often face grave consequences upon return to their origin country. Without a viable return option, these groups face strong incentives to invest in cultural capital. Immigrants with the easiest return options, particularly those facing only a brief and inexpensive journey to their origin country, are at the other end of the spectrum.

The experience of the United States, in summary, illustrates that the goal of ensuring cultural integration is not always best pursued by a policy of limited immigration. The immigrants who inspired the nation's most restrictive immigration policy moved rapidly toward the mainstream, and by the second or third generation had blended seamlessly into society. Cultural integration, like many fundamentally economic processes, is governed by incentives, and the fault of restrictive immigration policy, when combined with porous borders, is to weaken the incentives that many immigrants face to take strides toward the mainstream in their host country.

References

American Community Survey (2007) United States Department of Commerce. Bureau of the Census. American Community Survey (ACS): Public Use Micro-data Sample (PUMS), 2007 (Computer file).

Borjas, G.J. (2003) The Labor Demand Curve Is Downward Sloping: Reexamining the Impact of Immigration on the Labor Market. *Quarterly Journal of Economics*, 118(4), 1335–1374.

Cutler, D.M., Glaeser, E.L., and Vigdor, J.L. (1999) The Rise and Decline of the American Ghetto. *Journal of Political Economy*, 107(3), 455–506.

Cutler, D.M., Glaeser, E.L., and Vigdor, J.L. (2008) Is the Melting Pot Still Hot? Explaining the Resurgence of Immigrant Segregation. *Review of Economics and Statistics*, 90(3), 478–497.

Drachsler, J. (1920) *Democracy and Assimilation: The Blending of Immigrant Heritages in America*. New York, The Macmillan Company.

Espinosa, K.E. and Massey, D.S. (1997) Determinants of English Proficiency among Mexican Migrants to the United States. *International Migration Review*, 22(2), 28–50.

Massey, D.S. and Denton, N. (1988) The Dimensions of Residential Segregation. *Social Forces*, 67, 281–315.

Qian, Z. and Lichter, D. (2001) Measuring Marital Assimilation: Intermarriage among Natives and Immigrants. *Social Science Research*, 30, 289–312.

Vigdor, J.L. (2008) *Measuring Immigrant Assimilation in the United States*. Manhattan Institute for Policy Research Center for Civic Innovation, Civic Report no. 53. http://www.manhattan-institute.org/html/cr_53.htm.

Vigdor, J. L. (2009) *From Immigrants to Americans: The Rise and Fall of Fitting In*. Lanham, MD, Rowman and Littlefield.

10

Conclusion: Cultural Integration of Immigrants in Europe

Yann Algan and Mariya Aleksynska

10.1 Introduction

While European countries are witnessing an especially vivid debate about immigrants' assimilation and integration into receiving societies, this book has provided an analysis of multiple dimensions of integration processes in a selection of European countries. It has offered a quite unique exercise of applying the same unified methodology to studying the same, or similar, questions related to immigrants' integration in some most important European immigration countries.

Against this background, the purpose of this concluding chapter is to summarize the very rich analysis and the main findings of the country-specific chapters. Despite the very different datasets and sampling techniques and sometimes different phrasing of the questions and measures, most of the country-specific researchers do find similar tendencies of immigrants' assimilation. In many cases the immigrants' values converge to the local context within a generation. We highlight these similarities, as well as the most interesting and striking differences found across countries.

Besides, with the aim of overcoming the cross-country data comparability problem, and also with the aim of providing a formal cross-country analysis and a robustness check, we repeat the exercise within the same framework using a unified database: the cumulative European Social Survey (ESS) from 2001 to 2009. While each country chapter gave an account of differences between various origin groups, we further offer an overview of differences across European destination countries. The value added of the survey is to provide the same variable definition for economic and cultural outcomes across the different countries. The survey reports information on different dimensions of integration of immigrants that are broadly consistent with the list of outcomes of the previous country chapters. Also, the same questions of the survey are asked to all individuals in all participating countries, with a particular effort made to ensure the cross-country comparability of questions and concepts (Card *et al.*, 2005). We contrast the aggregate results from using these data with the finer findings of specific country chapters. We also note in passing the aggregate results of assimilation processes in other countries, and on some other dimensions that have remained beyond the scope of this book.

10.2 Country-specific analysis of immigrants' assimilation: what have we learned?

The country-specific chapters offered an in-depth analysis of the economic and cultural assimilation patterns of immigrants from various origins, various cohorts, and generations. One of the striking results is that, despite the tremendous differences between migration histories and patterns across studied countries, despite large differences in collected data and sometimes different framing of the questions, but perhaps thanks to the same methodology used, we can speak about some universal patterns that emerge.

The most common and universal feature concerns the language progress and the general secularization among immigrants. Despite popular perceptions, second-generation immigrants of all backgrounds do have a higher propensity to speak a destination country's language at home, or to report a better use of language, as compared to the first-generation immigrants. It is important to recognize this process, as it suggests the success of assimilation. However, it is also true that in many countries differences with the native born still remain, and equally important questions for further research are why this is the case, how to further reduce these differences, and in which instances such reduction is desirable.

In all countries, second-generation immigrants report a lower religiosity, measured by the frequency of praying and/or of church attendance. This happens for immigrants of all religious backgrounds, although the speed of secularization may vary. Among first-generation immigrants, usually Asian and Black (African or Caribbean) groups report a higher religiosity, and not Maghrebis. The latter group, however, has the slowest convergence rate to the religiosity of the native born in several destination countries.

Another common pattern concerns the civic incorporation of immigrants. In some countries we can observe even an overshooting of behaviours. That is, there is a higher political incorporation of some second-generation immigrant groups as compared to the first-generation immigrants and to the native born. For example, this is the case of MENA (Maghreb and North Africa) immigrants in Switzerland. Also, a lower satisfaction with democracy of Western Europeans or Latin Americans, that is, individuals from countries with democratic traditions, is reported, as compared to Asians or Africans.

As the author of Chapter 7, on Switzerland, suggests, most important differences remain, however, in gender-related attitudes, not religious or political outcomes. Indeed, on the side of the differences, perhaps the largest variation is observed across marital arrangements, education, and employment patterns across the studies countries. These differences are especially pronounced when examined separately for the two genders.

In terms of marriage outcomes, in most of the countries, first-generation immigrants have a higher incidence of marriage than the native born, and usually a lower age at first marriage. The most-speaking examples include Turkish males in Germany, among which up to 76 per cent report being in a formal relationship, versus 50 per cent of the native born men. In terms of age of marriage, Maghreb, Eastern European, and Southern European women show a general pattern of early marriages across the studied countries. These differences, however, almost universally disappear for second-generation immigrants. Thus, on these dimensions, immigrants' outcomes converge to those of the native born within a generation. With very few exceptions, such as women of Italian, Spanish, or Turkish origin in Germany, second-generation women do not have significantly different rates of marriage than the native-born women. Some groups even report a reversal of these patterns. Notably, UK-born Black African women have lower marriage rates than native-born women. Also, second-generation Maghreb-origin women in France actually report later marriages as compared to the native born.

Overall employment rates for first-generation immigrants are higher than for the native born in Spain, although at the expense of the worse jobs. Female labour force participation is higher among immigrants than among natives in Italy and in Germany (except for Turkish women), and a full convergance in the participation rates of the native-born women is observed for second-generation immigrant women. In contrast, immigrant female employment is lower than among natives in Sweden, France, Switzerland (except Southern European women), and the UK (although the authors consider only Asian and Black females). These differences, however, attenuate, when conditioned on the number of children, or on marital status. At the same time, in these countries, too, the catch-up is observed across the board. In general, female employment depends strongly on the origin. In most of the receiving countries, females from Eastern Europe have highest employment rates.

In terms of education outcomes, education of first-generation women is higher than that of the native-born women and of first-generation men in Sweden and in Italy. In Sweden, women's education drops to the level of the native-born women within a generation. In contrast, in Italy, second-generation women have even more schooling, especially Asian and African women.

Overall schooling is lower among first-generation immigrants than among the native born in Spain, Germany, and France. It improves significantly across generations in Spain, especially for Moroccans, and in Germany, where second-generation women also have more schooling than men. For France, education outcomes of second-generation men actually worsen. They, however, improve for women, especially within groups that were particularly disadvantaged in the first generation, such as Asians, Maghreb, and South European.

Finally, some of the country-specific data allowed for the analysis of self-reported national identity, in countries like Great Britain, Germany, or France. In these three countries, an impressive convergence of behaviours is reported, as second-generation immigrants report a much higher degree of self-identification with their residence country than the first-generation immigrants. Remarkably, in Britain, Muslim groups (the Pakistanis and Bangladeshis) whose loyalty to Britain is often questioned, are the ethnic minorities who are most likely to report a British national identity. Even more strikingly, in France, second-generation immigrants of Maghreb origin feel no less likely 'French' than the native born. In France, it is actually second-generation immigrants from Southern Europe who have the highest maintenance of their own national identity. In Germany, especially Poles and Russians show a great commitment to Germany, whereas Turks and Greeks still feel closely bound to their country of origin.

10.3 Unified cross-country analysis of immigrants' assimilation in Europe

In what follows, we use the European Social Survey to provide a further summary of assimilation processes based on the unified cross-country dataset. This also allows checking the robustness of the country chapter results. First, we can control for country of residence fixed effects that could drive the cultural and economic integration processes. Second, the information given by the country of origin fixed effects allows us to control partly for the sample composition of immigrants. Let's say, for instance, that we are interested in comparing the cultural integration of immigrants of Maghreb origin across European countries. This analysis is likely to be biased by the fact that all Maghreb immigrants do not come from the same country of origin, and the inherited specificities from the home country could determine the economic and cultural integration process of immigrants in their destination country. The cross-country dataset allows mitigating such biases.

Our analysis covers most of the European countries and most of the outcomes considered in country chapters of the book. Furthermore, we also enlarge the analysis to a wider set of Western European countries covered by the ESS: Austria, Belgium, Denmark, Finland, Greece, Ireland, the Netherlands, Norway, and Portugal. Unfortunately, data on immigrants are not available for Italy. We also explore the richness of the data to include a few other outcomes of immigrants that remained beyond the scope of the country chapters, such as various measures of trust, perceived discrimination, and preferences for redistribution. These outcomes have been shown as particularly rooted in cultural heritage (Algan *et al.*, 2011; Luttmer and Singhal, 2011; Putnam, 1993; Guiso *et al.*, 2006). We also group the studied outcomes slightly differently from the rest of the book, speaking about economic, cultural, and civic dimensions. Full sample description and variables description is available in Appendices I–IV.

10.3.1 *Methodological setting*

In line with the country specific chapters, we are interested in measuring the gaps between native-born and various subgroups of immigrants in various outcomes. Wider gaps are informative of bigger differences in behaviours, and if these gaps diminish from one generation to another, or for the same generation over time, such tendencies are usually taken as signs of assimilation. For example, if the assimilation process is perfect, for second-generation immigrants there should be little differences in the outcomes as compared to the native born. The existence of the gaps signals the persistence of original traits, which can be taken as the lack of assimilation, especially when this concerns economic and civic outcomes. Such a view is coherent if the goal is to achieve the convergence of outcomes of immigrants and native-born. The persistence of the gaps may, however, also be taken as evidence in favour of integration, especially when it concerns cultural outcomes, if integration is viewed as the right to preserve and freely exercise own features.

To compute these gaps, we estimate the following specification:

$$Outcome_{ijko} = \beta_1 FirstGenImmLess20 + \beta_2 FirstGenImmOver20 + \\ + \beta_3 SecondGenImm + X_i'\alpha + D_j'\gamma + r_k'\rho + o_m'\phi + e_{ijko} \qquad (1)$$

where $Outcome_{ijko}$ is one of the economic, cultural, or social outcomes of interest, of an individual i, living in country j, in year k, and of origin o; β_1, β_2, and β_3 measure the impact of being a first-generation immigrant with less than 20 years of residence, a first-generation immigrant with more than 20 years of residence,[1] or a second-generation immigrant (an individual who has both parents born abroad), as compared to native-born individuals with parents who are both native born. *FirstGenImm-Less20*, *FirstGenImmOver20*, and *SecondGenImm* are dummies equal to 1 if an individual belongs to a corresponding group, and 0 otherwise. The comparison between coefficients β_1, β_2, and β_3 allows an understanding of whether there are differences in gaps between these immigrant groups as opposed to the native born.

As we work with the pooled ESS data over a relatively short period of time, the estimations provide a rather static picture of differences in gaps that exists in the early twenty-first century. Different immigrant generations today may, however, be quite different from each other, both in the composition of their origins, in sorting across destination countries, and in migration reasons. We partly correct for the migration cohorts by including the fixed effects for the survey year, r_k (which, controlling for the years since migration, is analogous to controlling for the year of entry) and a cohort dummy equal to 1 for younger generations (individuals aged less than 30).

In each estimation, we also control for a set of individual-specific parameters, X_i, which include age, gender, education (except the education equations), and fathers' education. The latter is an exogenous proxy for individual's potential socio-economic predisposition that helps to control for intentionally omitted income variable, which we use as one of the outcomes. All regressions also include dummy variables for one of the six origin groups, o_m,[2] and a set of host country dummies D_j.

---

[1] Splitting first-generation immigrants in these two subgroups by duration at destination has the convenience of splitting them in two almost equal parts.

[2] These are Maghreb and North Africa (MENA); Africa; Asia; South America; developed OECD countries; as well as Eastern Europe, Former Soviet Union, and Former Yugoslavia. See Appendix IV for the list of countries that constitutes each subgroup.

As a second step, we repeat similar regressions in a pooled sample of the native born and first-generation immigrants only, taking all European countries as a unique destination, and focusing on the impact of immigrants belonging to a specific origin group. In these regressions, we are additionally able to control for duration of stay of first-generation immigrants:

$$
\begin{aligned}
Outcome_{ijk} = \sum_k \beta_k OriginGroup_k {}^*FirstGenImm + \\
+ YearsOfResidence {}^*FirstGenImm + X_i{}'\alpha + D_j{}'\gamma + r_k{}'\rho + e_{ijk}
\end{aligned}
\tag{2}
$$

Small numbers of second-generation immigrants reporting the birth country of their ancestors precludes from doing a similar analysis for second-generation immigrants.

10.3.2 *Cultural integration*

We start by analysing the various dimensions of cultural outcomes of immigrants. These are family arrangements, such as the marital status and the age gap between spouses, but also the language spoken at home, the frequency of praying, and the frequency of socialization.[3] Table 10.1a reports gaps in these outcomes based on estimating (1) for various sub-types of immigrants as opposed to the native-born, in all European countries grouped together. Table 10.1b further distinguishes gaps for first-generation immigrants from different origins, and is based on estimating equation (2).

From Table 10.1a, first-generation immigrants have a higher probability of being married, as compared to the native-born of the same age. This is a result that corresponds to the findings of country-specific chapters. Table 10.1b further shows that higher marriage rates among first-generation immigrants are mostly due to higher marriage rates among immigrants from MENA and Asia. Back to Table 10.1a, second-generation immigrants actually have lower marriage rates than the native born. This result has occurred only in some specific instances through country-specific chapters, and only for some specific origin groups.

In terms of age gap between spouses, there is little overall difference between first-generation immigrants and the native born, although differences actually appear among origin groups: MENA, African, and Asian couples have higher age gap than native-born couples.

---

[3] The ESS does not report the country of origin or the years of education of the spouse, and we cannot compute the interethnic marriage rates or education gaps, contrary to the different chapters.

Table 10.1a Average gaps in cultural outcomes between immigrants and the native born in the EU.

Variables	First-generation immigrants with >20 years of residence		First-generation immigrants with <20 years of residence		Second-generation immigrants		No. obs	R-sq
Married	0.101***	(0.015)	0.027*	(0.015)	−0.069***	(0.018)	101,749	0.150
Age gap between spouses	0,174	(0,182)	0,081	(0.177)	−0.386**	(0.191)	70,633	0.016
Language of the country spoken at home	−0.330***	(0.014)	−0.130***	(0.012)	−0.060***	(0.013)	101,749	0.197
Frequency of praying (days a year)	44,625***	(4522)	28,767***	(4633)	18,364***	(5320)	100,622	0.150
Frequency of taking part in social activities	−0.174***	(0.030)	0.018	(0.030)	0.045	(0.039)	100,362	0.039

Table 10.1b Average gaps in cultural outcomes between first-generation immigrants, by origin, and native born.

Variables	MENA		African		Asian		South American		OECD		East. European, FSU, FY		No. obs	R-sq
Married	0.102*	(0.044)	0.019	(0.048)	0.115*	(0.047)	-0.051	(0.047)	-0.010	(0.040)	0.036	(0.042)	95,093	0.144
Age gap between spouses	1.844**	(0.525)	1.413*	(0.590)	2.036**	(0.535)	0.392	(0.562)	0.142	(0.465)	0.294	(0.459)	66,403	0.017
Language of the country spoken at home	-0.281**	(0.050)	-0.128*	(0.053)	-0.357**	(0.053)	0.089	(0.049)	-0.094*	(0.046)	-0.199**	(0.049)	95,093	0.213
Frequency of praying (days a year)	109.299**	(15.544)	151.549**	(16.727)	120.797**	(17.449)	72.706**	(16.406)	17.718	(14.174)	23.206	(14.749)	94,024	0.156
Social activities	-0.051	(0.087)	-0.160	(0.097)	-0.190	(0.098)	-0.129	(0.096)	-0.056	(0.080)	-0.204*	(0.081)	93,789	0.534

Each line represents a separate regression, where the first column defines the dependent variable, and other columns' headings define the independent variables of interest. All regressions additionally include age, gender, education, parental education, destination country. and survey round fixed effects, and are estimated accounting for the survey design and population weights. Reported coefficients represent the gaps in outcomes. Robust standard errors in parentheses. Significant at * 5%, ** 1%.

Regrettably, though, we do not have any information on the nationality of the spouse, which could have enabled more insight into this question. For second-generation immigrants, the age gap is smaller than for the native born.

Much larger cross-generational differences are observed for the language outcome. Language is measured in a dichotomous way, where 1 is assigned to individuals who report any official language of a country as first-mentioned language spoken at home, and 0 otherwise (data on official country languages come from CIA fact book).[4] Speaking the language is among the most important outcomes for immigrants, as it not only reflects assimilation, but it also, in its turn, affects the speed of assimilation along other dimensions (Chiswick, 1991; Dustmann, 1994). The gaps in language spoken at home are significant and initially large for all types of non-native-born individuals. In a notable way, for this outcome, the gaps between any immigrant group and the native born never disappear completely. This, in itself, is not necessarily a negative phenomenon, as those individuals who report a non-official country's language as the first language spoken at home may still be fluent in an official country's language; and simply be multilingual. What is interesting, however, is a particularly strong 'closing' of these gaps, the nearer we get to the 'native born with both native-born parents' status. First-generation immigrants with less than 20 years of residence have a 33 percentage point lower probability of speaking the official language of a country when at home, as compared to native-born. This gap is still statistically significant for second generation, but the magnitude drops dramatically to six percentage points, and to significant three percentage points for individuals with one foreign-born parent. This result also confirms the previous country-specific findings.

Figure 10.1 plots the gaps in probability of speaking the country's official language at home as the first mentioned language, for first and second-generation immigrants, by destination country. We observe a similar pattern for all destination countries: second-generation immigrants have lower gaps in speaking the language of the country than the first-generation immigrants (all effects are placed below the 45° line). In some countries, like Greece or Portugal, the progress between generations is particularly strong.

---

[4] We use the term 'probability' of speaking the language by immigrants, rather than 'per cent' of people who speak another language at home; as even among native-born individuals, 2 per cent report a language other than official as their first language spoken at home.

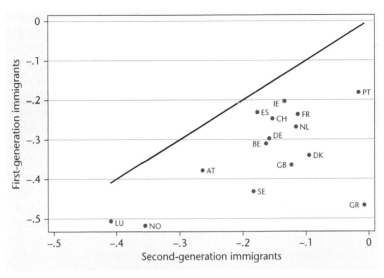

Figure 10.1 Gaps in speaking the destination country's language at home among first and second-generation immigrants.

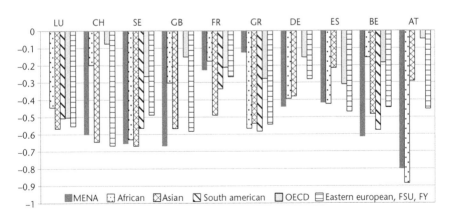

Figure 10.2 Gaps in the probability of speaking the language (first and second generation).

Figure 10.2 also shows differences in language gaps by destination and origin pair, suggesting a large variation in outcomes.[5] Not surprisingly, first-generation South-Americans in Spain have no language gaps as compared to the native born, while the highest gap is observed for Africans in Austria. More generally, immigrants from MENA and Asian countries have relatively high language gaps regardless of the destination. But there is also a large heterogeneity across the destination countries. Take the situation of immigrants from Maghreb. The gap in the probability of speaking a different language at home ranges from 22 percentage points in France, 42 percentage points in Germany, to 80 percentage points in Austria. By and large, there is more heterogeneity in these gaps across the destination counties than within the same country of destination between the different immigrants. This result may be due to several reasons, such as the existence of several languages spoken in a country, difficulty of learning a particular language for any of the origin groups, or a different sorting across countries. To the extent that we obtain these estimates by controlling for country of origin fixed effects, they seem to reflect, in a large part, genuine specificities in the integration process of each destination country.

We now turn to religiosity, considered to be perhaps the most persisting cultural trait. We measure religiosity as the frequency of praying, relating it to answers to the question: 'Apart from when you are at religious services, how often if at all do you pray?' The answer takes on values of 1 for every day, 2 for more than once a week, 3 for once a week, 4 for at least once a month, 5 for only on special holidays, 6 for less often, and 7 for never; and we convert them into days per year. Table 10.1a first shows a much higher frequency of praying among first-generation immigrants relative to natives, although it drops significantly between newcomers and those with over 20 years at destination. Table 10.1b also shows that the frequency of praying is significantly higher among immigrants from Africa and Asia, and to a lesser extent from MENA and South America, relative to the native born. There are no differences in religiosity among OECD, Eastern European, former Yugoslavia, and former Soviet Union immigrants. Besides, the overall gap persists among second-generation immigrants. However, it further drops significantly: second-generation immigrants report praying almost three times less than newly-arrived first-generation immigrants. This result also confirms previous country-specific findings, despite

---

[5] Reported gaps are computed by estimating equation such as (1), by destination country, for a sub-sample of ten largest immigration countries. First-generation immigrants are pooled together.

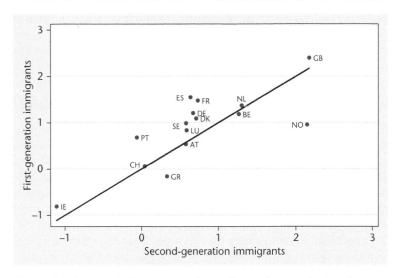

Figure 10.3 Gaps in religiosity among first and second-generation immigrants.

common perceptions of high persistency of religiosity traits. In fact, higher praying may serve as a source of strength and the search of answers to profound questions, which may be particularly important at the time of big life changes (Lehrer, 2010), such as immigration and settlement in a new country; it may thus diminish once more stability and familiarity with new conditions is acquired. Also, immigrants may become more secularized when being exposed to more secularized societies.

Figure 10.3 further shows heterogeneity of changes along this dimension across destinations, suggesting that not only differences between first and second-generation immigrants may go in different direction depending on the destination country in question, but also that in some countries, such as Ireland, both first and second-generation immigrants actually pray less than the native born.

10.3.3 *Integration in civic life and feeling of discrimination*

In a similar fashion, this section offers insight into gaps in civic outcomes, such as being naturalized, the probability of being civically involved into various types of activities, expressing various types of trust, being satisfied with the way democracy works, and having particular preferences for redistribution. We also address the question of perceived discrimination.

Becoming a citizen of a destination country can—albeit arguably—be considered as one of the most ultimate outcomes for immigrants. It is framed by the policies of the destination countries, as much as by the migration reasons and migration intentions. While naturalization means acquiring equal rights of a citizen and thus opening ways to further assimilation on many economic, cultural, and civic dimensions, it may also be considered by itself as a civic act, a conscious step towards becoming a full member of the hosting society (Gropas, 2008; Chiswick and Miller, 2009a). As such, it can be viewed as a behavioural civic outcome in its own right. In this chapter, the outcome citizen is measured on a 0–1 scale, with 1 representing having the citizenship of the country of current residence.

Tables 10.2a and 10.2b show that among all types of non-natives, as well as first-generation immigrants of all origins, there are significantly high percentages of non-citizens. But as with language, the closing of the gap on this dimension is rather pronounced. The probability of being a citizen for second-generation immigrants is twice as high as for first-generation immigrants with more than 20 years at destination. However, it is still 20 percentage points lower than that of the native-born, for whom the probability is 100 per cent. This finding raises particular concerns, as it signifies either a lack of assimilation on the part of immigrants along this dimension, or a lack of opportunities provided by receiving countries for gaining citizenship for second-generation immigrants born in the country, or both.

Figure 10.4 shows that second-generation immigrants are at a disadvantage compared to the native born in a sizeable number of countries. The gap in naturalization among second-generation immigrants almost disappears in Great Britain, Ireland, Greece, and France; however, it remains statistically significant in all other countries of the sample, and is especially high in Luxembourg, Switzerland, and Germany.

A closely related measure of belonging to a 'polity' is a notion of immigrants' civic participation. We measure it with the help of a dummy variable equal to 1 if a respondent reports doing in the last year at least one of the following: being a member or volunteering for a political party, a trade union, or another organization or association; taking part in a legal demonstration; signing a petition; or wearing a badge. Table 10.2a shows that there is an 18.3 percentage point lower probability of being involved in civic life among first-generation immigrants with less than twenty years at destination, and it is attributable to all origin groups (Table 10.2b). However, this gap vanishes quickly, and

Table 10.2a Average gaps in civic outcomes between immigrants and the native born in the EU.

Variables	First-generation immigrants with >20 years of residence	First-generation immigrants with <20 years of residence	Second-generation immigrants	No. obs	R-sq
Citizen	-0.709*** (0.013)	-0.400*** (0.014)	-0.204*** (0.012)	101,723	0.458
Civic participation	-0.183*** (0.016)	-0.023 (0.016)	0.011 (0.020)	101,749	0.118
General. trust (1–10)	-0.037 (0.074)	-0.191** (0.074)	-0.319*** (0.090)	101,505	0.096
Trust in police	0.400*** (0.077)	-0.001 (0.075)	-0.238** (0.095)	101,063	0.062
Trust in country's parliament	0.503*** (0.080)	0.111 (0.079)	-0.191* (0.097)	98,933	0.069
Trust in politicians	0.461*** (0.076)	-0.053 (0.076)	-0.188** (0.092)	100,207	0.078
Trust in the Eur. parliament	0.788*** (0.082)	0.374*** (0.082)	0.243** (0.096)	91,559	0.075
Satisfaction with democracy	0.130*** (0.014)	0.049*** (0.015)	0.027 (0.019)	101,749	0.052
Preferences for redistribution	-0.032** (0.016)	0.006 (0.015)	0.007 (0.018)	101,749	0.071
Perceived discrimination	0.071*** (0.012)	0.013 (0.010)	0.092*** (0.016)	101,283	0.058

Each line represents a separate regression, where the first column defines the dependent variable, and other columns' headings define the independent variables of interest. All regressions additionally include age, gender, education, parental education, origin fixed effects, destination country, and survey round fixed effects, and are estimated accounting for the survey design and population weights. Reported coefficients represent the gaps in outcomes. Robust standard errors in parentheses. Significant at * 5%, ** 1%.

Table 10.2b Average gaps in civic outcomes between first-generation immigrants, by origin, and native-born.

Variables	MENA		African		Asian		South American		OECD		East European, FSU, FY		No. obs	R-sq
Citizen	-0.457**	(0.054)	-0.316**	(0.056)	-0.284**	(0.058)	-0.370**	(0.054)	-0.605**	(0.051)	-0.266**	(0.053)	95,072	0.534
Civic participation	-0.150**	(0.043)	-0.166**	(0.050)	-0.267**	(0.047)	-0.156**	(0.046)	-0.155**	(0.041)	-0.275**	(0.041)	95,093	0.120
Gen. trust (1–10)	0.213	(0.207)	0.086	(0.219)	0.266	(0.217)	0.123	(0.215)	0.331	(0.181)	0.466*	(0.189)	94,861	0.096
Trust in police	0.443	(0.228)	0.321	(0.250)	0.563*	(0.248)	0.058	(0.240)	0.324	(0.207)	0.427*	(0.216)	94,442	0.062
Trust in country's Parliament	0.535**	(0.207)	0.605**	(0.234)	0.874**	(0.219)	0.201	(0.220)	-0.006	(0.188)	0.305	(0.193)	92,473	0.069
Trust in politicians	0.898**	(0.212)	0.828**	(0.228)	1.084**	(0.232)	0.513*	(0.233)	0.347	(0.189)	0.648**	(0.199)	93,660	0.079
Trust in the Eur. Parliament	0.766**	(0.206)	0.784**	(0.219)	0.953**	(0.218)	0.238	(0.230)	0.500**	(0.187)	0.476*	(0.195)	85,532	0.076
Satisfaction with democracy	0.176**	(0.034)	0.184**	(0.039)	0.221**	(0.034)	0.093*	(0.036)	0.119**	(0.032)	0.140**	(0.032)	95,093	0.053
Preferences for redistribution	0.015	(0.043)	0.055	(0.049)	0.014	(0.049)	0.063	(0.045)	-0.026	(0.041)	0.013	(0.043)	95,093	0.072
Perceived discrimination	0.132**	(0.037)	0.129**	(0.043)	0.001	(0.036)	0.039	(0.039)	-0.075*	(0.032)	0.023	(0.034)	94,662	0.048

Each line represents a separate regression, where the first column defines the dependent variable, and other columns' headings define the independent variables of interest. All regressions additionally include age, gender, education, parental education, destination country, and survey round fixed effects, and are estimated accounting for the survey design and population weights. Reported coefficients represent the gaps in outcomes. Robust standard errors in parentheses. Significant at * 5%, ** 1%.

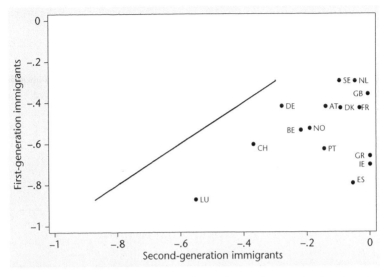

Figure 10.4 Gaps in citizenship among first and second-generation immigrants.

within one generation immigrant outcomes fully converge to those of the native born.

We further turn to various measures of social capital and attitudes, such as trust in others, trust in a country's police, parliament, politicians, and in the European parliament. The analysis of these outcomes was not possible in all country-specific chapters due to data limitations. Table 10.2a shows that newly arriving first-generation immigrants actually are no different in trusting people in general, as compared to the native born. However, first-generation immigrants with longer stay, and also second-generation immigrants both have significantly lower propensity for trusting, with the gap reaching 31.9 percentage points for the latter group. Even more pronounced reversals are observed in other measures of trust: while newly arriving immigrants tend to trust more than the native born in the police, the parliament, the politicians of the receiving countries, this trend is fully reversed for second generation. In a similar way, satisfaction with democracy is higher among immigrants of first generation regardless of their origin, but not among second-generation immigrants.

Figure 10.5 shows that the gap in distrust widens for second-generation immigrants in almost all countries, exceptions being Sweden, Spain, and

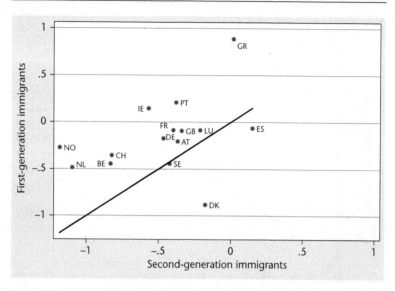

Figure 10.5 Gaps in generalized trust among first and second-generation immigrants.

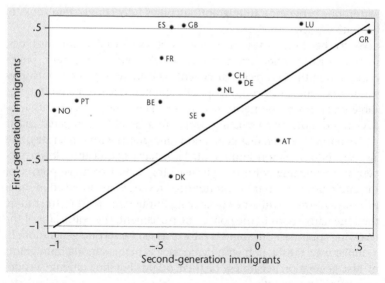

Figure 10.6 Gaps in trust in the police among first and second-generation immigrants.

Denmark. From Figure 10.6, the widening gaps in distrust in the police are observed almost universally, except Denmark and Greece. Second-generation immigrants distrust the police significantly more than the native born and the first-generation immigrants.

The obtained results on trust are rather alarming. Newly arriving immigrants tend to have a significantly more positive outlook than others, and hence more trust, both because they are self-selected, and because they have high hopes associated with migration decisions. The fact that this positive outlook vanishes quickly is, inevitably, due to disillusions that immigrants encounter. It may also, however, signal potential problems with the acceptance and integration policies of the receiving countries.

This latter idea is partly explored by analysing the question on perceived discrimination: 'Would you describe yourself as being a member of a group that is discriminated against in this country on grounds: nationality, religion, colour and race, language, ethnicity, and gender?' The answer takes on the value of 1 for yes and 0 for no. In a descriptive way, Figure 10.7 shows the variation in the grounds for perceived discrimination for immigrants in all destinations grouped together. First-generation immigrants feel in general discriminated against more than any other group, and are followed by second-generation immigrants in this perception. The main reason for perceived discrimination is nationality, followed by colour/race and religion. Nationality is the top

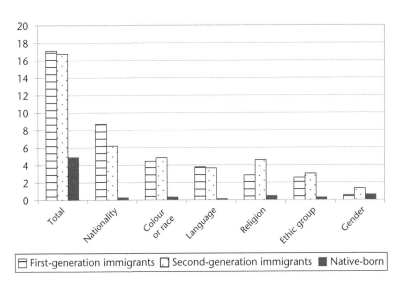

Figure 10.7 The dimensions of discrimination.

319

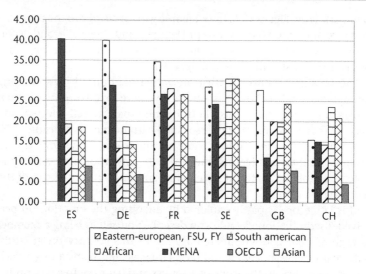

Figure 10.8 Who feels discriminated, and where?

preoccupation for first-generation immigrants, while the discrimination for colour, religion, or ethnic origin is more prevalent among second-generation immigrants.

For a selection of countries, Figure 10.8 also reports where immigrants feel the most discriminated against, all grounds for discrimination grouped together. It shows that the feeling of discrimination is spread out in a different way among immigrants depending on the destination country. Immigrants from MENA feel the most discriminated in Spain (40 per cent), Germany (29 per cent), France (26 per cent), and Sweden (24 per cent). They feel much less discriminated in Switzerland (15 per cent) and Great Britain (11 per cent). Africans feel the most discriminated in Germany (40 per cent), followed by France (34 per cent). All, including other-OECD immigrants, report significant degrees of discrimination.

Table 10.2a reports the corresponding estimates of gaps in perceived discrimination. Newly arriving first-generation immigrants have a seven percentage point higher probability of feeling discriminated compared to the native born, while this probability is nine percentage points for second-generation immigrants. Table 10.2b shows that immigrants from MENA and Africa display the highest perceived discrimination, which is higher by 13.2 and 12.9 percentage points than the perceived discrimination of natives, respectively.

From Figure 10.9, in almost two-thirds of the sampled countries, second-generation immigrants feel significantly more discriminated

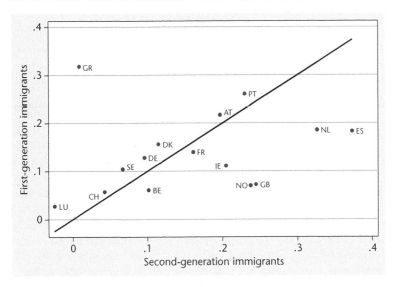

Figure 10.9 Gaps in perceived discrimination first and second-generation immigrants.

against as opposed to the first-generation immigrants. Interestingly, countries where second-generation immigrants feel least discriminated are also the same countries where they have more trust in the police (Greece and Luxembourg). In other countries, the finding of increased feelings of discrimination, coupled with the finding on widening gaps in trust, once again raises concerns about the success of integration processes of immigrants. Since the perceived discrimination reflects immigrants' experiences with the attitudes and behaviours of native born (potentially also of the police, administration, and politicians) in the receiving societies, this finding hints at the failure of immigrants' acceptance. 'Culture clash' or 'culture club' (Manning and Roy, 2010) is a two-way process; and pure willingness to assimilate on the part of immigrants may not enough: it is also the receiving societies that may have to accomplish the work of accepting and integrating them.

Finally, the last line of Table 10.2a reports differences in preferences for redistribution. We find a significantly lower redistribution preference among newly arriving immigrants, while no significant differences among other groups.

10.3.4 *Economic integration*

This section turns to immigrants' economic assimilation. We estimate the gaps in outcomes such as probability of being unemployed or inactive, probability of being employed in a low-skilled job, as well as gaps in incomes.

Tables 10.3a and 3b suggests that both recent and second-generation immigrants have a significantly higher propensity of being unemployed. The unemployment gap, although slightly lower for second-generation immigrants, is actually rather persistent. Among first-generation, the highest employment penalty is observed for immigrants from MENA (5.6 percentage points), Asia (5.3), and Eastern Europe (5.5). There is also a cross-country heterogeneity in the evolution of the employment penalty across types of immigrants. Figure 10.10 shows that the persisting—and widening—unemployment gap seems to be mostly driven by France, Switzerland, and Belgium, where second-generation immigrants have particularly higher probability of being unemployed, as opposed to the native born and to first-generation immigrants.

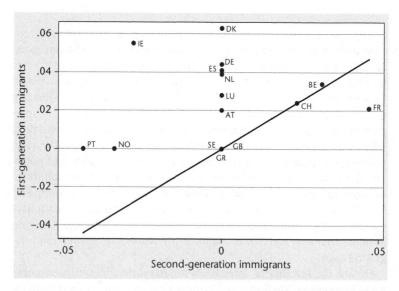

Figure 10.10 Gaps in unemployment among first and second-generation immigrants.

Table 10.3a Gaps in economic outcomes between immigrants and the native born in the EU.

Variables	First-generation immigrants with >20 years of residence		First-generation immigrants with <20 years of residence		Second-generation immigrants		No. obs	R-sq
Unemployed	0.026***	(0.008)	−0.000	(0.007)	0.021*	(0.011)	101,749	0.020
Inactive	0.011**	(0.005)	0.008*	(0.005)	0.003	(0.008)	101,749	0.005
Occupation: low skilled	0.049***	(0.010)	0.009	(0.010)	−0.011	(0.011)	101,749	0.051
Individual income (log)	−0.158***	(0.029)	0.052**	(0.025)	0.043	(0.034)	81,931	0.217

Each line represents a separate regression, where the first column defines the dependent variable, and other columns' headings define the independent variables of interest. All regressions additionally include age, gender, education, parental education, origin fixed effects, destination country, and survey round fixed effects, and are estimated accounting for the survey design and population weights. Reported coefficients represent the gaps in outcomes. Robust standard errors in parentheses. Significant at * 5%, ** 1%.

Table 10.3b Gaps in economic outcomes between first-generation immigrants, by origin, and native-born.

Variables	MENA		African		Asian		South American		OECD		East. European, FSU, FY		No. obs	R-sq
Unemployed	0.056*	(0.025)	0.051	(0.027)	0.053*	(0.026)	0.047	(0.027)	0.031	(0.022)	0.055*	(0.025)	95,093	0.018
Inactive	−0.007	(0.021)	−0.016	(0.021)	−0.031	(0.020)	−0.018	(0.022)	−0.026	(0.019)	−0.020	(0.020)	95,093	0.006
Occupation: low skilled	0.014	(0.032)	0.027	(0.035)	−0.019	(0.037)	0.081*	(0.036)	0.015	(0.029)	0.055*	(0.021)	95,093	0.053
Individual income (log)	−0.293**	(0.083)	−0.273**	(0.097)	−0.287**	(0.087)	−0.103	(0.089)	−0.057	(0.076)	−0.208*	(0.083)	76,582	0.224

Each line represents a separate regression, where the first column defines the dependent variable, and other columns' headings define the independent variables of interest. All regressions additionally include age, gender, education, parental education, destination country, and survey round fixed effects, and are estimated accounting for the survey design and population weights. Reported coefficients represent the gaps in outcomes. Robust standard errors in parentheses. Significant at * 5%, ** 1%.

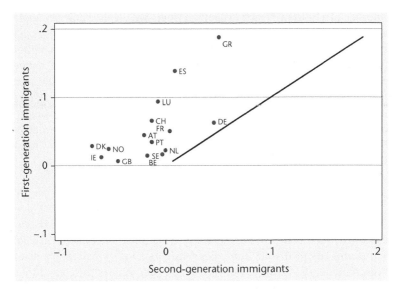

Figure 10.11 Gaps in probability of occupying a low-skilled job.

For those who are employed, the distribution of jobs across type of skill is of interest. We consider gaps in probabilities of being employed in low-skilled, elementary occupations (ISCO classification codes 9), versus all other jobs. Recent first-generation immigrants have a significantly higher probability of performing these jobs, regardless of their potentially higher level of education. This result is mostly driven by South American and Eastern European immigrants. The literature suggests various reasons for this, such as the potential mismatch of occupations and qualifications (Chiswick and Miller, 2009b), or different valuation and non-recognitions of diplomas at destination (Dumont and Monso, 2007). Remarkably, however, the biggest progress towards assimilation along the economic dimension is observed in occupation distribution. Figure 10.11 shows that for all destination countries, second-generation immigrants have a significantly lower probability of performing an elementary job, as opposed to first-generation immigrants and, in the majority of countries also, as opposed to the native born (except Spain, Greece, and Germany).

Finally, we also consider differences in incomes. Unfortunately, the European Social Survey does not contain information on earnings, or on individual incomes. Thus, we use the household income and divide it by the number of household members, but as the information on the number of children is not available either, we are not able to apply equivalence scales and treat each member of the household as an adult. Hence, our measure of gaps in individual incomes is rather crude, and also reflects the differences in the compositions of native and immigrant families. Results of the regression analysis show that immigrants' initial individual incomes are much lower than of the native born, but that the catch-up is strong, and that immigrants with over 20 years at destination actually have higher incomes than native born. In contrast, second-generation immigrants are no different from the native born across this dimension.

10.3.5 *Gender differences along selected outcomes*

Country-specific chapters paid particular attention to differences in outcomes between males and females, especially in what concerns marital status and labour market outcomes. Thus, as a very last step, for most important gender-sensitive outcomes we repeat some of the estimations such as (1). We pool together first-generation immigrants with various durations of stay and interact both types of immigrant dummies with a 'female' variable. This variable equals 1 for female respondents, and 0 otherwise.

Table 10.4 summarizes the results. Indeed, there is a considerable degree of heterogeneity in outcomes across genders, albeit our aggregate results only partly support country-specific findings. Specifically, both first-generation and second-generation females have a higher probability of being married than males of the corresponding generation and than the native-born females. Second-generation men, however, have lower marriage rates. In terms of education, first-generation males and females do not seem to be significantly different either from each other, or from the natives. The diverging pattern in education, however, is confirmed for second generation: while men have less schooling than the native born, women have more schooling than the native-born women and than the second-generation men. Individual income of immigrant females tends to be higher than that of males. These regressions, however, do not condition on the nationality of the spouse, which may be driving the result if, say, immigrant women are more frequently married to native-born richer men. In terms of unemployment, there is little evidence of a particular penalty for women. In contrast, first-generation females have a higher tendency to be employed in low-skilled jobs than both first-generation men and native-born women.

Table 10.4 Gender differences along selected outcomes.

	Married	Education	Individual income (log)	Unemployed	Occupation: low-skilled
First gen. immigrant	0.093***	−0.235	−0.150***	0.014*	0.015
	(0.015)	(0.148)	(0.030)	(0.008)	(0.010)
Female	−0.040***	−0.430***	−0.121***	−0.002	0.025***
	(0.004)	(0.035)	(0.008)	(0.002)	(0.003)
First gen. immigrant *female	0.033**	−0.002	0.057*	0.002	0.045***
	(0.016)	(0.154)	(0.029)	(0.009)	(0.012)
Second gen. immigrant	−0.075***	−0.638***	−0.049	0.020	0.010
	(0.020)	(0.177)	(0.044)	(0.016)	(0.013)
Second gen. immigrant *female	0.096***	0.644***	0.122**	−0.024	−0.013
	(0.027)	(0.228)	(0.056)	(0.019)	(0.017)
No. obs	95,093	101,751	90,465	101,749	101,749
R^2	0.139	0.168	0.112	0.018	0.016

Each column represents a separate regression, where column headings define the dependent variable. All regressions additionally include age, parental education, origin fixed effects, destination country, and survey round fixed effects, and are estimated accounting for the survey design and population weights. Robust standard errors in parentheses. Significant at * 5%, ** 1%.

10.4 Discussion

All in all, the aggregate results of the cross-country analysis go hand in hand with general findings of country-specific chapters, despite difference in samples and questions. This is very reassuring. While assimilation patterns are highly heterogeneous, and vary across destination, origin, and generation of immigrants, in the majority of cases, convergences of immigrants' behaviours to those of the native born are observed. This is the success of assimilation that is worth highlighting.

At the same time, a concern remains as to why, given the same birth country and language of schooling (although maybe not the same schools), the outcomes of some second-generation immigrants are actually still different from those of the native born. Some outcomes may be persisting. For example, country studies stressed low schooling outcomes for Turks in Germany, lower female employment rates of both immigrant generations in Sweden and (among some origin groups) in the UK. Some other outcomes may even diverge. For example, from

Chapter 2 on France, there is a worsening of education outcomes of second-generation men in France. In our turn, we reported persisting cross-generational unemployment gaps in France, Switzerland, and Belgium, as well as diverging patterns of trust, or a disillusion effect, for numerous countries.

Undoubtedly, the appropriateness of convergence in cultural dimensions is open to debate. However, its desirability in economic terms and in terms of equal opportunities for males and females is rather uncontestable.

Potentially, some of the problematic areas may be linked to the apt inclusion of all immigrant groups, especially families and women, into the life of the receiving society, and to the proper exposure to local practices. In part, better inclusion may be linked to the naturalization laws, as acquiring the citizenship of the country of residence gives a sense of security of status, and a sense of belonging. However, non-naturalization rates among second-generation immigrants may be as high as 30 per cent in Switzerland, or 25 per cent in Germany. In part, better inclusion may also be linked to attitudes towards immigrants on the part of the native born. For example, in Spain, Great Britain, Norway, the Netherlands, France, and Belgium, second-generation immigrants report a lower trust in the police and a higher degree of perceived discrimination than the first-generation immigrants. Future research should look at the interaction between country specific policies and those assimilation patterns. Besides, it is not impossible that immigrants' assimilation is interdependent with the perception of the security of their status, and with the acceptance of immigrants on the part of the native born. Successful integration may imply a two-way process. While such analysis has been beyond the scope of this book, clearly, more research into the direction of inter-linkages and interactions between immigrant outcomes, perceptions of the native born, and specific country conditions is needed.

One of the questions that consistently came out of this research is also the question of a benchmark with respect to which the convergence of behaviours should be measured. In the majority of cases, we analysed the progress of immigrants as compared to the native born in specific countries. Further research may also be enriched by stepping away from the use of an 'average' native born as a benchmark for immigrants, and encompass a more regional or ethnical perspective. Lastly, a question that we leave for further research is to what extent the native born, in their turn, adopt certain values and attitudes of immigrants. Is there a convergence of all individuals to some medium, universal values?

Appendix I Sample statistics: focus on destination countries.

Country	Native-born as % of the sample	First-generation immigrants as % of the sample	Immigrants with >20 years of residence, % of first-generation immigrants	Second-generation immigrants as % of the sample	Total number of observations
AT	83.2	7.3	53.3	9.5	6,862
BE	83.0	7.5	47.9	9.6	7,099
CH	69.0	18.4	48.0	12.6	7,717
DE	85.9	7.3	64.7	6.9	11,316
DK	90.2	4.7	57.2	5.1	6,012
ES	91.7	6.6	91.2	1.8	7,763
FI	96.8	1.4	85.2	1.7	7,983
FR	81.0	7.9	33.3	11.1	7,265
GB	84.5	8.2	52.4	7.3	8,531
GR	83.8	8.0	82.6	8.1	4,810
IE	90.4	6.0	72.5	3.7	5,924
LU	51.6	29.4	57.8	19.0	3,129
NL	86.6	7.3	47.3	6.2	6,056
NO	90.2	5.5	66.5	4.3	6,938
PT	94.2	3.9	67.0	2.0	7,939
SE	81.7	10.0	46.2	8.3	7,634

Appendix II First-generation immigrants by origin, as percentage of total number of first-generation immigrants, by destination.

Destination/Origin	MENA	African	Asian	South American	Eastern European, F. Soviet Union, F. Yugoslavia	OECD	Total
Austria	11.13	1.39	3.38	0.80	48.51	34.79	10,000
Belgium	19.92	8.83	5.83	1.70	7.70	56.01	10,000
Switzerland	5.56	4.24	5.21	4.71	14.99	65.29	10,000
Germany	17.05	2.43	5.72	0.85	59.68	14.26	10,000
Denmark	12.98	5.26	21.75	1.05	16.49	42.46	10,000
Spain	18.86	3.54	3.73	42.83	15.52	15.52	10,000
Finland	2.61	3.48	13.04	0.87	59.13	20.87	10,000
France	36.43	13.13	3.85	5.25	6.48	34.85	10,000
The UK	2.87	21.38	29.27	6.31	5.88	34.29	10,000
Greece	13.21	3.63	3.37	3.11	67.10	9.59	10,000
Ireland	1.42	6.23	7.37	0.85	15.01	69.12	10,000
Luxembourg	0.54	5.10	2.28	1.09	8.79	82.19	10,000
The Netherlands	19.52	6.28	20.88	15.79	8.32	29.20	10,000
Norway	3.14	3.40	25.13	3.40	17.54	47.38	10,000
Portugal	0.32	51.46	2.27	27.83	11.65	6.47	10,000
Sweden	8.83	3.69	14.36	4.87	19.37	48.88	10,000

Appendix III Descriptive statistics by immigrant status (means).

	First-generation immigrants, >20 years of residence	First-generation immigrants, <20 years of residence	Second-generation immigrants	Native born
Socio-economic indicators:				
Years of education	12.74	11.82	12.63	12.07
Unemployed	0.09	0.04	0.08	0.04
Inactive	0.03	0.02	0.03	0.02
Occupation: low-skilled	0.15	0.11	0.07	0.09
Cultural indicators:				
Married	0.57	0.63	0.42	0.55
Age gap between spouses	2.73	2.38	2.23	2.28
Speaking an official language of a country as first language at home	0.61	0.80	0.86	0.98
Frequency of praying (converted into days per year)	12.900	13.557	97.90	82.57
Perceived discrimination	0.22	0.15	0.22	0.05
Frequency of socialization (on the scale from 1 to 7)	5.01	4.88	5.21	4.96
Generalized trust (1–10)	4.99	4.74	4.42	4.82
Trust in police	6.51	6.20	5.69	6.02
Trust in country's parliament	5.32	4.77	4.29	4.37
Trust in legislation	5.95	5.30	5.01	5.00
Trust in politicians	4.19	3.69	3.41	3.42
Trust in the European parliament	5.29	4.53	4.54	4.43
Trust in the United Nations	5.42	5.02	4.95	5.18
Civic indicators:				
Citizen	0.42	0.69	0.89	1.00
Civic participation	0.33	0.47	0.50	0.46
Satisfaction with democracy	0.82	0.71	0.66	0.65
In favour of redistribution	0.65	0.70	0.72	0.69

Note: Tabulations are done accounting for survey design and population weights.
Source: Authors' calculations based on the ESS.

Appendix IV List of countries in immigrants' origin subgroups.

MENA: Algeria, Morocco, Egypt, Jordan, Kuwait, Lebanon, Libya, Saudi Arabia, Syria, Tunisia, Turkey, Yemen, Arab Emirates

East European, FSU, FY: Armenia, Azerbaijan, Byelorussia, Ukraine, Russia, Estonia, Latvia, Lithuania, Georgia, Kyrgyzstan, Tajikistan, Turkmenistan, Uzbekistan, Moldova, Albania, Bulgaria, Czech Republic, Romania, Poland, Hungary, Slovenia, Slovakia, Croatia, Macedonia, Serbia and Montenegro, Bosnia and Herzegovina

African: Angola, Burkina Faso, Benin, Burundi, Congo, Central African Republic, Côte d'Ivoire, Djibouti, Ethiopia, Ghana, Guinea, Uganda, Gambia, Kenya, Cameroon, Liberia, Madagascar, Mali, Mauritania, Mozambique, Malawi, Namibia, Niger, Nigeria, Rwanda, Sudan, Sierra Leone, Somalia, Chad, Togo, Tanzania, Zambia, Zimbabwe

Asian: Afghanistan, Pakistan, Bangladesh, Brunei, China, Hong Kong, India, Iran, Iraq, Korea, Laos, Mongolia, Macao, Nepal, Philippines, Sri Lanka, Thailand, Vietnam

South American: Argentina, Bolivia, Brazil, Chile, Colombia, Belize, Costa Rica, Cuba, Dominican Republic, Ecuador, Jamaica, Honduras, Mexico, Nicaragua, Panama, Peru, Surinam, El Salvador, Uruguay, Venezuela, Guatemala, Paraguay

OECD: Austria, Australia, Belgium, Canada, Switzerland, Denmark, Germany, Spain, France, Ireland, Italy, Iceland, Finland, Great Britain, Greece, Portugal, Norway, the Netherlands, New Zealand, Japan, Luxembourg, the USA, Sweden

References

Algan, Y. and Cahuc, P., and Sangnier, M. (2011) Efficient and Inefficient Welfare states. *IZA DP 5445*.

Card, D., Dustmann, Ch., and Preston, I. (2005) *Understanding Attitudes to Immigration: The Migration and Minority module of the first European Social Survey.* CReAM Discussion Paper Series 0503. London, University College London.

Chiswick, B. (1991) Reading, Speaking, and Earnings Among Low-skilled Immigrants. *Journal of Labor Economics*, 9, 149–170.

Chiswick, B. and Miller, P.W. (2009a) Citizenship in the United States: The Roles of Immigrant Characteristics and the Country of Origin. *Research in Labor Economics*, 29, 91–130.

Chiswick, B. and Miller, P.W. (2009b) *Educational Mismatch: Are High-Skilled Immigrants Really Working at High-Skilled Jobs and the Price They Pay If They Aren't?* IZA DP 4280.

Dumont, J.-C. and Monso, O. (2007) Matching Educational Background and Employment: a Challenge for Immigrants in Host Countries. In: *International Migration Outlook*, SOPEMI. Paris, OECD.

Dustmann, Ch. (1994) Speaking Fluency, Writing Fluency, and Earnings of Immigrants. *Journal of Population Economics*, 7, 133–156.

Gropas, R. (2008) Is Naturalisation a Factor in Immigrant Activism? In: D. Vogel, (ed.) *Highly Active Immigrants—a Resource for European Civic Societies*. Frankfurt, Peter Lang, pp. 145–160.

Guiso, L., Sapienza, P., and Zingales, L. (2006) Does Culture Affect Economic Outcomes, *Journal of Economic Perspectives*, 20(2), 23–48.

Lehrer, E.L. (2010) Religion, Human Capital Investments and the Family in the United States. In: R. McCleary (ed.) *The Oxford Handbook of the Economics of Religion*. Oxford, Oxford University Press.

Luttmer, E. and Singhal, M. (2011) Culture, Context and the Taste for Redistribution. *American Economic Journal: Economic Policy*, 1, 157–179.

Manning, A. and Roy, S. (2010) Culture Clash or Culture Club? National Identity in Britain, *Economic Journal*, 120 (542), F72–F102.

Putnam, R. (1993) *Making Democracy Work*. Princeton, NJ, Princeton University Press.

Index

Bold entries refer to figures and tables.